Migrant Workers in Contemporary Japan

JAPANESE SOCIETY SERIES
General Editor: Yoshio Sugimoto

A Social History of Science and Technology in Contempory Japan, Volume 2
Shigeru Nakayama

Gender and Japanese Management
Kimiko Kimoto

Philosophy of Agricultural Science: A Japanese Perspective
Osamu Soda

A Social History of Science and Technology in Contempory Japan, Volume 3
Shigeru Nakayama and Kunio Goto

Japan's Underclass: Day Laborers and the Homeless
Hideo Aoki

A Social History of Science and Technology in Contemporary Japan, Volume 4
Shigeru Nakayama and Hitoshi Yoshioka

Scams and Sweeteners: A Sociology of Fraud
Masahiro Ogino

Toyota's Assembly Line: A View from the Factory Floor
Ryoji Ihara

Village Life in Modern Japan: An Environmental Perspective
Akira Furukawa

Social Welfare in Japan: Principles and Applications
Kojun Furukawa

Escape from Work: Freelancing Youth and the Challenge to Corporate Japan
Reiko Kosugi

Japan's Whaling: The Politics of Culture in Historical Perspective
Hiroyuki Watanabe

Gender Gymnastics: Performing and Consuming Japan's Takarazuka Revue
Leonie R. Stickland

Poverty and Social Welfare in Japan
Masami Iwata and Akihiko Nishizawa

The Modern Japanese Family: Its Rise and Fall
Chizuko Ueno

Widows of Japan: An Anthropological Perspective
Deborah McDowell Aoki

In Pursuit of the Seikatsusha:
A Genealogy of the Autonomous Citizen in Japan
Masako Amano

Demographic Change and Inequality in Japan
Sawako Shirahase

The Origins of Japanese Credentialism
Ikuo Amano

Pop Culture and the Everyday in Japan: Sociological Perspectives
Katsuya Minamida and Izumi Tsuji

Migrant Workers in Contemporary Japan:
An Institutional Perspective on Transnational Employment
Kiyoto Tanno

MODERNITY AND IDENTITY IN ASIA SERIES

Migrant Workers in Contemporary Japan

An Institutional Perspective on Transnational Employment

By

Kiyoto Tanno

Translated by

Teresa Castelvetere

Trans Pacific Press

Melbourne

First published in Japanese in 2007 by the University of Tokyo Press as *Ekkyō suru koyō shisutemu to gaikokujin rōdōsha*.

First published in English in 2013 by:
Trans Pacific Press, PO Box 164, Balwyn North, Victoria 3104, Australia
Telephone: +61 (0)3 9859 1112 Fax: +61 (0)3 8611 7989
Email: tpp.mail@gmail.com
Web: http://www.transpacificpress.com

Designed and set by Digital Environs, Melbourne, Australia. www.digitalenvirons.com

Distributors

Australia and New Zealand
James Bennett Pty Ltd
Locked Bag 537
Frenchs Forest NSW 2086
Australia
Telephone: +61-(0)2-8988-5000
Fax: +61-(0)2-8988-5031
Email: info@bennett.com.au
Web: www.bennett.com.au

USA and Canada
International Specialized Book
Services (ISBS)
920 NE 58th Avenue, Suite 300
Portland, Oregon 97213-3786
USA
Telephone: 1-800-944-6190
Fax: 1-503-280-8832
Email: orders@isbs.com
Web: http://www.isbs.com

Asia and the Pacific
Kinokuniya Company Ltd.
Head office:
3-7-10 Shimomeguro
Meguro-ku
Tokyo 153-8504
Japan
Telephone: +81-(0)3-6910-0531
Fax: +81-(0)3-6420-1362
Email: bkimp@kinokuniya.co.jp
Web: www.kinokuniya.co.jp
Asia-Pacific office:
Kinokuniya Book Stores of Singapore Pte., Ltd.
391B Orchard Road #13-06/07/08
Ngee Ann City Tower B
Singapore 238874
Telephone: +65-6276-5558
Fax: +65-6276-5570
Email: SSO@kinokuniya.co.jp

ISSN   1443–9670 (Japanese Society Series)

ISBN   978–1–920901–60–8 (Hardcover)
        978–1–920901–24–0 (Softcover)

The author and the publishers gratefully acknowledge a Grant-in-Aid for Publication of Scientific Results provided by the Japan Society for the Promotion of Science (JSPS) towards the translation and publication of this volume.

Contents

Part III: The Divisions Between the Economic System
and Legal Society Concerning Transnational Persons

Figures

Tables

Preface: Employment realities for foreigners of Japanese descent and public indifference

Introduction

The attention garnered by studies of immigration in the 1980s re-sulted not only from the fact that they highlighted changes in the international division of labour, but also from their treatment as illustrative of one moment in the ongoing demise of welfare states. The volume edited by Nash and Fernandez-Kelly was a piece of interdisciplinary research that directly examined this international division of labour and also the relationship between immigration and changes emanating from within developed societies which are stuck in a bottleneck (Nash and Fernandez-Kelly, editors, 1983). Sassen provides one of the high points in this current of research (Sassen [1988] 1982). In Japan also, Kirirō Morita was compara-tively early in noting the relationship between the international division of labour and immigration. Morita (editor) (1987) deals with this issue in Japan.

In the 1990s, however, immigration came to be discussed exclu-sively in terms of the relationship between globalisation and people's immediate world, and the moment that happened the discussion was cast either in terms of the concept of post-colonialism – with its keywords of 'subaltern' and 'diaspora' – or in the context of ex-tremely abstract spatial concepts. Exponents of Orientalism, such as Said, are representatives of the former tendency, while examples of the latter are to be found in urban theory. As the former group have a strong literary and philosophical aspect, they cannot be said to exert any considerable influence on empirical research, unlike the latter who are exerting a large influence on this research, including in Japan. The fact, for example, that even someone like Hideo Aoki, who is a representative of research into the urban underclass in present day Japan, selects as research themes the ways in which the masses see and feel towards foreign workers in the urban underclass and the stratification of the labour market, while also quoting the urban theory of Friedman and others is indicative of the influence of this trend (Aoki 2000: Chapter 5).

It is undeniably important to display sensitivity towards the mood and feelings of a period. The author is, however, more interested in questions such as what kind of changes is the social institution trying to bring about under globalisation and, furthermore, what kind of lifestyle are the changes in the social institution that appear under globalisation demanding of people living in Japan? This is why the author would like to return to the issue of relationships in the division of labour – the most basic social system – and take a look at changes in the social institution. In this book, the indicator of this change will be foreign workers. This is why the author believes that this book is not simply to be located within the field of research into foreign workers. With the entry of foreign workers into the world of the Japanese employment system – known for its lifetime employment and seniority-based promotion, this employment system found exclusively within Japanese society, is now importing a labour force from overseas as well. This book hopes to show that: the Japanese employment system has become a 'transnational employment system' which transcends national borders in order to bring in the labour supply that it needs; and also that this employment system was formed as a unique reorganisation of the relationships within the division of labour under globalisation.

The 'division of labour' and the employment system: fundamental concepts of social organisation

In Adam Smith's words, the division of labour results from the mutual realisation of the idea "give me what I want, and I will give you what you want" (Smith [1937: 14] 2000: 38).

> And thus the certainty of being able to exchange all that surplus part of the produce of his own labour, which is over and above his own consumption, for such parts of the produce of other men's labour as he may have occasion for, *encourages every man to apply himself to a particular occupation, and to cultivate and bring to perfection*

*whatever talent or genius he may possess for that particular species
of business* [author's emphasis] (Smith [1937: 15] 2000: 40).

Consequently, people engaged in various occupations (people
divided by differences) become increasingly specialised in just their
own areas of work and collectively make up one organism: society.
In Smith's division of labour, the ability to engage in exchange is
a premise, and there is also an assumption that those carrying out
these activities are all equals.

Subsequently, Karl Marx problematized the fact that in the
labour contract between employers and workers – even in exchange
relationships that placed them on an equal footing – workers would
continue to be exploited. He also thought that this exploitation
would be perpetuated as long as modern civil society continued to
be viewed in terms of contractual principles. Takeyoshi Kawashima
treats Japanese society as being in this previous state, as described
by Marx. He makes the critical observation that,

> In Japanese society, relationships of a competitive nature between
> independent actors and mutual recognition of this – the social basis
> for rights – have for a long time existed only in the weakest form.
> Japanese society is organised along the lines of various forms of
> collectives, and people have always existed as members of a variety
> of these collectives; it is only within an extremely limited sphere
> that people have existed as independent individuals (Kawashima
> 1982a: 230).

Kawashima regards it as a problem that equal relationships between fellow citizens, which form the basis of modern civil society,
failed to be established, even in a token manner, from the outset in
Japan. He argues that Japan was a society in which the 'principle
of "united as one"' was at work, under which the expectation was
that even while the division of labour went ahead, the interests of
the individual would always be to contribute to the interests of the
group.[1] Kawashima bases his substantiation of the fact that these
relationships in the division of labour have an exclusively collec-
tivist nature on a rural community survey, but even in present day
Japan where the agricultural population has declined to ten per cent,
many other scholars are pointing out that the collectivism referred

to by Kawashima is being transformed into company-ism, and that this is continuing under the ongoing influence of globalisation.[2]

Incidentally, if the author were to be asked, 'What is the true nature of today's globalisation?' the answer would probably be, 'the reintroduction of disparities.' The author believes that globalisation is the very cause of the breaking up of Japan as a middle class society. It is true that the dual structure of full-time and part-time workers has long been in existence. However, even though there has been a dual structure in which full-time workers who enjoyed the so-called lifetime employment and seniority-based wages were not a majority of the working population (it was not in reality a lifetime employment and seniority-based wages society), there was the myth that if one could persevere, acquire university graduation credentials and enter the labour market, then one would be able to gain secure employment (the establishment of employment and seniority-based wages as ideology). Globalisation has brought about the decisive collapse of this myth.[3] Respect for the rights of full-time workers in workplaces provided the foundation for the welfare state, which took the families of full-time workers as its social model. Taking a hand to full-time employment inevitably leads to a reorganisation of the welfare state. The destruction of the myth of lifetime employment and seniority-based wages is then followed by a rapid expansion of a workforce premised on disparity in the labour market: temporary workers; contract workers; part-time workers; *furītā* (part time jobbers); and finally foreign workers. Moreover, the labour force which is premised on these disparities is seeing ongoing reforms of the labour market on a scale that cannot be ignored. As a consequence, new companies and restructured companies that rely on a differentiated workforce are starting up and, at present, companies that have grown by riding this wave have begun to make up the mainstream of the business community.

Meanwhile, a segment of company-dominated society that demands the existing type of collectivism stubbornly persists. Moreover, the storm of restructuring that raged at the turn of the century, in the form of employment insecurity, is introducing the principle of competition to people who are attempting to stay within the area of lifetime employment and seniority-based wages (the prevalence of a results-oriented approach is a sure indication of this), and also demands – even more than in the past – that they be steeped in the company's colours. This has not only occurred within the company organisation itself; the same logic carried over into subcontracting relationships also. A good example would be the promotion of the integration of subcontractors by parent companies pursuing economies of scale (the classification of subcontracting companies). Meanwhile, subcontractors also seek to cultivate new clients outside their own company (increasing independence of subcontracting firms). Subcontracting firms have had no alternative but to establish a management base that does not rely on the parent company as they have experienced being screened out by the latter. However, subcontracting firms that are technologically independent are still fine. It is to be expected that subcontracting firms that are just anticipating costs will naturally make use of the differentiated work force around them as part of their work force portfolio.

The consequence of all this is that society will demand a legal system that increasingly fails to recognise the rights of individuals. This follows from the fact that *companies are first able to make use of a differentiated work force when disparities appear within those things that ought to be safeguarded such as the nature of what it is to be a worker and people's human rights.* It is not the existence of disparities within workers' lifestyles and their intentions regarding the ways in which they work that has created the expectation of a variety of ways of working. At the time of drawing up work contracts, disparities regarding people with different natures are introduced, allocating the parties to the contract to a specific 'status.' People simply match their lifestyle to the income that this status brings them. These days, people are not able to be perceived as subjects who are people with human rights; in an existence where one's duty is to contribute to the interests of the group and of society (in this regard, the Japanese society identified by Kawashima persists), they are further defined as a work force lacking any individuality. This contradiction ends up being distorted and expressed by the people who are newly arrived from overseas. The work of this volume is to make this point clear.

Erased existences: contract workers

It should be clear from the previous discussion that changes in the ways that foreign workers are used indicate changes to the composition of the Japanese workforce. Let us first look specifically at how foreign workers are used in present day Japan.

With the collapse of the bubble economy of the 1990s, Japan struggled with a prolonged period of economic stagnation. The impossibility of any expectation that there would be an increase in economic growth was clear to everyone. Once it became clear to companies that they could no longer expect any growth in the Japanese economy, continuing to employ full-time workers simply became a burden. In companies that paid seniority-based wages, and particularly in the case of highly-paid middle-aged workers, restructuring became an unavoidable issue. Contract workers had been widely used in large industries with fluctuating demand, such as coalmining, shipbuilding and steel, since the period of modernisation beginning in the Meiji era. Contract workers had also always existed, as a work force for blue-collar workplaces, in the key post-war industries, such as the manufacture of transportation equipment (the automobile industry) and the manufacture of electrical machinery, equipment and supplies. Even if contract workers had long been a part of blue-collar workplaces, their numbers can be thought of as having remained fairly constant within set limits. In Japan's industrial society, characterised by its complex subcontracting structure, there is also a strong perception that the problem of contract workers is one found in subcontracting companies. As restructuring also starts to occur in large companies it has, however, become by no means unusual for significant numbers of contract workers to be used even in companies which are the main exponents of the subcontracting structure. Workers of Japanese descent are the clearest present day example of this contract work force. The workers are awarded a legal status for the duration of their stay in Japan, on the logic of their family line; they face no limits to the jobs that they can take because their employment qualifications place them in a particular employment category, and as such they work in a totally different environment from that experienced by foreign workers, who are largely from Asia and do not possess employment qualifications.[4] This is why it is not possible to discuss foreign workers in general on the basis of the conditions of workers of Japanese descent. And yet, workers of Japanese descent congregate to an unusually large degree in the contract labour market where they are received in what is the characteristic pattern for foreigners who work as contract workers. Now, let us embark on the main argument of this book.

Figure 0.1: Changes in the composition of employees in one auto-mobile-related company

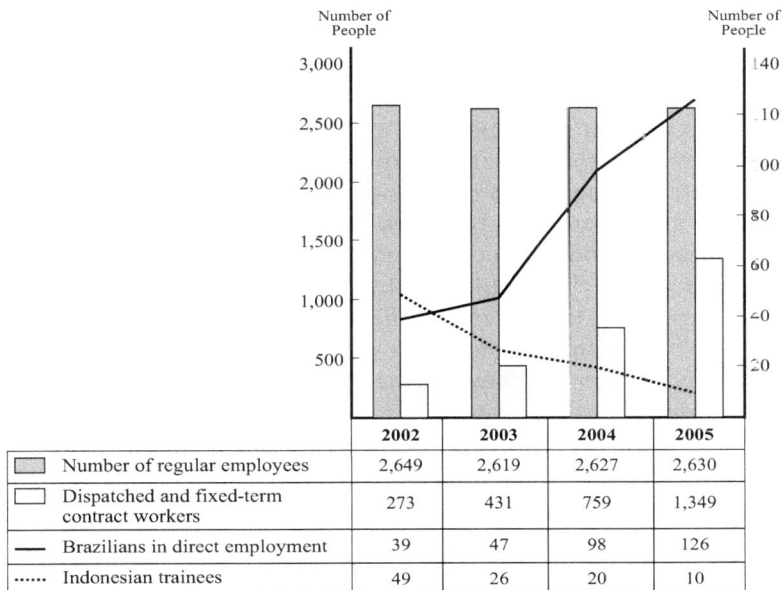

	2002	2003	2004	2005
Number of regular employees	2,649	2,619	2,627	2,630
Dispatched and fixed-term contract workers	273	431	759	1,349
Brazilians in direct employment	39	47	98	126
Indonesian trainees	49	26	20	10

Figure 0.1 shows the changes in the composition of employees at an automobile parts maker. This parts maker has around 2600 full-time workers and boasts sales of 1100 billion yen. Since Japanese industrial statistics define small- and medium-sized companies in the manufacturing industry as those on a scale of fewer than 300 workers, this parts maker is certainly a large company. Figure 0.1 is limited to a recent four year period, but at a glance one can see that while the level of full-time workers remains stable at around 2600, the numbers of temporary workers, such as dispatched workers and those on fixed term contracts are increasing. The number of directly employed Brazilians is also increasing at roughly the same rate as the incremental increase in irregular employment.[5]

Figure 0.1 must be read with care. This is due to the fact that workers who work for the contracting company (the workers in Figure 0.1 who appear as dispatched workers and those on fixed term contracts) are not counted as workers in this company's factory. Although they are working in the factory, they are not under the management of the personnel and labour management divisions. They are managed by the Supply Division which oversees the procurement of parts. Why is it that although they are human beings, they are procured as parts? This is because the work contract agreement is for line work and as such the agreement treats them as production costs for the manufactured goods in this line (a way of thinking that sees this form of agreement as appropriate because they are producing a certain number of goods in their monthly output). Seen from the management perspective of the factory, the agreement with the work contracting company is an agreement about production costs and processing fees; it is not a dispatch agreement that would see the placing of specific people in the factory, much less an employment agreement (that is to say, there are no contractual relationships with people as their subject). Consequently, the people denoted in the agreement reached between the factory and the work contracting company represent a labour quantity of the number of people necessary to the manufacturing process and the production of the goods that are the subject of the agreement. In specific terms, contract workers are not understood to be one or two people but one or two workers; that is, units of manpower that are measured in terms of amount of work. They only appear as a dimension of the overall volume of essential work. That is to say, *the foreign workers working in the contract area are not perceptible in the factory records in terms of who has done the work, but only in terms of the number of man hours of work in the factory.*[6]

One representative example of this absence from the formal record, observed in a company that the author was shown around in Hamamatsu, is the application of the one surname 'Matsuo' followed by numbers 1, 2, 3, 4 and so on for all workers of Japanese descent on the time cards used for labour management. This was a system for determining how many 'Matsuo' were in attendance altogether on the basis of seeing whether 'Matsuo 1' or 'Matsuo 2' was away; it did not perceive workers as subjects in possession of any will or rights, but attempted to measure the whole group as a work volume.[7] Allocating Japanese names such as 'Matsuo' to foreign workers' time cards is also, needless to say, a means of disguising the fact that there are foreigners working in the company when labour standards inspectors (or other outsiders like the author) visit the factory. However, those in charge of labour management in the company where the author was given access to the time cards were not proud of this situation; it was rather a case of everyone having misgivings about it while also seeing it as an inevitable reality in attempts at cost reduction. The factory manager of a listed company made the following stark remark to the author: 'Inspectors are well aware of the reality within companies; it is because they do not know which factory documents to scrutinise that we end up with figures suggesting that there are no foreign workers despite the fact they are actually working there.'

When we differentiate workers in the factory and the work force, we are left asking what exactly accounted for the rapid growth in irregular employment between 2002 and 2005 in the company in Figure 0.1. The rapid increase from 273 to 1349 does not mean that this rapid increase in irregular employment occurred in the company in question. This calls for a more detailed explanation. The increase in 'dispatch and fixed term contract workers' from 273 to 431, between 2002 and 2003, and from 431 to 759 between 2003 and 2004 give the outward appearance of a numerical increase when one counts the people sent from the contracting company who are working in this company as people. Although around 750 workers were working there in 2002, the figures show a mere 273 because the workers sent by the contracting company were merely counted as manpower. In contrast to this, Brazilian workers are directly employed by the company as Brazilian workers and their employment agreement is one in which they are employed on a fixed term contract.[8] Brazilian workers also work for contracting companies, but Brazilians who work under these contracts are hidden amongst the dispatched and fixed contract workers in this figure.

The two dividing lines of nationality and gender

Two dividing lines of nationality and gender separate workers working for contracting companies. Generally speaking, it is a characteristic of contract work that age and academic background make practically no difference with regard to the same work. Differences in nationality and gender, however, lead to differences in pay. This would better be described as a difference in unit costs at the time of the drawing up of the contract agreement by the factory and the contracting company, more so than a difference in pay. The factory and service contractors usually conclude two contracts – one that is visible and one behind the scenes. The visible contract is, as was described in the preceding section, a written contract according to which one unit is contracted for X goods at Y yen in pay in the contract line. Under the terms of the behind the scenes contract, Z yen in contract wages are paid per hour for each worker received. The Z yen of the behind the scenes contract is generally known as the contract unit price.

Table 0.1 shows the contract unit price concluded with a service contractor by a different factory from the one discussed above. The following is a straightforward explanation for the reasons behind differences in contract unit prices. The first thing to notice is the emergence of a seventy yen disparity in the prescribed pay (this forms the standard amount) between Japanese and foreigners and also between males and females. This reflects the fact that foreign contract workers do not participate in social insurance (health insurance) schemes.[9] This lack of inclusion in health insurance is a premise at the time of the contract agreement. The difference in unit price between males and females does not necessarily stem from differences in the workplaces where they are employed. In general, most men are sent to workplaces requiring heavy physical labour, but there are also workplaces in which men and women do the same work. Even in the latter, the unit prices are 1770 yen per hour for Japanese men and 1350 for foreign women. The difference in contract unit price between men and women is directly tied to wages that reflect the market price for obtaining workers. It might seem a good idea to assemble only cheap female labour, but the Labour Relations Adjustment Law has a bearing on this. For example, with the enforcement of the Gender Equality in Employment Act the ban on employing women late at night was lifted, however, this was accompanied by the provision that in order to employ women late at night a room, separate from that used by males, had to be provided for women to take their breaks. This is why the work force in Table 0.1 was not replaced with an all-female work force.

There has, however, been a change towards a reorganisation of the work force which relies more heavily on female labour in this factory. The reason for this lies in the considerable changes to the composition of the goods being manufactured in this company as a consequence of fierce international competition. The factory is reducing workshops that make goods that are large and heavy, and increasing lines producing easy to export, high value added

*Table 0.1: Differences in contract unit price on the basis of nation-
ality and gender (unit: 1 yen)*

	Japanese male	Foreign male	Japanese female	Foreign female
Within fixed hours	1,770	1,700	1,420	1,350
Overtime	1,970	1,900	1,620	1,550
Fixed late night	1,970	1,900	1,620	1,600
Holidays	1,970	1,900	1,620	1,600
Non-prescribed late night	2,170	2,100	1,820	1,750
Legally prescribed holidays	2,070	2,000	1,720	1,650
Outside legally prescribed holidays	2,270	2,000	1,920	1,850

As at 2003

goods that are lighter in weight. The modification of the goods
being produced in this type of factory does not represent a shift
to female labour as a result of a simple quest for cheap labour; it
was the increase in work consisting of detailed operations that do
not require manual strength that led to the heightening demand for
female labour.[10] This change in products is also leading to extremely
large seasonal fluctuations in the number of workers working in the
factory. Due to periods of heavy work pressure and off-seasons, the
number of workers in the factory varies from 100 to 300 per cent
in the space of a year. From the company perspective, if they were
unable to respond to large-scale changes in the size of the work
force required, they could not continue manufacturing in Japan.
They could maintain stable production of large and heavy goods,
but these have little value adding and given Japan's high wages it
is not possible to compete with rival Asian factories. This is why
this company is moving the production of heavy goods to their
Chinese factory.

However, the foreign workers in Table 0.2 are foreign workers
of Japanese descent. Let us now consider the problems caused by
the Immigration Control and Refugee Recognition Act (hereafter:
Immigration Control Act). The reason why we cannot avoid
looking at the Immigration Control Act is because it is this law
that decides the right to stay of all foreigners. The Immigration
Control Act is said to be based on U.S. Immigration Law. Lawyer
Emiko Miki, a friend of the author, says that 'Annex 1 and Annex
2 make distinctions on the basis of whether people are real or sham
immigrants, and that each of these distinctions is then differentiated

on the basis of even more minute considerations.[11] There are two Annexes and these are schedules, within the Immigration Control Act, of the rights of foreigners to stay in Japan. Annex 1 covers the right to stay with work entitlements (generally, the visa issued on the basis of the rights contained in Annex 1 is called a 'work visa'). By contrast, Annex 2 is a right to stay that confers residence on 'long-term residents;' 'permanent residents;' and 'spouses of, for example, Japanese nationals, long-term residents and permanent residents.' Consequently, while in Annex 1 the right to residence is issued on the basis of a job, there are no restrictions on employment in the residence rights conferred under Annex 2.[12]

Seen from the perspective of the right to stay, there are three types of foreign workers engaged in unskilled labour in Japan. There are the trainees and technical trainees[13] under the control of Annex 1; the workers of Japanese descent who fall under Annex 2; and other foreign workers who do not have any rights. Workers of Japanese descent in Annex 2 present the most troublesome problem. Like other workers they are ineligible to vote, but they have complete freedom regarding choice of work and they also possess the social right to receive social assistance such as livelihood protection if they should fall on hard times. Whilst they are foreigners, if they are considered immigrants to Japan, then it is natural that they should be guaranteed social rights.

Meanwhile, because the state maintains its stance that Japan has not, to date, accepted unskilled workers – even though workers of Japanese descent congregate in service contracting agencies (which characteristically offer atypical and irregular employment) – this ends up not being seen as a problem of foreign workers (since it is merely the casual consequence of the freedom of work choice). Also, the foreigners in Annex 1, who are given residence rights on the basis of their type of work, fall within the domain of the Ministry of Health, Labour and Welfare, but the foreigners in Annex 2 cannot be placed within labour policy.[14]

Takamichi Kajita argued that the admission of workers of Japanese descent is occurring via the side door (Kajita 2001 & 2002), but the author feels that neither the side door nor the back door have been opened yet. Questions regarding which door has been opened are simply trivial matters. Regardless of whether the door has essentially remained shut to date, the rather far more fundamental issue is that it can be argued that – whether at the side or the back – the door is open. This type of problem emerges because it functions as an administratively 'useful lie' surrounding foreign workers. The usefulness of the lie is:

> Avoiding the application of the law by saying that what happened did not happen and that what did not happen happened…in any case, once the "law" no longer meets social demands, that is when "lies" manifest their usefulness (Suehiro 1988: 20-22).

Because the state will not alter its stance of not acknowledging the admission of unskilled workers, although workers of Japanese descent are actually being hired as unskilled workers, the lie that they are not workers has arisen and they continue to be omitted as the subjects of policy.

Fluctuations in the regular and irregular employment loopholes

As the terms *furītā* (part time jobbers) and *nīto* (*neet: not in employment, education or training*) and also employment instability show, burgeoning irregular employment drew widespread attention in Japan from the late 1990s to the first half of the 2000s (Genda 2001; Kosugi 2002; Nomura 1998). We can bundle these together as having been debates about the social problem of declining stable employment and increasing irregular employment. However, from the point of view of an author who regards irregular employment as the central issue, this period was also one of an opening up of a hitherto unimaginable circuit in irregular employment. It is to this point that we will now turn, focussing on the example of the company dealt with at the beginning of this chapter.

Let us confirm the size of the differences in costs between regular and irregular workers for this company. Table 0.2 is a comparison of workers doing basically the same magnitude of work. Blue-collar work in this company is divided into four ranks from A to D.[15] To date, work in ranks A to C has been undertaken by regular workers with workers on fixed term contracts, dispatched workers and those from contracting agencies being employed to do rank D work.[16] Recent high school graduates end up working on D rank work

Table 0.2: A cost comparison of regular and irregular employees
'in a primary subcontracting firm

	Cost per time	Establishment percentage
Regular employees	2,430 yen	100%
Directly employed Brazilians	1,700 yen	100%
Indonesian trainees	1,557 yen	100%
Temporary employee replacements and contractors	1,850 yen	68%
Workers with fixed term employment contracts	1,388 yen	75%

because although they are regular workers, they do not yet have any experience of the workplace. This D rank for high school graduates can, however, be upgraded the following year to C rank. Table 0.2 is a calculation of the respective costs to the factory of employing regular workers, directly-employed Brazilians, Indonesian trainees and workers on temporary contracts in D rank work (hourly costs), and also of how much of each respective part of this labour force remains after a year (fixed percentage).

Workers who would be paid 1388 yen per hour if they could be employed on temporary contracts end up costing 1850 yen per hour (1850 is the contract unit cost) when they are sourced from employee placement and contracting agencies because of the added costs in the form of commissions for these organisations. In the case of trainees, the amount of money that is paid directly to them is small, but they end up costing 1557 yen – more expensive than workers on temporary contracts – because in addition to directly shouldering the classroom learning costs of trainees, the manufacturer pays other expenses to the organisation that takes the trainees.[17] Conversely, in the case of the direct employment of Brazilians, the employment agreement is directly concluded with this factory (company), but these workers are under a service contractor in all matters ranging from the management of their lives in the dormitories to labour management on the work site. Alongside the amount of money paid to the workers – an hourly wage of 1400 yen, practically the same amount as workers on temporary contracts – 300 yen per person per hour is paid for the service contractor who manages them. The company claims to employ them directly, but in reality they are treated as contract labour. Why is it that although directly employed,

Brazilian workers are under the management of service contractors? Firstly, this is because the direct employment of Brazilians amounts to no more than half-yearly fixed term contracts. For this reason, even though it is called direct employment, it does not mean regular employment with pay raises and promotions (the direct employment of Brazilians does not mean Brazilians are regular employees). Secondly, there is the influence of the fact that the company does not recognise or anticipate that these workers will be able to achieve regular employment or become regular employees. These are companies that belong to the first tier of the Tokyo Stock Exchange, and they see investment in the development of the capacities of their regular employees as worthwhile. On this point, the following explanation, given by a labour management official at one of these companies, is instructive:[18] 'there can largely be no expectation of investment by the company in the development of the capacities of Brazilians or that Brazilians are in a position to become the subject of capacity development by the company.'[19] The lack of expectations on the part of the company regarding these workers becoming the subjects of capacity development results from the fact that they have been made into irregular workers, despite being employed directly.

Major differences, in regard to this point, between the Brazilian and Japanese workers on fixed term contracts have been emerging in recent years. For example, in 2005, the Toyota Motor Company announced that it was promoting around 900 of its 12,000 fixed term contract workers to regular employee status. This type of trend can also be seen in parts companies, in subcontracting companies and – while the absolute numbers are small – promotions of fixed term contract workers can also be seen at a higher percentage than is the case amongst parent automobile makers. In one plant (factory) in Figure 0.1 and Table 0.2 about half of the fixed term contract workers have taken the examination for promotion to regular employment. There are about fifty successful applicants each year, with around twenty-five per cent of workers on fixed term contracts gaining regular employment. The explanation for this state of affairs lies in the preference on the part of companies to obtain a work force that is clearly committed to work by promoting irregular workers rather than ending up with workers such as *furītā and nīto* who have doubts about working. Previously, the academic credentials showing that one had graduated from high school or university were used as barometers for gauging one's will to work; these days, however, the barometer indicating a person's will to work is sought in the fact that they are currently in work. Furthermore, using fixed term contract workers who are midway through their training period provides a ready-to-use supply of labour.

However, Brazilian workers, despite the fact that they were the same type of fixed term contract workers, did not receive this same treatment.[20] Within irregular employment, the road to promotion to regular employment is open to Japanese, but only a road to ongoing irregular employment is provided to foreigners.[21] Nevertheless, in the past, with the exclusion of technical experts in some professional jobs, the thinking was that a person's life would be largely decided according to which company they entered upon graduation. Even if one is temporarily an irregular worker, arrangements are available for becoming a regular worker in a major company. In this sense, the border between regular and irregular work is becoming blurred.

Why have we remained indifferent to foreigners?

The problem of foreign workers continues to be presented in newspapers and magazines as a problem of public order, crime and the education of the children of foreigners. Also, as the example of the factory introduced in this book shows, even the companies that take in foreign workers harbour doubts about their manner of work and social treatment. The headline, 'The foreign worker problem: the current state of foreign workers and an intensification of measures regarding illegal employment,' appeared in the June 2006 edition of the official bulletin of the Japanese government, *Trends of the Times*. Alongside an acknowledgement of the necessity for foreign workers, the article stressed that the present situation was replete with problems, the problem of illegal employment being particularly serious, and that even though it was necessary to accept this there would need to be careful consideration regarding the acceptance of any more foreign workers in future (*Trends of the Times* 2006: 12–19).

Everyone acknowledges that there is a problem and understands that at the same time Japanese industry has a need. This recognition was clear in works being published more than ten years ago, and in this sense we have seen no progress whatsoever. The acknowledgement of and understanding that there is a foreign worker problem notwithstanding, the same arguments as ten years ago continue to be repeated. One of these is that we Japanese are indifferent to this problem. Another is that this results from researchers' attention being taken up by only those problems occurring in their immediate environment (alternatively, that they are only interested in theories that explain the existence of foreign workers). A further explanation of this indifference is that it results from the fact that researchers are not conducting research on a level that grasps the fiction that foreign workers are not workers despite the fact that they are working (alternatively, the usefulness of the lie). There is no accumulation of a body of argument, despite the frequent treatments of this problem, because time after time these deal with individual cases and fail to question fundamental principles. The conclusion (repeated each time) is that something must be done about the foreign worker problem; this is the steady state of things (the question of what then ought to be done is never made clear).

Why is it that this is the only possible conclusion? Do the reasons for this not lie in the fact that we only see foreigners as a foreign labour supply and also that we suffer from an extreme lack of consciousness of the fact that the companies that we have looked at in this section are individually all doing precisely the same things on a national level to acquire the labour supply that they need? The necessary labour supply viewpoint has at its forefront management ideas such as just how many foreigners are needed in total and what kind of mechanisms are needed to distribute this volume of foreigners. Japan is not alone in this, as is suggested by Cornelius et al.'s book, *Controlling Immigration*, which discussed immigration policy in developed countries (Cornelius, W. A., et al. 1992). However, we cannot hope to deal with the immigration problem, the problem of foreign workers, simply as a management concept.

To begin with, if the service contract agencies that are directly employing workers of Japanese descent were to recognise the rights of workers working for their companies textbook fashion, they would find that they had very little scope for continued survival. It is said that if they had to sign up all of the workers in their companies for social (health) insurance, they would all – with the exception of a number of large contracting companies – face insolvency. Even if one does overtime, it is not unusual for the overtime to be paid not as a bonus but under the cover of just a few hours of fixed wages. What also enables the company to respond to sudden fluctuations in production is its failure to comply with the Labour Standards Act

(LSA) which states that a minimum of thirty days' notice is to be given at the time of dismissals; and it is able to do this because the lack of labour unions or employee organisations for these workers leaves them with no means of complaining to the company.

Since the factory attempts to take on only the labour that it needs, even if its own company abides by the LSA, they are not concerned with the fact that the party that supplies this labour is not complying with the LSA. The state strives to stay abreast of foreign workers in factories through the Labour Standards Inspection Office and the Public Employment Exchange, but because the actual employment destination of foreign workers is contracting agencies, no matter how much attempted control of factories there is, there will always be workers who are not accounted for. The way in which this sort of thing is actually happening was explained at the beginning of this chapter. Foreign workers have been embedded within a mechanism that the state cannot control, and the practical use of service contracting agencies, which first becomes possible as a result of the evasion of the law somewhere along the line, leads to a social arrangement in which the system of acquiring the necessary labour supply when it is needed functions as the economic system's 'living law.'[22]

The structure of this book

While empirically making clear the relationship between the employment of foreign workers and social problems, this book constructs a coherent theoretical framework for explaining foreign workers. The theoretical frameworks that will be suggested are firstly 'transnational employment systems' and secondly 'the fiction (lie) surrounding workers who cross national borders.' The former is a treatment of the logic of an economic system that transcends borders and connects demand and supply for labour while the latter is an appraisal of the logic of Japan's political system which accepts workers who have transcended national borders.

In Part One of the book, 'An examination of the logic of obtaining people who transgress national borders,' the first chapter, 'Globalisation and labour market reform,' makes clear the type of labour supply that foreign workers are expected to provide under calls for deregulation. Chapter 2, 'Broker sociology,' looks at a number of cases of brokers who find foreign workers to come to Japan and examines their function. Chapter 3, 'Fluctuations in the employment structure and foreign workers,' discusses the mechanism that reorganises the lifestyles of the foreign workers introduced to the Japanese labour market by brokers as these men and women respond to news coming out of the Japanese corporate world. Chapter 4, 'Reasons for segmentation of the foreign worker labour market' discusses the divisions along ethnic lines that occur within the labour market even as it attempts to adapt to the Japanese labour market. Chapter 5, 'Foreign workers in industrial organisations,' reveals that the transnational employment system came into existence in the midst of three overlapping games: a game of establishing the terms for a legal category of foreigners; a game of establishing the terms for their inclusion in the labour market; and a game of establishing the terms that would enable the construction of their own communities. And, furthermore, that these are embedded within the culture of company organisations and also the culture of regional communities.

Part Two, 'Transnational workers and Japan,' paints a clear picture of the transnational employment system. Chapter 6, 'The contract age and workers of Japanese descent,' makes general observations and explains the increasing demand for workers of Japanese descent as a result of major changes to the nature of employment contracts. Chapter 7, 'Industrial reorganisation and regional labour markets under globalisation,' shows, with reference to the automobile industry in Aichi Prefecture, that disparities are emerging in the reliance on a foreign labour supply on the basis of the position that a company holds in the subcontracting organisation. Chapter 8, 'The labour market for Brazilians in Japan,' deals with the service contractor industry that sends off Brazilian workers to companies, and argues that a system for turning out all of the required labour is being constructed amidst the ongoing division of labour in this industry. Chapter 9, 'Microanalysis of the labour market for workers of Japanese descent,' depicts the kind of employment environments and social lifestyle environments forced onto individual foreign workers, via an ethnographic study of a particular service contractor where the author has conducted a survey.

Part Three, 'The division between the economic system and legal society concerning transnational persons,' discusses the social foundation of foreign workers who straddle national borders. In Chapter 10, 'The birth of an integrated migrant worker industry,' it is argued that the transnational system changes with the passage of time and that it will not lead to migrant labour becoming firmly established in Japan, where it is seen as a customary practice. Chapter 11, 'The sociology of the law of special permission to stay,' deals with the problem of the normalisation of illegal workers. This discussion covers: what is the fundamental legal base of foreign workers; how is the law applied administratively; and what sort of contradictions do the provisions and the administrative application of the law bring about? The final chapter, Chapter 12, makes clear that the legal status of people of Japanese descent, which has been discussed in this book, has arisen in close connection with the definition of Japanese nationality. It also elucidates the logic of the Japanese government which while considering people of Japanese descent to be foreigners, sees them as special foreigners.

Part I
An Examination of the Logic of Obtaining People Who Transgress National Borders

1 Globalisation and reform of the labour market: the peripheral work perspective

Introduction

There are attempts, both public and private, to carry out major reforms targeted at the labour market which is made up of a very diverse labour supply. This chapter will address the question: what is the logic that attempts to justify the appearance of disparities among the participants in the labour market?

Marx began the *Communist Manifesto* with the now famous words 'A spectre is haunting Europe, and the name of that spectre is communism' (Marx and Engels [1,848] 1951). If we were to re-write this in the present day, it would probably become 'A spectre is haunting the world, and the name of that spectre is globalisation.' It may be that globalisation – which has the movement of capital without borders as its premise – is the essential form of capitalism, rather than the post-war welfare state structures which were established on the premise of the nation state and a national economy. However, globalisation is causing various forms of confrontation not only in developing countries but even in developed countries which are supposed to be enjoying its benefits. This chapter treats the globalisation of the market place from the point of view of the peripheral work which occupies the lowliest position in that market, and uses this as the basis for considering the political nature of the logic that promotes globalisation.

The author considers the characteristic feature of present day peripheral work to be the 'fixed term of employment' that accompanies 'irregular work' – in contrast to the 'unspecified limits of employment' in the case of 'regular work.' That is why the logic that pushes forward 'fixed term employment,' with its disparities in terms of rights compared to regular employees, advances its logic with a focus on approaches that come particularly from the arguments found in 'law and economics.' This approach's point of view is not confined to labour problems; it finds its way into various aspects of globalisation such as environmental issues and international disputes.

Does globalisation increase the number of beneficiaries?

It is argued that globalisation, with its principle of 'liberalisation,' based in turn on deregulation, is the means by which the bottleneck of the post-war welfare state structure can be surmounted. Calls for deregulation contain criticisms of the welfare state, in particular, along the lines that the welfare state is giving rise to a specific class of people with vested interests and that the dismantling of these now institutionalised vested interests is linked to increasing social welfare. For example, once deregulation had been used to bring about the same establishment criteria for nursery schools and kindergartens, in order to decrease the number of children on waiting lists, areas that had previously been accepting children into nursery school experienced an increase in the number of children requiring nursery teachers to look after them, and this led to an inevitable decline in the service being received. However, areas with pre-school children who had previously been completely unable to receive this service experienced benefits in that there was now somewhere where they were able to leave their children. This logic asserts that although the service received by existing beneficiaries had declined as a result of deregulation, with the creation of a new group of people who had previously been unable to receive this service (new beneficiaries), an increase in the total number of beneficiaries has been effected. However, in this case, *whatever the standard of service experienced by the children who can be left (which, depending on the situation, could even be conditions that are detrimental to the developmental environment for children) the logic employed says that there have been benefits.*

We cannot overlook an additional aspect of deregulation theory. This is the classic liberal ideology of 'personal autonomy' and 'will' on the one hand and the concept of a new order that includes the state and also international organisations. This problem is characteristically seen in the Kyoto Protocol which is environmental regulation on a global level. As the United States, which is the largest emitter of carbon dioxide, failed to ratify and as the number of ratifying countries needed to issue the declaration was not reached, it is still not an effective world framework. However, via the establishment of rights to emit carbon dioxide, ways of thinking that attempt to reduce the greenhouse effect on the whole planet are condensing new thinking. The establishment of rights to emit carbon dioxide turns the creation of pollution (external diseconomy) into a negotiable good and it is not the external diseconomy itself that is regulated; the problem is dealt with via an accumulation of goods by people who are most effectively able to dispose of them through market activities in the course of which these goods are transacted. Bruce Yandle calls methods of resolution that rely on active state intervention, such as support for equipment that reduces pollution and the taxation of polluters of the external economy, Pigovian. He describes a contrasting method in which activities that give rise to an external economy, such as the establishment of rights to emit carbon dioxide, are transformed into a negotiable right and the transacting of negotiable rights, goods, is allowed in the market. The method of dealing with the issue through this market activity is referred to as Coasian (Yandle 2003). This demonstrates a strong faith in both the definite existence of people who are considerably more efficient than states and governments in handling goods and also in transactions between people who are capable of dealing efficiently – that is, in the fact that the market is the most efficient vehicle.[1]

It is 'law and economics' that suggest a powerful framework for attempting to construct a new order with 'personal autonomy' and 'will' as their principles. Law and economics, based on the conviction that market exchange (transaction) is the most economised method, offer a framework; a law in which the market brings about maximum social utility via these lowest costs. Law and economics keep developing theoretically as they interact with the New Institutional School in economics[2] and with economic sociology.[3] Economics approaches consider even the law and social relationships to be methods for achieving economic goals while sociology thinks that social relations, which are not reducible to economic goals, influence the achievement of those goals. In contrast to these, Law and Economics in Jurisprudence stresses the normative nature of law and positively attempts to create a society that orients itself on the basis of this normative power.[4]

Dean Lueck maintains that globalisation, with its reestablishment of rights-based relationships, is the way to respond to and overcome the failure of the market and the failure of the state (government). Accordingly, he develops his theory on the premise that because of the reestablishment of rights, mentioned previously, the greatest social utility can be gained by having goods and issues that have become a problem dealt with by the people who are the most knowledgeable about them, and not by the government (Lueck 2003). By hypothesising that there are no transaction costs, law and economics lend theoretical support to the Coase Theorem which argues that since the conditions of distribution of resources and rights in the initial stages of market transactions do not pose a problem for the achievement of efficiency, in order to regain the original function of the market, it can be argued that what is needed is the abolition of government regulation (Coase, [1960] 1992). However, even taking this type of theoretical background into account, there remain a number of misgivings about the adaptation of the assertions within law and economics to real social problems. The first is how long would it take for problems to be dealt with? Secondly, even if problems are ultimately dealt with, how would the people who suffered disadvantage during the time that it had taken to achieve this be compensated? Finally, absolutely no account is taken of the fact that while the social harm done may be very small, as a whole, it would most likely be concentrated in specific areas.[5]

This 'law and economics' way of thinking has also been evident in the arguments surrounding labour market reform in recent years. Naohiro Yashiro insists on reform of the labour market arguing that:

> Seen from the point of view of the union of daily employees, there are many elements of employment instability in the fluidization of employment, but for the part-time and dispatched workers at the base of employment practices that are by nature fluid, it presents a considerable number of plus sides such as the expansion of mid-career recruitment opportunities (Yashiro 1997: 86–87).

Tatsuo Hatta takes Yashiro's argument further saying:

> In recent years, there has been deregulation of employment agreements and as a result of the increasing ease of obtaining contract employees and temporary employee placement there has been an expansion of irregular employment. It is said that this has increased the income divide. However, the nineties, when this deregulation occurred, was a period

of mass unemployment as a result of recession. If there had not been deregulation of irregular employment in this period, the majority of companies would have been likely to have had hesitations about any new employment. As a consequence of irregular employment having become easier due to deregulation, many companies enthusiastically expanded their irregular employment thus bringing about a fall in unemployment. In the sense that it increased the number of employed people and reduced the number of unemployed, this deregulation led to a narrowing of disparities (Hatta 2006: 26).

The author understands the questioning of the application of exactly the same logic that he displayed in the case of nursery schools to places of employment.[6] However, in the same way as in the example of establishing nursery schools on the same basis as kindergartens so as to reduce the number of children on waiting lists, this logic is a market organization that leads to lower (or poor) standards and a means of measuring an increase in the number of beneficiaries and overall social utility. The author cannot help feeling that, on this point, law and economics are exerting a powerful influence on arguments that deal with far reaching social problems.

Labour market reform and foreign labour

This section examines the foreign worker labour market using the statements made by the management side in recent years regarding this reform. It also considers, from the standpoint of foreign workers, the influence that globalisation is exerting on peripheral workers. Even following the collapse of the bubble economy in the 1990s, and in spite of the prolonged period of economic slump, there were business people suffering from a shortage of labour. Possibly reflecting these sorts of voices, the Japan Federation of Employers' Associations first made clear the need for the introduction of foreign workers in their 2001 'Report of the Research Committee on the Labour Problem (*Nikkeiren Report*)' (*Nikkeiren Report* 2001: 26–28). However, what one must pay attention to here is the context in which the Japan Federation of Employers' Associations considered it essential to bring in foreign workers. It was not simply in order to address a shortage of labour. They argued for the necessity of foreign labour as one of a variety of employment measures for companies. The following year, the 2002 'Report of the Research Committee on the Labour Problem' made a more systematic case for the type of labour market that the management side wanted to see. The labour market that they were seeking at this point would have the following four desired conditions: '1) a migratory nature – a market that did not hinder workers' voluntary movements:' '2) flexibility – a labour market capable of efficiently matching the supply and demand for labour, such as flexibility in response to technological innovation in areas like IT;' '3) specialised in nature – a market that stimulates a rise in specialist abilities;' '4) diversity – a market that makes full use, for example, of foreigners, older people and women. (*Nikkeiren Report* 2002: 39).

> We consider it possible – in the midst of an increase in older workers, a decline in younger workers and further increases in the presence of women in the workplace – that the maintenance and creation of employment can be realised precisely by aiming in future to use the long-term, continuous employment of core employees as the mainstay and combining a variety of forms of employment to increase productivity while avoiding any increase in total labour costs (*Nikkeiren Report*: 34).

As this shows, it is assumed that the 'market diversity' being sought in the form of foreign workers is hypothesised as operating for the purpose of stabilising the employment of core employees. The various parts of the labour force that shoulder the burden of diversity, are fixed in roles that differ from those of core employees; there is no consideration of foreign workers, older workers or women going on to become core employees.

The treatment of irregular employment as fixed (as not shifting towards regular employment), even as it is being expanded, by the 'Report of the Research Committee on the Labour Problem,' which shows the employers' point of view, is entirely natural to the extent that it takes a labour-management cooperation line. However, how could the fixing of stable regular workers and insecure irregular workers possibly be justified when we look at this from a stance other than that of management? Looked at from a social point of view, when regular employment declines and irregular employment increases it is difficult to maintain a sense of social justice if there is no route open for returning to regular employment even if one might temporarily be plunged into irregular employment. Also, because regular employment continues to be limited to the regular employment category irregular workers are compelled to undergo severe competition because they are in irregular employment. Yashiro, who calls for labour market reform, has modelled the present institution as:

> The wage structure inside companies in addition to relying heavily on institutions and customary practices is also closely related to the expectations of the employees, and large-scale changes to these things is not necessarily easy to bring about. For this reason, a company carries out a rearrangement of its portfolio from the company's special human capital to its general capital, and carries out a stock adjustment (quantity adjustment) of excess human capital (Yashiro 1997: 135–136).

The more one takes the stand of the model that they are actually based on, arguments for the reform of the labour market, in contrast to the criticisms of the welfare state carried out by original deregulation arguments, envisage the descent of the employment of the vast majority of people into the field of fixed instability, meanwhile converting the class with vested interests in the welfare state into a smaller, protected privileged class.

Does a foreign worker labour market exist?

In recent years, in documents such as the 'Report of the Research Committee on the Labour Problem' encountered in the preceding section, foreign labour has been discussed as the diversification of employment measures. What does this mean?

Hiroyuki Chūma has conducted a thorough analysis of the realities of the actual use of in-house contracting firms; service contractors. This analysis clearly showed that business people were using service contractors as one of a variety of employment options (Chūma 2001). The subject of Chūma's research is the use of subcontracting firms in one particular industry, the electrical appliances industry, but Hiroki Satō, working before Chūma, has shown that the same can generally be said of the manufacturing industry (Satō 1998). Service contractors, in which large numbers of foreign workers, and particularly workers of Japanese descent, are employed, are rapidly expanding their sphere of activity in company-dominated society as an institution that provides a diversity of employment options.[7] How then are we to understand the spread of the activities of these sorts of subcontracting firms? The author perceives the foreign worker labour market in the way shown in the related groupings in Figure 1.1.

Firstly, the formation of a labour market of a standard scale became possible because of the discovery, by the existing institution – that turned out workers on fixed term contracts and seasonal workers, that is, the service contractors – of foreign workers as an internal factor (institutional factor) in the labour market. However, with the changing employment environment and the heightening of the dual problems of employment instability and the *furītā*, as well as the introduction of Japanese workers into the institution that foreign workers had come to occupy (service contractors), the situation changed completely. This type of change in the labour market was further prompted in response to the globalisation of company-dominated society. Because companies are drawn into global competition, they keep restructuring employment in order to maintain their international competitive power and they also demand further cost reductions in dealings with subcontracting companies. As a consequence, increasingly fewer workers are able to find employment in the stable employment sector, and they are forced to move from stable to insecure employment. These sorts of changes in company-dominated society leave workers who have recently been forced to move to insecure employment and families whose principal breadwinners have ended up in insecure employment with no choice but to work on the same worksites as foreign workers, in order to secure the maintenance and stability of their families' household incomes (This is discussed in detail in Chapter 7). In short, changes in a company regulate its workers' thoughts about work and also those of their families, and lead to their inclusion in the insecure employment labour market. The very inclusion of Japanese in the peripheral labour market goes on to have an impact on the employment plans and strategies of small- and medium-sized subcontractors and the service contracting industry.

Furthermore, when we think of changes in the peripheral labour market as a reaction to changes in company-dominated society we should not lose sight of the decisive nature of policy changes. The revision of the 1990 Immigration Control and Refugee Recognition Act made public the introduction of foreign workers into Japan.[8] Changes to the application of the legal system on a national level

Figure 1.1: Systematic groupings of the state, the labour market and the business world with regard to the peripheral labour force

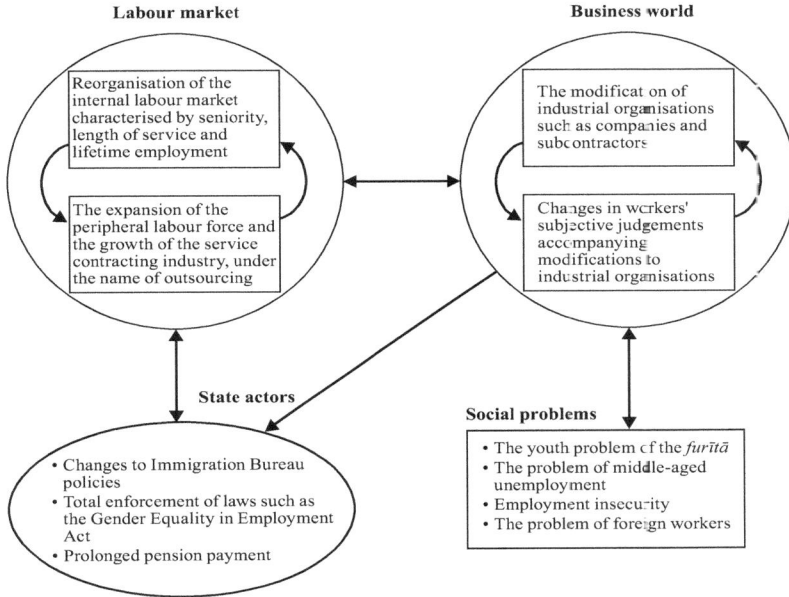

Labour market   **Business world**

Reorganisation of the internal labour market characterised by seniority, length of service and lifetime employment

The modification of industrial organisations such as companies and subcontractors

The expansion of the peripheral labour force and the growth of the service contracting industry, under the name of outsourcing

Changes in workers' subjective judgements accompanying modifications to industrial organisations

State actors

Social problems

• Changes to Immigration Bureau policies
• Total enforcement of laws such as the Gender Equality in Employment Act
• Prolonged pension payment

• The youth problem of the *furītā*
• The problem of middle-aged unemployment
• Employment insecurity
• The problem of foreign workers

Note: Eggertsson (1996: 12) has been adapted and revised in line with the issues in this book.

also had a significant influence on the growth of rivalry between the foreign labour force, represented by people of Japanese descent, and the Japanese peripheral labour force. The changes that fuelled this rivalry were the lifting of the ban on late night work by women that accompanied the complete enforcement of the Gender Equality in Employment Act and the extension of the retirement age and return to work that accompanied the increase in the age of commencement of payment of the pension. In brief, this was the influence of the changes to the institution brought about by state actors.

While the actions of these groups – 'the labour market,' 'company-dominated society' and 'state actors' – were having an influence on one another, the problem of the peripheral labour force was coming into existence.

Incidentally, if we were to approach this in terms of the links between the groupings in Figure 1.1, then we would have to say that the foreign worker labour market is already on the verge of demise. This "demise of the foreign worker labour market" does not imply the imminent disappearance of the foreign workers working in Japan.[9] Foreign labour as a social phenomenon – workers who are foreign nationals working in Japan – and a foreign worker labour market, in the sense of a labour market made up of these workers (a foreign worker labour market as a phenomenon), will doubtless continue to exist. However, the foreign worker labour market is a labour market that has been formed with a narrow and selective focus on foreigners by companies that were unable to attract Japanese into the labour market. That is, the principle behind the establishment of the foreign worker labour market was to introduce foreigners because they could not get Japanese workers. This principle has now vanished.

What has replaced the old principle of a substitute labour force for the Japanese labour force is 'the contract principle' (This is examined in more detail in Chapter 6). In using contract labour from the service contracting industry, companies are merely entrusting them with daily contract jobs while continuing to have workers working in the factory. This is why they are able to ensure a workforce matched to fluctuations in the work that comes in. By replacing suspensions of work orders (business orders), factory dismissals – unlike the dismissal of workers – can be concluded simply on the basis of talks or the reaching of a mutual agreement between the contracting party and the service contractor. As Japanese workers also enter this labour market of service contracting companies, the position of foreign workers becomes extremely weak. This is because the existence of foreign workers in the factory does not signify that they were selected by the company, but rather by the contracting company.

Considering all of these matters, an analysis of the labour market which focusses solely on foreign workers no longer holds true as a theory of foreign worker labour markets. The overall trend of a peripheral labour market that includes foreigners is exerting a strong influence on the foreign worker labour market, and it is precisely in a theory of the peripheral labour market that includes other peripheral labour that the issues in foreign worker problems are likely to be detected in future.

From the welfare state to the contract age: towards globalisation

What does it mean when the principal behind the foreign labour market changes to a contract? This section treats 'contract' as a keyword.

It goes without saying that the progress of globalisation has had a profound influence on the collapse of the welfare state. In the labour field, the retreat of the welfare state is strik_ngly evident in the decline of regular employment and the increase in irregular employment. Takashi Uchida (2000: 1) pointed out that:

> Policies curtailing the role of the state and emphasizing market mechanisms usher in a new age and activities that had to date been seen as being qualitatively different from contracts are increasingly being entrusted to the market; that is, to contacts. Right now, it is not merely business transactions that are being affected by contracts. As a result of the Public Nursing Care Insurance Law enacted on the first of April 2000, the nursing care service, which had until now been supplied via administrative "measures," is now determined to be supplied via a contract between the insured party and a designated business person. Even welfare services such as aged care will be supplied on the basis of contracts.

This, according to a legal scholar, is the essence of globalisation. What we can read into this is that *the state in the global era*, where even the logic of the welfare state to date as the provider of welfare is replaced by a contract between welfare recipients and a welfare service provider, shifts the focus of its own role to establishing contract rules and the smooth exercise of the rules. This outlook also emerges in Yashiro's point of view, which:

> regards as desirable the legalisation of rules concerning dismissal procedures [substantial regulation of the adjustment of dismissals] such as, for example, company efforts to assist in the smooth change of employment conditions and occupation for workers rather than entrusting decisions about the necessity for and size of dismissals to labour management negotiations [author's insertion] (Yashiro 2003: 234).

Considerable confusion ensued as a result of the conversion of all manner of relations to a contractual footing in the period of transition from a feudal to a capitalist system. The enclosure of land under the Enclosure System brought about the demise of common land. Employment agreements that existed in form only led not merely to difficulties in the reproduction of workers, but also to a demand that women and youth do the same work that was being done by adult males. It is no exaggeration to say that this process was one of contracts bringing about the ongoing destruction of all social relationships.[10] This is, however, different in nature from the flood of contracts in the present global era. Contracts do not simply destroy social relationships. Prescribed social concerns also come into play as the state establishes and implements rules, and this leads instead to contracts incorporating social relationships.

What then are contracts that incorporate social relationships (transactional relationships)? They are 'continuous contracts' (continuous transactions). The parties concerned achieve long-term goals as they keep renewing these contracts. For this reason, there is not rigid determination of the contents of each specific round of contracts. This is because given the likelihood of unanticipated environmental changes in long-term transactions, the taking of rigid decisions would result in an inability to meet any changes in the environment. Instead, there is no mention in the wording of written contracts, and the trust between the parties concerned plays a weighty role.[11] The subject (goals) then are achieved by building long-term and continuous relationships with particular partners while establishing different structures depending on the nature of the contracts.

The contract exchanged between the point of production (the factory) and the service contractor can also only be expressed as a transaction based on a continuous contract. In the official written contract, the pay for each product is derived from the contracting cost per hour for an individual worker, with a written contracting agreement drawn up using this pay as the standard value. In distinction to this official written contract, actual negotiations about unit costs are then conducted as the pricing of workers on the basis of what an individual worker produces (temporary worker price setting) and an accord about the contents of the contract with regard to contract tasks between the point of production and a service contractor. What we should perhaps call a hidden contract is concluded via a process in which labour costs are determined on the basis of an individual worker's output.

Publicly, a contracting agreement is concluded on the basis of an official written contract setting out the unit cost of wages for labour. However, the contents of the contract regarding contract tasks are decided via an unofficial, hidden contract premised on continuous transactions. The spread of contract tasks being carried out by the use of this kind of agreement reaching in company-dominated society – with manufacturing industry at its heart – demonstrates flexibility on the point of responding to changes in the economic environment. On the other hand, as Figure 1.1 shows, it is precisely because this is a business world that displays considerable flexibility regarding its environment that young workers inevitably end up as *furītā* while middle and older workers, who are on high wage levels because of seniority-based wages, are simultaneously made the targets of restructuring. What is more, the emergence amongst foreign workers of social problems such as the rampant situation in which they have no insurance or pension despite having resided in Japan for an extended period of time becomes inevitable.

Changes to the labour market system present as a reduction in the segment of workers in long-term employment (regular employment) and an increase in short term contract employees and the contracting labour force (this has also led to workers being on short term employment contracts). Stable labour-management relations are dismantled and the areas pervaded by the logic of short term costs expand. Under these conditions, the labour market ends up being organised and its degree of diversity increased through the introduction of people who are there on the basis of a different logic from that of foreign workers – *furītā*, women and older workers; those in insecure employment.[12]

Conclusion

Finally, this section concludes with a discussion of the limitations of deregulation as a response to globalisation. Responding adaptively to the actions of others leads to some degree of complementarity arising between the actors. This problem of complementarity is dealt with in detail in the following chapter, but since complementarity functions efficiently societies in which it is at work display favourable performance levels (Aoki, Okuno & Muramatsu 1996). Even looked at theoretically, however, it is not possible to show that this is a good situation.[13] This is because although the efficiency viewpoint can assert the legitimacy of a particular institution on the grounds that in addition to safeguarding a certain degree of equality it is capable of achieving efficiency, when the achievement of efficiency invites inequality, it is not possible to assert the legitimacy of the institution. Also, as Robert O. Keohane and Elinor Ostrom show, in contrast to the ease with which agreements are reached in international relations when there is a diversity of interests amongst the players (states) engaged in transactions, attempting to reach agreement at the community level – on issues such as irrigation facilities, common land and the management of common land – it is homogeneity amongst the players that becomes a major factor in attaining agreement (Keohane and Ostrom 1995). Not only is this not able to show that theories which indicate that performance is a favourable quality are fair in terms of social justice, it suggests that under a different standard of analysis, favourable qualities can lead equally to heterogeneity or homogeneity amongst the players.[14] In short, arguments based on efficiency do not, in fact, provide a consistent explanatory theory.

It is to be expected that the logic of seeking efficiency will yield good performance in terms of company management. However, those areas that organise the people who contribute to the management of the company, such as sub-contracted workers, contract workers and workers on temporary contracts, make use of large numbers of the socially weak – foreigners, older workers, women, ethnic minorities within the country, single fathers, single mothers and so on. Furthermore, places like call centres that make use of the growth of communication technology to gather consumer complaints, despite cutting costs by virtue of having been established in distant lands and third world countries, are left with the reality that consumers cannot see or comprehend this composition at all.[15] Why is the failure to value the labour force as workers who have delivered good performance to these sorts of companies justified? Moreover, why is it that we can approve of the wretchedness, misfortune and uneven distribution that is the lot of specific categories of people?

The very restoration of a human existence to contract workers, who have been incapable of being seen as anything other than a labour force lacking any individual existence, is a challenge shared by every country that is confronting globalisation If we were to expand Coase's Theorem, on the basis that it discovered the fundamental significance of increasing the wealth of a society, then there would be no problem with the widening of the gap between the poor and the wealthy in any given society (alternatively, the gap in employment) as long as this produced an increase in wealth (as long as employment is increased, regardless of the sort of employment). However, the adaptation of Coase's Theorem is not a problem. Atsushi Tsuneki and Yoshikazu Shishido point out that:

> Since the Coase Theorem asserts that the distribution of property rights has no influence on efficiency, it is possible to regard it as illustrating the foundation of the fact that handing down judgments based on a standard of fairness regarding the distribution of tangible property rights that the judiciary has traditionally emphasised, is of no consequence. It sends a powerful message on this point also.

As this shows, this is because the adaptation of Coase's theorem is not directly linked to the destruction of the standard of fairness that has operated to date (Shishido and Tsunehiki 2004: 30).

The problem lies in the inability of this theory to establish a minimum for the type of condition in which an individual lives in society. Stated more accurately, it is both the law and economics that set the minimum. As Hideo Fukui and Fumio Ohtake (Fukui and Ohtake eds 2006) state in their Introduction, they use law and economics to break down existing labour policy into labour market policy and social welfare policy. They set forth a schema which seeks the thorough penetration of the market principle in the former and aims for the safeguarding of workers' existence as people should they fall out of the labour market via a general social welfare policy. However, the general social welfare policy that they have in mind merely argues for livelihood protection. Thinking about the state of households currently under livelihood protection, it is extremely difficult to expect that they would re-enter a competitive labour market and, particularly, that the labour market that they re-entered would be one of regular employment. Even so, can it be said that social welfare has increased? Given the example of the deregulation of nursery schools, where is the sense in talking about welfare in the case of a theory that is incapable of questioning the developmental environment for children? The limitations of deregulation theory, which has become inseparable, like two sides of the same coin, from globalisation, lie in its inability to consider a social existence for people as individuals.

Suehiro published his essay entitled 'Constitutional government and violence' in *Kaizō* (volume 13, number 6). Published in an era when, following the end of the period of Taishō Democracy, Japan had plunged into militarism, it contains the argument:

> It is highly desirable, if possible, that all disputes should be resolved peacefully by the courts. However, for this to happen, it would be necessary to have a policy that induces the parties concerned to seek resolution of all disputes in the courts....No matter how desirable peaceful resolution by the courts may be in the interests of social peace, as long as they do not give people satisfactory results, it is not to be expected that they will seek resolution of disputes from the courts (Suehiro 1994: 279).

Even the most magnificent institution cannot be used if it cannot provide what it takes to satisfy the individuals in that particular society; this is a term that, on the contrary, implies bringing about the widespread resolution of violent disputes. The same analogy constantly dogs the assertions of law and economics.[16] No matter how great the potential of an argument for increasing the overall efficiency of society, if it cannot discuss the level that would be capable of satisfying the individuals in that society, then the magnificent theory is useless except for placing on the table.

2 Broker sociology: pinpoint immigration and 'regional labour markets'

Introduction

This chapter locates the movement of international labour from the viewpoint of the changing form of industrial organisations and examines the subjective world of workers that arises from the use of 'broker structures' to deploy the essential labour force within these changing organisations. Sassen's concept of 'local labor markets' is the starting point for this examination of the conditions that structure the subjective world of workers. Sassen's argument is generally likely to be used in big contexts such as globalisation. In this case, however, we will not be dealing with the big theme of globalisation. As to the reason for this: in the process of formulating her own arguments about the movement of international labour, Sassen has accumulated an extensive number of case studies. Similarly, because this book is an attempt to consolidate into one system the knowledge that the author has come across in the research that he has conducted thus far on foreign workers, the argument focuses here on local labour markets as a concept that can withstand empirical analysis.[1]

The limitations of theory and of actual proof

The author thinks that the reason why Sassen's theory about the migration of international labour has been widely accepted lies in the fact that it made clear the areas that could not be explained by neoclassical economic theory. Namely, the clarification of migration that cannot be achieved using the 'anticipated income' differential that exists between the sending and receiving countries, which has developed from the initial work of Harris and Todaro (1970). If it were possible to explain the migration of labour (immigrants) using the wage differential that they could hope to acquire, then there should be far more movement certainly from the poorest countries to wealthy, developed countries. The actual movement of international labour, however, is at variance with this. The movement of labour from Asia to Japan is not from Asia's poorest countries, Bhutan and Nepal; it is from China, Thailand and also from Korea and the Philippines. Why is it that movement occurs not from the poorest countries but from newly-developing to developed countries? Also, why is it that even though movement occurs from similarly newly-developing countries, it only comes from certain of these sending countries? If we take the case of Japan, why is that although the economies of China and India are in the same take-off phase, while we have movement from China there is none from India?[2]

It was Sassen who explained this clearly (Sassen 1983, 1988=1992). Sassen clarified the immigrant labour vector by her inclusion of two explanatory variables: the developments in communication and transportation brought about by the influx of capital that accompanies development; and the influx of the culture of developed capitalist countries that then accompanies the movement of capital. Explanations using the anticipated wages differential are unable to explain the reason why, despite being able to head for all of the developed countries, the immigrants who cross national borders only go from certain sending countries to specific developed countries. Sassen resolved this by taking into account both the movement of capital and the influx of ideology.

While neoclassical economics realised at an early stage that it could not explain the movement vector using wage differentials, it attempted to resolve this point by introducing the economics of information.[3] Even though differences exist regarding whether the explanation lies in the effect of ideology or the transmission of information, there are only slight differences in the theoretical frameworks of both Sassen and neoclassical economics.[4] The clear difference between the two is not in their frameworks, but rather in their interpretations of immigrants. The former treats the immigrants' condition of being in a comparatively inferior position with regard to information resources in the host society as arising out of inherent power problems in their position of not possessing all of the same rights as the citizens of the host country. The reason for using the disparity that derives from this problem of power is not because the true nature of the movement of capital leads towards equilibrium, but because it attempts to detach itself from equilibrium. Sassen interprets this as immigrants creating their own space within the movement of capital as it attempts to detach itself from equilibrium.[5] In contrast, the latter sees incomplete information as a temporary detachment phenomenon and also fundamentally treats the immigrant phenomenon as a point en route to a process of equilibrium.

Incidentally, the foreign worker problem has been a fact since the latter half of the 1980s, with considerable empirical research having been conducted into it. One of the reasons why Sassen's research began to invite interest in Japan was because there was a visible internationalisation of people there. However, the more researchers develop an interest in dealing with individual cases, the fewer researchers there will be who, even if they read Sassen, depend on it to explain immigrant labour in Japan. There are two matters related to this. Firstly, because empirical researchers are far too interested in individual cases, they are indifferent to the overall structure of the societies that either send or receive immigrants. Secondly, there is also the fact that the Japanese reality cannot be explained well using Sassen's arguments.[6] What the author feels, in particular, is that the phenomenon of 'pinpoint migration,' which will be discussed more fully in the following section, cannot be explained by Sassen's theory of the movement of international labour which is based on the movement of capital. While the author may have doubts about explaining Japan using the schema of Sassen's theory of the movement of international labour, her estimation of the value of approaching the labour market for foreign workers from the viewpoint of local labour markets is appealing. Accordingly, this work will approach the structural principle of the labour market for foreign workers from the viewpoint of local labour markets and pinpoint migration.

'Pinpoint migration' – the characteristic of present day migrants

In using the local labour market concept when dealing with migrants, Sassen began with four experientially observed findings. Firstly, when making decisions about whether or not to live in certain cities, labour market variables which will affect them, such as the unemployment rate, do not influence immigrants if fellow countrymen are present. Secondly, the residence or the arrival of immigrants has practically no influence on wage rates in the labour market. Thirdly, the acquisition of work by immigrants is not just in growth industries but also in declining industries. Finally, rather than choosing wages by the hour or by the week, from the outset, immigrants find margins in whether to enter or leave the workplace (Sassen 1995: 91).

Sassen's theory of local labour markets is constructed with these four findings as preconditions, and it is precisely these preconditions that the author views as obstacles to its application to Japan. The third and fourth findings presented by Sassen can be observed in practically the same manner in Japan. However, even if the first condition can be recognised in part, it has to be said that the second condition is significantly different in Japan. To the extent that the first condition is discussed as a problem of subjective decision making by immigrants, it can – as will be discussed later – be recognised in Japan too. However, when it is discussed in relation to labour market variables, this condition can be dismissed in Japan. This is because while the case of foreigners of Japanese descent who are legally employed foreign workers is a particular model, in a Japan where it is difficult for foreigners to rent a house on their own, without the help of an employer, the connection between the presence of foreign workers in the regions and labour market variables is evident. Because the influence of the presence of migrants on the labour market for one's own citizens can be seen in competitive relations in the field of unstable employment (discussed in detail in Chapter 7) and also a considerable influence on regular employees,[7] the second condition can be seen to have some relevance to Japan.

What then would be the appropriate characteristics for approaching the problem in Japan? If the author were to be asked, 'What characterises present day immigrants in Japan?' the answer would probably be 'pinpoint migration.'[8] What then is 'pinpoint migration?' Let us start with an explanation of this term.

Large numbers of Brazilians of Japanese descent live in Ōta City and Ōizumimachi in Gunma Prefecture; Hamamatsu City in Shizuoka Prefecture; Toyohashi City and Toyota City in Aichi Prefecture. There are also large numbers of Peruvians of Japanese descent living in Yamato City and Fujisawa City in Kanagawa Prefecture. When carrying out questionnaire surveys in these areas with large concentrations of foreigners of Japanese descent living in them, one encounters a very strange phenomenon. When one asks the question, 'What's the name of the area where you live?' even though it is a question that calls for a city-town-village response, all that one gets is the name of the district (the name of a town or a street) and it is not at all unusual to come across people who are unable to give the names of towns or municipalities. In short, even though someone may know the area name 'Homi,' they will not know the name of Toyota city and someone who knows the name of the area 'Shōnandai' will not comprehend the name 'Fujisawa city.'

Why has this phenomenon appeared? To begin with, it is easy to imagine that this is because the world in which these men and women live their lives is made up of a narrow, specific area. The reality is that in the worksites where foreigners of Japanese descent work infringements of the Labour Standards Act are a daily occurrence; indeed, a given. The logic of the companies that allow them to work for high wages is consistent: they give work to these men and women who willingly put in long hours of work for the company. This is why overtime and working on holidays becomes a given in their case. To the extent that workers take up employment on this basis, their world is likely to consist merely of the round trip between factory and home. Consequently, even though they may have lived in Japan for a long time, they end up not knowing anything about places other than the area within the neighbourhoods in which they live. In this way, the manner in which they are employed shrinks the world in which they live their lives and inevitably narrows the volume and sphere of information that makes up this world.

This, however, is not the only problem. From the outset, from the time of their arrival in Japan, these men and women knew nothing about Japan let alone about the cities that were their destinations. They came, from the beginning, with 'Homi' and 'Shōnandai' as their targets. They came to Japan from places like Brazil and Peru, from the other side of the world, with just one spot in all of Japan in mind. The emergence of the movement of people, who come in this way from the other side of the world with the aim of reaching one spot, can only be because information about this one spot has made its way to the other side of the world. Sometimes, information is received about a number of places, but this is information about those particular places; it is not information or knowledge about Japan. It is only ever information about one point.

In this book, it has been decided to call this pattern of migration by present day immigrants, in which they move on the basis of this

information about a single point, 'pinpoint migration.' There follows
a discussion of how 'pinpoint migration' comes into existence.

The path by which pinpoint migration is created

If the movement of Brazilians and Peruvians of Japanese descent,
who are characterised by pinpoint immigration, began following
Japanese development investment in these two countries, and also
in reaction to this, then the movement of immigrants between Japan
and Latin America can be explained using Sassen's schema of the
international movement of labour and capital. Let us begin with a
consideration of this point.

Japanese direct investment in Brazil in the post-war period be-
gan in 1951 and by the end of the 1950s Tōyō Spinning Company;
Nerima Spinning Company; Kurabo Spinning Company; Dainippon
Spinning Company; Tsuzuki Spinning Company; Howa machinery;
Yanmar Diesel; Kubota Ironworks; Ishikawajima-Harima heavy
Industries; Nippon Tokushu Tōgyō (NGK Spark Plugs); Ajinomoto
Company; Nippon Usiminas (Nippon Steel Corporation's local
joint-management enterprise); and the Toyota Motor Corporation
had moved in (Koike 1995: 165).

Furthermore, in the 1970s, with a view to food security, agricultural development of one of the food supply centres for Japan
began with Japanese government aid to develop the Cerrado in the
centre of Brazil.

Notwithstanding the occurrence of this type of conspicuous
capital investment from the 1950s to the 1970s, immigration as a
reaction to capital investment did not occur in this period. What
needs to be kept in mind, in particular, is that Japanese investment
in Latin America did not give rise to the development of exchanges
that created links between Japan and Latin America. To this extent,
Sassen's schema is to be dismissed with regard to immigration
between Japan and Latin America.

How then did the relationships of exchange that made immigration by people of Japanese descent possible begin? In surveys of
travel agencies run by people of Japanese descent in Latin America
conducted by the author and others, the opening up of pathways
for employment in Japan for those of Japanese descent was via the
following types of opportunities.[9]

In the 1980s, strained trade relations existed between Japan and the United States as a result of the constant excess of exports from Japan. Japan exercised voluntary restraint in the area of the manufacturing industry, that is, in the export of items such as iron and steel and automobiles. The memory of Japan having been constrained to promise an opening up of the market to manufactured goods from the United States is still fresh. One of the points at issue in the service area at this time was reform of the 'Japan-America Airlines Agreement.' The issue of 'beyond rights' was posing particular problems. The United States sought the right for its planes going to Japan to pass through Japan on their way to South East Asian destinations such as the Philippines. The Airlines Agreement conferred beyond rights on the United States, in the interests of reciprocity, and this meant that Japan also had beyond rights. However, in Japan's case, there were no attractive markets for its United States bound aeroplanes to fly on to. Nevertheless, reform of the 'Japan-America Airlines Agreement' ended up recognising beyond rights as a result of its relationship with other trade issues and under a form of semi-coercion on the part of the United States.

The consequence of beyond rights brought about by this reform of the Japan-America Airlines Agreement was the opening up of a transport relationship which directly linked Japan and Latin America. In short, *the establishment of a direct transport relationship between Japan and Latin America cannot be treated as a problem of the movement of capital between the two countries or as one of the problems that accompany this; instead, in this instance, a transport relationship was concluded from conditions that derived from the relationship with a third country, the United States.* It was an unintended result. The author considers this to have the same meaning as the existence of a mercantile stage in the early stages of the establishment of the capitalist mode of production. In short, it makes no difference whether the establishment of a transport relationship results from the movement of capital or incidental events which precede this. The issue is that the very moment that a transport relationship has been established, capital will use this to carry out its self-propagation.

However, the establishment of a transport relationship between two countries does not automatically deliver a labour force to the place where it is needed. Figure 2.1 shows changes in the population

*Figure 2.1: Changes in the population of people of Japanese descent
in Toyota City*

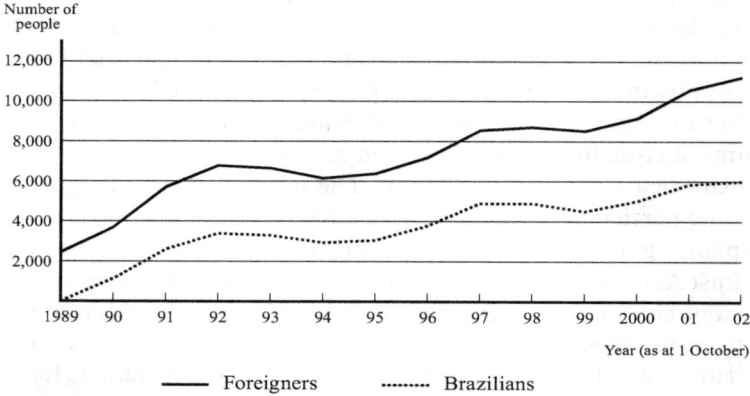

Source: Prepared using statistical documents for Toyota City for each respective year.

of foreigners in Toyota City, which contains the Homi Apartments
where foreigners of Japanese descent live in large numbers. In
1989, before the revision of the Immigration Control and Refugee
Recognition Act, there were 96 Brazilians residing in the city, but in
1990, the year of the revision of the Act, there was an immediate and
rapid increase in numbers to 1,179. However, the boom in Brazilians
of Japanese descent working abroad had begun before this time.

As Figure 2.2 shows, in 1988, before the revision of the Immigration Control and Refugee Recognition Act, the Japanese
Consulate in São Paolo alone issued a total of 8,602 visitor visas to
Japan, while in 1989 the number was a total of 18,309. There were
48,195 cases and an immediate increase in the number of visas
issued in 1990, the year in which the Immigration Control and
Refugee Recognition Act was revised, but other factors were also
at work in this.[10] Firstly, there is the fact that there had already been
a wave of large numbers of immigrants coming to Japan before the
revision of this act. Secondly, at the point in time when travelling
abroad for work began, foreigners of Japanese descent were not
living in the areas of Japan with the greatest need for labour.

The author believes that the gap between the increase in foreign
workers on a national level and the increase in foreign immigrants

Figure 2.2: Changes in the number of cases of visas issued by the Consulate-General of Japan in São Paolo

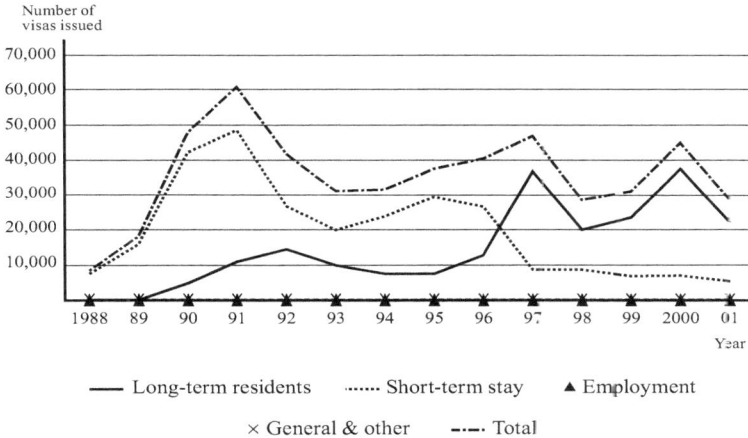

Number of
visas issued

```
70,000
60,000
50,000
40,000
30,000
20,000
10,000

       1988  89   90   91   92   93   94   95   96   97   98   99  2000  01
                                                                        Year
```

——— Long-term residents   ······ Short-term stay   ▲ Employment

× General & other   —·—· Total

Source: Compiled using documents from the Consulate-General of Japan in São Paolo.

at the local level, of the sort that one can discern from Figures 2.1 and 2.2, can be explained by adopting the following point of view.[11]

This point of view is distinct from country to country movements; it is a viewpoint according to which *as a result of a system beginning to function at the regional level that brings labour into a specific region from other countries, the population of foreigners in that region begins to increase for the first time.* And this is precisely what the author thinks of as the immigrant local labour market. Let us examine this mechanism in the following section.

Brokers and 'local labour markets'

Even if there are differences such as the development of transportation accompanying the movement of capital or the commencement of transportation as the unexpected product brought about by international relations, once transportation is opened up, the situation changes completely. The employment of workers of Japanese descent began to increase just at the time when Japan was recovering from the recession induced by the high value of the yen, which was brought about by the Plaza Agreement.[12] There have been several different currents in the boom of workers travelling abroad to Japan which began in this way. However, the following kinds of common characteristics were detected by the author and others in what they heard on the ground in Brazil.

The people who played the role of bringing in overseas workers (the first brokers) were either trainees in Japanese companies that had moved into Latin America around the middle of the 1980s or people who were employed by private organisations that provided opportunities for experiencing Japan to people who themselves or whose grandfathers had been born in Japan.[13] There were also other people who had failed in agricultural companies in Latin America and who worked as fixed term contract workers in Japan, but what characterised those who took the route to operating as brokers was that they were largely former trainees or people who had been employed by private organisations. The invitation to these people by the company would have been along the lines of, 'As there are people in Latin America who would like to go to Japan to work, won't you hire them for us?' (This point will be discussed again in Chapter 10.) This was, by chance, happening in the period when direct flights from São Paolo began operating as a result of the Japan-America Airlines Agreement.[14] Those who were approached by companies did some of the recruiting themselves of people who wanted to go to Japan to work, and those who felt that they could not manage it on their own, gathered people who aspired to go to Japan via their acquaintances. As acquaintances in this sense meant for the purpose of gathering people, use was made of human relationships such as prefectural association organisations that were spread throughout the societies of people of Japanese descent in Latin America.[15] This gathering of people by making use of the human relationships in prefectural association organisations became one of the causes of the progress, at a stroke, of links with the travel industry. Travel agencies serving people of Japanese descent in Latin America, up until the 1970s, had organised recreational travel for each prefectural association, alongside domestic travel as their main business. There was also a small amount of overseas travel; however, this was mainly first trips to the groom's ancestral village, in one's prefecture, by a bride after marriage with the prefectural association again serving as the main unit. Thus, the prefectural association organisations and the travel agencies serving people of Japanese descent were closely

Figure 2.3: Service arrangements from Brazil to Japan

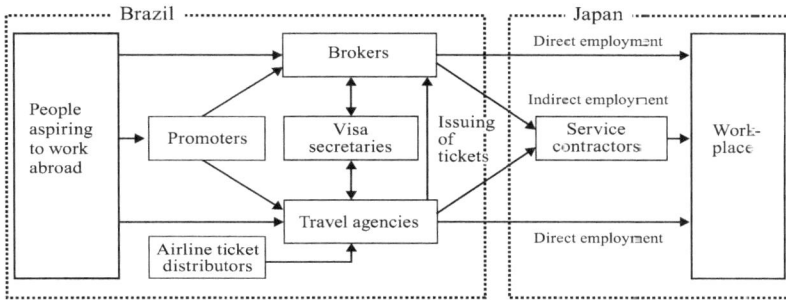

Source: Higuchi 2002: 80.

connected; the big travel agencies were operated by the leaders of the prefectural association organisations and of the federation of prefectural association organisations. Throughout the 1990s, the representative community newspapers for Brazilians of Japanese descent, such as the *São Paolo Shinbun, Nippaku Mainichi Shinbun and the Paulista Shinbun*, carried daily reports on the problem of Japanese employment leading to the breakdown of the Japanese descent community.[16] However, while lamenting the demise of their communities these same community leaders were making this their very business.

It was the movement of large numbers of people, first made possible by the linking of people who had been selected by Japanese companies (factories) to act as brokers with existing organisations in Latin America, that facilitated the boom in the employment of foreigners of Japanese descent in Japan. Consequently, the recruiting system as a labour export mechanism that centred on local travel agencies serving people of Japanese descent ended up establishing one system of division of labour relationships (Figure 2.3). Movements by way of these division of labour relationships, ended up sending workers to regions where Japan's export industries, such as automobiles and appliances had developed. This meant that, from the point of view of people who wanted employment in Japan, participation in this system would lead to being able to go to Japan to work. However, as a result of this, actual movements, such as where in Japan one would work, were decided on the basis of relationships between service contractors and individual brokers/travel agents.

The information about Japan that the workers who actually went there to work were able to get via these labour export mechanisms was consequently about the specific factories or service contractors with whom the individual brokers/travel agents had dealings.

Before people of Japanese descent came to Japan to work, service contractors had been housing recruited workers in their own company dormitories in the regions and sending workers to factories that had contracted the labour for their production line. Securing somewhere to live for the workers being sent across (company dormitories, in the case of independent contractors) was a necessary condition for the service contractors to conduct their operations. In the 1990s, when the population of foreigners of Japanese descent began to increase in Toyota City, the central branch of the corporation servicing the residential city (present day UR City Organization Central Branch UR; referred to as the Public Corporation hereafter) made a decision. It decided that it would rent out any vacant residences that could not be filled in the Homi Apartments, which were leased by the Public Corporation, to legal business people. As a result of this, the service contractors who were sending people of Japanese descent found that they were able to secure dwellings in which to house these people in Toyota City and the system for supplying workers of Japanese descent thus began operating there. In the industries of Toyota City, with its well-developed automobile industry, the sending over of workers by service contractors had already been occurring. However, the situation which saw workers of Japanese descent coming into Toyota City in the mid-1980s, when the numbers of people of Japanese descent in Japan began to increase, did not come about solely as a result of the service contractors carrying out their business activities in the city. Only once the conditions for being able to secure housing were in place did it become possible for Toyota City's industries to turn Brazilians on the other side of the world into a reservoir of labour and to bring a labour force that traversed national boundaries into the local labour market.

The brokers who connect the organisational gaps

As mentioned previously, the movement vector has been explained using Sassen's argument that the specific system for recruiting

Figure 2.4: Business commencement dates for travel agencies, brokers and service contractors

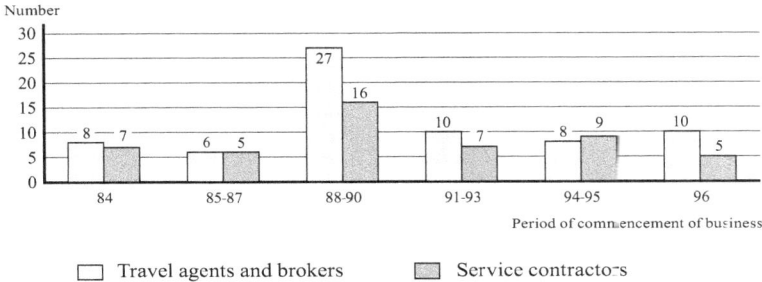

Number

	84	85-87	88-90	91-93	94-95	96
Travel agents and brokers	8	6	27	10	8	10
Service contractors	7	5	16	7	9	5

Period of commencement of business

☐ Travel agents and brokers   ▨ Service contractors

labour is formed inside the international movement of capital and work. Brokers form the tip of this recruiting system and they are an important prerequisite for bringing in the necessary labour force that crosses national borders. And the brokers do not end up being simply brokers; the labour export mechanism was perfected when brokers changed the very nature of existing organisations with which they were linked – in this case, the change from Japanese travel agencies serving people of Japanese descent as the recreational part of the prefectural association organisations into travel agencies serving people of Japanese descent as bodies for dispatching foreign workers. That is to say, it was once the operation of the labour supply mechanism began working that the movement of large numbers of people was possible.

It can be comprehended at a glance that this causes a layering effect. Locally, the year of commencement of travel agencies serving people of Japanese descent that recruit workers from within this group and the changes in migration by these workers are layered onto the year of commencement, in Japan, of contracting agencies that dispatch to factories people of Japanese descent, who have been sent by travel agencies serving people of Japanese descent. As Figure 2.4 shows, we can detect the same trend in the increase of travel agencies and brokers recruiting people of Japanese descent locally in Latin America and the increase in service contractors who send people of Japanese descent to factories.[17] It was precisely because of the establishment of this kind of labour exporting mechanism that there was a boom in the employment of foreign workers

of Japanese descent in Japan before the revision of the Immigration
Control and Refugee Recognition Act in 1990, as seen in Figure 2.3.

What possible meaning could a labour export mechanism operating to effect the division of labour have had for Japanese manufacturing industry with its multilayered subcontracting structure?
Let us look at the example of the introduction of labour of Japanese
descent by Toyota City (effectively by the Toyota Motor Company)
before the comprehensive application of the division of labour
structure to all parts of the industrial structure. As mentioned above,
the beginning of the increase in the numbers of people of Japanese
descent in Toyota City occurred after the Public Corporation for
the Homi Apartments started leasing to people legally in Japan
in 1990. Around the same time, companies in N Town in Toyota
City – on the basis of human relationships cultivated in the course
of interaction with different types of companies in the chamber
and industry association – began bringing in people of Japanese
descent directly from Brazil. Small- and medium-sized companies
that had found it impossible to assemble Japanese workers as a result
of the unprecedented shortage of workers occasioned by the bubble
economy, with the proprietors who, by chance, had connections with
Brazil, set about constructing the labour recruitment system with
travel agencies serving Brazilians of Japanese descent as the point
of contact. However, simultaneously with the collapse of the bubble
economy, this system spontaneously vanished. This was because
the point in common between the companies jointly bringing in
Brazilians – the shortage of labour – disappeared. In short, when
there was a situation of labour shortage in one company, but one of
declining production and an excess of labour in another the need
for simultaneous recruiting activities in all companies no longer
existed (this will be dealt with in detail in Chapter 7).

Did these companies then no longer rely on foreigners of Japanese
descent for their labour force? The answer is no. The group of
companies from N Town ended up selecting two strategies in
response to the dispersal of the times of labour need. Firstly, they
put together a system whereby instead of concluding contracts as
a group with travel agencies in Brazil to have the labour that they
periodically needed sent over, each individual company contracted
with its respective travel agency and had labour sent over as required.
Secondly, individual companies ended up bringing in workers from

the contracting industry. This relied heavily on the contracting industry in Toyota City that was supplying workers of Japanese descent. However, as soon as the use of service contractors began, companies learned that they could assemble a labour force simply by issuing instructions that the labour they needed be sent to them when they needed it. The use of workers of Japanese descent that had come via service contractors differed from the labour force that had initially been sent across; it had now become a labour force assembled with a short term perspective.

Self-exercise of a niche and regional labour markets

When a foreign work force functions as one regional labour market, it is necessary to examine its mode of incorporation into the labour market of the host society (Portes 1997). However, when viewed from the point of view of broker sociology, the mode of incorporation is not simply a matter of the manner of subsumption into the host society within the labour market. This mode of incorporation is also related to the nature of routes available to people, who are included into the base as immigrants, to rise in the host society. On this point, we can find strange areas in common between the brokers for those who are legally employed and the brokers for those who are not legally employed. There follows a brief explanation.

The author defines the characteristic of brokers as being that of intermediaries who recruit labour and distribute it to the areas where there is a need. In other words, brokers possess the dual functions of being recruiters and also distributors. Brokers earn a fee both from those demanding and also from those supplying labour. They demand an agent's introduction charge (a recruiter's fee) from those supplying the workers, for having introduced them to the work, and an introduction to the workers fee (a distributor's fee) from the party demanding labour, for having mediated to source the workers.

There are also cases, such as in that of women working in the entertainment area, where the burden of both the recruiter's and the distributor's fee is foisted onto the workers. Figure 2.5 depicts the situation for workers from Thailand and Colombia who are employed in the sex entertainment industry and who have been saddled with both of these fees. From the concentration of the amount of debt with which they have been burdened at around three to four million yen, it can be that there is a price; in short, that the market is being constructed. It is also important to acknowledge that it is not just brokers but also friends and acquaintances who are demanding similar amounts of money from them. In a functional sense, as Figure 2.5 shows, we could also call friends and acquaintances brokers[18] (Tanno, Mutō, Nishioka and Niikura 2003).

It is thus difficult to distinguish brokers on the basis of their attributes; the most appropriate thing to do may be, as we have in this section, to assume that they function as intermediaries possessing the dual aspects of recruiters and distributors of labour. Naturally, in the case of workers of Japanese descent who can be legally employed in Japan the situation is a little different. This is because workers pay an agent's fee to brokers, but those demanding this labour themselves pay a fee (rent) to brokers. Naturally, there are also cases of the burden of paying the fee (rent) incurred by those demanding labour being pushed arbitrarily onto the workers. However, these workers have more employment opportunities than people who start off not being permitted to work, such as those who are employed as undocumented workers. The amount of fees that brokers receive is, therefore, small. Workers who come across from Latin America have to pay expenses of around $2,400, which includes $1,400 for their ticket and a work referral fee[19] of $1,000[20] or thereabouts.

The question is: in what ways are the brokers, who are the intermediaries in the labour market, connected with the host society? Both the brokers for legally employed workers and those for undocumented workers display similar characteristics on this point. In the case of brokers for undocumented workers, by investing funds that they have acquired through illegal activities (the broker business) in legal economic activities (the management of restaurants in the host society) they provide the career path for immigrants at the moment when the act of brokering emerges from the hidden economy into the visible economy. It can be confirmed that workers of Japanese descent are handed over to ethnic entrepreneurs (immigrant business operators) – whose travel agencies and service contractors have independent interpreters and recruiting staff, and who are themselves the managers of their own travel and contracting companies – who provide their fellow countrymen with groceries, various daily goods and the media necessary for daily life in Japan. In the case of legally employed

Figure 2.5: Amount of debt burden on arrival in Japan

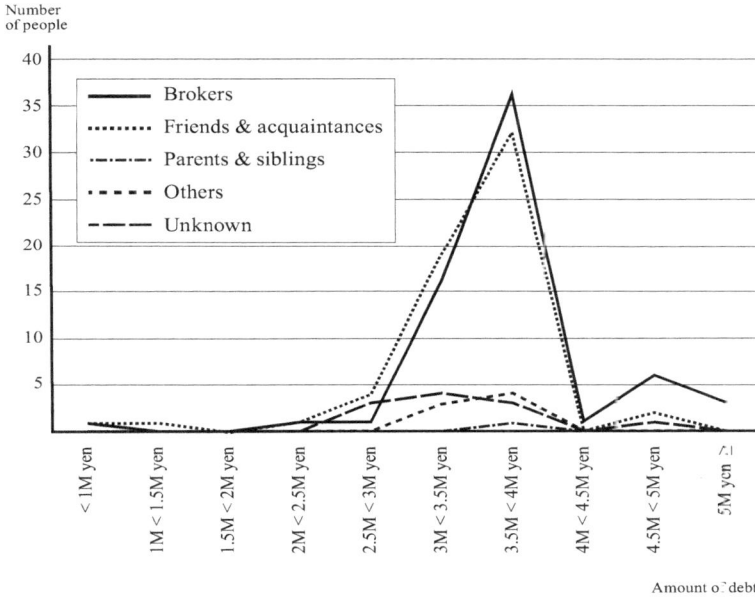

workers also, being a broker provides one career path as a step for rising up through the economic classes.

This broker business as a career path fulfils an important function in terms of constructing a niche in regional labour markets. In conditions where there are virtually no other opportunities for rising higher in the host society, becoming a broker (or stepping into the broker business) provides an effective means of getting nearer to success. As a consequence, criticising brokers in communities of foreigners is the equivalent of being a failure. From the brokers' side, criticisms of them can, at best, only be regarded as the howling of defeated dogs. Thus, within the immigrant community, the existence of brokers while being acknowledged as that of people who constantly exploit us, also continues to be an existence that is one option for action by individuals – what they would like to become. Because of the constant production of brokers with this ambivalent existence, there is an automatic reproduction of the niche within regional labour markets.

Conclusion: regional labour markets and Japan's immigrant workers

As we have seen thus far, the foreign worker labour market carries out its function as a market via the mediation of brokers. Functioning as a market means allocating labour to the points of production (factories) that need labour and work to foreigners who want jobs. In addition to performing this fundamental function as a market, their use of foreigners brings about even more value adding at the points of production.

When new technology is introduced at the point of production, this is always connected with politics. This is because the introduction of new technology at the point of production alters the nature of the division of labour both within and without the organisation (Sable 1981). The employment of foreigners can avoid the politics (disputes) that accompany the introduction of this new technology.

Eishi Fujita has arranged the changes that occurred in the Japanese automobile industry from the 1980s to the 1990s from the perspective of technology in the workplace (Fujita 1999). If we use Fujita's arguments, Japanese manufacturing industry in this period had its sights set precisely on thorough labour saving and the thoroughness of this labour saving gave rise to a vast amount of work that could not be mechanised. Also, looked at the other way around, because thoroughgoing labour savings by nature aim at the slimming down of regular employment, illegally employed workers inevitably end up being used as the labour engaged in work that cannot be mechanised. One ought not to lose sight of the big social context: this led to an expansion of the niche market and workers of Japanese descent who were brought in through service contracting companies acquired a market segment.

The social context directs the actions of people acting within it along a certain vector. However, this simply defines the orientation: the kind of system that will end up functioning in a particular context, in practical terms, is largely prescribed by the historical circumstances of that society. The majority of employment of foreigners is employment in which dismissal is easy and which is particularly heavy work. If the function being sought is simply the ease of dismissal, then the labour market could also be constructed via a system other than that of service contractors. However, as the example of workers of Japanese descent who can work legally in Japan shows, the legal employment market for foreign workers in Japan has converged with the service contractors. (There is a logical interpretation of why this convergence has occurred in the following chapter.)

In order to understand regional labour markets, they must be grasped not as abstract, but as actual ideas whose emergence has been governed by particular (historical) incidents. Both the opening up of pathways linking the movement of people between Japan and Latin America, following the conclusion of the Japan-America Airlines Agreement, and the functioning in the host society of the role of a broker who organises regional labour markets as a route to upward mobility are things that are largely controlled by the particular circumstances of Japanese society. In this sense, the regional labour market for foreign workers, while occurring against the backdrop of the large world historical context of globalisation, is also embedded in the particular major social factors making up the host country.

3 Changes in the structure of employment and foreign workers: labour market and lifestyle complementarity

Introduction: Fluctuations in the employment structure during the bubble period

Since the 1980s, Japan has seen an increasing number of foreign workers largely from Asia, referred to as newcomers, whose purpose is to find work. During the period of labour shortages, the employment of foreigners was most striking in small- and medium-sized factories and on construction sites. These days, the employment of foreigners is a commonplace sight even in the factories of the export companies that represent Japan.

Incidentally, the employment of foreign workers has continued apace in the area of blue-collar work as a result of the absolute shortage of labour, but the logic of the companies that needed to hire foreign workers changed considerably in the 1990s. This chapter examines the impact that these kinds of changes in the economic and social environment have had on foreign workers. In order to do this, let us begin with a look at the changes that have occurred in industrial society.

Japan's industrial society consists of a dual structure that creates considerable wage differentials between parent companies and the small- and medium-sized companies that are their subcontractors. It is not simply differences in productivity that lead to the social structure being established on the basis of the wages gap that appears between parent companies and the small- and medium-sized companies. This is because the movement of workers and the changing of jobs from small- and medium-sized companies to the parent company have been hindered by two rules: 1) that the labour market in the parent companies is only open to recent graduates and 2) that there is no mid-career recruitment between companies that do business with one another or within conglomerates of people who have worked for the partner companies. Under the lifetime employment system, to join a company is also to enter a concrete labour market. The former rule, determining which labour market in the hierarchy of industrial society an individual will enter at the time of their initial participation in the labour market and the latter rule, which orients any change of job by workers solely downwards in the hierarchy, have been the means by which the dual structure has become the structural mechanism that constantly preserves disparity.[1]

The bubble economy that began in the latter half of the 1980s brought about an absolute labour shortage. As a result of this type of environmental change, the business-to-business rules regarding movements between occupational categories and changing jobs were broken by parent companies. At the same time as parent company recruiting methods were ceasing to focus solely on new graduates, the conditions for the recruitment of people in mid-career changed to being 'people whose most recent previous position was not working for a business partner or a company in the conglomerate. Because this change in the rules could be an acknowledgement of the movement of low wage workers into high wage workplaces, it embodied the possibility of shaking up the dual structure of wages. Since the parent company also understood that the existence of the dual structure was the basis for its own continuation, it established the restriction that, in the case of blue-collar workers, they would be employed as full workers after having spent either one or two years as trainee workers during which time they were not able to earn anything more than trainee wages. In view of the overwhelming wage differential, however, there was, despite the existence of the traineeship period, a succession of people from small- and medium-sized companies wanting to change jobs by seeking to move to the parent company.

Moreover, in the Japanese manufacturing industry, when the line in the parent company factory is fully operational or when there has been an accident and there needs to be an increase in temporary personnel, the parent company asks the subcontracting company to supply support personnel (Nishiguchi and Bourdais 1999). Companies also tend to use support personnel as substitutes for regular employees (main workers). Against a backdrop of power relationships, subcontracting companies cannot refuse requests from parent companies for support personnel as these form part of usual practice between companies. Because of these requests, the more the parent companies restructured the more job vacancies there were in small and medium subcontracting companies; not even a period of recession could dampen their demand for labour.

However, the movement of labour from small- and medium-sized companies into the parent companies was not the only means by which the latter were able to secure the labour that they needed. Even after the bursting of the bubble economy, the severe shortage of blue-collar workers in the automobile and appliances industries persisted. The reason for the unpopularity of blue-collar work in these industries was due to the existence of late night work. This led to the twenty-four hour factory operating system upon which the automobile industry was centred being changed to a continuous two shift system thus removing late night work and making it easier to recruit workers.[2]

This series of changes in industrial society have also had a considerable impact on the employment destinations of foreign workers. What exactly is the influence of changes in these company-to-company rules; changes in the employment system of the parent company; and also of the economic environment that surrounds companies?

The labour market for foreign workers is divided into workers of Japanese descent who are able to work legally and the remainder who are undocumented workers, and the rules for finding work are completely different in each case. Undocumented workers, who are working concealed from society, and who could be called illegal workers, cover a very wide range: people who have come to Japan from Latin America on forged documents pretending to be of Japanese descent and have then overstayed; women from the Philippines who have come to Japan as entertainers and then overstayed; South Koreans who come to Japan as migrant workers and rely on the Korean community resident in Japan; women from Thailand and Colombia who entered Japan via crime syndicate and mafia routes and who are in conditions of organised prostitution; and, furthermore, people who have come to Japan from Asia as trainees and then fled from these positions partway through. Each one of these people has entered a unique labour market and they cannot be discussed using generalisations. Accordingly, workers of Japanese descent, who are legal workers, will be considered as coming under one employment system, but undocumented workers will be discussed with reference to case studies that the author has conducted, as a basis for making comparisons between them and people of Japanese descent with regard to changing and getting jobs.

The labour force's interface devices

Let us start with a discussion of the work force of Japanese descent, the legal workers. The majority of workers of Japanese descent, whether in direct or indirect employment, are employed as blue-collar workers. Up until the time of the bursting of the bubble economy, every company, including those in Japan's manufacturing industry, directly carried out activities to recruit workers in the cities of Latin America with the aim of resolving the labour shortage. Since the collapse of the bubble economy, however, every company in Japan's manufacturing industry has stopped its own direct recruiting of the workforce and now, in the 2000s, it is exclusively service contracting companies which dispatch workers to the worksites of manufacturing companies that are carrying out recruitment in Latin America.[3] It cannot be denied that these changes are linked to the fact that it has become possible to recruit a labour force without going to Latin America, as a result of the constant presence within Japan of workers of Japanese descent who form a regular labour force. However, just as recruitment activities in Latin America have shifted to service contractors, we see a similar shift also in the methods for employing workers of Japanese descent away from direct employment by manufacturing companies towards indirect employment through service contracting companies. As mentioned above, the change from a three shift system in factories to a system of two continuous shifts has made it easier to secure Japanese blue-collar workers. Similarly, with the end of the absolute labour shortages of the period of the bubble economy, parent companies are now able to satisfy their need for blue-collar workers via temporary workers such as fixed term contract workers and seasonal workers and also support personnel from subcontractors. The meaning of foreign workers in industrial society has changed. In the latter half of the 1990s, at the time of the renewal of labour contracts, workers who had formerly been gathered together in Latin America for direct employment were re-employed on the premise of re-registration with service contracting companies. The prevalence of this state of affairs is a pointed illustration of the changing trends mentioned above in the employment of people of Japanese descent (Toyota City 2001).

The mere mention of the words from direct to indirect employment is enough to convey a sense of the creation of insecurity for people of Japanese descent, but the matter is not that simple. The direct employment of people of Japanese descent whilst referred to as direct employment was, in most cases, employment for a fixed period of time in the form of labour contracts as fixed term contract and seasonal workers. This was not 'employment for an indefinite period' under which they would have been known as 'regular employees.' There were also workers in their midst who had been employed for long periods of time, but they were people who had ended up in long-term employment as a result of the accumulation of stints of fixed term employment; they had not initially been employed with a promise of long-term employment. The employment of people of Japanese descent had belonged within the category of insecure employment, also referred to as employment on the margins or peripheral employment, from the period predating indirect employment via service contracting companies.

What sort of role was a labour force of people of Japanese descent expected to play in companies? In international comparisons, it is frequently the low internalisation rate of products and the concomitant small scale of employee numbers that are cited as examples of the defining traits of Japanese manufacturing (Dore 1967; Kagono, Nonaka, Sakakibara and Okumura 1983; Smith 2000; and Nishiguchi 2000). Japanese manufacturing has, from the outset, proceeded via outsourcing particularly the blue-collar areas and has had a larger number of irregular employees compared to regular employees. Japanese companies have aimed to secure a labour force that suits their scale of production by placing orders with these outsourcers and by adjusting up or down the number of irregular employees. These can be read in terms of the types of relations set out in Figure 3.1.

Whilst making predictions about future demand for their products companies also attempt to make their current funds, plant and equipment and labour force correspond to the funds, plant and

Figure 3.1: Current and future relationships in companies

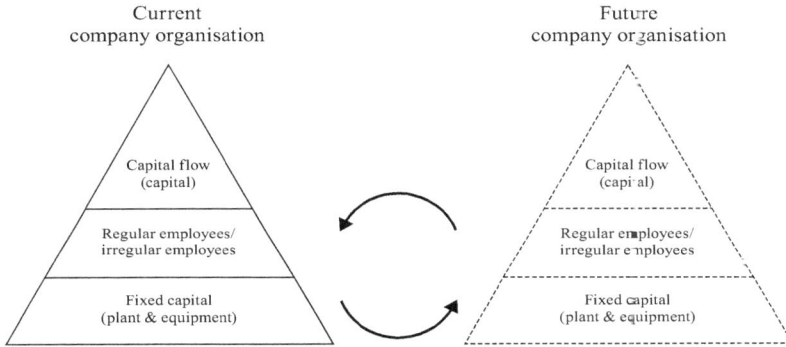

equipment and labour force that will be needed to carry out production activities to meet future demand. The demand for their own companies' products is constantly changing, including seasonal changes. Employment in the reliable portion of production activities and in product development, which has a bearing on the competitive power of their products, as well as in those areas that are related to quality control, is shouldered by regular employees. Companies have, however, coped by allotting blue-collar employment, which is exposed to fluctuations, to irregular workers. These are, in concrete terms, part-time, fixed term contract and seasonal workers. Fixed term contract and seasonal workers, in particular, are almost invariably rounded up for fixed terms of employment of six months or a year. In factories periodically employing fixed term contract and seasonal workers, the necessary labour force was regulated via a dual regulatory mechanism consisting of adjustments in the rate of renewals for those renewing contracts every month and adjustments to the recruitment of fixed term contract and seasonal workers. The direct employment of people of Japanese descent has been as fixed term contract or seasonal workers.

How does this change once there is a shift to indirect employment? The employment of workers on fixed term employment, of which fixed term contract and seasonal workers in direct employment are representative, is, as has been discussed, superb as a system for acquiring the necessary labour force in response to demand for products from one's own company. For the parent company, which produces multiple products that enable it to offset any drop in demand for a particular product with demand for other products and which is able to stabilise the overall operating ratio of its factories, it is a particularly effective labour recruitment system. However, within the multilayered subcontracting structure of Japan, the further down one goes, all the way down to the low level subcontractors, there is a tendency to specialise in specific parts for specific products amongst what is an array of parent company products. Subcontracting companies that find themselves in these sorts of relationships end up singlehandedly shouldering the burden of the fluctuations in product demand that the parent company is offsetting. This is why employment for a limited period in which the duration is fixed, seen by parent companies as an effective measure, ends up being a measure that contains within it the risk, in subcontracting companies, of being saddled with a surplus labour force. In other words, parent companies are able to deal with fluctuating employment numbers by using fixed term employment, but subcontracting companies end up being saddled with a surplus labour force despite using fixed term employment.

What then are the necessary conditions for subcontracting companies to be able to construct a system in which they will not carry a surplus labour force? Subcontracting companies cannot describe their own future vision without reference to the parent company's future vision. This is because they cannot maintain a long-term and stable future vision if they do not adjust employment numbers up or down to deal with sudden fluctuations in production in the parent company. Subcontracting companies are seeking to be going concerns that match the daily operating conditions in the parent company (Commons 1995: Chapter 5). Not only do subcontracting companies have to match their own current operating conditions to those in the parent company, for the benefit of the parent company's daily operations, their labour demand also must be made to comply with daily operating conditions in the parent company. Thus, as shown in Figure 3.2, a subcontracting company's labour force demand must be determined whilst blending, in a complicated fashion, the parent company's current operating conditions and future vision with one's own company's current operating conditions and future vision.

The labour force demand interface mechanism that acts as a mediator between these sorts of companies is the service contracting

*Figure 3.2: Company activity concept map for subcontracting
companies*

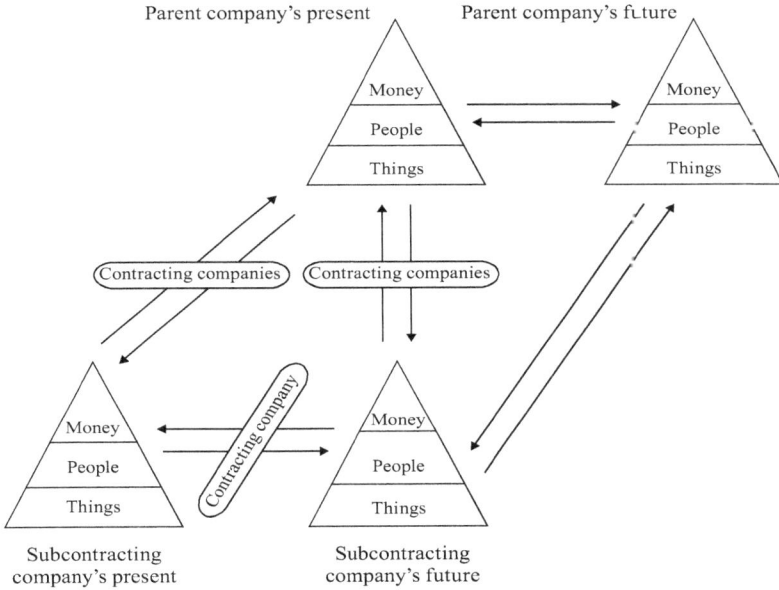

Parent company's present   Parent company's future

Money

People

Things

Money

People

Things

Contracting companies   Contracting companies

Money

People

Things

Money

People

Things

Contracting company

Subcontracting
company's present

Subcontracting
company's future

company.[4] As a result of being compelled to convert labour contracts
for individual companies into contracting agreements, subcontracting companies forego the freedom that they would have been able to
secure via labour contracts. This is the function of assembling only
the labour force that they deem to be necessary. Through indirect
employment, subcontracting companies use foreign workers to gain
the facility that parent companies have gained via the use of fixed
term and seasonal workers. It is actually not unusual for the cost of
workers in factories who have been dispatched by service contracting companies to be dealt with as factory purchasing costs.[5] Being
able to treat these as the same procurement costs as when buying
parts enabled companies, unlike the case with employment and
dismissal costs for workers, to bring about increases and decreases
in the numbers of workers needed in a speedy manner. There are
also numerous cases amongst workers of Japanese descent of people
being employed under these procurement costs in factories even
though they were directly employed. This is why it is not unusual

for these workers, even in direct employment, not to be covered by work insurance or social insurance (health insurance and the welfare pension).

The progress of settling and diversified and complex migrant labour

Let us begin with a look at how current workers of Japanese descent in indirect employment are deployed throughout Japan. Figure 3.3 gives a clear representation of this. Independent service contractors are able to dispatch the prescribed number of workers to factories by mediating between a reduction in personnel in one factory and an increase in personnel in another place. However, because a subcontracting company has to assume the risk (only the labour force portion) that it sustains singlehandedly, it is impossible for one company alone to deal with these fluctuations. This is why, some way or another, the sort of relationships between independent service contractors as those in Figure 3.3 are formed. These are sometimes formed amongst the proprietors of service contracting companies and they are also sometimes established amongst interpreting staff of Japanese descent who manage blue-collar workers in service contracting companies (see Chapter 9).

Service contractors dispatch workers to a variety of blue-collar jobs while concluding these sorts of relationships amongst one another. Along with the increasing diversification of varieties of jobs, there is also growing diversification of wages and working conditions for workers. When considering this diversification, we must focus our attention on the diversity, variety, of migrant workers that are being produced as spin-offs accompanying the increasingly long-term nature of migrant work for people of Japanese descent. Accordingly, let us now use a consideration of the variety of migrant workers for thinking about how migrant worker spin-offs become rational.

Migrant work by people of Japanese descent will be treated here as the synthesis of two propositions or, alternatively, as an exercise in conditional probability. In other words, Proposition Q – 'that migrant work by people of Japanese descent is rational (people of Japanese descent can become wealthy through migrant work)' – will be examined (Table 3.1) as a compound proposition which contains both Proposition p – 'that it is rational to stay on living in Latin

*Figure 3.3: Dispatching from contracting companies and employ-
ment networks*

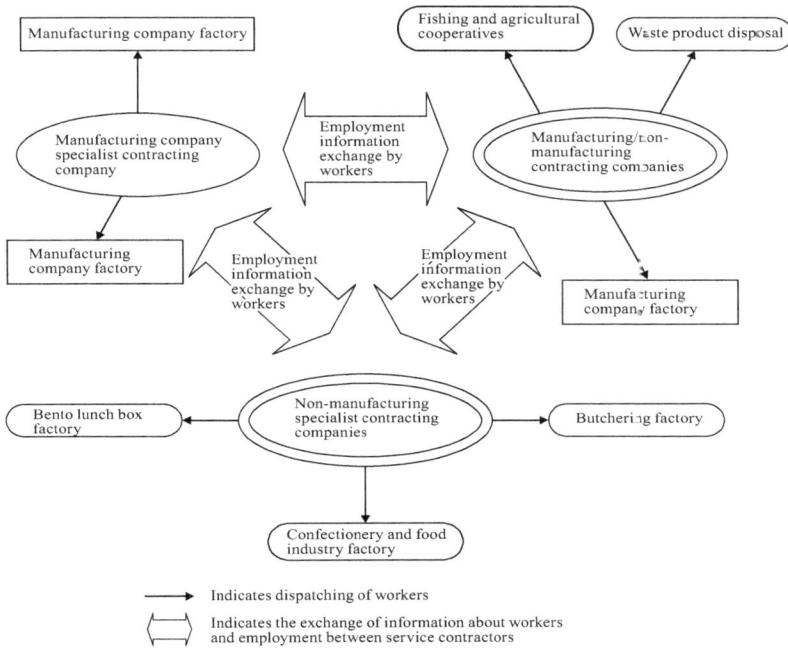

| Manufacturing company factory |
| Fishing and agricultural cooperatives |
| Waste product disposal |

| Manufacturing company specialist contracting company |
| Employment information exchange by workers |
| Manufacturing/non-manufacturing contracting companies |

| Manufacturing company factory |
| Employment information exchange by workers |
| Employment information exchange by workers |
| Manufacturing company factory |

| Bento lunch box factory |
| Non-manufacturing specialist contracting companies |
| Butchering factory |

| Confectionery and food industry factory |

⟶ Indicates dispatching of workers

⟷ Indicates the exchange of information about workers
and employment between service contractors

America (plenty of good jobs can be found in Latin America)' – and
Proposition q – 'that it is rational to travel to Japan (it is possible
to find plenty of good jobs by going to Japan as a migrant worker).'

Generally, whether migrant workers are people of Japanese
descent or Japanese nationals coming into cities from rural
villages, the term 'migrant worker' describes finding work by
moving temporarily to another place where job opportunities are
plentiful because there was a lack of sufficient job opportunities
to support one's family in the area from which one came. These
cases can be thought of as cases in which for migrant work to be
rational (Proposition Q is the rational proposition), then there
would be a lack of work if one were to remain in one's home area
(Proposition p is false), but there would be job opportunities if one
were to travel to another place (Proposition q is true). This means
that: if one were to be blessed with abundant job opportunities

Table 3.1: The rationality of migrant work as a conditional hypothesis

Traditional migrant work (short term migrant work)			Current migrant work (increasingly long-term migrant work and residency)		
Proposition Q Migrant work is rational	Proposition p Jobs exist in South America	Proposition q Jobs exist in Japan	Proposition Q Migrant work is rational	Proposition p Jobs exist in South America	Proposition q Jobs exist in Japan
o	x	o	o	x	o
x	x	x	o	x	x
x	o	x	x	o	x
x	o	o	Δ	o	o

Note:

o indicates that a proposition is true

x indicates that a proposition is false

Δ indicates that there are times when the proposition is true and also times when it is false while continuing to live in one's home area (Proposition p is true), and if going elsewhere in search of work were to represent a job opportunity that entailed only costs (Proposition q is false), then the rationality of going elsewhere in search of work would vanish. Migrant work in search of jobs in other places where one's prospects are unknown regardless of the fact that there are job opportunities in one's home area (a combination of Proposition p being true and Proposition q being false) and migrant work in which there would be no jobs even if one were to stay in one's home area and similarly no prospect of work even if this person were to go elsewhere (both Proposition p and Proposition q are false) render movement very risky; alternatively, because it is not possible to calculate the benefits that one would gain by moving, this could not necessarily be called a rational economic act.

On the other hand, when it would be possible to find work either by staying in one's home area (Proposition p is true) or by moving (Proposition q is true) – that is, in the case of migrant workers of Japanese descent, if one were to have abundant job opportunities even if one chose to remain in Latin America and also the prospect of similar conditions if one were to come to Japan – being in either place would represent a rational act in terms of finding work. In these cases, major impetuses that are not simply job opportunities emerge and the rationality of migrant work is determined from other points of view. If we take a look at the actual situation, around the time that migrant workers from Latin America began appearing in the mid-1980s, coming to Japan for migrant work was for no other reason than a search for job opportunities, therefore, had there been sufficient work in Latin America, there would not have been any movement even if it had been possible to find work in Japan.[6]

However, once large numbers of one's family and friends have left for Japan as migrant workers, the question of whether to go off as a migrant worker or not ceases to be limited to a mere calculation of economic opportunity and the very method of calculating economic opportunity itself changes. As migrant work has taken on an increasingly long-term nature, growing numbers of people in the ranks of those left behind as a reserve army of migrant workers in Latin America have a family member who has spent some time living in Japan. If it is possible to get oneself to the place where family are living, then it becomes possible to go to Japan, even if one does not have work at the time of arriving there. Moreover, if it becomes possible to be a migrant worker who is a lodger, then one can make do even on a low amount of total wages from which living costs in Japan and savings must come (there is a reduction of harmful conditions in which Proposition q becomes rational). In short, migrant work for a lower rate of pay became a rational act because somewhere to live had already been secured.

If we view this change in migrant work by returning to the migrant work propositions given in Table 3.1, as migrant work and residency have become more long-term in nature, the form of Propositions p and q has also changed and as a result migrant work as a compound proposition (Proposition Q), which was once irrational, has also emerged as rational in some cases. Migrant work which had not been possible up until now – that is, in which there is the long-term possibility of finding work even though there are no immediate prospects of employment (Proposition q is false in the long term) – becomes possible (Proposition Q, which had been false, can change to become true). Due to the effectiveness of these propositions, cases that had previously been unimaginable – in short, migrant work by people who find it difficult to get work by staying in Latin America, but who are not likely to have much prospect of work as a result of having come to Japan (Proposition p is false and Proposition Q in which Proposition q is also false) have also become rational. The consequence of all of these developments, the increasingly long-term nature of migrant work, has caused changes to the social environment and has brought about a change in the economic rationality of migrant work.

Intermediaries who are migrant workers of Japanese descent

The diversification of migrant work has brought about an even greater amplification of complexity as a result of the reaction of service contractors, who are their employers, to changes in workers. Consequently, the employment of workers of Japanese descent is extending into broader spheres both geographically and in terms of areas of work. This section examines how migrant work has changed as a result of the responses of service contractors to changes amongst migrant workers.

The dispatching of workers to key industries such as automobiles and appliances, the areas in which the majority of people of Japanese descent are employed, is well known. There are two reasons for the concentration of dispatching in these sectors. One is the fact that recruitment advertisements for all areas in Japan are published in the newspapers for people of Japanese descent (including *International Press, Tudo Bem, Nova Visião and Folha Mundial*) which are sold in the areas where most of these people live. The second is that the fact that workers of Japanese descent, to a large extent, move to those areas where there is even a slightly better hourly rate has led to the creation of a largely uniform national wage rate. Between 1997 and 2000, the hourly wage rate was 1,300–1,400 yen for men and 900–1,100 yen for women. The workplaces able to pay these wages were, needless to say, limited to the industries with the highest rates of productivity. As mentioned in the previous section, however, with the appearance of people who have come over as migrant workers despite the fact that they have no work in the short term and also of people who will work even for low wages, service contractors were able to begin dispatching workers to new areas of work, which they had previously been unable to enter because the high hourly wage rate for people of Japanese descent would have meant pricing below cost.

The movement of workers that mediates between service contractors and the workplaces that receive the workers dispatched by the service contractors, as shown in Figure 3.3 (above), depicts the situation following the appearance of people willing to work for amounts below the going wage rate. It is essential to ask, before proceeding any further: what kind of workers are these workers who are prepared to work for less than the going wage rate? The hierarchy that most likely comes to mind when one thinks about the wages and job opportunities for workers of Japanese descent is: 1) male workers able to perform even manual labour for which the wages are high and the job opportunities plentiful; 2) young female workers for whom there are lower wages but more job opportunities than for men; 3) mature age workers; and 4) elderly workers. As the number of migrant workers living with family members has increased, people corresponding to 3) mature age workers and 4) elderly workers, who can be recruited for conditions under which the amount of pay is inferior to the going rate, have come into existence. Being able to dispatch to workplaces with considerably lower contracting unit costs has made it possible for service contractors to show a profit, and they have been able to increase the number of places to which they dispatch workers beyond what had previously been possible. This expansion in places to which they dispatch workers has been to workplaces such as factories producing bento lunchboxes for convenience stores, agricultural and fishing cooperatives and industrial waste management plants.

The diversification of both wages and workplaces also has an impact on the state of migrant work for the workers themselves. The same logic that applies to Japanese part-time workers has made it possible for migrant workers to stay in Japan when, as family members, as long as they earn an income that is ancillary to the household finances their actions are regarded as rational and this has given rise to the household form of migrant work. Workers of Japanese descent have created a nationally uniform wage rate by frequently moving around, but service contractors endeavour to bring about a settling down in one place of those workers engaged in high contracting unit price employment by making use of the employment of family members. This is because, from the service contractors' point of view, increasing the staying on the job rate of workers who are able to do the work will increase the trust placed in them by the client companies to whom they dispatch workers. Because most client companies receive dispatched workers from a number of service contractors, the diversification of workplaces, to the extent that it ultimately brings about an increase in the rate of workers staying on the job, is a necessary strategy for each service contractor representing an important moment in terms of prevailing in the competition against other companies.[7]

What inevitably emerges as a result of these developments is a safety net made up of relationships in which residences are shared. In human society, we normally observe parents supporting their children until the latter are adults, and eventually when these children are older, they support their own children while also supporting their parents, who can no longer work (Tachibanaki 2000). This is a kind of archetypal private safety net in which those members within the family group who are earning wages support the generations within that same family membership group who cannot earn wages. We can detect the kind of mechanism that this type of safety net creates, within a short time span, in the residence patterns of people of Japanese descent. Whether they are directly employed or indirectly employed, workers of Japanese descent, whose basis is short, fixed term employment, are dogged by the

*Figure 3.4: Concept map of residence sharing by workers of Japan-
    ese descent*

Residents

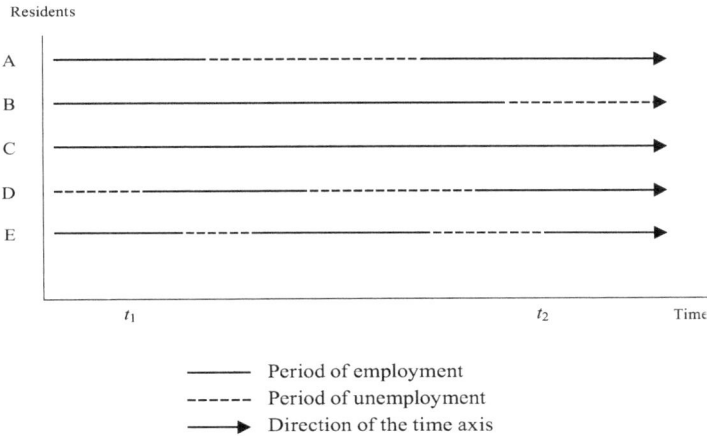

```
A  ———————————————————————————————————— ►
B  ———————————————————————————————————— ►
C  ———————————————————————————————————— ►
D  ———————————————————————————————————— ►
E  ———————————————————————————————————— ►

   t₁                          t₂        Time
```

    ——————— Period of employment
    --------- Period of unemployment
    —————► Direction of the time axis

threat of sudden dismissal. Service contractors who employ people
of Japanese descent house these workers in their dormitories and,
as long as there are people living there who work for their company
and that they pay the rent, service contractors do not object to other
people living there also. This is because when there is a sudden
request for increased personnel from a client, this arrangement also
enables the service contractor to lay his hands on a reserve army of
workers (Tanno 2000a).

Figure 3.4 shows a concept map of the safety net in a dormitory
for workers of Japanese descent. For the sake of convenience, Figure
3.4 is taken to be a case of five workers living in one dormitory. If
we were to apply what has been discussed thus far to this figure,
for point in time t1, for example, A, B, C and E are working, but
of these fellow residents, D is unemployed. At point in time t2,
however, A, C and D are working, but B and E are unemployed.
They have constructed a system whereby, in the midst of frequent
bouts of unemployment, even those who are unemployed will not
lose a place to live as long as the fellow residents pay the rent.
The dormitories of people of Japanese descent end up fulfilling
the function of a safety net by constructing households based on
multiple workers capable of becoming the main wage earners or
alternatively households which include workers whose earnings are

incidental in order to avoid the risk of unemployment also leading
to the loss of a place to live.

As a result of this diversification of the employment of migrant workers we now frequently have migrant workers who lack
prospects of work when they set off as migrant workers. This is
migrant work as reunion with family, relatives or acquaintances.
Employment in Japan on this basis has led to the appearance of what
is referred to as a shift to 'a tendency towards overconsumption
by migrant workers' or 'the enjoying the lifestyle type' (Ishi 1995;
Mori 1993 and 1995). It would, however, be premature to think that
migrant work in general had changed on the basis of these results. It
is simply that it has become difficult to see the true nature of migrant
workers of Japanese descent as a result of the diversification from
the old type of migrant worker who came to Japan and worked with
a goal in mind to the migrant worker who does not necessarily wish
to be the main breadwinner.

Service contractors have understood these changes amongst
workers and have also expanded their business opportunities. Once
it is possible to share living quarters, as in Figure 3.4, the need
vanishes for all those who come as migrant workers to earn an
income sufficient to support one's family. Migrant workers who
take their wives or elderly relatives along with them do not find
that these family members become a burden on the wage earner,
rather they have come to provide a safety net during times of
unemployment. As far as the employment of people of Japanese
descent is concerned – from the era of an absolute shortage of
manpower during the bubble economy to the midst of economic
recession – these changes have been convenient for both workers
and service contractors.

Safety net and community

As has been argued, the diversification of the types of work in which
foreigners are employed also represents progress in the safety net for
foreign workers. In the case of people of Japanese descent, service
contractors and workers of Japanese descent have come to mutually
treat one another as a resource with service contractors aiming to
expand their sphere of business (client companies) and workers
aiming to acquire a safety valve within short term employment.
The industrial workplaces that are on the receiving end of these

mutual changes in service contractors and workers and also of a labour force have changed too. The companies that receive workers exclude (dismiss) workers lacking a sense of purpose, in the name of line contracting. Just as there are times when directives are issued to replace workers in client companies, there are also times when workers themselves quit because an atmosphere has arisen within the workplace that makes it difficult for them to remain there. Thus, a mechanism for screening workers, a mechanism for coping with the changes in workers, is functioning efficiently in workplaces.

Unlike companies, however, the regions and local government areas in which foreigners live cannot make decisions about who they will allow to live there. This is where a gap emerges between the usefulness of employing foreign workers, from the point of view of companies, and residence by foreign workers as far as regional society is concerned. The mechanism whereby this gap emerges is simple. Foreign workers' safety nets are made up of a membership that is fixed in the short term, but given the form of employment in which foreigners are engaged, premised on insecure employment, these are networks that could not survive without a constant changing of members in the medium and long term. In the case of workers of Japanese descent, the most typical expression is a phenomenon that could be called 'invisible settlement and residence' (Tanno 1999a and 2000a). 'Invisible settlement and residence' refers to the emergence, in the regions, of a situation in which, it is not possible for residents to form the usual neighbourly relationships with people of Japanese descent, despite the fact that the latter are long-term residents. What kind of social structure gives rise to this kind of situation?

The author believes that it is possible to approach this gap through the fissure between the logic of production activities and the logic of regional and living space. Production activity, an economic activity, is one in which people as the protagonists (hereafter referred to as individuals) set to work on the labour target, using tools, to produce goods or services. However, these production activities are not carried out by individuals in isolation from society. It is usual for individuals to be engaged in production activities within an organisation according to the rules of that organisation. Decisions about which work targets individuals will be working on are made based on the internal division of labour within the organisation to which the individual belongs. Similarly, the issue of which products the particular organisation (in practical terms, individual companies or public bodies) to which an individual belongs produces is determined on the basis of the state of the social division of labour within the society concerned. Within these relationships, production activities are accomplished resulting in the production of goods and services (Engestrom 1993 and 1999; Kuutti 1996; and Nishiyama 1997). Current production activities consist of the use of goods and services which are the products of production activities as future raw materials and they also, simultaneously, result from the use of goods and services which are products of past production activities. Production activities (which are also simultaneously reproduction activities) are thus reorganised in a cyclical process. Figure 3.5a depicts the nature of these relationships.

The lives of individuals are not, it should be said, made up exclusively of production activities. There are long-term, non-economic activities of raising the next generation and short term non-economic activities of recuperating for work the next day that occur in the living space. In the long term, even in the living space, individuals do not exist in isolation. Individuals living in regional communities are members of formal organisations such as residents' neighbourhood councils; they are members of the PTA; and, while it may not be an organisation, they live lives as participants in a set of relationships with other members of the neighbourhood. A common set of rules exists between individuals and the regional community for the people who live there. Regional communities, as assemblies of regional residents made up of individuals, ask administrative bodies to deal with and resolve problems whenever disputes arise regarding the region. Regional problems (social problems) are not only the result of direct appeals to the administration by residents; they also result from the world of discourse – that is, newspapers and television. Similarly, regional problems are outputs of present day regional society, but – just as in the case of goods and services which are the products of economic activity – they will become future inputs in the form of issues that regional society must resolve. Figure 3.5b depicts non-economic activity in these living spaces.

Economic and non-economic activities function as the two sides of society. Society reproduces itself by consuming the outputs of economic activities as subsequent social inputs. At the same time as the results of this economic activity are used as goods in the reproduction of economic activity, they are also used in people's

Figure 3.5: *Fundamental structure of economic and living space activities*

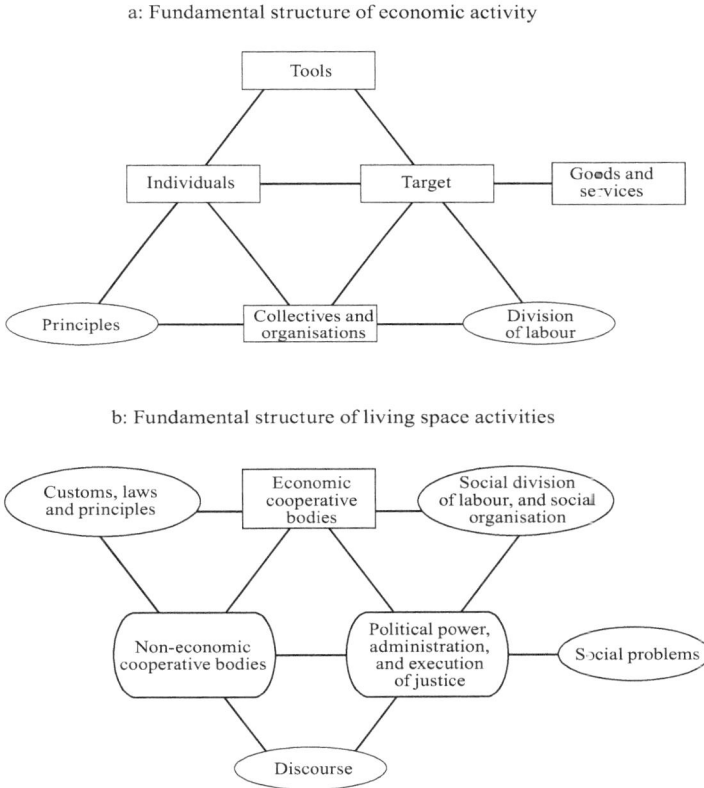

a: Fundamental structure of economic activity

b: Fundamental structure of living space activities

reproduction as consumer goods in their living spaces. Economic and non-economic activities, while causing their respective regional and social problems, also respectively carry out activities to grapple with these problems in the form of issues for social resolution. In short, Figure 3.5a and Figure 3.5b form the superstructure and substructure of an entire society. This is exemplified in Figure 3.6.

Companies deal with their labour force within this kind of structure while making service contractors the point of contact – that is, the interface – between the company and the labour market. Intermediary organisations (service contractors) do not simply pro-

Figure 3.6: The reproductive structure of activities, including social problems

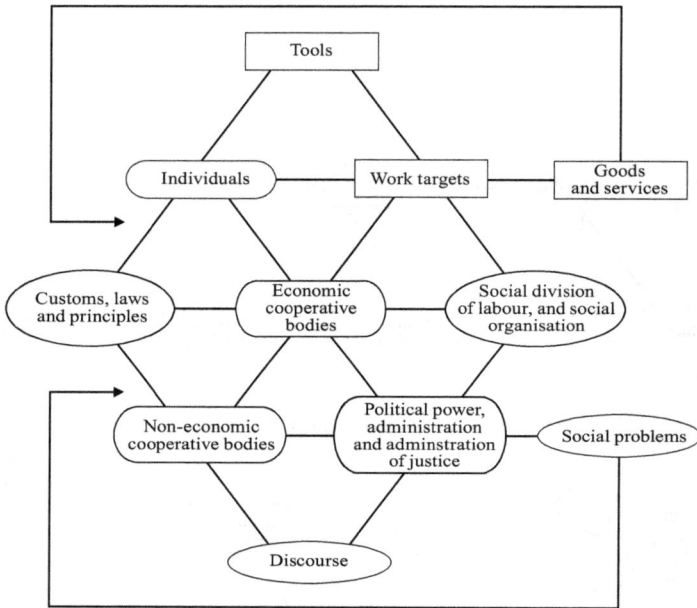

vide a flexible labour force to industrial society; they also play the role of gatekeepers who usher into the market workers who will adapt to the company environment. The problem is that having foreigners living in the regional societies concerned becomes a necessary condition in order for companies to be able to source the labour force that they need at the times when they need it. A flexible labour supply first becomes feasible when there is external diseconomy in the regional society. At the same time as imposing a burden on regional society, this fact also places an extraordinary burden on foreigners by putting them in a situation in which they have no choice but to rely on a private safety net.

Complementarity between the labour market and lifestyle

What has the spread of foreign workers throughout Japan come to look like? The increase in the population of foreigners living in Japan does not simply indicate that there has been an increase in companies employing foreigners. It is not always the case that a company that had until last month been employing foreigners will still be employing foreign workers come next month. Whilst foreign workers come and go at the level of individual companies, the total number of companies for the region as a whole that employ foreigners goes on increasing. The reason why individual companies do not continue to use the employment of foreigners just because they once did is because as far as the company is concerned, the employment of foreigners is merely one of a variety of choices at its disposal.

In 1995, in their *'Japanese Management' in a New Era*, the Japan Federation of Employers' Associations (hereafter *Nikkeiren*) raised the issue that it was possible to change from the type of company organisations that had existed to date, with the lifetime employment system at their heart, to flexible company organisations whilst continuing to aim for employment stability by having temporary and transferred employees and also contract employees brought in on an individual project basis or for a fixed period of time working alongside lifetime employment employees. *Nikkeiren* also raised the issue that company-dominated society needed this change (Japan Federation of Employers' Associations 1995). Flexible workplace organisations to match this sort of economic environment are produced by a combination of the internal and external labour markets, but *Nikkeiren* refers to these as 'employment portfolios.' It is in the area of white-collar employees that *Nikkeiren* is attempting to advance the creation of employment portfolios. In light of the fact that blue-collar work is seeing the growth of the subcontracting structure, which is by nature stratified, and that regular employees and workers from outside the company – support personnel, fixed term contract workers, seasonal workers and part-time workers – are working in the same workplaces, we could say that the creation of a portfolio approach is already complete.

Foreign work, the consequence of these employment portfolios, whilst influenced by the economic environment in the form of business ups and downs, is simultaneously exposed to competition with other portfolio labour forces. During the era of absolute labour shortages in the bubble economy period even though the creation of employment portfolios progressed, there was no sense of foreign workers being forced into competition against other portfolio labour forces. In recent years, however, conditions have changed considerably.

Since the progressively declining birth rate and the ageing of the population lead to a decline, in the long term, in the population able to supply a labour force, this may be increasing demand for a foreign labour force.[8] However, in order to secure the employment of workers who will work in the new system of delayed retirement and re-employment that accompanies the current raising of the age at which payments of the age pension commence, parent companies are reducing the work that they send out to subcontractors and they are also beginning to establish contracting departments and send older people to the shop floor. The decline in the volume of orders placed with subcontractors and the inclusion of older workers in the contracting labour force has led to a result that seems to snatch work away from foreign workers; in short, it has led to a shift away from foreign work towards Japanese work.

This same pattern has also become strikingly obvious in female work. In the midst of the fluidisation of employment, one might even say 'employment insecurity,' there is the shadow of anxieties about work restructuring for husbands who used to be the traditional wage earners in families (Nomura 1998; Yashiro 1999). This is why it has become easier for the housewife stratum to enter the labour market. Furthermore, as a result of the full implementation of the Gender Equality in Employment Act (hereafter the Equality Act) in 1999, late night work by female workers also became possible. With their gaze firmly on these changes, companies established new fixed term contract worker lines made up solely of female workers by developing jigsaws that would also be easy for women to work with and machine tools that required little physical strength to operate.

Once there was an increase in the available labour force resources – as a result of the existence of a labour force that could be used to reduce total wage costs to below the level of the cost of using part-time foreign workers and also as a result of taking advantage of the Equality Act to extend worker recruitment to include women for workplace environments in areas that used to be male workplaces – it was natural for companies to use those resources that would be most advantageous to their company activities. Thus, we can see the trend of a Japanese national labour force replacing a foreign labour force. This is the case of one lot of peripheral work being left behind and replaced by another type of peripheral work; it is, effectively, competition within the area of insecure employment – that is, amongst older people, women and foreigners.[9]

When the economic environment changes and foreign workers in the marketplace become merely one of several resources as far as companies are concerned, considerable changes also emerge in the lifestyles of workers. Under conditions of labour shortages in which there is no option but to rely on foreign workers, companies cannot help but be concerned about how to make workers stay. When, however, foreign workers are simply one choice as far as the company is concerned, the company prefers to avail itself of the most advantageous choice on a case by case basis. Once this is the case, the retention of foreign workers ends up being a constraining factor on the optimum action for the company to take in terms of making the most advantageous choice on a given occasion When varied choices are available it is rather workers who do not remain who suit the social context in which the company finds itself.

The diversity of foreign workers that has been discussed thus far is the flip side of these sorts of changes to industrial society. We can, for example discern a clear shift in the case of employers' views of foreign workers from assessments of foreign workers as working diligently even for low wages to these workers being seen as selfish workers or as workers who are no replacement for Japanese workers. In the survey conducted by this author and others (Kajita (ed.) 1999) individual employers gave the following reasons for these changes in the nature of workers: 1) because with the passage of ten years since the beginning of the employment of people of Japanese descent, a new generation has replaced the older one; 2) because their knowledge of Japan has increased during their long period of working in Japan; 3) because they have achieved their goal of living with their families; and 4) because they have shifted from being migrant workers whose aim was to send money home and to save to migrant workers who enjoy being consumers. We can indeed observe a change in generations in migrant workers and also an accumulation of experience of having worked in a variety of workplaces through the prolongation and repeated experiences of being a migrant worker. There are also a significant number of migrant workers who not only send for relatives who are looking for work, but also migrant worker households which have sent for wives and children thus comprehensively moving the place where they live to Japan. It is as a result of this that we have come to see a shift away from traditional migrant workers who saved and sent remittances to migrant workers who display a marked preference for consumption in Japan.

This may well represent an alteration in the nature of workers, but it would not do to overlook the fact that it is a change in the labour market which now seeks the kind of workers who enjoy immediate consumption rather than migrant workers with a clear goal-orientation that provides the backdrop to this alteration. Employment that might be able to be substituted using a different means of employment always carries the risk of unemployment. It is only workers who are able to accept unemployment who can continue working in this type of employment environment. What then is the kind of lifestyle attitude displayed by those personalities that are able to accept unemployment?

People who send money home or who attempt to return home again one day with the bulk of their savings, however small these savings may be, adopt a preference for increasing their working hours and for reducing consumption in order to speed up the realisation of their goal by even just a little and they also try to find employment in work with the lowest possible incidence of unemployment. In the midst of the constant existence of the risk of unemployment, however, they have no option but to discard their hoped for goals and live with unemployment. Similarly, in an environment in which it is certain that they will be visited by unemployment, are workers whose preference is to realise their goals of sending money home and saving going to lose their will to work and leave the market? Migrant workers who started off with the goal to send money home and to save have no option but to undergo a change of nature and become migrant workers whose goal is consumption. Workers whose intention had been consumption in Japan from the outset can continue working in Japan even faced with the risk of unemployment because consumption itself, which is the fruit of their work, is their goal. In this manner, workers who are industrious and diligent by nature become few in the labour market as a whole and workers who, at a glance, have no gaols, who have consumption as their goal, stand out.

As will, however, be clear from the explanation thus far, these changes in the labour market are actually the result of actions by the protagonists – companies, Japanese (regular employees as well as older and female workers) and foreign workers – all of whom live in the same period against the backdrop of the same economic environment; actions which each actor, with their own sense of autonomy, has taken to match the environment. It is possible to infer from this that complementarity exists between the lifestyle of foreign workers and the labour market.

The changes in foreign workers are apt to be explained in terms of changes on the part of workers that have accompanied the increases in length of stay and experiences as migrant workers (Mori 1995). There is, of course, no doubt about the fact that the workers' patterns of conduct have changed. We should not, however, overlook the existence of a social context that gave direction to these individual changes in the conduct of workers (Lave 1993 and Nardi 1996). This section has pointed out that changes in the labour market environment within which foreigners were employed had a part in the shift in foreign workers' orientation from having a preference for diligence to a preference for consumption; and also that the changes in the lifestyle patterns that led towards a preference for consumption are the result of a complementarity between the protagonists of each of these actions – companies, Japanese and foreign workers. If we take the complementarity between these environmental changes and the protagonists of the actions into consideration, we are able to understand that the change in workers of Japanese descent which might have seemed irrational was, instead, a consequence of the properties suited to survival in a changed environment.

The complementarity between changes in the networks found amongst undocumented workers and the living environment

The environments surrounding undocumented workers and workers of Japanese descent differ vastly. There are commonalities on points such as the fact that, just as in the case of people of Japanese descent who are legal workers, networks become a sort of key as there cannot be any recourse to systems for changing and transferring between jobs via formal organisations such as the Public Employment Exchange and the Gaikokujin Job Center (*Nikkeis*), both in the public sector, or service contracting companies which are in the private sector. Accordingly, this chapter will now consider the labour market for undocumented workers when seen as a network from the standpoint of cases of workers from Pakistan, Bangladesh and Iran on whom the author has been working.

It has been stated that the labour environments for people of Japanese descent and undocumented workers are widely divergent, but this serves to indicate that there are disparities in the methods of changing or transferring between jobs and does not exclude the fact that these two groups are squarely located within the same employment system. In reality, people of Japanese descent and undocumented workers are to be found working in the same workplaces (Igarashi 1999) and there are also service contractors and brokers who dispatch both people of Japanese descent and undocumented workers.[10] However, service contractors and brokers dispatching undocumented workers face labour management issues and tend to target only specific ethnic groups. Because of this, it is difficult for undocumented workers who suddenly find that they are unemployed to transfer and work for a different service contractor or broker. Particularly in the case of workers from countries with a caste system, there is no attempt at communication between workers who, although sharing the same nationality, belong to different castes and there are also cases where on the basis of one's standing in terms of caste, there have been refusals to carry out the instructions given in the workplace by interpreting staff, who form the point of contact with Japanese. Service contractors who dispatch undocumented workers have a well-developed knowledge, gleaned by experience, about this sort of culture and they assemble workers from groups having not only similar language, but also religious and cultural backgrounds.

Incidentally, although there are cases of undocumented workers being dispatched from service contracting companies, job changes and job transfers for undocumented workers are not movements within the labour market based on the attributes seen in the case of people of Japanese descent (the visa status of people of Japanese descent); they are characterised by work being acquired via movements centred around networks. Accordingly, there is a need to consider the system of job movements and transfers that is mediated by these networks. The author uses the term ethnic networks to define 'networks in general that are constructed by foreign workers,' including the majority which are built on the basis of regional bonds and blood relationships, but also religious solidarity with areas in other countries and market type relationships in which money is taken for introductions to work (Tanno 1998). Let us now use these ethnic networks to think about the movement of undocumented workers.

A mechanism that could be called chain migration can be observed in the host country within the movement of undocumented workers. Whenever a worker moves from a job, because he is returning home or because he has found work at another workplace, the job vacancy is communicated as employment information to acquaintances who share regional or blood bonds. Then a new worker fills that position. This does not just occur when someone moves to another job; employment information is circulated and the necessary workers assembled also when there has been an increase in the volume of work and there is a need for additional workers.

When an employment vacancy arises, whether as a result of workers moving or an increase in work, proprietors speak to the workers in their own companies asking, 'You wouldn't know anyone suitable?' The workers who are asked this question put out a call to people from the same areas as them and to their relatives. We see that as a result of doing things this way, changing jobs for undocumented workers actually ends up being not a case of the newly employed workers having been chosen by the proprietors, but by the workers who put out a call to them. This type of shift is defined as a shift based on 'indirect trust.'

Within the ethnic networks, there are also ethnic brokers who sell employment information to workers looking for work. The shifts that occur via these ethnic brokers are also shifts based on precisely this same indirect trust. As proprietors inform ethnic brokers of their need for workers, the latter sell this employment information to workers seeking work as a commodity. It is, of course, the proprietors who, ultimately, interview workers and decide whether they will or will not be employed. In these cases also, however, a proprietor's choice of workers is preceded by the initial choice of ethnic broker by that proprietor. Even when a change of job occurs via a broker, the question of who provided the introduction carries considerable weight.

Naturally, movements by undocumented workers are not completed solely through movements based on indirect trust. When leaving one's job becomes inevitable as a result of conflict with the proprietor, there are incidences of workers setting off to look for

work themselves without either waiting for an invitation from relatives and people from their own region or using an ethnic broker. In
these cases, workers looking for work simply turn up at companies
and bargain asking, 'Have you got a job for me?' Occasionally, a
worker's sense of the advisability of moving is influenced by chance
factors such as encountering an employer who was looking for
workers or an employer who is looking for workers and has work at
the wage level that the worker had been hoping to find. If workers
should find a place of employment on their own and succeed in
winning that proprietor's trust, then the possibility of a whole new
employment market opens up for their ethnic network.

Let us now take a look at how changes of employment mediated
by ethnic brokers actually occur. When ethnic brokers get telephone
calls from workers in search of employment, they ask about the
kind of work that the latter are seeking. The substantial issues in
these discussions concern the wage level of the work being sought
by workers and also the regions in which they wish to work. If
ethnic brokers have the sort of employment information that those
looking for work are after, then discussions occur about passing
on this information. The employment information that is passed
on usually consists of the names of several workplaces. The reason
for this is the result of the accumulation of factors such as, firstly,
the fact that there is no guarantee that the proprietor will definitely
hire the workers who come in for interviews; and, secondly, that
as it is standard for proprietors to talk to several ethnic brokers,
there may possibly be other workers also coming in for interviews.
In any case, multiple pieces of employment information are given
in exchange for money to those seeking work, but the method of
payment in these situations is deferred payment. The reason for
deferred payment is because of the possibility that despite attending
an interview, on the basis of the employment information, there
may not be any offer of employment from the proprietor. There
are even times when no job is found after having exhausted all
of the employment information that was received. In these cases,
additional employment information is given after making contact
again.

Between 1995 and 1999, the author carried out interviews with
seven sets of Pakistani brokers and two sets of Iranian brokers. Table
3.2 illustrates the sums received by ethnic brokers interviewed thus
far as introduction fees in exchange for employment information

from people seeking employment. The introduction fees that ethnic brokers demand from people seeking employment are certainly not inexpensive. The discrepancies between the introduction fees arise from decisive differences, foremost amongst which is the number of companies to which applications can be made on the list handed over to job seekers in exchange for the introduction fee. In the case of Table 3.2, the payment of a 100,000 yen introduction fee would yield the names of more than five companies to contact. Similarly, information about places of employment paying high wages incurs a correspondingly high information fee. Some brokers used the figure of half of the monthly salary that workers can hope to receive if they are employed by a particular company to set the cost of their employment information.

Because the payment of ethnic brokers occurs as a post-payment, brokers need to guard against acts of betrayal by workers who lie and attempt to avoid paying the information fee despite having found work using employment information from the broker. This is why ethnic brokers keep a lookout for any acts of betrayal on the part of either proprietors or job seekers, both of whom are their customers, while periodically visiting their client companies to check on the clients' needs for further recruitment activities to find new workers. However, it is via these surveillance activities that the labour market for undocumented workers constantly transforms the demand for labour into employment information which is then conveyed to job seekers and these activities also become the mechanism that connects the demand for and supply of labour.

There are many points of similarity between the systems for movement and changing jobs for undocumented workers from Pakistan, Bangladesh and Iran. Firstly, one sees the frequent calling over of relatives or people from the same region and also introductions to work opportunities amongst people sharing these connections. Secondly, people returning to the home country generally assume the role of taking back remittances for their relatives or people from the same region who are staying on in Japan. Thirdly, as a result of the cessation of mutual visa exemption agreements, their compatriots from abroad have been refused entry into Japan and this has made it difficult for these groups to find any employment channels outside that of using brokers.

When there had been a simultaneous flow of people entering and leaving Japan, those leaving would hand over their old jobs to

Table 3.2: Work introduction fees for ethnic brokers

Information fee	Pakistani brokers							Iranian brokers		Total
	Pa1	Pa2	Pa3	Pa4	Pa5	Pa6	Pa7	Ir1	Ir2	
Less than 30,000 yen	o	o						o		3
More than 30,000 yen, but less than 50,000 yen		o								1
More than 50,000 yen, but less than 80,000 yen	o		o	o	o				o	5
More than 80,000 yen, but less than 100,000 yen			o	o						2
More than 100,000 yen, but less than 150,000 yen			o			o	o	o	o	5
More than 150,000 yen		o								1

Note: Pa2–Pa7 are the numbers allocated to each group of Pakistani brokers interviewed and Ir1 and Ir2 were similarly assigned to Iranian brokers.

those arriving and, furthermore, those leaving would be entrusted with the savings of their relatives and people from the same region and assume the role of taking these back to the home country. This occurred because holding onto cash in U.S. dollars, rather than making remittances using foreign currency remittances from banks or postal money orders, allowed people to avoid reducing the value of the wages that they had earned in Japan. With the existence of a flow of people simultaneously leaving from and arriving in Japan the acquisition of work and the sending home of remittances had been simultaneously carried out within the ethnic group. The cessation of the mutual visa exemption agreements (in 1988 for Pakistan and Bangladesh and 1992 for Iran) destroyed the very foundations of this mechanism. As the flow becomes solely one of people leaving the country and leads to a reduction in the scale of the ethnic group to which one belongs – in terms of employment information that had once been acquired by relying on relatives and people from the same region – the longer the periods of unemployment become. As a result of the decline in the number of members, there has been a reduction in the amount of employment information that the network had formerly been able to amass and it is now no longer able to fulfil this function. At the same time, those who had been relied on by proprietors to round up people now face a situation in which even if they have employment information, there are no members to whom it can be passed. This presented a type of employment mismatch. Ethnic brokers were the ones who resolved it. By converting employment vacancies into employment information that could be exchanged for cash, they brought about a reunification of the demand for and supply of labour that had become disconnected through its reliance on relatives and people from the same region.

The provision of employment information by brokers functions to unite labour demand and supply, but it does not assume the role that the ethnic networks used to carry out of sending remittances back to the home country. Remittance brokers stepped in to fill this part of the role. When employment information came to be mediated by brokers, they also came to mediate the sending of remittances, an activity that was always to be found alongside employment. Remittance brokers are also known as 'underground banks.' Under conditions in which the mutually beneficial employment references of relatives and people from one's own region and also the act of sending remittances have become difficult, brokers – by carrying

out these functions – have made possible the existence of undocumented foreign labour, in the form of migrant workers. Employment
references and remittances have shifted from cooperation within
lifestyle/living communities to things seen to by service industry
specialists. This type of service industry is showing signs of extensive development. While on the one hand the flow of people into
Japan has been stemmed, the increasing lengths of stay in Japan
have been accompanied by increasing numbers of people who are
marrying Japanese and the emergence amongst these people of
ethnic entrepreneurs starting up businesses within Japan (Higuchi,
Tanno, Higuchi 1998; Higuchi & Tanno 2000). The types of businesses in which they are engaged are wide ranging, and while there
are many Halal food shops aimed largely at providing a service to
fellow countrymen, we have also seen exporters of second-hand cars
to Asia and Latin America; and, more and more, individuals moving
into media businesses that convey information about Japan to their
countries of origin or, conversely, that are contracted by newspaper
and communications companies to collect data on matters such as
the political situation in their home countries. It is the switch in the
movement vector – from the coexistence of a flow of people into
Japan and one of people leaving Japan to an exclusive flow of people
leaving – that has had a considerable influence on the structural
conditions of this sort of change. It goes without saying, however,
that there is, in the advance of this growing reliance on brokers and
experts, an expansion in the nature of relationships within Japanese
society that has accompanied the increasing length of stay of both
brokers and individual entrepreneurs.

Conclusion: complementarity and 'the resultant symbiosis'

Employment via the networks for undocumented workers has
antithetical special characteristics when it comes to ways of entering
the labour market for people of Japanese descent. It is possible
for any worker of Japanese descent to be employed in the labour
market to which entry is restricted on the basis of being a person
of Japanese descent. In this sense, labour of Japanese descent is
treated as an abstract labour force. However, employment via
networks for undocumented workers does not allow the employment
of just anybody. It is a labour market that only opens up once one
has relationships within that network. Looked at as labour markets,

there is this decisive difference between the labour market for legal workers and that for undocumented workers. Despite this difference on the point of the organisational principles of markets and networks, however, they possess identical functional traits. These identical functional traits are that they provide only the labour that is required by businesses and that when this labour is no longer needed, they remove it speedily from the production site. If we look exclusively at these traits of markets mediated by the service contracting companies of people of Japanese descent and networks mediated by brokers for undocumented workers, then, as Herbert A. Simon points out, labour market and network 'internal structures, despite differing in their internal organisation, display extremely similar behaviour as systems' (Simon [1996: 16–17] 1999: 21).

Similarly, the reason why companies make use of service contracting companies, networks and ethnic brokers is not because these are the very best options. Companies always feel it necessary to maintain a flexible labour force: insecure employment. Service contracting companies and brokers have functioned as a route for building an insecure labour force even before the newcomer foreigners start working in Japan. Companies have carried out their employment activities at the time of employing foreigners by using the existing employment system. In the case of direct employment, major companies have used the system that they would use for hiring temporary workers while small- and medium-sized companies have used brokers and the direct workers dropping in unannounced looking for work. In the case of indirect employment, large as well as small- and medium-sized companies have made use of service contracting companies. The reason why these sorts of systems have been used by companies lies in the fact that, as the established systems, these were computable measures. For companies that deal with all management activities as costs, new employment methods whose costs are not known are not regarded as the optimum option. They will seek the optimum option from amongst computable, existing measures. This is why path dependency is at work in the employment system for foreigners.

Wilfred Pareto has argued that, 'the form of a society is decided by all of the factors at work in the society. At the same time, the form of a society also reacts against these factors. It is possible to say that as a result of this a certain mutual determination arises (Pareto [1917: 2060] 1987: 4).' We can perceive that in the labour market for foreign workers, or in the very employment structure, the mutual determination of mutually intertwined and complex relationships regulates the micro actions of foreign workers while, simultaneously, the labour market conversely is regulated by the individuals carrying out these actions.

As we have seen in this chapter, foreign workers have also changed in nature along with the changes in the employment environment. They continue to be consistently pushed into peripheral labour, but the meaning of the use of foreign workers by companies occasionally changes and there is a mechanism at work producing increasing numbers of workers who conform to changes in the companies.

As the social environment that surrounds companies changes, companies also go on changing. At these times, there are also changes in the labour market and in the character of workers who enter this market to earn wages. In the midst of these continuous changes, because regional residential issues concerning foreign workers occur, the existence of foreign workers cannot be grasped in terms of a goal-oriented symbiotic concept. In biological terms, the changing state of workers that occurs in response to these sorts of company changes is a matter of coevolution (Inoue and Katō 1993). The result of coevolution has been the emergence of a 'resultant symbiosis' between companies and foreign workers, and furthermore between them and the middlemen who link both of them (service contracting companies in the case of people of Japanese descent and ethnic brokers in the case of undocumented workers); one in which, on the one hand, flexibility is made possible by the presence of the other party and one that, on the other hand, sees the acquisition of increased net wages and business opportunities.

Both parties have ended up being able to play a game of acquiring short term benefits while placing the burden on the other party. Even workers, who would be required to pay half of the health insurance contributions, regard the fact that companies escape the burdens of labour and health insurance, which they are supposed to pay under employment contracts, and their subsequent lack of membership in these schemes as having the advantage of increasing their own net income. Similarly, it is possible for foreign workers to earn higher net wages from contract employment and employment in which they are dealt with as factory purchasing costs rather than by being covered by seniority wages. Given that foreign workers are restricted to participating in a labour market in which they are never far from the dangers of unemployment, the employment environment for them is structured in such a way as to turn an option that promises only increased risks and costs in the long term, as far as both industrial society and foreign workers themselves are concerned, into the most logical step in the short term. Thus, transformations in foreign workers reflect structural changes in Japanese society which provide the backdrop to these transformations.

4 Reasons for segmentation of the foreign worker labour market: strategic complementarity and the logic of systematisation

Introduction

1990 saw the revision of the Immigration Control and Refugee Recognition Act and the legalisation of the employment of foreign workers. Although referred to as legalisation, the possibility of working in all areas of employment applied only to workers of Japanese descent; the employment of other foreigners as workers in unskilled work has continued unrecognised, as in the past. There are, however, workplaces that rely for their workforce on foreign workers whose visa status does not confer work rights, and the employment situation of these types of foreign workers shows a tendency towards concentration by ethnic group in certain industries and employment sectors. The appearance of these types of divisions between ethnic groups results from the fact that the power of 'strategic complementarity' – which in addition to enabling people to achieve their own goals by following the pattern of behaviour of the majority of other people can keep costs low – is at work in the form that employment takes in the labour market, in the methods for recruiting workers and in the collective action of workers staying in Japan. This chapter uses the keywords of the relationships between forms of employment and recruitment methods and group actions as well as strategic complementarity to locate foreign workers in Japan. Moreover, it will show that the process of continuing centralisation of the employment of workers of Japanese descent in indirect employment has conversely led to the progress of the diversification of employment destinations within indirect employment. Furthermore, there will be a consideration of the kinds of differences that appear in the actions of foreign workers according to their abilities to work in this type of market, on the basis of differences in labour union participation.

Foreign workers in a period of economic slump

As can be seen from the increase in the unemployment rate following the bursting of the bubble economy, Japan, which is in a period of economic stagnation, is not at all short of manpower. Even in this kind of economic environment, however, there are workplaces that require foreign workers. Japan's industrial structure has a bearing on this. There are sizable gaps in the pay and the welfare entitlements (health insurance and age pension) received by workers in large companies compared to those in small- and medium-sized companies in Japanese industrial society. Because of this, when we talk about a dual structure economy in Japan it is not Michael P. Piore et al.'s division into an internal labour market and an external labour market (Berger and Piore 1980), but the gap between large companies and medium and small companies that is usually being indicated (Sumiya 1966 and Ujihara 1989). As is also clear from the fact that minimum wages are determined region by region and by type of occupation, there are differences in pay between the regions and between industries. In order to see the gap between large companies and small and medium companies clearly, we need to look at the wage differential when the same industries in a certain region have been differentiated according to the scale of workers in the plants. Toyota City in Aichi Prefecture is known for housing the headquarters of Japan's largest automobile company, and the city chooses economic statistics that have been differentiated to include only the automobile industry as its own statistics. First, using this data, let us confirm the extent of the wage differential due to company scale within similar industries.[1]

Let us look at Table 4.1. There are large yearly differences in the wage differential and also differences in the yearly changes on the basis of the scale of the company, but there is consistently a more than twofold difference in the wage differential between enterprises with over 1,000 employees and the smallest enterprises on the scale of one to three employees. When comparing enterprises on the scale of up to around fifty employees and those with over 1,000, there is a constant wage differential of around twofold. As a result of

Table 4.1: *Yearly cash income differentials by the scale of employee numbers in the automobile industry in Toyota City (Unit: 10,000 yen)*

Employee numbers	Year										
	1988	1989	1990	1991	1992	1993	1994	1995	1996	1997	1998
30–39	289.0	268.8	317.0	338.7	382.5	394.6	371.3	366.2	391.5	445.6	411.6
50–59	313.4	341.8	345.4	361.7	382.9	403.7	400.0	406.2	399.1	423.3	394.9
100–199	349.2	376.8	374.9	403.0	455.5	435.8	440.1	456.3	440.0	449.3	491.9
200–299	367.9	413.2	373.3	438.4	437.7	472.7	496.2	485.0	518.4	523.6	504.4
300–499	454.4	467.8	497.6	479.2	553.2	530.4	562.3	598.3	543.1	584.9	559.7
500–999	491.7	497.3	559.4	589.8	617.6	598.3	592.2	594.2	613.4	638.5	645.6
Over 1000	578.2	605.6	637.4	657.3	659.6	639.3	660.4	700.6	725.9	777.3	776.0
Total	519.3	541.4	572.1	591.8	606.6	589.5	610.9	643.4	662.6	702.8	700.7

Source: compiled using yearly publications of Toyota City Statistics

the existence of this wage differential, it is more profitable to send goods that would be costly to produce at one's own company to a subcontractor. The same logic that brings about the relocation of a factory overseas in search of cheap labour is to be found in the subcontracting structure. It could be said that the highest ranking companies in the industrial structure maintain high wages by having only the portion of workers who are highly paid specialising in highly productive work. Because there are these large wage differentials within the same industry in the same region, small-scale companies – in terms of the number of employees – find themselves in a trap of not being able to gather the labour supply that they need solely from amongst the Japanese population, even when the unemployment rate is high. This is because they are unable to pay the level of wages that Japanese workers demand. Even in a time of economic slump, there are workplaces in Japan that cannot assemble a Japanese workforce; this applies primarily to blue-collar workers for small- and medium-sized companies.

In this sort of situation, foreign workers tend inevitably to be seen as cheap labour. However, amongst workers of Japanese descent, who are legal workers and who have largely come to Japan from Latin America, employment information is widely disseminated via Portuguese and Spanish language newspapers that are published in Japan. As employment opportunities are abundant, there is a considerable amount of moving between jobs and this leads to the wages that are directly received by these workers being, on average, around 1,400 yen per hour for men and 1,000 yen per hour for women; higher than the wages for Japanese part-time and casual workers. In addition to high wages, there are also instances of workers of Japanese descent being employed for longer periods in their workplaces; if they convert to a monthly basis, then they achieve a monthly wage level of around 300,000 yen for men and even women earn 200,000 yen. However, the wages of these men and women are comparable to the costs of employing Japanese regular workers, along the lines of the figures in Table 4.1. The amount of money in Table 4.1 shows the amount of cash wages; it does not include costs such as those for the legally designated welfare expenses associated with welfare pensions and social insurance (health insurance), which the company must shoulder when employing regular employees. The wages of workers of Japanese descent appear to be high at a glance; however, they are in reality low. Table 4.2 was published by a service

Table 4.2: A comparative table of Japanese workers and workers of Japanese descent from a service contractor's brochure

	Outsourcing costs		Regular employee costs
	%	Yen	Yen
Wages	100.0	299,500	300,000
Bonuses	33.3	99,833	0
Legally mandated welfare costs	15.2	45,524	0
Extra-legal welfare costs	5.2	15,574	0
Labour management costs	2.0	5,990	0
Retirement payments	7.2	21,564	0
Total	163.0	487,985	300,000

contractor, who sends workers of Japanese descent to factories, in a brochure distributed to new clients entitled 'A Proposal for the Practical Use of Outsourcing.' When the employment of workers of Japanese descent is compared with that of the regular workers for whom they are used as substitutes, we understand that, as far as the company is concerned, the high wages of workers of Japanese descent appear cheap.

The segmented foreign worker labour market

Wage differentials also exist within the single category of workers of Japanese descent. We can see wage differentials between Brazilians and Peruvians of Japanese descent, and moreover between workers of Japanese descent from places other than Latin America – for example, those from the Philippines. Whilst these are all people of Japanese descent, their labour market is segmented. The reason for this segmentation lies in the fact that the labour market is not a conceptual place where the demand for and the supply of labour intersect, but a system set up by real society for distributing a workforce to the workplaces that require labour. The rise and fall of wages are events internal to the labour market as a discrete system. This is why even though they belong to the same category of workers of Japanese descent, gaps appear between these groups.

Let us look at this from the perspective of the employment system for workers of Japanese descent. It is the sector that dispatches workers from outside of companies – what we call the service contracting industry – that places workers of Japanese descent at the points of production, such as factories, requiring a workforce. In the same way as manufacturing factories recruit seasonal and contract workers for fixed periods of employment such as six months or a year, service contractors, who have subcontracted a factory line, assemble workers of Japanese descent for fixed term employment and station workers on the line that they have contracted. Factories allow their lines to be contracted because demand fluctuates, and workers on fixed term contracts are needed in order to respond to these fluctuations. In this way, workers of Japanese descent are positioned in factories via the practical system of service contractors. Service contractors are responsible for all aspects of labour management and therefore, in addition to being able to speak the workers' mother tongue, have to use Japanese-speaking personnel in order to ensure mutual understanding between the Japanese factory staff and the service contractor's staff. Usually, service contractors carry out labour management by employing people of Japanese descent who can speak Japanese as interpreting staff. When people from a variety of countries are employed as workers it also becomes necessary to hire a variety of people as interpreting staff. This is why, in order to reduce management costs, service contractors tend to impose specialisations on groups of workers from certain countries amongst the workers that they send out.[2]

There is a tendency for Brazilians of Japanese descent, who in the context of workers of Japanese descent have numerous employment opportunities, to enjoy high wages because of employer efforts to prevent the movement of these workers. There is a significant relationship between this and the growth of ethnic media, which results in the existence of abundant employment information. By contrast, in the case of Peruvians of Japanese descent, their employment opportunities are reduced as both employment information lessens and wages decline. Because service contractors employing people from the Philippines have been few from the outset, Filipinos of Japanese descent have extremely limited employment opportunities in comparison to workers from Latin America. There are also considerable numbers of these workers from the Philippines employed as trainees, a feature that is not seen amongst workers of Japanese descent from Latin America. Although they all belong to the same category of being of Japanese descent, the employment routes for

Filipinos of Japanese descent are different from those for workers of Japanese descent from Latin America.

What then is the reason for the disparity in the employment opportunities – that is, the amount of employment information – that exists between Brazilians of Japanese descent and Peruvians of Japanese descent, despite them both having come from Latin America and having followed practically the same employment route? People of Japanese descent belong to the legal employment category, but there are illegal workers even within their ranks. Firstly, there are people who have forged their documents and come to Japan masquerading as people of Japanese descent and, secondly, there are workers of Japanese descent who are fourth genereation.[3] The majority of the former are made up particularly of Peruvians of Japanese descent. Firstly, this is largely related to the visa system. Since Brazil does not have a visa exemption agreement, just as Japanese people need to get a visa for each occasion when they travel to Brazil, whenever Brazilians come to Japan, they also need to present the documents required by the Japanese government to get a visa otherwise they cannot enter. However, as Peru has a visa exemption agreement, Peruvians are able to enter Japan without specifically getting a visa if they are coming as tourists.

Secondly, this situation also reflects the historical circumstances of Peruvian society's severe attitude towards "enemy aliens" amongst their citizens during the Second World War. Many Japanese immigrants and their children had had no choice but to burn any documents showing that they had personal links with Japan, in order to escape persecution within the society of a foreign country. Over seventy per cent of the population that is of Japanese descent in modern day Peruvian society is made up of Okinawans, but as a result of the Battle of Okinawa that occurred on that island there are also many cases in Japan of documents pertaining to people's descent having been destroyed by fire. Because of this, the need for time to restore family registers created structural conditions amongst Peruvians of Japanese descent which facilitated an outbreak of document forgery. It is actually unclear just how many people are masquerading as Peruvians of Japanese descent. However, as a result of the exposure of a series of cases in which enterprises had been dealing with workers who had claimed fake Japanese descent, large companies and contracting companies, in an attempt as far as possible to minimise their chances of being exposed, have sought to satisfy the demand for labour not with Peruvians but Brazilians of Japanese descent.[4] The substantial differences in employment opportunities for Peruvians and Brazilians, even though they both have the same Japanese ancestry, reflect the disparate levels of confidence in the passports that these men and women hold.

As was briefly explained previously, the low wages and scant employment opportunities for Filipinos of Japanese descent are firstly the result of the lack of development of service contracting companies and also of a travel industry that does the footwork for the contracting industry and assembles workers. Consequently, and secondly, the lack of development amongst this group of ethnic media of the kind that people of Japanese descent from Latin America can use has also had considerable bearing on the situation. As the conditions for participating in the labour market are determined by the existence of service contractors, where service contractors exist, high wages are received even where employment is insecure. Filipino workers are further limited in terms of the possibilities that might be provided for changing jobs through the ethnic media after having entered Japan. Even though these workers belong to the same category of Japanese descent, there are few service contractors who dispatch Filipinos of Japanese descent, and because these workers find themselves in a structure in which there is no free flow of employment information, it is difficult for them to change jobs with the result that they do not make their way into the higher paid market place for contracting work. The following section is a discussion of why it is that there has been no development of a contracting industry amongst Filipinos of Japanese descent.

The foreign worker labour market and strategic complementarity

The foreign worker labour market is not only legally subdivided on the basis of legal employment and undocumented employment, but is also segmented along the lines of individual ethnic groups. What are the reasons for this? Why is employment for workers of Japanese descent concentrated in the service contracting industry which dispatches external factory workers to factories and why does being dispatched by the contracting industry not extend to undocumented workers? Furthermore, why is it that even amongst the workforce of Japanese descent, employment is concentrated in the contracting industry for workers of Japanese descent who are from Latin America while workers of Japanese descent who are from the Philippines are even more likely to be employed as low paid trainees than undocumented workers?

The reference point for the ordering of the labour market, which accounts for the hierarchical nature of foreign workers, is generally to be found in one's visa status – whether one is eligible to be legally employed or not. We can, on this basis, give a rational explanation for the employment system that exists amongst the majority of workers of Japanese descent and undocumented workers, as well as for the appearance of wage differentials. We cannot, however, explain the differences in the employment opportunities that are apparent for Brazilians and Peruvians of Japanese descent despite them both belonging to one category as people of Japanese descent; as indeed we cannot explain the existence of trainees in the ranks of Filipinos of Japanese descent.

It is the author's belief that these points can be dealt with from the viewpoint of 'strategic complementarity.'[5] A good example of strategic complementarity that actually exists in society is provided by the stairs at railway stations during rush hour and escalators in department stores (Bulow, Geanakoplos and Klemperer 1985; Okuno 1993). Railway stairs during times of congestion become crowded whenever a train arrives, but they are naturally divided into, on the one hand, sides on which most people are going up and, on the other, sides on which most people are going down the stairs. Irrespective of whether there are announcements by the station staff or not, a natural order emerges. We see the same thing in the case of escalators also: one side is left clear for people who are in a hurry; usually either the left or right side is left completely clear. Why does this type of order emerge? Whether in the case of the congested railway station or of the escalator, the goal of the actors in both locations is to move forwards. For the subjects of these actions, advancing by going against a human wave would be a high cost action in the sense that it would render the achievement of that action difficult. Taking the side that the majority of people are taking reduces the costs and enables one to achieve the goal of moving forwards. In short, by aligning one's own action strategy with the strategy of the majority of people, one can easily achieve one's own objectives. The order that emerges in this fashion, results from following the strategies of others, of a large number of others, and from the influence of one's own action strategy on the others around one in a mutually interpolatory manner. Because this mutual complementarity exists between the decision making of each person, it is rational for the decision making of each individual actor to intentionally (strategically) select the same action as the majority of people. This type of choice is one of the choices of strategic complementarity.

As mentioned previously, the foreign worker labour market is not an abstract labour market where labour demand and supply confront one another; it is a social entity that has been set up by the system for dispatching factory workers from outside companies, known as the service contracting industry. Around the time of the beginning of workers of Japanese descent from Latin America going overseas to work, the mid-1980s, it was not only service contractors but also every manufacturing company that went directly into cities such as São Paolo, Londrina, Curitiba, Campo Grande, Lima and Buenos Aires; they published newspaper advertisements, carried out recruiting activities and made local community leaders into their agents who would assemble people hoping to go to Japan to work.[6] Various possible routes existed up until the time that they were delivered to the factories, the points of production. However, the employment of workers of Japanese descent within Japan stopped being a temporary phenomenon, and as their presence in Japan became a constant, Japanese companies refrained from employing them directly. Naturally, the fact that the demand for labour declined as a result of the recession, brought about by the collapse of the bubble economy, coupled with the newfound ability to assemble a Japanese workforce in workplaces where it had until then not been possible had a significant bearing on this. However, we should not overlook the fact that strategic complementarity is also at work in employment markets for workers of Japanese descent.

In the midst of the labour shortage during the period of the bubble economy, there were manufacturing industry companies that directly employed workers of Japanese descent and assembled the number of people required for the operation of their companies from their ranks. There were also companies in the manufacturing industry that assembled the workforce required in their factories by indirectly employing workers of Japanese descent through the service contracting industry. Migrant workers who had regarded working in Japan as a temporary move, whose intention had been to work for a while and then return home, were advised 'move to the higher price, even for a ten yen difference.' They changed jobs with a finely tuned sense for the highest hourly rate. As a result of this, the wages of workers of Japanese descent rose and led to a situation in which they were only able to find work in high productivity workplaces. However, as the bubble economy collapsed and the economic slump continued 1) a result of the slump in total demand, every factory reduced the number of workers that it required (the total number of personnel required to operate the factory). Also, the increase in the unemployment rate that was the social manifestation of this meant that 2) it became easy for companies to employ Japanese workers. The beginnings of the reduction in the need for directly employing foreigners occurred in the midst of an absolute labour shortage in large-scale companies that had used a foreign workforce.

Big companies whose names carried weight in society were now able to assemble the workforce that they needed using Japanese labour. However, even in a context in which the unemployment rate is rising and job applicants are lining up at public employment exchanges, the shop floors of small- and medium-sized companies with their large wage differentials are unable to assemble the labour force that they require solely from the ranks of Japanese workers. This is not related to economic trends; there is a chronic shortage of blue-collar workers for small- and medium-sized companies. Service contractors are dispatching labour to numerous workplaces, principally to those that cannot meet their labour needs even during a period of economic slump.

Also, the decline in direct employment has not only come about because of attempts to assemble a purely Japanese workforce. Companies that had directly employed foreigners in an effort to reduce the labour shortage realised that the costs of the direct employment of foreigners – that is labour management costs – were anything but low. The simple matter of assembling the necessary labour at the point of production can be achieved via the service contracting industry and labour management can also be left to them. The higher the awareness of the costs, the greater the requests made of the service contracting industry.

The problem is that as demand is concentrated in employment using the contracting industry, the places to which workers are sent by the service contracting industry become progressively and increasingly more diversified. Originally, the service contracting industry, by virtue of the fact that its business was to act as a mediator between the increase in personnel at a particular factory and the decrease in personnel at another factory, provided workers to a variety of destinations. With the passing of the period of labour shortages and the ability of the major companies to assemble the workforce that they need using Japanese workers, not only did direct employment fall but wages also peaked and then started on a falling trend.

Meanwhile, the increase in families staying that accompanied the increasing length of stay of workers, led to the emergence of a labour force with a variety of age ranges living in Japan. When it became possible for older foreigners to work, service contractors were able to send labour to workplaces where up until then this would have entailed pricing below cost. By combining labour recipients with high contracting unit costs and those with low contracting unit costs, service contractors are able to dispatch a wide age range of employable workers. When it is possible to employ a worker's family unit, changing jobs becomes difficult for the workers of Japanese descent – that is, moving them to another job again as a family unit – and as a result a highly settled workforce can be secured. There is thus a mechanism at work whereby the greater the number of companies that source their foreign workers (source their workforce) from service contractors, the larger the increase in the number of workplaces with workers of Japanese descent working in them.

Similarly, as individual companies shift from direct to indirect employment through service contractors, the demand for and numbers of service contractors also increases. Accordingly, unit cost competition between service contractors also appears. Consequently, if individual companies take into account that other companies are aiming to secure the workforce that they need by using the service contracting industry and adopt the same strategy themselves, then all of the companies that have adopted the strategy of using the service contracting industry are able to obtain the supply of a cheaper foreign worker workforce than if their own company had been the only one to make use of the service contracting industry. It is easy to see strategic complementarity at work here. Thus, as a result of individual companies adopting the same indirect employment strategy as other companies the transactions market for the service contracting industry has widened. The expansion of the market is not merely one of quantitative expansion; it has given rise to a diversification of customer markets and has provided employment opportunities for a whole range of age groups.

The hierarchical nature of foreign workers brought about by strategic complementarity

The more that the vast majority of companies make use of the contracting industry, the more diversified the workplaces employing workers of Japanese descent become. As a result of the employment opportunities that the diversification of the workforce provides to a variety of age groups, the transactions market of the service contracting industry displays the following features, as seen in Table 4.3: ① in-company factory employment that manages the factory floor in-company; ② manufacturing line contracting, on a line unit contracting basis, of the manufacturing line of the customer factory; ③ fluctuating employment within the factory (a) whereby a contract is concluded with the factory and workers are dispatched, but there is no unit set for the line; ④ fluctuating employment within the factory (b) in which the dispatching of workers to the factory is not carried out on the basis of a contract, but through a verbal agreement; and ⑤ a broadening that even includes fluctuating employment outside the factory in which the workers' wages and the contracting unit costs of the service contracting industry fall below the market price. As a result of this, service contractors have been able to dispatch to a variety of workplaces ranging from export industries such as automobiles and electronic appliances to Japanese boxed lunch factories servicing convenience stores; the boxing of cut flowers in agricultural cooperatives; the sorting of different types of clams in fishery cooperatives; and even industrial waste treatment plants.

While continuing to dispatch to these different transactional markets, service contractors are attempting to stabilise their own management. Anyone would imagine that if it were possible to increase the weighting of types ① and ② markets, which represent stable customers, then the management of the service contractor would also be stable. However, the trust of customers is vital in order to access these stable markets. Acquiring the trust of

Table 4.3: Segmentation of the market in which people of Japanese descent are used

Market segment			Market characteristics	Distribution
Stable employment	① In-company factory employment	Secure employment	① In-company management of the factory floor	4 companies
	② Manufacturing line contracting		② Unit contract agreement of the manufacturing line	4 companies
Insecure employment	③ Femployment within the factory, a	Insecure employment	③ Dispatch of workers contracted with customer (a)	14 companies
	④ Fluctuating employment within the factory, b		④ Dispatch of workers on the basis of a verbal agreement (b)	11 companies
	⑤ Fluctuating employment outside the factory		⑤ Employment below the market price for foreign worker wages	6 companies

Note: Distribution = Distribution of business people in author's survey customers is not something that can be achieved overnight; it is a drawn out matter requiring time. This is why there is a tendency for new markets to broaden into unstable employment markets, or alternatively markets with low contracting unit costs.

Incidentally, in the multilayered subcontracting structure of Japanese industrial society, stable transaction markets would be companies close to the parent company which is located near the top of the industrial structure. It is precisely because they are close to the parent company that companies making up types ① and ② transaction markets differ from subcontracting companies that are in charge of specific goods and parts; they take charge of multiple goods and produce multiple parts. This is why they are in constant need of a stable workforce. These types of companies are practically all listed stock companies that are concerned about their "social reputation." Although indirectly employed, it would not do for there to be undocumented workers in their factories or for there to be any uncovering of illegally dispatched workers in their companies.

For this reason, in more stable transactional markets, the wishes of the companies receiving the dispatched workers are taken into account and workers with documents about which there can be no doubts are selected for preference. At the beginning of the 1990s, there were a series of arrests of Peruvians who had entered Japan on forged passports. This had a big influence on Peruvians of Japanese descent. Where companies were able to express a preference for either Brazilians or Peruvians, they preferred Brazilians. This is why in areas inhabited by both Brazilians and Peruvians of Japanese descent the former have come to enjoy more opportunities for employment in workplaces with better conditions (higher wages and a lower risk of unemployment).

Service contractors dispatch workers to a multitude of workplaces in different transactional markets. It is because large companies with their stable production levels and good conditions are concerned about their social reputations that the market for dispatching a foreign workforce has centred on Brazilians of Japanese descent. Peruvians of Japanese descent, as a function of the more limited employment opportunities open to them than to Brazilians of Japanese descent, end up largely occupying labour markets with poor conditions in terms of wages and unemployment. *International Press*, which boasts the highest publication figures amongst the newspapers published in Japan for people of Japanese descent, is published in both Portuguese and Spanish editions. The publication figures for these two editions differ as a result of the difference in size of the population of Brazilians of Japanese descent and Peruvians of Japanese descent living in Japan, but an additional difference is that of the volume of help wanted advertisements. Instrumental complementarity leads to an expansion of markets; gives rise to further diversification inside markets; and heightens structural divisions. As a result of the expansion of better market conditions for Brazilians of Japanese descent, there is a converse expansion also of markets with poor conditions. As a consequence of the blocking of any expansion into labour markets with good conditions for Peruvians of Japanese descent, all of the labour markets to which they are relegated are even poorer than those for Brazilians of Japanese descent, and because of this the expansion of markets for them is also more limited than it is for Brazilians of Japanese descent. This is why despite being indirectly employed via the same service contracting firms, Peruvians of Japanese descent are more likely to end up in labour markets with high risks of unemployment.

Incidentally, does the factory, which is the point of production, see the employment of workers of Japanese descent in terms of a workforce that they have chosen made up of people of Japanese descent or, alternatively, is it a matter of the factory having selected a contracting company? The author thinks that the effect is that they have selected a service contracting company. The clearest indication that this is the case is the existence of Filipinos who work as trainees despite the fact that they also are of Japanese descent; there are practically no trainees in the ranks of workers of Japanese descent from Latin America. This is simply because the wages for trainees are extremely low compared to indirect employment with service contracting companies. Travel agencies run by people of Japanese descent have been established and carry out labour recruiting activities locally with service contractors who introduce the Japanese workplaces to which workers will go. The establishment of the indirect employment of people of Japanese descent from Latin America is the result of the development of this sort of tangible system. As indicated previously, service contractors need to take responsibility for all labour management issues. Dispatching workers means having to employ interpreting staff who carry out duties that range from those of management staff – the labour management of workers – to helping with daily life. As far as service contractors are concerned too, unless a supply area is one where they can acquire a stable labour supply at times when they need new workers, it has no appeal to them as a labour supply source. For this reason, compared to Latin America, the Philippines with its small population of people of Japanese descent has not developed a contacting company recruiting system, and the opportunities for Filipinos of Japanese descent to enter the contracting industry labour market are limited. It is in this context that we see the emergence of people who come to Japan as trainees when they seek employment opportunities over here.

The organisation of foreign workers with segmented employment opportunities

Seen from the viewpoint of the organisation of foreign workers, we can detect a strange 'twisted phenomenon between employment opportunities in the labour market and the organisation of workers. This is manifested in the fact that it is undocumented workers, far more than workers of Japanese descent who are legally employed, that increasingly join labour unions. Why is it that this twisted phenomenon arises? In the author's opinion, it is Japanese labour laws and pressure from the labour administration that induces this result. The labour contracts for foreign workers, who end up as indirectly employed external workers, are largely for short term, fixed periods of employment; and, in sharp contradistinction to the 'unlimited employment' of Japanese regular workers in the same workplaces this remains the case even when foreign workers are directly employed in these workplaces. They form the so-called insecure labour sector.

Although not an issue faced solely by foreign workers, when matters of dispute arise between workers in the insecure labour sector and employers (companies), there are many cases of unfair dismissals.[7] Because the rationale for employing the insecure labour sector is to match fluctuations in production volumes, it carries a high risk of sudden dismissal and unemployment. Whilst workers are under contract, employers are obliged to give them one month's notice before they can be dismissed. Employers are also supposed to be able to explain why those particular workers were selected for dismissal.[8] However, it is not at all unusual for workers to be notified suddenly of their dismissal, without any explanation whatsoever. Furthermore, in the insecure employment sector there are also numerous issues such as workers being unable to take the paid leave to which they are legally entitled and not being paid overtime despite having done overtime. However, because they find themselves in an insecure position, even if they are dissatisfied, it is usual for these workers not to raise any objections with their employers unless they are being dismissed. This is why all issues present as illegal dismissal issues.

As can be seen from the Spring Wage Talks (*Shuntō*), the company unions found largely in the big companies are the most powerful Japanese labour unions. The rate of union organisation falls off as the scale of employee numbers decreases. It can be imagined that in the case of insecure employment, which is irregular employment, the usual situation is for there to be no labour union in these smaller workplaces. Hence, even if one is dismissed suddenly, it is largely the case that there is no possibility of raising objections with the employer. As there are regional unions that individuals can join in Japan, there are many cases of workers in the insecure employment sector joining these regional unions when they have labour issues-related grievances about their employers with this leading to negotiations.[9] However, in cases where labour union negotiations with the employer still fail to reach a resolution, mediation and arbitration is sought from regional labour committees and the matter goes to trial.

Labour trials for foreigners fighting unfair dismissal generally hand down a verdict accepting the dismissal after acknowledging that it was an unfair dismissal. The matter ends with workers receiving pay covering the period from the time of their unfair dismissal to the verdict and the workers then retiring. In cases of the workers having found a new job by the time that the verdict is handed down, the period of unemployment from the time of unfair dismissal to the time of finding a new job becomes the subject of compensation for lost opportunities resulting from unfair dismissal. Because of this, in the case of Brazilians of Japanese descent for whom work opportunities are easy to find, even if they win at the trial, after making allowances for what they can gain and the costs of the trial, it ends up being more logical to find new work for themselves. On the other hand, for Peruvians of Japanese descent, because their work opportunities are limited and they tend to be unemployed for longer periods of time, courtroom disputes are logical actions that bring gains greater than the costs; and the commitment to unions, which have the know-how for appealing to the courts, can be observed as a group phenomenon amongst Peruvians of Japanese descent. Whilst belonging to the same category of workers of Japanese descent, differences in the labour market cause differences in participation in labour unions between Brazilians and Peruvians of Japanese descent.[10]

We can see an even greater commitment to labour unions than is the case for workers of Japanese descent by undocumented foreign workers who are at even greater risk of unemployment than workers of Japanese descent. Undocumented workers stick to labour unions because unlike workers of Japanese descent, they do not get employment information via formal organisations (the public employment exchange, an official organisation; the employment centre for people of Japanese descent; the contracting industry, a private organisation; and ethnic media in their mother tongues) and consequently when they land in trouble their resources for seeking help are limited to either foreign aid groups in the form of NGOs or labour unions.

Let us look at similar conditions within different examples.[11] There are differences in the levels of involvement in labour unions between migrant workers from Korea who are newly arrived foreigners, whose numbers have been increasing since the 1980s, and those who have already established communities within Japan. In the case of the former, their first point of participation in a labour union occurs when workers seek help with resolving matters such as incidents of work-related injuries or unfair dismissals. The resolution of the issues concerned results, in most cases, in dismissal from the workplace where they had been working to date, but even when they move to the next workplace, most workers continue as members of the labour union. In the case of migrant workers from Korea, however, large numbers return to Korea upon resolution of their issues; there is a recurrence of the practice of joining a labour union after the incidence of a work-related injury or unfair dismissal followed by returning home after the resolution of this issue, and this becomes a perpetual cycle in which a comparatively large proportion of members of the labour union fail to acquire workplace rights.

Conclusion

The reason why foreign workers have left their countries of origin in search of work opportunities in Japan is because they could not find adequate employment opportunities of the kind that they desire within the economic environment in their homelands. Immigration is the act of attempting to achieve one's economic goals by effecting a change in the very environment within which one finds oneself. Because immigrants change the environment itself, when they find themselves in trouble, they are unable to resolve even the sorts of issues that had they been in their countries of origin, they would have been able to solve by making use of social capital. In order for immigrant workers to capitalise on the economic opportunities that they themselves have attempted to acquire, they are compelled to construct a new environment around themselves. This new environment is, however, not something that can be constructed through individual effort. Particularly when migration has occurred on a group basis, then whatever the intentions that motivate each individual to act might be, it will instead be the vector produced by the whole group that ends up prescribing the direction of individual actions. This chapter has used strategic complementarity as the approach for viewing the process of the establishment of a vector which provides a new direction for these actions.

However, the strategic complementarity that provides direction for the actions of individuals results from interaction between this strategic complementarity itself and the broader society. In short, the diversification of the destination points, the factories, to which service contracting companies dispatch workers of Japanese descent, is conditioned by economic slumps and declines in the demand for labour. If there were to be an absolute shortage of labour such as to give rise to bankruptcies, then direct employment would increase in order to resolve this shortage and as a result the situation would be different from what it is now. Also, if there were to be recognition of the right to work for foreigners other than those of Japanese descent, then it would be difficult for workers of Japanese descent from Latin America to continue in their current position of being employed as the highest paid foreign workers. More than twenty years have passed since the legalisation of work by workers of Japanese descent under the revisions to the Immigration Control and Refugee Recognition Act. If we consider the start of the employment of labour of Japanese descent in Japan from the middle of the 1980s, then a period of more than twenty five years has already elapsed. The amount of time that has elapsed from the commencement of this type of hiring certainly does not imply any improvement in the Japanese language proficiency of the workers working in Japan. Rather, the third generation of migrant workers, following the first and second generations, have come to form the core of the labour supply and as this changing of generations progresses, an increasing proportion are marrying Japanese people from outside their Japanese descent communities. The change of generations is leading to a much larger increase in the number of workers who cannot speak Japanese. Meanwhile, the accumulation of know-how regarding work matters is advancing amongst those who cannot communicate in the places of production. Because of this, it could fairly be surmised that a situation different from that which exists at present will arise in the event of any broadening of the right to work.

We do not know what type of new directions the labour market will take in future. Similarly, even if change occurs not in the form of the environment, but on the part of the protagonists – in short, if the present intention of seeking work opportunities changes to an intention directed at struggling for the right to long-term stays in Japan – the mutual complementarity at work in the labour market will inevitably change into something else. Whatever the situation that we postulate, immigrant workers will feel a disproportionately large influence from even minor changes because of the limited social capital that they are able to mobilise. It will also be the case that social capital expands along with the passage of time. Therefore, it is imperative that we understand these conditions not using a static model that holds them to be constant, but as existing within a perpetually dynamic model. Strategic complementarity places its focus on the interaction between the action of individuals and the behaviour of the whole. It is in this regard that strategic complementarity is able to explain some of the changes that have occurred in the actions of migrants.

5 Foreign workers inside industrial organisations: a Game Theory approach

Introduction

In an attempt to begin by understanding the present situation accurately, the author treats the segmentation and diversification of workers as a game. Similarly, this chapter will show that this game of segmenting and diversifying workers is strongly regulated by Japan's *kigyō shakai* (company-dominated society). The key concepts in this chapter are 'order without commands' and 'forced free riders.' These concepts will serve to reveal both the connecting mechanism that links the labour problems of foreigners in workplaces with community problems and also the people, hidden behind this, who are 'truly' benefitting by using foreign workers. At a glance, the residential problems of foreigners in regional society present themselves as foreign residents being reduced to the status of regional free riders because of issues surrounding the putting out rubbish and noise. However, if one attempts to approach this problem from the position of the foreigners who are the visible free riders, these efforts will end in one straying into a bottleneck. The bottleneck takes the form of arguments that end up blaming individual foreign workers or their direct employers. In order to approach the problem of foreign workers without getting bogged down in this bottleneck, this chapter endeavours to grasp just who the invisible free riders are; the people enjoying the advantages of using foreign labour – the visible free riders.

Explaining the diversification of foreign workers

Chapter 3 discussed the division into a variety of patterns of staying that accompany the increasing length of stay of foreign workers: from stays characterised by total devotion to work and sending home remittances to lifestyles in which consumption in Japan is the goal.

The author has been critical in his discussion of the change to a 'lifestyle enjoyment type' – 'a change to the intent to consume' – by foreign workers of Japanese descent, arguing that we cannot conclude from this that foreign workers in general have changed. This does not, however, mean that the author does not acknowledge the existence of lifestyles of the 'lifestyle enjoyment' kind or 'tendencies towards excessive consumption' amongst workers of Japanese descent. What the author wishes to say is that while styles of staying in Japan that have consumption as their aim do exist, so too does the former type of migrant work which has sending remittances as its aim, and as both ends – 'the consumption goal' and 'the saving and sending remittances goal' – continue a variety of intermediate forms will also emerge. How can we approach the issue of the emergence of these intermediate forms? It is the author's belief that an effective approach could be made using Game Theory. Accordingly, this chapter will use Game Theory to consider the divergence and coexistence of diverse foreign workers.

Games are sets of rules on the basis of which the players act. In Game Theory, it is assumed that having made gains when a certain strategy (Strategy 1) and a another strategy (Strategy 2) were adopted, fellow players, who share – mutually acknowledge – the list of gains, select the strategies that maximise the gains that they themselves can acquire, while taking into account how one's own list of gains changes depending on the strategy adopted by one's opponent. Games presented as a list of gains are not simply a matter of rules that individuals have internalised. For example, the fact that if technological innovations occur and the tax system and trade conditions change, then the list of gains can be rewritten is a reflection of the social system that surrounds the players. Furthermore, just as whether the game becomes a cooperative or a non-cooperative game is determined by the trust between the players who assess the shared list of gains, the rules of the game also extend to the nature of the relationship between the players. That is, we can think of games as complexes of systems which regulate individuals' internalised intentions and the options that individuals can take in society.

Wages games, staying games and rights games

Let us examine the kinds of games that are being used concerning foreign workers. The majority of workers of Japanese descent are indirectly employed through service contracting companies. The point has already been repeatedly made that employment via service contracting companies may be insecure but, in terms of pay, these workers earn larger amounts than Japanese part-time and casual workers. The ability of workers of Japanese descent alone amongst all foreign workers to take part in this labour market blessed with high wages, in an almost monopolistic manner, is largely influenced by the visa status that has been issued to these men and women. The strategies are determined by who will be made into a worker by the legal system that decides the work qualifications of foreign workers and by the contracting industry that offers high hourly rates of pay to foreign workers. The legal system, that decides the work rights of foreign workers and who will be acknowledged as a worker, along with the contracting industry, that offers high hourly rates of pay to foreign workers, determine the strategy of entering a high wage labour market despite the insecure nature of employment and the strategy of possibly entering a labour market that is insecure and where there is no hope of high wages.

In reality, because the destination companies in key industries will terminate dealings with service contracting companies that send them workers if there are revelations of the commission of crimes such as the employment of undocumented workers or illegal workers, there is no attempt to hire anyone other than people who can work legally.[1] For this reason, whether foreign workers, who are the players, can adopt the strategy of working in a high wage job is entirely dependent on the legal system. We will call this game that is centred on wages the 'wages game.'

The wages game first decides whether or not one can enter the high wage service contracting industry labour market. In the wages game in Figure 5.1, many workers of Japanese descent are positioned before the yes arrow and undocumented workers before the no arrow. Following the determination of one's participation in the labour market, according to the wages game, a game concerning lifestyles while staying in Japan comes into play. Workers of Japanese descent, legal workers; undocumented workers; those who hope to return home one day having put something aside who are saving and trying to cover the living costs of their families actually living in their country of origin are probably all sending money home. Workers with these sorts of 'save and send' goals do not look for high levels of quality in their lives in Japan, which is a place where they are living temporarily.

Figure 5.1: Diversification of foreign workers as Game Theory[2]

Choice of wages and hourly pay

Wages game

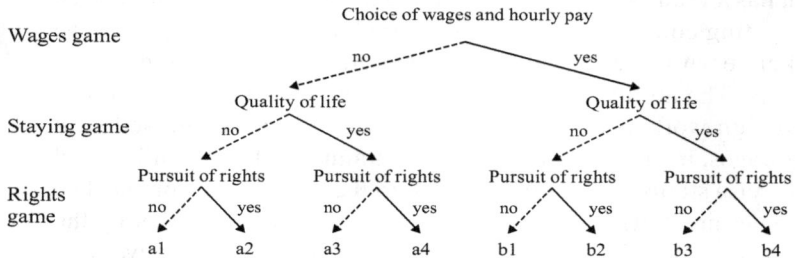

Note: a1: foreign workers in the 'urban underclass;' a2: undocumented employees who have saving and remittance goals and are organised; a3: foreign workers who have acquired a Japanese spouse; a4: organised undocumented employees who see Japan as the place where they live and assert their rights; b1: lone people of Japanese descent; b2: people of Japanese descent who have saving and remittance goals and are organised; b3: people of Japanese descent who are inclined to be excessive consumers; b4: protagonists who seek ideal rights

Meanwhile, if working abroad becomes prolonged and workers send for their spouses; marry in Japan; and the social and economic situations in their countries of origin worsen, it should perhaps not be surprising that the desire to seek a better quality of life will surface as the 'saving and remittance' goals lessen and the relative importance of Japan as the place where one lives increases. We will refer to games in which the environment for seeking a better life and this as a goal may or may not emerge as the 'staying game.' The staying game is at work amongst both workers of Japanese descent, who are legal workers, and also undocumented workers, giving rise to four patterns.

The staying game is a game concerning whether or not foreign workers staying in Japan find themselves in a setting in which they seek 'quality of life.' However, it is not possible to extrapolate from this and make any immediate decisions about whether or not foreign workers acknowledge Japan as the place where they will live their lives in the long-term. The reason for this lies in the fact that the increase in the relative weighting of Japan as the place where they live that accompanies the decline of the saving and remittance goals has not necessarily been the result of workers actively choosing this state of affairs. The explanation for this change contains, rather, a strong aspect of adaptive behaviour to the state of affairs in which the individual actors, who have been in insecure employment for a long period of time, find themselves. There is no active attempt to understand relations with Japan, the host country, in the staying game. The third game comes into play with regard to this point. This is the 'rights game' in which, by asserting their own rights, an attempt is made to establish Japan as the place where they live.

The first game, the wages game, contained an aspect of institutional choice regarding which the individual worker could not make any selection: whether they could be employed as legal workers. That is, whether they could participate in the high wages service contract labour market.[3] In the case of the staying game and the rights game, however, this issue is one of preference rather than choice: how do individual workers rank their own stay in Japan or, alternatively, what are the circumstances that they would wish to prevail during their stay?[4] Generally speaking, the fact that eight preference patterns (a1, a2, a3, a4, b1, b2, b3 and b4) emerge from the three layers of games indicates the existence of differing types of rationality amongst foreign workers. This is because there are variations in the very question of what each individual considers to be rational based on differing preferences, such as the kind of circumstances that they accept or the kind of circumstances to which they aspire.

Let us now give tangible illustrations of the kinds of images of foreigners that are linked to the eight patterns which diverge on the basis of differences in choices, preferences and rationality. Fundamentally, **a1** denotes the most vulnerable foreign workers; close in nature to the foreign workers that Akihiko Nishizawa calls 'the urban underclass' (Nishizawa 2002). There are differences between **a2** and **a4**, regarding whether or not they continue to subscribe to the saving and remittance goals, but these categories correspond to organised undocumented workers who speak out while taking part in labour unions and NGOs. In the case of **a3**, this covers mainly people of Japanese descent, permanent residents or the spouses of long-term residents in positions that are stable and legal and for whom Japan is the place where they live. This group does not join movements that advocate for rights. 'Lonely people of Japanese descent' who live solely to save and make remittances, whose lives during their stay in Japan end up being merely the sum total of the round trip between the factory and the dormitory; and who do not even socialise with any friends make up group **b1**. It is organised workers of Japanese descent who can be found mainly in the ranks of workers from Peru that make up group **b2**. People of Japanese descent who are of the 'enjoy life type' compose group **b3**. Finally, **b4** denotes workers who are in a superior position in the labour market and who, in addition to seeking quality of life, continue to firmly assert their own rights. These are the idealistic supporters of the rights movement for foreign workers. As seen in Chapter 3, however, because there is a tendency to eschew struggles for rights on the level of those enjoyed by Brazilians who have the best conditions amongst legal workers in the labour market, the author cannot confirm that these idealistic people exist as a group at this point in time.

The 'order without commands' established amongst subcontracting companies

As has been argued thus far, foreign workers diverge into groups based on the different patterns of behaviour observed between workers in the three levels of games: the wages game, the staying game and the rights game. However, the process of divergence amongst foreign workers has not simply come about because of the longer periods of stay of foreign workers and the increasing levels of experience and knowledge of Japanese society on the part of individual foreign workers. Since foreign workers also lead lives in Japan whilst being employed, the formation of patterns of behaviour amongst these men and women is closely connected with changes in industrial society (see Chapter 2). At a glance, it is also the goals of staying and goals of fighting for rights which are preferred and selected by individual foreign workers that, when viewed from another perspective, have been strengthened by the *kigyō shakai* (company-dominated society). Accordingly, this chapter will include an examination of industrial society – from a company organisation perspective – as it concerns foreign workers, paying particular attention to industrial society with its enterprise groups that are made up of multilayered subcontracting relationships.

The crucial point in games concerning employment and the formation of order as a result of these games is that the positional relationship with new companies alters the methods of employment according to the level of subcontracting in which one is positioned; that is, on the basis of considerations such as whether a particular company is a primary or a secondary subcontractor.[5] In order to consider the ways in which disparities in the employment methods that can be adopted by companies can create a specific order, let us first of all take a brief look at the differences in the practice of employment adjustment inside the subcontracting structure.

As far as parent companies are concerned, three routes form the main employment methods used to assemble the workforce required on their worksites: a permanent workforce (the regular workers); reinforcement personnel from subcontractors (workers from outside the company); and temporary workers (fixed term and seasonal workers). Even large group companies who have capital ties with their parent companies will use practically the same employment methods as their parent companies. However, most primary subcontractors are unable to source the portion of the temporary workforce to match fluctuating demand exclusively from the ranks of fixed term and seasonal workers. In other words, the main employment methods for primary subcontracting companies are: a permanent workforce (the regular workers); reinforcement personnel from subcontractors (workers from outside the company); and service contracting companies (an indirectly employed workforce). In companies under secondary subcontractors, reinforcement personnel from subcontractors disappear,[6] and the pattern becomes one of a permanent workforce (the regular workers); a workforce of part-time and casual workers (daily irregular employment); and service contracting companies (an indirectly employed workforce). Hierarchical differences emerge in the workforce that a company uses depending on the position that it occupies in the subcontracting structure (see Chapter 7 for a more detailed discussion).

Incidentally, in present day Japanese companies, with the thoroughgoing application of just in time approaches, one of these differences is information that is transmitted amongst subcontracting companies (transmission stimulus). This is the volume of work conveyed to subcontracting companies by parent companies (in practical terms, the volume of parts supplied). As the parent company also constructs a production system that, as far as possible, does not lead to a stockpile of merchandise it is affected by fluctuations in demand for its company's products brought about by a variety of factors including seasonal fluctuations. To this degree, the effects of fluctuations are felt on a daily basis from the parent company to the subcontractor at the very other end. However, in relation to the activity of producing goods on about largely the same scale as companies at the top of the subcontracting structure, the lowest ranked subcontracting companies within the subcontracting structure – because they are in charge of specific parts for specific goods (and occasionally for specific manufacturing processes for specific parts) – experience the same scale of large fluctuations as the lower ranked companies. It is here that the hierarchical differences in employment methods emerge.

The hierarchical order of the subcontracting structure that we see in the combination of regular and irregular employment as employment methods, is produced by the transmission of just one single piece of information – 'the volume of work' – and it is not something that the parent company has planned in detail regarding employment within the subcontracting company which exists at the very other end. Discrete decisions regarding the options that each individual company making up the subcontracting structure can itself take will lead to the spontaneous appearance of a particular order. To this extent, the hierarchical nature observed within methods of employment is a 'spontaneous order.' In the sense that companies, as subjects carrying out individual actions, have selected their own employment methods that they will use on the basis of individual decisions, this hierarchical order can be perceived as what Frederic A. Hayek calls 'order without commands' (Hayek [1960: 159–160] 1987: 40–43).

'Order without commands' and the social structure that reproduces irresponsibility

The social structure produced via order without commands exhibits functionally superior performance when considered from the viewpoint of fluctuating demand. Given that this is a structure that has been produced through connections that have emerged within the transmission of information about 'the volume of work' (that is, the volume of orders for parts), we might say that it is natural that it should deliver a functionally favourable performance. There is, however, nothing inevitable about functionally superior systems necessarily being superior also from a social justice viewpoint.

Problems that arise as a result of the individual selection of the most rational employment methods that a particular company decides that it can make are logically solely the problem of the individual company that took the decision. This is because there is no command from the parent company (the source of orders) to use any particular employment method (the application of this sort of pressure is in reality increasing, but this cannot be proven); it is nothing more than simply a case of having spontaneously used a particular method. Service contracting companies represent one of these methods and it is as a result of the use of service contracting companies that the employment of foreigners has appeared. In the case of subcontracting firms which have foreign workers working in them also, because they have sent their manufacturing processes to an in-house subcontractor in the contracting industry, even if problems do arise regarding foreign workers in the factories in their own companies, and even if these are internal factory issues, the logic will steadfastly be that these are problems in the outsourcing company and not in one's own company.

Let us give more specific consideration to this issue. The advantages gained by companies when they use an irregular workforce are not confined solely to having acquired the flexibility to be able to easily sever the employment relationship, unlike the case with regular employees. When we refer to irregular employment that supports production activity which is aligned with demand we always tend to place our focus on the flexibility aspect, but in companies occupying the bottom echelons of the subcontracting structure it is not at all unusual for there to be a reliance on irregular workers, in the form of part-time and casual employment, for the constantly required workforce. Unlike regular workers, there is no need to include these workers within the framework of seniority-based wages, but above all else, the main reason for using irregular workers for quantitative work is that companies can get away without any responsibility for indirect costs apart from wages (including legally-designated welfare expenses). Not being covered by social insurance has ended up becoming accepted practice in the case of the indirect employment of workers of Japanese descent via service contracting companies. In comparison to service contracting companies that dispatch Japanese workers who are covered by social insurance, the use of this practice makes lowering the cost (the so-called contracting unit cost) of dispatching workers of Japanese descent possible. It also increases the competitiveness of the indirect employment of workers of Japanese descent – that is, the competitiveness of the service contracting companies that dispatch workers of Japanese descent.

Indirect employment, which is a cost advantageous method, and above all the indirect employment of foreigners, which is the employment of legal workers, ought, properly speaking, to entitle these workers to inclusion in social insurance (health insurance and age pension). It is as a consequence of this lack of inclusion within social insurance having become accepted practice that the portion of costs of social insurance that are the responsibility of the company goes unpaid and these workers become a cheap workforce. As of 2007, service contracting companies argued that if they were to enter into social insurance, then the 1,200 yen per hour rate of pay for workers would result in a contracting unit cost of 1,920 yen whereas this cost would be 1,618 yen if they did not enter into social insurance.[7] In reality, contracts are drawn up on the basis of contracting unit costs that include workers within social insurance when Japanese workers are dispatched and with contract unit costs that do not include workers in social insurance when foreign workers are dispatched (this is confirmed by the company cited as an example in the Introduction). It is via the social dumping, as it were, of social welfare costs that it has been possible for the use of foreign labour to become a method for acquiring a cheap workforce.

Of course, it is fundamentally the service contractors as individual companies that ought to join up for social insurance (health insurance). However, the advantages of not having enrolled for social insurance, as they properly should have, are enjoyed by the whole subcontracting structure, including the parent company that is able to make use of a low cost workforce. *'Order without commands' thus reduces responsibility for social problems to the problem of individual companies. The whole structure that enjoys these advantages displays functionally favourable performance as a result of escaping its own responsibilities, but it simultaneously perpetuates a system that is the source of social injustice.* It is this 'irresponsible social structure' which produces order without commands that the author intends.

Coerced free riders

One of the problems produced by an irresponsible social structure to which we cannot turn a blind eye is that of the ghettoization of foreign workers. From the viewpoint of long-term Japanese residents, this problem that takes the form of a concentration of foreigners within a specific region is mostly perceived as deterioration in the living environment. This is a commonly observed phenomenon in areas where large numbers of foreigners reside, and is actualised in concrete terms as problems of 'putting out the rubbish,' 'noise' and 'illegal parking.' In the case of workers of Japanese descent, as a result of their strong tendency to live together in the regional cities that manufacturing companies are relentlessly developing, even the failure to participate in autonomous regions (neighbourhood associations) – something that would not have been a problem in the wider metropolitan area – becomes a weighty issue.

Why do these sorts of problems that are common to the regions in which foreigners live arise? Frankly speaking, the crux of the problem lies in the communication problems between foreign and Japanese residents. Communication between foreign and Japanese residents and also the formation of a united body, established via the act of communicating (a commune), requires the existence of the possibility of establishing a common framework of standards and recognition. However, the lack of the existence, over a long period of time, of this sort of common framework of standards and recognition between foreign and Japanese residents in the regions is giving rise to the problem of the ghettoization of foreigners in these areas.

The problems that arise alongside foreigners living in regional areas have to date been discussed by various commentators as being problems of 'coexistence.' However, the main arguments within these discussions have been: 1) coexistence arguments based on the stance that, morally and ethically, people ought to get along well with one another; and 2) coexistence arguments about the primacy of the community that insist on the formation of community. In both cases, the underlying premise is that people form communities and this results in the failure of analyses to cover the existence of those who make no attempt to participate in communities.[8]

In thinking about the residential problems of foreigners in regional areas, the author's view is that it is only by investigating what it is that gives rise to people who do not participate in formal regional communities that we will be able to answer the question of why problems to do with foreigners arise in regions where the majority of foreigners live.

We have, thus far, discussed the stratification of the foreign worker labour market from the viewpoint of Hayek's order without commands. The discussion will continue to be based on Hayek in this section also; it will be about 'coercion,' which Hayek regarded as an antithetical concept to 'freedom.' According to Hayek, 'coercion' does not mean forcing people to do things against their will. Hayek defines coercion in the following way – from the standpoint of relationships with others when an individual acts on a choice that he has made and also relationships with circumstances in which one cannot help making choices.

> Coercion occurs when one man's actions are made to serve another man's will, not for his own but for the other's purpose. It is not that the coerced does not choose at all; if that were the case, we should not speak his 'acting'... However, that I still choose but that my mind is made someone else's tool, because the alternatives before me have been so manipulated that the conduct that the coercer wants me to choose becomes for me the least painful one. Although coerced, it is still I who decide which is the least evil under the circumstances (Hayek [1960:133] 1987:4).

When we think about foreign workers as migrants, we think about individuals who have come to a host country as a result of having decided to work in a country that is not their own. To this extent, migrant labour is a decision based on the *free will* of the individual. However, as we have seen up to this point, the majority of foreign workers working in Japan are not able to enter anything other than the peripheral market of insecure employment and even though it is said that they can change jobs, they are restricted to the interior of the peripheral labour market.

In the case of people of Japanese descent, although we can observe frequent changing of jobs, this is the changing of workplaces where hiring is conducted by the service contracting company. It is said that these male and female workers choose their places of employment on the basis of how high the pay is and whether or not there is overtime and work on days off. However, 'changing one's place of employment' is generally synonymous with 'changing the service contracting company in which one is employed.' Although it is an individual's choice, it would not be an exaggeration to use the term coerced labour contract to refer to the following form of employment: one in which there is no possibility of choosing regular employment and no choice but to choose irregular employment; and which perpetuates a state of affairs whereby the individual cannot be covered by social insurance (health insurance), half of the business of labour management – all in the interests of maximising the profits of contracting companies and brokers.

Furthermore, the residential style of foreign workers who, as a result of their coerced labour contracts, work from early in the morning until late at night and consequently are unable to fulfil the role of being members of cooperative bodies as part of their lives in the communities where they live is also a form of coercion.

It is as a result of not putting in the effort that is required to maintain residential communities – 'they disregard the times for putting out rubbish;' 'they do not take their duty turns for putting out rubbish;' 'they do not pay neighbourhood association fees;' 'they do not play their part in neighbourhood associations' and so on – that foreign workers are liable to be regarded as free riders in the community. However, the nature of foreign workers as free riders in residential areas results from the coerced labour contracts and in this sense they are 'coerced free riders.'

Conclusion: an irresponsible social structure and coerced free riders

The issue is what kind of mechanism will give rise to relationships that produce social problems such as 'an irresponsible social structure' and 'coerced free riders?' The first thing that we must take into consideration is the legal framework that restricts the inflow of migrants. In the case of Japan, the main cause of the shift away from Pakistanis and Bangladeshis towards Iranians is well known to have been the Japanese government's 1988 termination of the mutual visa exemption agreement that had existed with the first two countries (Tanno 2002b), while the 1990 revision of the Immigration Control and Refugee Recognition Act had a very large influence on the influx of a labour force made up of people of Japanese descent. This is because the legal system applies not only to workers but also to companies that bring in a workforce. Similarly, when the full implementation of the Gender Equality in Employment Act makes late night work by women possible, there is also a shift from a foreign worker labour force to a Japanese labour force (this will be investigated more thoroughly in Chapter 7). Thus, the rules created by the legal system not only regulate the patterns of behaviour of direct actors, such as foreign workers and companies who are the subjects of analysis, but also have an influence that extends to the patterns of behaviour of third parties who become rivals; they regulate the behaviour environment ('the legal system game').

The influence of the legal system affects the whole of *kigyō shakai* (company-dominated society) and the business-to-business rules are also influenced by the legal system (the 'business-to-business rules game'). Changes to the legal system also have an impact on the type of role that an individual company plays within a company group, on the basis of the business-to-business rules. The role within a company group determines the type of workforce that will be required according to the type of role that an individual company plays within the subcontracting structure (the 'intra-company role game'). The actual demand for a workforce, in the form of the type of workforce that is wanted, is a signal regarding what the company is seeking in terms of the way in which the workforce is to work – as a labour market; and this determines the way in which both Japanese and foreign workers work (the 'Japanese workers' way of working game' and the 'foreign workers way of working game'). Their role within the subcontracting structure also determines the location conditions of individual companies and plants: where the factory is located within Japan or alternatively whether it moves abroad. Once the location conditions within the subcontracting structure have been decided, these form the basis for also determining the kind of workforce that an individual production point can use (the 'individual company's social and geographic conditions game').

Changes to the legal system do not only have an impact on the organisation of companies. It is inevitable that when changes occur in the demand for Japanese or foreign labour these will also lead to changes in the ways in which workers work. Examples of these types of changes are amendments to the legal system such as the full implementation of the Gender Equality in Employment Act and increasing the age of eligibility for the age pension; and these forcibly bring about changes in the relationships of demand in the labour market. Changes in these sorts of factors force practical reconsiderations of employment strategies, such as what kind of workforce they will use, on the part of individual points of production.

Figure 5.2 shows these types of relationships. There is a need to explain why this figure is entitled 'The coercive social structure

Figure 5.2: The coercive social structure surrounding migrant workers[9]

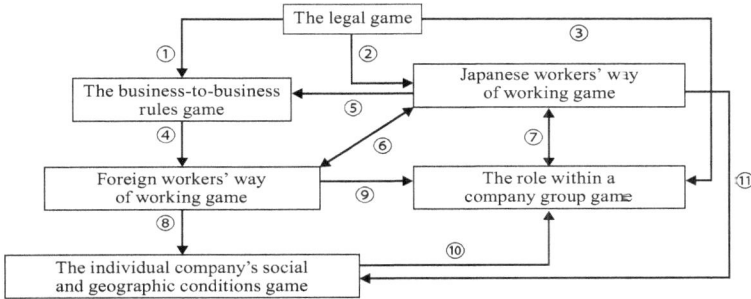

surrounding migrant workers.' The author, as stated earlier, has understood 'the diversification of foreign workers' in terms of three layers of games: the wages game, the staying game and the rights game. The diversification prompted by these games has not progressed completely according to their logic. The diversification of foreigners in Figure 5.2 is the area shown as the foreign workers' way of working game, and this interacts with the manner in which the games in the various other areas progress: the framework of the legal system (the legal system game); the industrial structure of the company and its location within the subcontracting structure (the business-to-business rules game and the intra-company group roles game); the geographic conditions (the individual company's social and geographic conditions game); and the way of working of Japanese people (the Japanese workers' way of working game). Through these sorts of game linkages a feedback loop is established between organisations and individuals. Organisations, including the market, continue to operate as the thought patterns – established at these points – of individuals, and organisations themselves are regulated. Organisations, including the market, are themselves regulated via the continuous interaction with individuals' ways of thinking which have been formed within them.

The implications of the various points in Figure 5.2 are as follows: points ①, ② and ③ that on the national level the legal system acts on companies, Japanese people and foreigners alike; point ④ that industrial groups and transactional relationships between companies are formed within the legal framework; and point ⑤ that industrial groups as a whole scrutinise the state of employment at times when there have been long-term changes in the lifestyle of Japanese people. One such example is the *Report of the Research Committee on Labour Problems* which is published annually by the Japanese Federation of Employers' Associations (*Nikkeiren*). Points ⑥ and ⑨ indicate that the position within the group occupied by companies that work for themselves within the subcontracting structure determines the type of demands that they make on the ways in which both Japanese and foreign workers work. Points ⑥ and ⑦ are bidirectional arrows. Point ⑥ shows that the state of workers is heavily influenced by company demands and that the demands made by the company are also regulated by the fact that Japanese workers, who have many options open to them, avoid workplaces that do not meet their wishes. On the other hand, it is certainly not the case that foreign workers have no impact whatsoever on the way of working of Japanese workers. As we shall see in Chapter 7, within the insecure employment layer, foreign and Japanese workers are in competitive relations with one another; and, as touched on in Chapter 4, the existence of a contracted workforce made up of people of Japanese descent is also exerting an influence on the policies of labour unions that organise regular workers. Point ⑦ shows these relationships. Points ⑩ and ⑪ imply that whether or not companies are able to assemble Japanese workers largely regulates the location conditions in which they will find themselves; the implication is that if they are unable to assemble Japanese workers, then space will open up for the employment of foreigners. What point ⑧ shows is that the location conditions and shift times under which Japanese workers do not want to work are heavily influenced by the company strategy of the parent company. We are thus able to appreciate that the problems of foreign workers working in Japan arise as a consequence of the mutual interaction of these respective primary causes.

There remains a final point that needs to be considered: whether this type of mutual interaction is the inevitable result of an 'invisible hand' or whether it is the act of a 'visible hand.' The author's views are indicated by the directions of the arrows in Figure 5.2. It seems clear that the factors that regulate the way of working of foreign workers are: the 'legal system game' which is the legal framework on the national level; the 'intra-company group role game' and the 'social and geographic conditions of individual companies game' which decides the kind of employment strategy adopted by a company; and the 'way of working of Japanese workers game' that determines both the manner in which Japanese people will be employed and the types of work. Is it possible then for changes in foreign workers' way of working to exert any influence on the various games that regulate their way of working? The author thinks that this influence is only partial and that it is not fundamental. The introduction of foreign workers has occurred as a result of the inevitability of companies having to respond to changes in the way of working of Japanese workers such as disliking night shifts and disliking workplaces that are regarded as hard, dirty and dangerous. However, while there are some cases of companies regarding the establishment of workplaces that appeal to Japanese people as a matter of priority, the priority given to responding to the requests of foreign workers is low.

This is why the author believes that the nature of this type of mutual interaction is definitely not the result of an 'invisible hand.' When the legal system framework which covers everyone living in Japan, particularly at the national level, and the industrial society which is established alongside the subcontracting structure are givens, it is the management strategy of the parent company that exerts a large influence at the time of deciding what kind of function and role individual companies and plants will play.

We cannot exclude the influence of the 'visible hand' that is at work in industrial society making use of foreign workers. If we omit the operation of the 'visible hand,' then discussing the visible free riders found in specific cities where foreign workers reside and in specific ghettos within these specific cities is meaningless. In order to confront this issue squarely, we must understand the nature of the games that regulate Japan's industrial society and pay attention to the existence of invisible free riders who are turning foreign workers into 'coerced free riders.' It is by understanding the social structure of the coercion acting upon foreigners living in Japan that it will become possible, for the first time, for us to conceive a national scheme concerning the practical problems of foreign workers.

Part II
Transnational Workers and Japan

6 The contract age and workers of Japanese descent: foreign workers and the reorganisation of the peripheral labour market

Introduction

Japanese research into foreign workers is in a sad state of disarray. Ethnicity scholars have no interest in workplaces and labour scholars evince no interest in ethnic differences. Consequently, research into Japan's foreign workers leads to the publication of papers at either extreme of research into foreigners: those that make no mention of worksites; or, research into peripheral labour that is devoid of ethnic differences.

Also, the affinity between scholarship and national ideologies is of more than just passing relevance as part of the background to scholarship trends and interests. Whether or not national boundaries are to be made obvious units of analysis must be questioned. In the case of labour research, when the principal research theme is organisation in the interests of the welfare of workers and its improvement, questions are raised about whether or not we can turn our interests to social formation that goes beyond the existing people who structure organisations.[1] Chapter 2 confirmed the fact that if we introduce the perspective of a transnational employment system, then the actual labour market is not something that is formed within a closed region but rather is established as a 'local labor market' (Sassen 1995) that is also connected in a manner in which regions transcend borders. The failure to reintroduce the perspective of workers who transcend concepts of nationality leaves us unable, in this day and age, to put an end to the degradation of the welfare of workers who are citizens with vested interests. It is, accordingly, the aim of this chapter to consider a framework for discussing the posing of problems in the peripheral labour market which keeps sight of the existence of foreign workers.

A historical outline of the migrant work phenomenon

The majority of research into foreign workers in Japan treats the foreign worker problem as a domestic problem for Japan as the receiving country. However, the author considers it essential to view the foreign worker labour market as being formed via the connecting of different regions within two countries. Accordingly, this work begins its investigations not within the national economy, but by asking how it was that two points on a map came to form a labour market and what the context for this was. Because the labour market begins to function after the materialisation of a concrete organisational system, let us attempt to understand the historical process that led up to the completion of this concrete system.

Figure 6.1 registers the changes in the foreigners employed in Japan following the 1990 revision of the Immigration Control and Refugee Recognition Act.[2] Foreigners intending to work are the foreigners who hold one of the fourteen varieties of visa status under the categories contained in Appended Table 1 in the Preface to the revisions of the Act which sets out who can work.[3] Workers such as those of Japanese descent are foreigners who reside in Japan holding residence qualifications, including those who come under Appended Table 2 – 'permanent residents,' 'spouses of Japanese' and 'spouses of permanent residents' – who are in addition assumed to be working in Japan. As is clear from the definition, the latter group, 'workers such as those of Japanese descent,' is not necessarily made up exclusively of people of Japanese descent, but the majority are, in fact, workers of Japanese descent from Latin America. Since the 1990 revision of the Immigration Control and Refugee Recognition Act made it possible for workers such as those of Japanese descent to work in all areas of employment, it can largely be argued that this revision entirely underlies the increase in unskilled workers. However, as Figure 6.1 shows, following the revision of the Immigration Control and Refugee Recognition Act there was also a definite increase in foreign workers looking for employment that required high levels of specialisation.

Incidentally, the particular use of the term migrant workers to describe workers from Latin America, who make up the majority

Figure 6.1: Conditions of work for foreign workers following the revision of the Immigration Control and Refugee Recognition Act

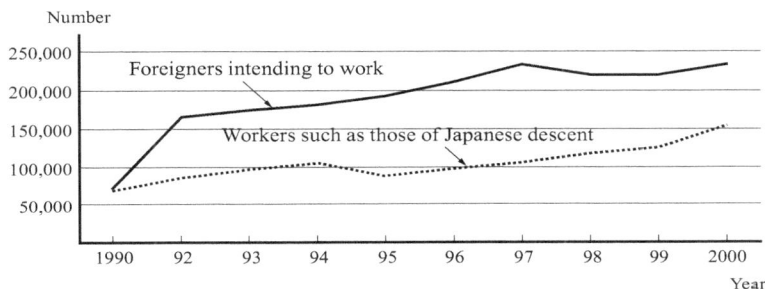

Number

of workers such as those of Japanese descent, is generally seen as having begun from the mid-1980s (Mori 1992). However, movement from Latin America to Japan had existed before this time. It is not the case that everyone who had originally migrated to Latin America settled there as a migrant. In fact, those who regarded the place to which they had migrated as their lifelong place of residence formed a minority of people. They were migrants who dreamt of 'returning home in glory' and as such very few went back immediately. However, people who determined to return to Japan having given up on migration after repeatedly trying it for five or ten years were not uncommon (Handa 1966; Handa 1970; Maeyama 1981; Zaihaku Okinawaken Jinkai 1987; Koronia Okinawa Nyūshoku 1995; and Gushiken 1998).

Similarly, not only people returning from their countries of emigration in Latin America but also 'proto-migrant workers' who returned to Japan temporarily to work because of failed agricultural or business ventures have always existed.[4] In around the mid-1980s, proto-migrant workers suddenly changed into a new form of migrant worker. This change was partly a result of changes in the attributes of the migrant worker protagonists, but it was also largely related to outside factors (external conditions) in the form of the economic chaos that occurred in the period of transition from military to civilian governments and also the opening up of direct flights to Japan.

The reader is referred back to Figure 2.2. This shows changes in the number of visas issued in Brazil. One can appreciate from this figure that while the migrant worker boom occurred during the period of the 1990 revision of the Immigration Control and Refugee Recognition Act, in 1992 the bubble economy withered just as it had begun. There are matters here regarding which it is essential to exercise caution. Firstly, even following the revision of the Immigration Control and Refugee Recognition Act the majority of people of Japanese descent entered Japan on short term visas and changed their status to a specific visa after they had started working. In response to this, immigration authorities adapted the operation of the system to match reality regarding people of Japanese descent whom they knew to be already working.[5] The change in visas issued from 1996 to 1997 reflects this. Secondly, after 1997, there was a large rally in visa numbers, but if we view this year as an exception, it appears that there is a reduction in the number of visas issued; that is, a reduction in the number of migrants between Japan and Brazil. There is also a problem here, however, in relation to the operation of the system. Special visas are issued for a period of either one or three years and, in recent years, a large number of the longer three year visas have come to be issued. Moreover, there has been an increase in changes of status by people holding long-term resident visas to permanent residents.[6] Because of this, there has been a decline in the number of people issued with a visa each time that they move between Japan and Brazil. Consequently, if we view the situation in terms of the number of visas issued, then this development is reflected in what appears to be a decline in movement between Japan and Latin America.[7] However, as is shown in Figure 6.1, the presence of workers such as those of Japanese descent living in Japan is leveling off and travelers who constantly traverse national borders continue to establish themselves as the labour force.

The emergence of migrant workers from Latin America

What exactly was the change from proto-migrant worker to migrant worker? At this point, we will begin – when thinking of migrant labour as one system – to consider it in terms of the kind of expectations that people have of this system and also in terms of the kinds of outcomes that the system brings about in response to these expectations. We will think of migrant labour in terms of the kind of relationships found in Figure 6.2. In short, in terms of the kind of expectations that link the migrant workers, who are the protagonists, to the migrant labour institution; and, whether or not their initial expectations concerning this institution have been achieved as a consequence. If expectations (hopes) lead to outcomes (actual outcomes), then the people who are the protagonists will probably continue to make use of this institution until their expectations fail to be met.[8] Similarly, the achievement of outcomes by a specific protagonist who uses this institution presents a model for realising expectations as far as other protagonists who have the same expectations are concerned, and this leads to the other protagonists also being won over by this system. As Thorstin Veblen also says, this is because 'The institutions are, in substance, prevalent habits of thought with respect to particular relations and particular functions of the individual and of the community (Veblen 1998: 190).

If we think of migrant workers as an institution, in the above fashion, then we are able to understand the changes that migrant workers were undergoing in the mid-1980s. The expectations of the protagonists – as seen in the fact that proto-migrant workers up until the mid-1980s were also known as 'loser migrant workers' – were to recover from the failure of agricultural and business ventures in Latin America and the outcomes that they sought were to be able to start their lives in Latin America over again after having paid back loans with the money that they earned by working in Japan. However, the expectations of and outcomes from the institution for protagonists in the case of the migrant labour that began in the mid-1980s were clearly different from those of proto-migrant labour. Migrant labour was now led by the 'expectations' that saving even just a little was acceptable and that they wanted to enjoy life while the outcomes that they sought were: 'owning real estate and cars' as well as 'earning funds so as to start a business.' *Migrant labour* for the purpose of regenerating the basis of one's life in the case of people who have failed and *migrant labour* that seeks savings and a better life each result in a considerable difference in the numbers of actors entering the institution. In other words, *the entry of only people who had failed meant that everyone in the Japanese descent*

Figure 6.2: System as function

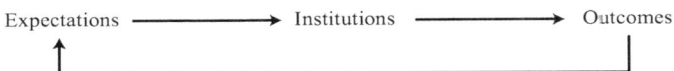

community was a potential user of the institution. What is the social significance of migrant labour as an institution when it engages increasing numbers of potential users? The author approaches this point using Mahasiko Aoki's concept of 'summary representation.' 'Summary representation' is the institution coordinating the hopes and behavioural choices of the protagonists through a process in which the protagonists, who carry out economic acts, consider themselves able to realise practically all of their own hopes (expectations) as outcomes (results) by using this institution (Aoki 2001: Chapter 5). This does not necessarily mean that by joining the ranks of migrant labour one will definitely be able to build up assets (savings and real estate). Summary representation merely assumes that if large numbers of people use an institution, this will produce specific results leading in turn to larger numbers of people joining the institution and the appearance in their midst of people who achieve the same results that others had been hoping for. For this very reason, in order for summary representation to be able to suffice (for *migrant labour* to gain social recognition as 'summary representation') people must accept it (*migrant labour)* as a model. The author and others have heard from interview surveys how the pioneer migrant workers even managed to establish businesses through their migrant labour (Kajita 1998; Higuchi 2002; the present work: Chapter 10). The unanimous story told by those who worked in Japan from around 1985 is that, 'the people who went to Japan to work from around 1984/1985 worked for two years and then returned home around 1986/1987. These people were able to buy houses with the money that they had saved in Japan creating a sudden migrant work boom.' Once the fruits of migrant work were visible in the form of an accumulation of property resources, migrant work as summary representation was destined for success.

Migrant labour as far as the various recipient companies are concerned

Migrant labour reached the peak of its boom during the period of the economic bubble and was welcomed into workplaces which, despite the availability of work, were experiencing an absolute shortage of manpower. This situation is reflected in the controversies at the time regarding whether to open up or close the country to foreign workers. Migrant workers were largely employed: in the case of direct employment, in workplaces offering fixed term direct employment in the form of fixed term contracts or seasonal work; or, in workplaces offering fixed term indirect employment through service contracting companies (in-house contracting companies). Thus, workplaces offering fixed term employment characterise the employment category in which these men and women were employed. Incidentally, at times when good business conditions saw the building up of orders in the workplaces to which these workers were sent, this type of fixed term employment category turned into employment of a more continuous nature, but if these receiving businesses stagnate once hard times return, workers in their workplaces will confront immediate crises of dismissals. This is because one's current employment is not protected by rights; it is simply no more than a case of it unexpectedly having turned into continuous employment. In this sense, these men and women clearly make up an insecure employment stratum of workers.

Kiyoshi Yamamoto has made the following remarks regarding this author's work in Tanno (2002a). Yamamoto sorts discussions of the separating out of the existing insecure employment stratum along the following lines. Firstly, the types of migrant workers who supplement the household economy type are rural women, and they become migrant workers in order to play this role in the family (Yamada 1934 and Hirano 1934). Secondly, the urban mixed industry stratum type forms the insecure employment stratum of the industrial category, which is formed when workers from the village are absorbed into the already formed urban mixed industrial stratum (Hirano 1934, Sumiya 1964 and Sumiya 1969). The third type is the fringe labour supply type which participates in the labour market when economic times are good, functioning to underpin the industrial category, but leaves the labour market during bad economic times to become housewives (Umemura 1964). In addition, Yamamoto (2002) was critical of the author's description of the formation of the mixed industrial class as resulting from the exclusion of the labour force of Japanese descent who had come to be temporarily placed working in factories.

We should not forget that for the fourth selection type of insecure employment, which as pointed out by Yamamoto was omitted, we have the household system provision type which was developed

Table 6.1: A model for separating the peripheral labour force

Separate types of labour supply	Peripheral formation mechanism
① Migrant labour: Supplementing the household economy type	Rurual women → industrial category
② Urban mixed industrial types	Village urban mixed industrial types → industrial category
③ Fringe labour supply type	Economic bubble → labour market → housewife during economic slump
④ Household system provision type	Village → urban labour market → the household system mediates surplus rural population during economic slumps
⑤ Migrant labour of Japanese descent type	Latin America → factories (industrial category) urban mixed industrial layer

Note: Compiled by partially revising Yamamoto 2002: 1.

into a schema by Kawashima. In the case of the household system provision type – in contrast to the explanation of the 'migrant labour and family supplement type,' 'urban mixed industrial stratum type' and 'fringe labour supply type' based on an economic moment – Kawashima pays attention to rural and urban movements brought about by major factors outside of the economy. The following passage from Kawashima provides a concrete expression of the essence of these movements.

> This has, naturally, bestowed a particular – that is, Japanese – trait on urban workers from rural areas. That is to say, as mentioned previously, the majority of wage labourers in Japan whilst living in another household far removed from their own families, remained attached by an invisible thread in the traditional family system to their families in the rural areas, and when they lost their jobs they were able to draw on these latent family relationships to return to their families. Consequently, Japanese wage labourers are not completely removed from the means of production (agricultural land in this case), and in this way unemployment has not shown up as the phenomenon of "unemployment" and this has impeded the development of modern labour laws for a long while in Japan (Kawashima 1982a: 62).

However, since the background and industries of that time differ for the various research subjects, the way to understand the peripheral labour supply on the basis of the labour force selection types shown in Table 6.1 is not to exclude consideration of other models for each of them. Similarly, in contrast to the '① migrant labour and supplementing the household economy type,' '② urban mixed industrial type' and '③ fringe labour supply type,' which are treated as problems of the accumulation of funds within Japan, ④ has an approach that starts from social relationships and, therefore, this lengthens the time period that it is possible to cover to some extent. Looking at main family-branch family relationships was a focus from the pre-war period until around the 1950s. However, all of these approaches construct their logic on the premise that the movement of workers occurs within the borders of just one country. In ⑤, the 'migrant labour of Japanese descent type,' however, the logic of labour force demand is a domestic issue, but the logic of supply of a labour force springs from a different dimension to that of the accumulation of funds within Japan. On this point, the migrant labour of Japanese descent type differs decisively from the four other varieties of types listed above.

The author, as in the organisation used by Yamamoto, sees the labour force of Japanese descent as forming a part of the urban mixed industrial stratum. However, when workers of Japanese descent became part of the urban mixed industrial stratum – just as there was a change amongst workers who came over from Latin America from proto-migrant labour to migrant labour – there was also a change, as far as employers were concerned, in the summary representation endorsed by migrant workers. It is also important to add the reservation that the 'urban mixed industrial stratum' referred to here is not at all the same as that referred to in Sumiya's definition. This is because the author merely uses it in the sense of people who work in occupational categories demanded by service contracting companies in which, whilst they may be wage labourers, the possibilities for changing to regular employment are few.[9]

Just as going off to work as a migrant worker meant the possibility of getting closer to success (that is, establishing summary representation) as far as migrant workers were concerned, this institution was a kind of summary representation also for the Japanese companies that accepted migrant workers. As stated previously, if looked at from the perspective of employment contracts, a labour force of Japanese descent has the consistent trait of being 'short term, fixed term employment.' And the core of summary representation as far as the employer side is concerned is expressed in these employment contracts that are for 'short, fixed term employment.' In other words, a labour force of Japanese descent is always a labour force that it is possible to withdraw from the point of production.

While this same short, fixed term employment continued, however, with the demise of the period of absolute labour shortages, there was a decisive change in summary representation in the form of expectations and outcomes functions that businesses sought from the employment of people of Japanese descent. This change was one away from seeing people of Japanese descent as a labour force that had to be secured ahead of others towards seeing this group as one part of the labour supply necessary to build the optimum combination (the construction of a labour force portfolio) from the midst of a mixture of multiple labour force resources. Table 2 makes this point clearly using evidence-based research.[10] With the collapse of the bubble, there has been an expansion of recruitment subjects for those in charge of human resources and labour both in terms of the quantity of work and work fluctuations. The summary representation that companies bestowed with regard to the labour force of Japanese descent changed from flexibility in lifestyle activities to a flexible personnel plan.

Adaptive evolution of the labour market and the growing lack of adaptation by individual workers

Thus far, we have considered changes in summary representation for the workers and also for companies. As both of these changes reveal changes in the labour force supply side and demand side, it would be safer to consider both as changing as they interact. Accordingly, this section will examine how changes resulting from the interaction of the demand for and supply of a labour force are in turn changing expectations (and their outcomes) regarding the institution of migrant labour.

The expectations regarding migrant work during the period of the bubble economy are shown in Table 6.2. It is important to note the existence of conditions that made possible the respective expectations and outcomes of both the labour force demand side and supply side. The reason for the almost total coincidence between workers' expectations and outcomes is due to the fact that because

Table 6.2: Expectations and outcomes of the labour force supply side and demand side regarding the institution of migrant labour in the bubble period, and the conditions producing outcomes

Labour force supply side	Labour force demand side
Expectations	
Building up assets	Resolving a labour shortage
Outcomes	
The building up of assets by some people	Resolving a labour shortage
Conditions that led to outcomes	
Inflation and weak local currency in one's own country	An economic environment in which one can sell what one makes

of the fall in the acceptability of the currency from workers' home countries, which were experiencing high levels of inflation, if they were able to get hold of foreign currency, then they would be able to increase the amount of currency that they retained in local currency exchanges given inflation and the exchange rate. Meanwhile, as far as the companies were concerned, the economic conditions, in which it was possible to sell all that was produced, brought about chronic labour shortages.

Whilst individual actors may have continued to hold the same expectations as in the period of the bubble economy, in the period of the collapse of the bubble economy both of the conditions that had produced outcomes changed (Table 6.3). In Brazil as a result of the exchange rate for US dollars having been pegged at parity with the Brazilian real during the bubble, inflation increased the final exchange value. Even if one obtained foreign currency, it now no longer increased beyond the value for which it had been bought. Unrelated to the Japanese economic environment, the summary representation of migrant work for success also began to decline. Meanwhile, on the labour force demand side also, the collapse of the bubble economy turned an economic environment in which it was possible to sell all that one could produce into a thing of the past, and transformed the economic environment into one in which some companies were winners and others losers. As a result, the companies that were winners sought even more flexible production activities so as to continue winning; and in the case of the companies

Table 6.3: Expectations and outcomes of the labour force supply and demand sides regarding the institution of migrant labour following the collapse of the bubble, and the conditions leading to outcomes

Labour force supply side	Labour force demand side
Expectations	
Building up assets	Flexible factory management
Outcomes	
Acquiring employment for the time being	Employment of diverse foreigners
Conditions that led to outcomes	
A better economic environment than in one's home country	Intensification of global competition/ progress of a declining birth rate and ageing population

that were the losers, the necessity of rebuilding their production system led them to require atypical employment.

Migrant work with a view to achieving success has become difficult as a result of changes in the economic environment in the counties of origin. Why is it that migrant work continues despite this? The answer lies in policies designed to check inflation in workers' countries of origin which have brought about a worsening of the employment environment there and, as a result, even though the bubble has burst, these foreign workers come to Japan with its relatively better employment situation. Meanwhile, as a result of the mythologising of migrant work to achieve success, despite the changes in the social environment that envelops migrant workers, the expectations of individuals regarding going abroad to work continue to be, as in the past, the building up of assets.[11]

The continuing intensification of global competition even following the collapse of the bubble gave rise to the emergence of one sole idea – the slimming down of organisations; companies that had been winners also shared in this thinking as the substitution of so-called irregular employment for regular employment spread throughout the whole of society. It has not at all, however, been the case that this has made every employment destination for foreign workers insecure. This is because, as a result of the progressively declining birth rate and ageing population, companies that wish to continue their production activities in Japan in the long term will begin to turn their labour force made up of workers of Japanese descent into a regular labour force.[12] Consequently, as on the one hand the shift towards increasingly insecure employment proceeds in the employment of workers of Japanese descent as a whole, there is the perceptible emergence of some secure workplaces – the internal polarisation of the employment of workers of Japanese descent has begun.[13]

The logic of a transnational employment system

The changes in the employment environment in Japan are also having an effect on the recruiting system in Latin America. This section examines the nature of these effects.

The system of recruiting a labour force of migrant workers in Latin America that began around the middle of the 1980s was systematically established in the latter half of the 1980s, and it created basically the same relationships of specialisation as the present system. A realistic picture of the relationships of specialisation in the labour market for workers of Japanese descent can be found by referring back to Figure 2.3. We are able to surmise that Brazil and Japan, two countries that are quite far apart geographically, form a single labour market via relationships of specialisation. The system that is formed via these relationships of specialisation will be referred to in this discussion as a labour force export mechanism. The distorted ruling structure of the Japanese descent community influences the background to the formation of this type of specialisation system. As an example of this we could give the fact that many of the leaders of associations of people from the same prefectures, which have provided support to the Japanese descent community to date, also operate travel agencies for migrant work that have the gathering of people as one of their prevailing characteristics.

The labour force export mechanism is constantly changing. In surveys conducted by the author in 1997–1998 (Kajita (ed.) 1999), the system resembled that found in Figure 2.3, but in the 2002 survey results hardly any relationships of specialisation could be seen amongst the travel agencies for working abroad; each of these travel agencies carried out its own business activities in a standalone manner. They were able to confirm their vertical integration, but it has become a system lacking horizontal integration. It is not, however, the case that all horizontal specialisation has disappeared. The horizontal specialisation found in Latin America

Figure 6.3: Labour force export mechanism as a network

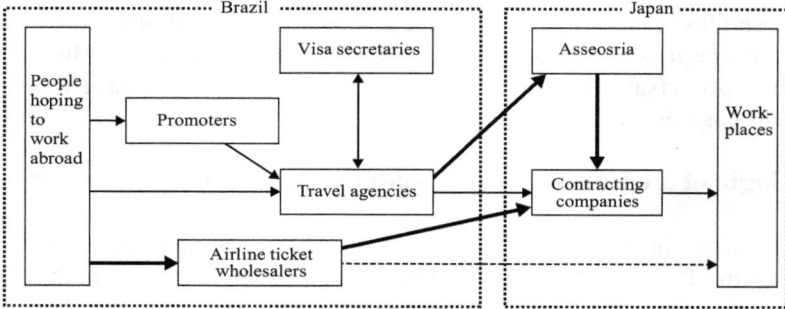

Note: Thick lines indicate the routes of frequently seen movements and thin lines those that have become scarce as movement routes. The arrow drawn from ticket wholesalers to workplaces, in addition to being a thin line, indicates the route taken by a small minority, but one that nonetheless exists, of workers who have temporarily returned to their home country with nothing but an airplane ticket, having secured employment in Japan.

has decreased, but there has been an increase within Japan of horizontal specialisation. Domestic horizontal specialisation within Japan is strongly related to the presence of brokers within Japan who have increased their influence anew. Brokers within Japan send faxed lists of workers of Japanese descent employed by their own companies to national contracting companies. When service contractors require a new labour force or when they cannot meet their needs despite having recruited within their own company, they have the labour that they need sent over by brokers. As a result of this, Latin American travel agencies for migrant work are now able to dispatch those workers who have visited their own offices in the hope of finding employment abroad even if they have not first received demands for a labour force from Japanese manufacturing companies or service contracting companies with whom they have dealings. Figure 6.3 shows this.

This sort of change is also related to changes that have occurred in the behaviour patterns of the actors (workers) who are using the system (labour export mechanism). Given that a population of 300,000 Brazilians alone ordinarily reside in Japan, the necessity for having to recruit a labour force made up of workers of Japanese descent on the ground in Latin America has largely declined and only a tiny minority of people remain who would be unable to get to

Japan without relying on a travel agency for working abroad.[14] This, in addition to the deepening of the Japanese recession, explains why travel agencies run by people of Japanese descent would find that their own companies could not stay in business if they were to wait for requests from the service contracting companies and Japanese manufacturing companies, with whom they are in partnership, to dispatch workers.[15]

As has been argued thus far, the labour market for workers of Japanese descent is largely regulated by labour force demand from Japan. When labour force demand is vigorous, each and every person of Japanese descent who can lawfully be employed is able to take part in the labour market. However, the minute that recession strikes, the market is transformed into something which clings dearly to network factors. Network factors are defined here in terms of the difficulty of entering the market without individual connections to specific gatekeepers. Prolonged worsening of the economic slump and recession as well as intensification in global competition brought about a complete change in demand for a labour force. There was a considerable decline in the help wanted requests reaching Latin America. However, the decline in help wanted requests reduced demand for travel agencies for people of Japanese descent; it did not destroy the horizontal integration amongst travel agencies. The reduction in help wanted requests strengthened the power of the labour force demand side (Japanese service contractors and factories) and brought about changes to the methods for selecting workers. In short, when anyone who was of Japanese descent could enter the marketplace as long as they had the attribute of being of 'Japanese descent,' then anyone would do. However, when the conditions being sought were Japanese conversational and reading and writing ability, previous experience of employment in Japan, and particular gender and age groups – that is, workers with specific attributes – then travel agencies turned to attempting to assemble a labour force that matched these attributes from amongst connections on whom they could rely. In this way, the labour force export mechanism in Latin America strengthened its aspect as a networking organisation characterised by vertical rather than horizontal integration.

The labour principle regulates the diverse domains of the various other interrelated principles, stretching from the labour-management relations principle, with its strong institutional hue, to the

Figure 6.4: The location of the law at work in the labour market

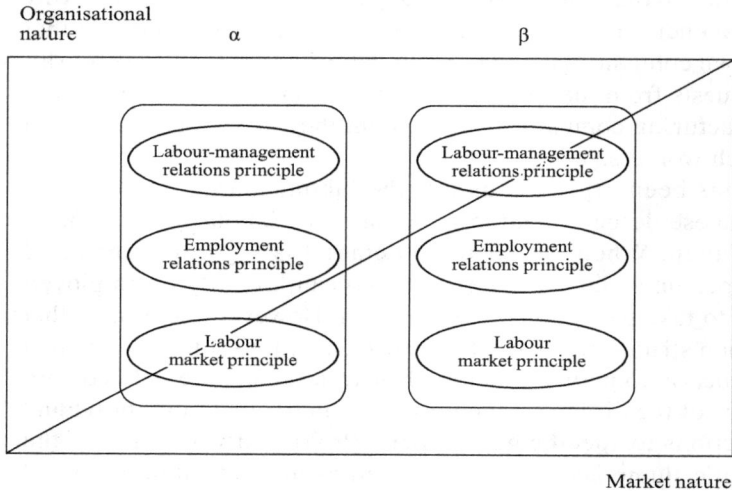

Source: Suwa 2002: 23.

labour market principle, with its strong market hue. Yasuo Suwa used Figure 6.4 to explain the logic of labour market principles: the issues that are highlighted will vary depending on the function sought from the labour market on each occasion by the principles at work at the level of the organisation that has undergone concrete institutionalisation and by the principles related to all of the actors who make up any market. According to Suwa, with calls for the liberalisation and deregulation of the labour market, at present, the position of the labour principle has shifted from α to β and each respective principle displays a more marked market preference (Suwa 2002).

We can see the same sort of ordering of the labour principle carried out by Suwa in the labour market for workers of Japanese descent also. As can also be appreciated from the changes to the labour force export mechanism, when there is vigorous demand for labour, anyone can take part as long as they satisfy specific categories; the labour market takes on stronger market elements. Conversely, there is an effort to assemble workers possessing specific attributes when the demand for labour becomes tight. The market character in which anyone can gain access vanishes and

*Figure 6.5: The relationship between organisation and market in
the labour market for workers of Japanese descent*

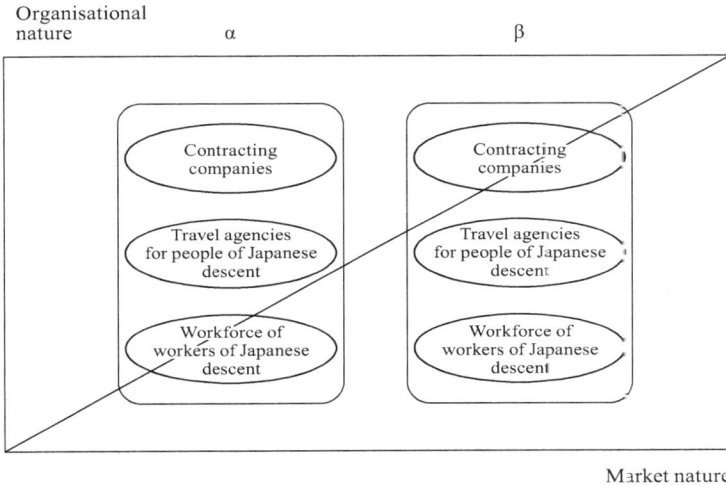

workers are sought from amongst the ranks of existing contacts who
are able to judge the attributes required. Consequently, the market is
changed by networks. We can see labour market β, shown in Figure
6.5, as having shifted to labour market α.

Conclusion

What exactly does the employment of foreigners mean to companies? A labour supervisor, in the area of transportation machine and
equipment manufacture, described the employment of foreigners to
the author as a 'grey zone.' On the point of not employing undocumented workers, this amounts to recognition of the fact that this may
not be illegal, but that the reality for these men and women working
as contract labour in the workplace is that they do not enjoy a legal
status; their existence is permitted because it has not been detected.

The labour force of Japanese descent is essential, but it came
about from company expectations regarding their desire to avoid
the costs of employing regular workers. It is a calculated form of
employment in which the aim is to evade paying benefits of any
kind other than the legally mandated welfare expenses, in order

to achieve lower labour costs.[16] Surely the practice of securing a labour force via a contracting agreement merely on the basis of compensation for work contains a contradiction in terms of the issues it raises for the legal category of contracts and also in terms of a company's accounts? However, the behavioural patterns forced onto workers who survive by means of the constant repetition of fixed-term employment have, as a result of the culmination of individual actions, produced exceptionally absurd outcomes for individuals and society. For example, this situation inevitably gives rise to problems such as the fact that foreign workers are uninsured – the issue that is drawing the most attention from local governments in terms of the various residential problems of foreign workers – and the participation of workers, who ought to be covered by social insurance, in national health insurance.

Being unable to participate in anything other than the fixed-term employment labour market creates a unique behavioural pattern for workers. This is that in their relationship with the workplaces that employ them and the labour market (organisations) there is no other way for them to assert their will apart from by leaving the organisation. There are no opportunities for nurturing the sort of altruistic relationships hypothesised by Albert Hirschman, such as voice and loyalty (Hirschman 1970). The secondary sector labour force, in the sense intended by Peter B. Doeringer and Michael Piore, are workers who have no exit strategy (Doeringer and Piore 1971).[17] It is the attribute of being 'foreigners' that determines that these workers can have no voice.

Incidentally, the growth of irregular employment in recent years has not only affected foreigners; it is common in industrial societies. However, the increase in irregular employment is not necessarily a bad thing. As the case of Spain illustrates, as long as there is a system that takes into consideration previous employment experience in regular employment in a way that is advantageous for workers when they take part in irregular employment, the increase in irregular employment will not, in any way, operate as a negative (Marsden and Ryan 1990 and Marsden 2003). The problem as far as foreign workers in Japan are concerned is that it is extremely difficult for them to move into the regular labour market (employment without fixed time limits). This is particularly striking in the case of workers of Japanese descent.[18]

Uchida uses 'the contract age' to refer to conditions that 'herald an age which has at its forefront policies that reduce the role of the state and stress market mechanisms; one in which activities that had to date been thought of as different from contracts are increasingly entrusted to the market – that is, to contracts (Uchida 2000: 1). Workers of Japanese descent who have no other course but to take part in indirect employment represent a conversion of workers into contract workers and as such they are the forerunners of the 'contract age' at the points of production.[19]

In the sense that the employment segment of workers of Japanese descent is leading the contract age, it is a new way of working. However, because the employment of people of Japanese descent continues to diversify and the employment destinations for the majority of people have narrowed to contracting companies, the labour market for workers of Japanese descent is displaying characteristics that are very similar to what Eiichi Eguchi previously called 'a liberalised labour market' (Eguchi 1980). Eguchi's intention in calling the labour market for the insecure employment stratum 'a liberalised labour market' was most likely as a contrast to Shōjirō Ujihara's 'frozen company labour market' characterised by seniority according to length of service and lifetime employment (Ujihara 1966). Eguchi primarily sought the characteristics of insecure employment in the openness of the market, but in the case of workers of Japanese descent who form the modern day insecure employment stratum, it is in the nature of the contracts with the points of production that we must seek this principal characteristic. Precisely because we are in the age of contacts, which in turn characterise the age of globalisation, people of Japanese descent who have been brought in from outside the national borders are being used as the vanguard of the contract age. The existence of these types of workers of Japanese descent requires from us a way of approaching the issue that does not conclude its considerations inside national borders when investigating Japanese worksites.

7 Globalisation, economic reorganisation and local labour markets: peripheral labour competition in the automobile industry

Introduction

In 1995, on the basis of survey results, the Ministry of Labour pointed out that wherever 'use could be made of Japanese "university graduates," "part-time workers" and "fixed contract workers," foreign workers currently being used for general work that did not fall under skilled or technical work would no longer be used.' It was also pointed out that, in terms of pay, foreign workers 'could not be described as cheap labour' (Rōdōshō Shokugyō antei kyoku 1995: 64–65). This is an indication that if the conditions were to exist for being able to employ Japanese people, then foreigners could be replaced. Following this, research was published showing that the foreign labour force had a substitution effect with regards to Japanese people (Tsutsui 2001). The author, on the other hand, thinks that following the latter half of the 1990s, foreign workers had the workplace positions that they had occupied in the Japanese labour market until then snatched away from them by Japanese and that they have been forced down into a labour market with worse conditions. This chapter is an attempt to substantiate this opinion empirically.

Toyota City in Aichi Prefecture is the research subject for this chapter. This chapter is based on the results of the *Survey of the Impact of the Progress of Internationalisation in Toyota City and in Regional Society* (*Toyota City Industrial Survey*) carried out amongst manufacturing plants affiliated with the Toyota Chamber of Commerce and Industry in 2000. The two-pronged survey technique consisted of: a postal questionnaire survey of 1,493 plants on the list of companies held by the Toyota Chamber of Commerce and Industry and interview surveys with 47 plants from amongst those who replied to the questionnaire survey that had experience of employing foreigners.[1] The discussion that follows will clearly show the manner in which the overall trends that emerged quantitatively from simultaneously conducted quantitative and qualitative surveys manifest themselves as actual problems amongst individual business people (companies) and workers.[2]

This chapter revises understanding of the *Toyota City Industrial Survey* from within one subcontracting structure by taking the view that the positions that companies occupy in the subcontracting structure reflect the ways in which each company employs foreigners. Company A, the parent company of the subcontracting structure that is the focus of this chapter, has its headquarters in Toyota City, but its main group companies are concentrated in the neighbouring city of Kariya. However, this chapter does not set out to study Company A. Similarly, the survey that forms the basis of this chapter is related to the foreign workers who live in Toyota City and to companies in the city, but although reference is made to local labour markets this is restricted to the labour market in Toyota City.

Outline of manufacturing industry in Toyota City

Toyota City is a regional industrial city with a population of 350,000 and its present city limits are the result of repeated amalgamations of towns and villages. The development of Toyota City has occurred around Koromochō in the environs of the old castle of Koromojō. Koromochō and the automobile industry are very closely related. This is given symbolic expression in the lining up side by side, in front of the city offices, of bronze statues of the mayor who originally lured Company A to Koromochō and the company's founder as people of importance who built the city's development. As of December 2002, the number of employees at Company A, the biggest in the city, was over 67,000 and because eight of the company's twelve factories in Aichi Prefecture were in the city of Toyota about seventy-five per cent of Company A's employees lived there.[3] Actually, 50,000 of the city's population of 350,000 work for Company A.[4]

The term *company castle town* carries connotations of a small elite of pivotal companies controlling most of the subcontracting and a vast majority of the workers. However, Toyota City with

Figure 7.1: Wage differences based on company scale discernible in automobile related industries in Toyota City

Individual
yearly income
(Unit: ¥10,000)

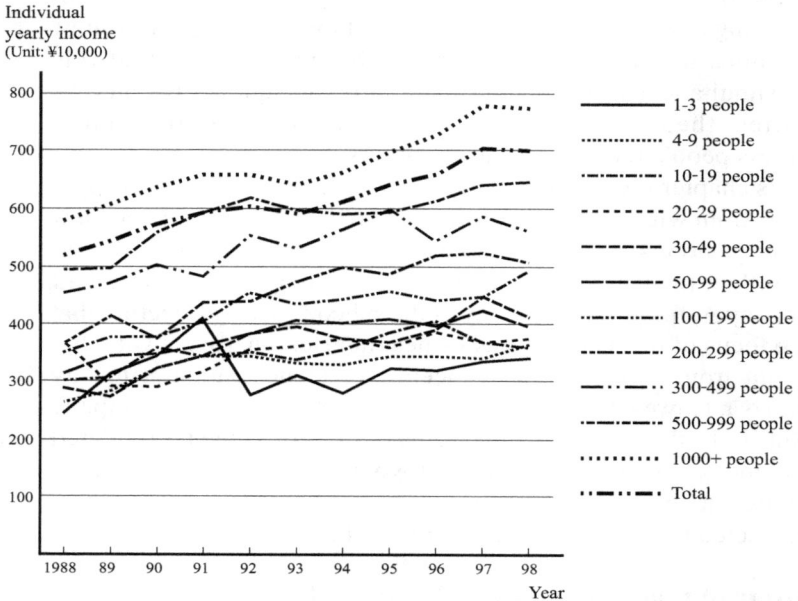

————	1-3 people
··············	4-9 people
—·—·—·—	10-19 people
- - - - - -	20-29 people
— — — —	30-49 people
—— ——	50-99 people
—··—··—··	100-199 people
—·—·—·—	200-299 people
—··—··—··	300-499 people
—·—·—·—	500-999 people
··········	1000+ people
··—··—··	Total

Company A in it, which has grown into a world company, has a majority of its workers employed by this corporate giant and a minority of workers employed in the small- and medium-sized companies which numerically account for the vast majority of plants. Table 7.1 conveys this concisely.

Toyota City only adopts industrial statistics produced by automobile related industries to use as its own city statistics. One of these sets of statistics classifies automobile related industries by the scale of employee numbers and gives the annual amount of money that plants pay to employees. Table 7.1, as suggested by the heading, divides the amount of money paid annually within each category by the number of workers to give the amount of money paid annually per person. Despite the fact that there is an approximately twofold wage differential between plants on a scale of over 1,000 workers and those with fewer than 200 workers, the amount of money paid annually per person within the whole of the automobile related industries approximates the wage level in companies of over 1,000.

This is a clear illustration of the extent of the impact of the corporate giant on the whole region.

It is not only the fact that workers in automobile related industries form the majority of workers in the region that makes the author's thoughts go immediately to automobile related industries when considering the industries and foreign workers in Toyota City. The questionnaire surveys were mailed to 1,493 plants and 740 of these responded.[5] These 740 plants can be broken down into 203 automobile and automobile parts manufacturing companies (27.7 per cent); other manufacturing plants (43.4 per cent); and 212 other plants (28.9 per cent). When looked at in terms of the number of plants, automobile related industries account for just a little over one in four. However, when looked at in terms of the scale of employee numbers, of plants that responded those with fewer than three employees made up 44.8 per cent and in the cumulative figures for plants employing fewer than ten people these plants accounted for 67.3 per cent of manufacturing industry in the city. One can easily imagine that foreign workers are irrelevant to these tiny companies and also that it is the large-scale automobile related industries that provide places of employment for foreign workers in this region.

Table 7.1 looks at whether or not plants with varying scales of employee numbers have any experience of employing foreigners. The figures for having some experience of employing foreigners were 11.8 per cent when the plant scale was fewer than thirty employees; 48.6 per cent for plants with over thirty and fewer than one hundred employees; and actually reached 66.0 per cent for plants with over a hundred employees. We see that an increase in the scale of employee numbers is accompanied by an increase in experience of employing foreigners. We can gather from Table 7.1 that the foreign worker problems in this region are employment problems in plants that are medium scale and above.

Table 7.2 shows the presence or absence of experience in employing foreigners by further dividing Table 7.1 by industry type. Automobile and automobile parts manufacturing plants make up 45.3 per cent of plants with experience of employing foreign workers. In contrast to this, other manufacturing plants at 16.0 per cent and other plants at 7.0 per cent form an extremely small minority. Of the total number of plants that responded, 21.6 per cent had some experience of employing foreign workers. However, 58.2 per cent of the plants with some experience of employing foreigners were

Table 7.1: The presence or absence of the experience of employing
foreigners, by scale of employee numbers

Number	Employment experience		No employment experience		Total
< 30	69	(11.8%)	518	(88.2%)	587
30–100	36	(48.6%)	38	(51.4%)	74
100 <	35	(66.0%)	18	(34.0%)	53
Total	140	(19.6%)	574	(80.4%)	714

Table 7.2: The presence or absence of the experience of employing
foreigners, by type of industry

	Employment experience		No employment experience		Total
Automobile and automobile parts manufacturing companies	92	(45.3%)	111	(54.7%)	203
Other manufacturing companies	51	(16.0%)	267	(84.0%)	318
Other	15	(7.0%)	197	(93.0%)	212
Total	158	(21.6%)	575	(78.4%)	733

automobile and automobile parts manufacturing plants. The prepon-
derance of automobile and automobile parts manufacturing plants
in the figures for plants with experience of employing foreigners
is tied up with the fact that many of these correspond to the plants
indicated in Table 7.1 as having over a hundred employees. The
employment of foreigners in Toyota City is heavily influenced by
trends in automobile related industries employing over one hundred
people. This is why when thinking about foreign workers in the
region we cannot overlook the strategy of the automobile industry
which exerts a very large influence on the regional economy.

Incidentally, a big change has emerged in the employment of
foreigners in recent years. Table 7.2 is based on the responses to
questions about when the employment of foreigners began or when
it ceased. It is easy to understand at a glance that 1990 was the year
in which the majority of plants began to employ foreign workers. It
is not difficult to imagine that there would have been an increase
in plants beginning to employ foreigners in this period; in the
midst of the economic bubble and when the Immigration Control
and Refugee Recognition Act was revised and work by people of

Figure 7.2: Initial and final years of employing foreigners

Number of
employees

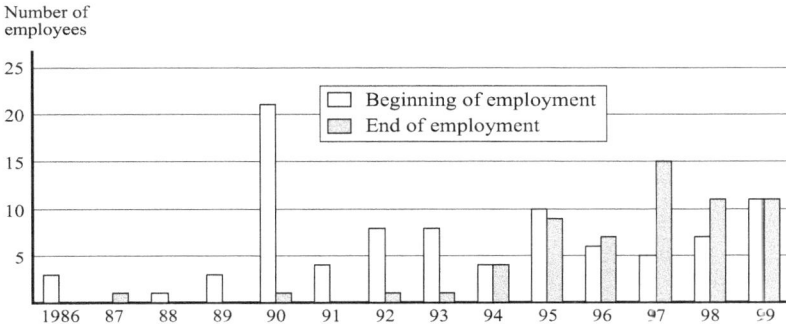

Japanese descent was legalised. At the same time, however, the number of plants that began employing foreign workers afresh following 1995, when Japan was clearly in recession, is not at all insignificant. What needs to be stressed above all else is that once there was a sudden increase in plants ceasing to use foreign workers, in 1995, the pattern that followed showed that the number of plants in which one could no longer see any foreign workers consistently surpassed the number of plants that were starting to use foreign workers. In terms of the number of plants, the situation in Toyota City saw a reduction in workplaces in which foreign workers worked.

How then have the plants that ceased employing foreigners been forced to change their form of employment? Have these changes meant a decrease in the volume of work or in the size of the labour force required? Or then again, has there been a progressive replacement of foreign labour with a different labour force as a result of having acquired a separate labour force that will work for them in place of foreigners? Alternatively, are the very places of work disappearing as a result of the offshoring = hollowing out of factories? The following section will begin to clarify these points using data from interview surveys.

The subcontracting structure of the automobile industry and foreign workers

In the preceding section, the position of the foreign labour force in Toyota City was discussed on the basis of the questionnaire survey

Figure 7.3: The employment of foreigners in the subcontracting company group related to Company A, the interview subject, in Toyota City[7]

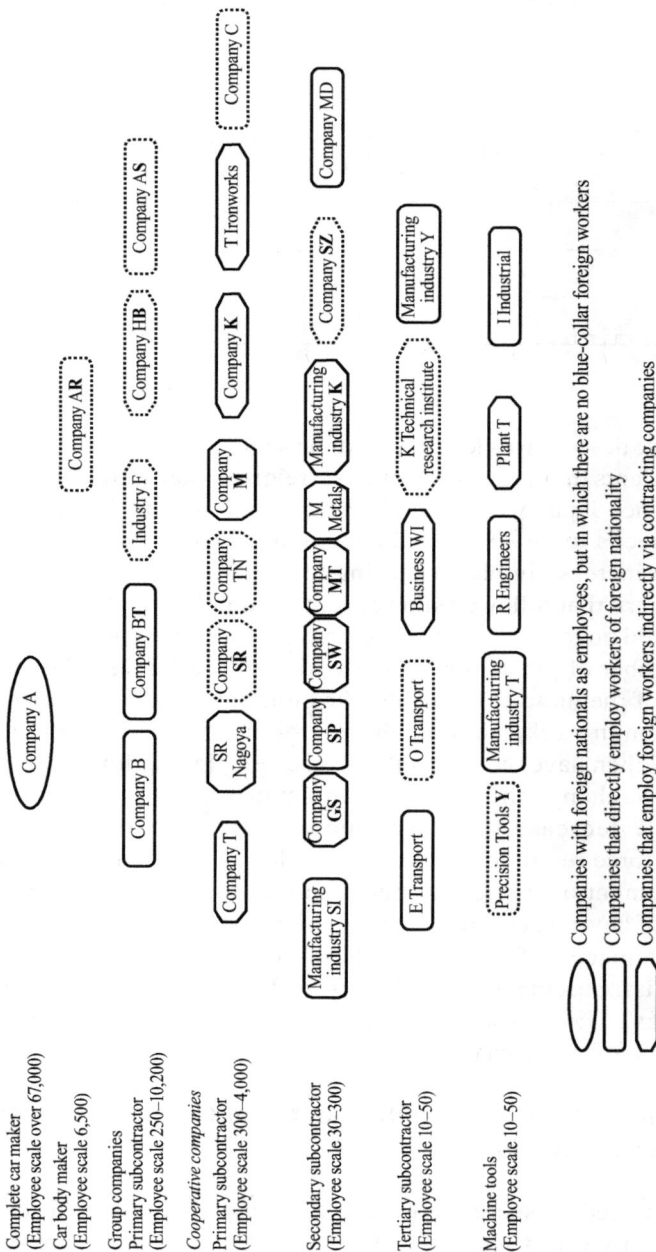

answers provided by plants. From this section on, the data that will be examined has been acquired via an oral interview survey conducted with personnel and labour supervisors who responded to the questionnaire survey. The questionnaire also contained instances of companies that had set up multiple plants and plants that were using (or had used) migrant workers. However, the replies that came back from these sorts of companies regarding personnel and labour were 'covered by responses from head office.' This is why plant surveys in the oral interviews take the form of company surveys. Since, at this point, we examine the responses that were made by the respective plants as individual companies, from here on companies rather than plants will form the basic unit of consideration.

Of the companies that form the focus of this survey Company A, the parent company, was the earliest employer of foreigners. However, Company A has not to date employed foreigners to work as blue-collar labourers. Thus far, the foreigners working for the parent company are only technical experts working as engineers and management cadets from overseas subsidiaries who have come to Japan for in-company training.[6] In the case of the companies whose subcontracting relationships are shown in Figure 7.3, it is the subcontracting companies under the car body maker Company AR that have used foreign workers as labourers.

In primary subcontracting, Companies B and BT use workers of Japanese descent through direct employment. Company T, SR Nagoya, Company M, Industry K and T Ironworks all have their labour force of Japanese descent dispatched from service contracting companies. In the case of Industry F, H Brakes, Company AS, Company SR, Company TN and Company C, however, foreign workers have disappeared from their factories in Toyota City.

When we look at secondary subcontracting, we see that the presence of foreign workers in Company S, Company SP and Company MD comes via direct employment, while in Company GS, Company SW, Company MT, M Metals and K Manufacturing Industry service contracting companies are used. It is only Company SZ that has stopped using a foreign labour force. In the case of tertiary subcontractors and machine tools makers, which are practically on the same scale of employee numbers, E Transport, Y Manufacturing Industry, T Manufacturing Industry, R Engineering and I Industrial directly employ foreign workers while Manufacturing Industry W and Plant

T use indirectly employed foreigners. Meanwhile, the employment of foreigners has vanished from O Transport, K Technical Research Institute and Y Precision Tools.

Thus workplaces for foreigners have disappeared from large-scale primary subcontractors and from small-scale tertiary subcontractors and machine tools makers.[8] Meanwhile, in the companies of secondary subcontractors, the foreign worker labour force remains, as in the past, an important available force for blue-collar worksites. A bipolarisation is occurring amongst companies under the same subcontracting relationships: companies that have in recent years stopped relying on a foreign labour force; and companies that are carrying out their production activities by relying on a foreign labour force.

The collapse of company-to-company rules regarding the employment and foreign workers

Let us now attempt to examine how foreign workers have been introduced into subcontracting relationships.[9] Plants in Toyota City provide representative cases of the introduction of a foreign labour force in 1990, the year in which the employment of foreigners suddenly soared. In 1990 – at a meeting of various industries in the Toyota Chamber of Commerce and Industry – six companies with plants in N Town of Toyota City, operating as the N Town group, jointly began introducing foreign workers of Japanese descent from Brazil. One of the managers in the group had a friend who owned a travel agency in Brazil and it was decided to assemble workers using that agency and then divide them between the six companies. Once they had begun dealing with the travel agency, this group set up an operational flow whereby the six companies would pool their new requests for help wanted every two to three months, send these to the travel agency and then bring in workers from Brazil.

In 1992, however, the N Town Group spontaneously ceased functioning. This was because, with the collapse of the bubble economy and the passing of the period of labour shortages, all of the companies making up the group simultaneously lost their need to carry out help wanted activities. The companies that made up the N Town Group ended up reaching individual agreements with the travel agent in Brazil to the effect that when they had positions to fill, the travel agent would place the help wanted ads and assemble a labour force on their behalf.[10] The companies in N Town Group began bringing in people of Japanese descent because workers in their own companies had left to work elsewhere. The companies that made up this group correspond to the lower level of secondary subcontracting in Figure 7.3. There are two main places to which Japanese workers would move from there. The first is a change of jobs to the service contracting industry. The second is a change of jobs to a higher level in the subcontracting company.

Let us look first at the pattern of moving to work in the service contracting industry. Apart from regular employees and part-time workers, there are also outside workers from service contracting companies working in factories in response to the fluctuations in production output. As they are in the same workplace, regular and contract workers have conversations with each other about pay. In the period of the bubble economy, an approximately twofold pay differential in total net income emerged between regular employees and workers from outside the company in secondary subcontracting companies. Factory workers had been unaware of the fact that despite doing the same work in the same workplace there were disparities in disposable income to the extent that: there were, on the one hand, subcontracted full-time employees who struggled even to find a few coins for cigarettes; while, on the other hand, subcontracted contract workers had money left to spend even though they were paying off car loans. Consequently, there was a steady stream of people leaving their jobs as regular workers and applying for help wanted positions in service contracting companies.[11]

Next, let us look at changing jobs to go to a more highly placed company within *keiretsu* companies [conglomerates]. As seen previously in Figure 7.1, there are big wage differentials depending on the scale of the company in automobile related companies. Given the existence of a disparity in the amount of wages, it might be natural to think that low paid people would flow into high wage workplaces. However, even after this 'dual structure' was pointed out in the 1957 *Economic White Paper*, it did not vanish, but continues to exist. It might be thought that the mechanism by which the dual structure continues to exist would vary according to the period or region, but from the 1980s to the 1990s, in companies related to Company A, agreement was reached amongst the *keiretsu* companies that 'they would not employ job seekers who had an employment history of having worked in the *keiretsu*.' Because of this, whether people seeking to start work in any Company A related area would start in a high or a low wage labour market was decided on the basis of the level of Company A related subcontracting at which they first entered the company: as recent graduates, from other industries or from another *keiretsu* – that is, from non-Company A related areas.

With the arrival of the period of unprecedented labour shortages due to the bubble economy keeping to the principle that 'they would not employ job seekers who had an employment history of having worked in the *keiretsu*' made it impossible for even the parent company to assemble the labour force that it needed. The automobile industry is well-known as an industry in which there are simultaneously large numbers of people employed and large numbers leaving. When able to extract sufficient numbers for its labour force from the external labour market, then despite the simultaneously large numbers of appointments and departures, it had been able to exclude people with a history of having worked in the *keiretsu* from the labour market. However, when the external labour market vanished, the parent company revised the rule that had held within the *keiretsu* that people with a history of having worked in the *keiretsu* would not be employed (the social linkages of this were discussed in Chapter 3). This took the form of 'we will not employ people whose most recent previous employment was in the *keiretsu*.' As a result of this, the path opened up for moving from a low to a high wage labour market.[12]

Recognising limitless mobility for workers within the *keiretsu* companies would have made it more difficult to maintain the dual structure within the *keiretsu*. The dual structure is also the source of cost competitive power because as far as the parent company is concerned it can decrease the product price by sending items that were unprofitable to produce in their own companies outside the company. The complete disappearance of the dual structure would also damage the parent company's profits. For this reason a mechanism for ensuring that worker mobility within the *keiretsu* happens no more than necessary is included in the new rule change. When people with a history of having worked in the *keiretsu* were employed, they did not immediately become regular workers, but had conditions imposed on them. They would be employed after having served either a six month or one year trial period as a trainee worker (during which they could only earn an apprenticeship wage) and then passing an exam;[13] both of these conditions applied in cases where more than six months had passed since having left a company within the *keiretsu*.

Incidentally, there were differing degrees of enthusiasm between the parent company and subcontracting companies for the existence of these people moving around within the *keiretsu*. The parent company's understanding of the issue was that whilst there certainly were trainee workers making their way up from the *keiretsu* subcontractors to employment in the main company, their numbers were extremely small and therefore should not have any impact on the management of factories in the subcontracting companies.[14] Contrastingly, the impact of the removal of one skilled worker was considerable in the case of subcontracting companies. It is precisely those people dissatisfied with low wages who aspired to move to work in the parent company who are workers with a sense of purpose; this is evident in the way that they take into consideration the wages that they could acquire in the long-term and determine to move. The impact on the workplaces of small-scale companies of the ongoing loss of workers with a sense of purpose is greater than imagined by the parent company. The six companies from amongst the secondary subcontracting companies in Figure 7.3 had experienced having workers from their companies lured away by the opening up of routes for moving to the parent company to change occupation.[15] The employment of foreigners in the automobile industry in Toyota City began side-by-side with these kinds of changes to the company-to-company rules.

Parent company demands within the subcontracting relationship and the labour market

The lower the level of the subcontractor within the subcontracting structure, the more that relying on a foreign labour force is rendered inevitable by conditions. Changes in the company-to-company rules that existed within *keiretsu* had a large impact on this transformation. It was not only the changes to the company-to-company rules that accentuated the sense of a labour shortage for subcontracting companies. By examining the factory management methods within *keiretsu*, this section will give more detailed consideration of the connections of the labour market within Toyota City's automobile industry.

Parent company, Company A, has eight plants that are affiliated with the Toyota Chamber of Commerce and Industry. There have

been various building periods from the time of the Motomachi
Factory – the original plant opened by the parent company in the
early period and the head company factory – to the Hirose Factory
that commenced operation in 1989. Similarly, the parent company
has a variety of factories: there are those that assemble whole cars,
but also factories like the Kamigō Factory that specialises in the
production of engines and the Hirose Factory that mainly produces
electrical components.

The type of car produced varies from factory to factory. Company
A, the parent company, is widely known for its TPS (Toyota
Production System) with its thorough implementation of just-in-
time practices. This production method in which the production
process proceeds in accordance with the *kanban* (signboard) is a system that minimises inventory in all areas including subcontracting.
This production method simultaneously synchronises production
activities with customer orders from dealers. Within the production
schedule, detailed predictions about demand are made and production systems to match these are set up, but orders certainly do not
come flowing in according to schedule. There are car types that
achieve higher than expected sales and also those for which sales
are lower than anticipated. For these reasons, differences always
appear between the operating ratios for each factory (plant).

The parent company responds to labour shortages arising from
these differences in operating ratios in factories (plants) by, firstly,
moving personnel between plants – from factories with a low operating ratio to factories with a high operating ratio. Any remaining
shortfall in the numbers needed is met by, secondly, requesting
reinforcement personnel from subcontracting companies, and any
further remaining shortfall is, thirdly, supplemented by recruiting
factory workers on fixed term contracts. The parent company also
has within it personnel from other types of industries that are in
recession and other makers experiencing poor performance. This is,
however, a labour supply provided on an ad hoc basis; it definitely
does not constitute part of the systematically configured labour
force in the company. This is why personnel from other industries
and other makers are not taken into consideration in this chapter.

Companies in the primary subcontracting group also respond to
labour shortages using a system along similar lines to that of the
parent company. For this reason, companies below the secondary
subcontracting level find themselves being asked to supply more

reinforcement personnel as the parent company's production activities pick up. When production activity is brisk in the parent company production activity in subcontracting companies is also pulled along by this, creating an active state. The companies related to Company A, including its subcontractors, are all gathered in Nishimikawa. Since demands for reinforcement personnel from the parent company to the subcontracting company occur when the labour market is tight for the region as a whole, if the labour market vanishes within the region, then subcontracting companies either rely on service contracting companies or they must inevitably rush to bring in foreign workers.

In terms of a labour market outside the region, methods such as recruiting fixed term contract workers from Kyūshū or Okinawa exist. At the time of the survey, however, the only companies amongst the automobile companies of Toyota City to be successful in recruiting fixed term contract workers were Company A and the pivotal company in its group, Company B. Despite being major companies within the company group, automobile body maker, Company AR, Company BT – a subsidiary of Company B – and HB all failed in their companies' attempts to recruit fixed term contract workers. The situation is the same inside primary contracting companies. The brand power of the company name exerts a large influence on the employment of fixed term contract workers. Despite the fact that they assembled complete automobiles just like the parent company and despite the fact also that they offered the same amount of recruitment pay and the same conditions as the parent company, Company AR and Company BT, with low social recognition of their names, were unable to assemble fixed term contract workers. Companies that had shifted to employing foreigners and, even if temporarily, ceased recruiting fixed term contract workers in the cities of Kyūshū and Okinawa thought that they might once again be able to recruit Japanese given the worsening employment conditions, but even though they started trying to recruit fixed term contract workers again, they failed.

This is why the irregular employment in the group of companies in Figure 7.3 is made up primarily of fixed term contract workers in Company A and Company B, whereas in other companies this labour force is made up primarily of a service contracting company and part-time female labour supply. Companies that have stopped using foreign labour up to the level of primary subcontracting companies are: those that have shifted from using directly employed foreigners to Japanese fixed term contract workers or Japanese part-time workers (from the direct employment of foreigners to the irregular employment of Japanese); or, those that have shifted from foreign workers from outside the company to Japanese workers from outside the company (from the irregular employment of foreigners to the irregular employment of Japanese). This kind of shift from foreigners to Japanese can also be seen partially below the secondary subcontractors. There are among small-scale secondary subcontracting companies, however, also companies that have terminated their contracts with service contracting companies, as in the case of Technical Research Institute K.[16]

The demise of the period of absolute labour shortages and the replacement of the foreign worker labour force with Japanese

The previous sections, have shown that the withdrawal of the foreign labour force from major companies has come about as a result of, firstly, one's own company replacing the direct employment of foreigners with Japanese workers from outside the company and, secondly, replacing the foreigners amongst the workers from outside the company who are sent from service contracting companies with Japanese. However, this is not all that there is to the replacing of the foreign labour force with a Japanese labour force. Let us now take a look at how a hierarchy is imposed in the blue-collar labour force in the workplaces of primary subcontractors in group companies; primary subcontractors in cooperatives; secondary subcontractors; tertiary subcontractors; and machine tool makers. We will also consider the kind of labour force that is being introduced from the perspective of the changes at around the time of the bubble economy.

As shown in Table 7.3, a new labour force is advancing into the jobs that had been the domain of indirectly employed foreign workers who had been sent by service contracting companies. These are women and older workers. The employment of women is not confined to subcontracting companies; it has also already begun in Company A, the parent company. Company A began employing women for fixed term contract blue-collar work from 1998. At first, there were concerns regarding whether they would be able to assemble a female labour force. However, the offer of exactly the same pay as for men led to this becoming a high-paying workplace for women and the assembling in no time at all of the required number of recruits.[17] The retention rate was also high.

Company A keeps a list of the people who have worked on fixed term contracts for the past three years and when it needs to recruit fixed term contract workers again it starts by doing a direct mail out to the names on this list. It does this because recruiting people who are happy to apply directly by mail, rather than dispatching staff to Kyūshū and Okinawa to recruit workers, is the most low cost form of recruitment. In the latter half of the 1990s, the rate at which fixed term contract work would be renewed was on average twice. Approximately just ten per cent of people extended their contract when the half year period of the fixed term contract work expired. In the 2000s, however, the level of female fixed term contract workers was forty people, but the retention rate exceeded eighty per cent. The blue-collar female labour force has become, as far the companies are concerned, an important strategic segment that ought to be secured.

However, whilst the female labour force, as fixed term contract workers, opened up a completely new segment of the fixed term contract labour market for these companies, somewhere to live had to be provided for them. This meant that new female dormitories were required. Because mixed living arrangements would give rise to problems of order within the dormitories, not even a single female worker could be placed in a male dormitory. For this reason, those in charge thought that female fixed contract workers were not a suitable part of employment practices that sought to match the ups and downs of production volumes because the number of dormitories would have to be increased. Company A's dormitory had a capacity of 4,300 people. From the summer season of 2000 to the winter season of 2001, the company continued operating on a system of 3,800 to 3,900 fixed term contract workers alone. Considered in terms of new employees and transfers within the company, personnel obstacles would emerge without a continuous margin of 400 to 500 and, therefore, fixed term contract worker levels that climbed to over 3,800 would be beyond the limits of dormitory capacity.

Company A is the only one using a female labour force as fixed contract workers. However, Company AR and Company HB have started hiring women as regular blue-collar employees. Because,

Table 7.3: Changes in the main attributes of blue-collar workers according to people in charge of personnel and labour in the different subcontracting levels seen around the time of the bubble economy

	Quantitative work	Fluctuating work
Parent company		
	Regular workers	Movement of personnel between plants, subcontracting reinfocement personnel, fixed term contract workers
Bubble period	Mainly male high school graduates	Men only
Post-bubble	Male high school graduates + people being re-employed	Men + women
Car body makers		
	Regular workers	Movement of personnel between plants, subcontracting reinforcement personnel, fixed term contract workers (task contract)
Bubble period	Mainly male high school graduates	Foreign fixed term contract workers + foreign contract workers
Post-bubble	Male high school graduates + female high school graduates + people being re-employed	Japanese contract workers
Conglomerates		
	Regular workers	Movement of personnel between plants, subcontracting reinforcement personnel, fixed term contract workers, task contracts
Bubble period	Mainly male high school graduates	Japanese fixed term contract workers + foreign contract workers
Post-bubble	Male high school graduates + female high school graduates + people being re-employed	Japanese + foreign fixed term contract workers, Japanese contract workers

Cooperatives primary subcontractors	Regular workers (contract and part-time)	Contracting compnaies
Bubble period	Male high school graduates + foreigners	Foreign contract workers
Post-bubble	Male and female high school graduates, female part-time workers + the elderly	Foreign contract workers + Japanese contract workers
Secondary subcontractors	Regular workers (contract and part-time)	Part-time and casual employment
Bubble period	Male high school graduates + foreigners	
Post-bubble	Male high school graduates, foreigners, female part-time workers	Female contract workers + Japanese elderly workers + female part-time workers
Tertiary and machine tools	Regular workers	Contracting companies
Bubble period	Male high school graduates + foreigners	Foreign contract workers
Post-bubble	Male high school graduates and day labourer foreigners	Foreign contract workers

Note: The movement of personnel between plants and subcontract reinforcement personnel are assumed to be Japanese workers therefore the expression of this attribute has been omitted. Main workers (contract company) in cooperative primary subcontractors and the regular workers (contract and part-time) in secondary subcontractors mean that that the fixed tasks in the factory are carried out by main workers and the workforce in parentheses. Similarly, fixed term contract workers (service contract) in car body makers mean that, as far as the company is concerned, fixed term contract workers and contractors represent an equally positioned workforce.

however, the hiring of women has only just commenced they have not reached the numbers that would make them a strategic force in the workplace. In the case of these two companies, the hiring of women is not simply a matter of putting a female labour force to practical use. Having perceived lower levels of physical strength as being a characteristic trait of women, the company reasoned that the lines created for women to work on were lines on which older workers could also be used.[18] In anticipation of requests from labour unions for extensions to the retirement age and for re-employment, companies above primary subcontractors, major companies, are thinking of the use of a female labour force and the creation of workplaces for older workers as going hand in hand.

The majority of the female labour force being used by small-scale primary subcontracting companies and those below secondary subcontractors are part-time workers. These companies had originally relied on a part-time female labour force, but the number of women available to work part-time shrank as the regional economy developed leading to the use of a foreign labour force to fill this area. In recent years, however, Toyota City has also been hit by the serious impact of employment insecurity and this has caused women to be assailed by fears about their husbands being discharged from their jobs. As a result of this, the housewife stratum has entered the labour market. The entry of this type of cheap labour force has seen the emergence of an area that can be used to replace the expensive, indirectly employed labour force from service contracting companies.[19]

Not all companies can, however, make use of the part-time housewife labour force. As part-time housewife workers have a simultaneous existence in which they run a household, their work hours are limited and their workplaces and dwellings need to be close by one another. In companies that are close by residential areas, this housewife stratum can be included as part of the labour force, but in companies in industrial parks that are located far away from residential areas no practical use can be made of a part-time labour force. Furthermore, because of the conditions for qualifying for tax exemptions for dependents the number of hours that they can work in a year are also limited meaning that no overtime can be expected of them either. Therefore, the pattern of labour force use in small-scale cooperative primary subcontracting companies and secondary subcontractors is that most part-time workers are deployed in the quantitative work areas of the factory on day shift and foreign workers from service contracting companies are deployed to do overtime and night shifts. Be that as it may, given that foreign workers had also been employed in both of these areas of work before the entry of the part-time housewife stratum into the labour market, they have had their work snatched away from them by the entry of this group into the labour market.

Companies that cannot make use of the housewife stratum in the labour market include factories that are far from residential areas, such as those that are located in industrial parks. These types of factories are still using a foreign labour force from service contracting companies. A shift can, however, be seen in some, albeit a small number, of these companies also from a foreign to a Japanese labour force. In these cases the first thing that happened was that the companies replaced their business partners with service contracting companies that would send them older Japanese people. The two contracting companies that are promoting the sending out of older Japanese in Toyota City are the subsidiaries of a major electronics maker and a communications business. Since these two companies are not able to put re-employed workers to work in their own companies, they have set up a service contracting section in their subsidiaries to dispatch workers.[20] Secondly, there has been the appearance of older people being re-employed by service contracting companies after having retired from the parent company. There is an abundance of light work that even older people over fifty-five can do in factories and this work is shifting to low-cost Japanese older contract workers. There are, however, two aspects to the second of these developments, the inclusion of retirees from the parent company: what the subcontracting companies call 'employment as hostages' (meaning that dealings cannot be cut as long as they are taking in retirees from the parent company); and the issue of securing highly productive workers.

Even in the large-scale primary subcontracting companies, in the period of the bubble economy, and up until around 1995, there was not much reliance on recent high school graduates. This has undergone a complete change with the fixed term appointment of recent high school graduates in primary subcontracting companies occurring largely as planned in recent years. When the bubble economy burst and the state of prosperity vanished, the labour force options increased for companies and foreign labour became one of a whole variety of options. The increasing labour force options available to those in charge of personnel and labour during and after the bubble period can also be understood from looking at Table 7.3. As a result of this, unlike the securing of workers during absolute labour shortages, such as during the bubble period, companies are now strategically attempting to construct 'labour force portfolios' with the optimum combination of blue-collar workers. They do this by using a labour force that they are now able to secure that is cheaper than a foreign labour force – part-time female and older workers – for the day shift, and also by allotting foreign workers to work that requires early starts and overtime, which Japanese do not want to do.

However, the construction of an optimum labour force portfolio within a company, depending on the position of the company in the subcontracting structure, leads to the bipolarisation of the conditions for the employment of foreigners. On the one hand, we see companies withdrawing from the employment of foreign workers and, on the other, there are conditions such as those in Companies B and BT, where workers of Japanese descent are employed as fixed term contract workers. In order to consider this type of phenomenon, the next section will examine the impact of a company's business outlook on the composition of its labour force.

Parent company management strategy and subcontractors' 'backward looking employment strategy'

The very first thing that we must do in considering the business outlook of the company group portrayed in Table 7.3 is to examine the business strategy of the parent company. Company A, which weathered the severe management crisis of 1950, subsequently favourably expanded its management scale. It endured the oil shock and was criticised by the United States for its flood of exports, but it had been its assertive search for overseas markets that had enabled it to survive. However, due to the trade war between the United States and Japan and also the resultant enactment of local contents legislation in the United States, beginning in the 1980s, Company A drastically hastened the overseas transfer of its production base. At present, Company A's factories have begun operations in South and North America, Europe, South East Asian countries such as Thailand and the Philippines and also in China. Due to this, the position of its Japanese factories has changed considerably. Until recently, the Japanese factories had produced for both the domestic and overseas export markets. Nowadays, however, its various factories scattered throughout the world produce cars aimed at the regional market of the place where the factory is located.

In the year before the Japan Federation of Employers' Associations brought attention to the need for 'employment portfolios' combining the diverse labour force as 'Japanese management for a new era,' the think tank that draws up Company A's labour management raised the issue of the necessity, in an age of internationalisation, for a universal direction regarding personnel and labour management policies that ought to be adopted by the Company A group as whole (the Institution for Industrial Relations and Labor Policy, Chūbu 1994). While continuing to assume the maintenance of long-term employment, this pointed out the challenges that the automobile industry would inevitably confront in competition at the global level.

This document makes future forecasts from the point of view of the type of impact that globalisation will have at three different levels: firstly, car makers; secondly, *keiretsu* core makers; and, thirdly, the whole Japanese automobile industry as a collection of individual makers. The first forecast is 'the development of the intensification and the internalisation of manufacturing' within car makers. The second is 'the implementation of the streamlining of the industry' via the 'coordination of car makers and the powerful parts and equipment makers with car makers sitting at the core of the automobile industry.' The third is the 'autonomous reorganisation of parts and equipment makers as a result of adjustments and job cuts due to the struggle for a shrinking pie.' Let us look at the fact that the first and second level forecasts have become trends in industrial society and have made steady progress in Toyota City.

Even in the Nishimikawa area, which houses the favourably performing Company A, there is a feeling of a sense of overcapacity from the parent company through to the subcontractors. While on the one hand there is an excess of productive capacity in the region, competitive power on the global level is being sought by all including by subcontractors. At the present time, parent company, Company A, is rushing, in the name of a 'universal global price,' to do business with companies that have quoted the cheapest price of any company in the world on the internet for generic products. There is also pressure on subcontractors to seek competitive power on the global level. In 1999, Company C, a primary subcontractor, took over the factory of another company in the same industry. It did this because it was requested to take over this factory by its parent company, Company A. As the company, with its small scale production, was not productive, Company A was encouraging its subcontractor to integrate production. At the time, Company C was on the side of those making the takeover, but it does not know when its own company will become the subject of a takeover itself. It is aware of the possibility of the integration of its domestic plants and the transfer of control for some of these to overseas factories into which the parent company has expanded. Under these conditions, the employment of foreigners is no longer seen in Company C, but this does not mean that there are no longer any foreigners working in Company C. In 1997, anticipating a fierce competitive environment, Company C transferred a portion of its production workers to its newly established subsidiary. This newly established subsidiary is an in-company contracting company. A portion of production workers are dispatched, in form only, from this contracting company to work in the factory. All workers of foreign nationality were made to transfer to this in-company contracting area and Company C then moved around the necessary labour force according to the demand from its plants which were scattered throughout various areas.

In order to prevail in global competition in the midst of excess automobile productive capacity in the Nishimikawa area, Company A ruthlessly set about efforts to reduce costs in the design stages for new cars released into the market. As a result, Company SW, which is in charge of part of the modularisation of interior upholstery including sun visors, had reduced the number of parts from 300 to 180, by as much as forty per cent, when the model change from the Starlet to the Vitz occurred despite the fact that they remained responsible for the same parts. A reduction in the number of items is, naturally, a reduction in the work manufacturing processes and this means that there is also a reduction in the number of workers that will be required. Moreover, because of this reduction in the number of items Company SW has not sent out the portion of work that it would conventionally have sent out to its subcontractor as this is now being done in its own company.

The reduction in the number of items that accompanied the development of modularisation in the midst of a sense of overcapacity, led to a reduction in the work sent out to subcontractors and heightened the pressure to be competitive amongst subcontracting companies. Half of the secondary subcontractors admit that whenever they win a contract, they become embroiled in a contest over unit costs. Conditions in which, due to the steady appearance of a postponing of the retirement age and reemployment in Company A and its primary subcontracting companies, work that used to be sent out to subcontractors is now being done within the parent company by these workers who have postponed their retirement and by re-employed workers; that is, there is a striking progression of further internalisation of manufacturing within the parent company and a further reduction in work for the subcontractors. Efforts by companies to prevail in global competition and the logic of companies facing an ageing society are further aggravating competition between subcontracting companies.

Incidentally, options for overseas expansion, matching the global expansion of the parent company, also exist for subcontracting companies. However, even if subcontracting companies advance independently into the same areas as the parent company, just as is the case domestically in Japan, it is not necessarily a given that the parent company will deal with them. When subcontracting companies do expand to the same overseas destination as the parent company, it is the parent company that decides which subcontractor will be allowed to expand overseas. At the time of overseas expansion by a subcontracting company the parent company decides whether this should be a joint venture with a local parts maker or whether it should expand on its own. In the event of the former option, integration, the parent company's inclination is also strongly reflected in decisions about the percentage of investment in the local company. As far as globalisation of a subsidiary is concerned, this is only possible following intense screening by the parent company. Under this kind of pressure, the parent company's bullish performance notwithstanding, there cannot be any clear future outlook for subcontracting companies. Seen from the parent company's viewpoint, a subcontracting company, since it is in an environment in which it may be taken over by another company if its productivity is judged to be low, cannot advance a long-term personnel and labour management policy. The most rational behaviour for the company is for it to be able to secure the minimum number of regular employees that it needs for its intermittent business, and then to keep securing the remainder from time to time as its cheapest labour force. If it can employ part-time workers, then part-time workers are fine, but if this is not possible, then it is all right to hire the most reasonable labour force that it can from amongst the options available. In this chapter, the state of employment in subcontracting companies, which absorbed as they are in competing under these sorts of cost pressures, attempt to get away with assembling a labour force cheaply as and when needed without having any long-term outlook, is defined as a 'backward looking employment strategy.'

While, on the one hand, the backward looking employment strategy continues to exist, Company B and its subsidiary Company BT, both group companies, are, in contrast to this, employing foreign workers through direct employment and with social insurance benefits. This is because, thinking in the long term, they consider a reliance on foreign workers to be inescapable in order to be able to continue production activities domestically within Japan in a situation in which there will be insufficient production workers. Since an understanding of labour management is not something that can be acquired in a day, the direct employment of foreigners by these two companies represents the acquisition of know-how as they anticipate the future. We find simultaneously within the one subcontracting structure the existence of the direct employment of foreign workers as a 'backward looking employment strategy' and also the direct employment of foreign workers in order to establish labour management that anticipates declining birth rates. Depending on the position in which a company finds itself, there are two types of companies: those that use a foreign labour force with a short term outlook; and companies that are snapping up a foreign labour force with a long-term outlook. This means that there are both companies that are withdrawing from the employment of foreigners and those that are once again making use of a foreign labour force. It is the author's belief that the practical state of hostility that exists between companies that have in recent years taken the plunge and once again made use of a foreign labour force and companies that have ceased using a foreign labour force, as was shown in Figure 7.2, reflect this.

New labour paradigm or long-standing fundamental problem?

Subcontracting companies in Toyota City receive eight *kanban* each day. If parts are not delivered to the business partner within the time designated on the *kanban*, a ten million yen penalty is levied for every ten minutes of lateness. Delays in the supply of parts from the subcontractor because there is no more stock cause the line in the parent company to stop. In reality, if the line in the parent company stops, the amount of loss cannot be compensated at the rate of ten million yen per ten minutes, but the application of this sort of penalty certainly leads subcontractors to abide by the *kanban*. It may be that the trust that emerges as a result of the sort of long-term business relationships that people who stress the economics of the system point to make possible the Toyota Production System. We should not, however, overlook the existence of a penalty in the form of a stick to explain the reliable obedience to the *kanban*.

Due to the fact that timelines have been observed sufficiently to avoid being penalised, the Toyota Production System, made it possible to build a production system that stretches between companies and carries no stock. A system that produces no more than the volume of production that meets demand, not only with reference to surplus parts and goods in progress, but also for the finished product – complete automobiles, represents the industrialisation of orders for durable consumer goods. Not holding any stock, as the flip side of this, is not producing anything in anticipation. When an organisation carries out production activities in a way that matches demand, although it may construct a workplace with various manufacturing processes deployed in a U-Shaped line, it will bring about changes in the labour force that match trends in demand.

In reality, fluctuations in production volumes in companies connected with the production of multiple types of cars, at the primary subcontractor level and above, hardly ever display a gap of more than five per cent in a three month period. This may be the situation in primary subcontractors and above which are responsible for multiple products, but in the case of secondary contractors and below – particularly the tertiary subcontracting level and below – which are responsible for specific parts for specific car models, there are occasionally considerable divergences.[21]

Production matched to trends in demand reduces *faux frais* (incidental expenses) as much as possible.[22] This system which minimises *faux frais* converts incidents that occur in a large organisation, such as the production of automobiles, into trans-actional relationships in objects between small, individual internal organisations. This is what makes it possible to hold only the resources needed at one particular point in time. The Toyota Production System and its practical application, the 'Cell Production System' are drawing attention as possible methods for restoring Japanese competitive power. In recent years, the Cell Production System, in the form of low-cost automation, has been rapidly introduced with positive results into precision machinery industries such as electrical appliances and cameras. However, we should keep in mind that this production method, that could be called 'a form of production that is reliant on people (Shirai 2001),' has a strong affinity with the practical use of in-house contracting businesses (service contracting companies). The indispensable premise of the industrialisation of taking orders is a labour force that can readily be dismissed. This is because the labour force must also exist in a just in time format. *In the same way as the production of automobiles inside one large organisation progresses as the transaction of parts between individual companies, service contracting companies, made up of companies that receive a labour force and those that dispatch it, supply only the labour force that is required by the receiving company by converting the required labour force into a volume of contract work.* This amounts to valuing the cost of the labour force only using the short term market price that does not include reproduction costs. The service contractor's pamphlet to new customers (Table 4.2), which contains the message that expenses amounted to the portion of monthly pay only, shows very concisely that these considerations are based on a value that does not include reproduction costs.

As our investigations in this chapter have shown, the new paradigm concerning present day foreign workers is nothing other than the classic problem of essentially reducing *faux frais* (incidental expenses). This reduction of *faux frais* is being carried out by assembling a labour force that is different in nature – with qualitative differences in the amount of wages and in the geographic and time ranges in which they can work: part-time women; re-employed older workers; Japanese fixed term contract workers and workers from outside the company; and foreign fixed term contract workers and workers from outside the company. The long-term economic slump in the Japanese economy has brought about the entry of various types of labour forces into the labour market. This has made it possible for companies to use a labour force that meets the geographic conditions of their location and also the characteristics of quantity that they require. Consequently, unlike the traditionally held view that foreign workers are stealing the workplaces of Japanese workers, we see the emergence of the phenomenon of Japanese workers stealing the workplaces of foreign workers. The replacement of foreign workers with Japanese workers is the replacement of foreign workers with cheaper Japanese workers and has been expressed via the overlaying of cost issues onto the problem of the reduction of *faux frais*. It is the progress of globalisation that makes this issue of cost momentous.

Conclusion

This chapter makes it clear that a new competition has appeared in the peripheral labour force due to the march of globalisation in the midst of a sluggish economy. There is something else that also needs to be pointed out. This is how the employment of foreigners is accounted for inside companies. Fourteen of the companies looked at in this chapter, included in Figure 7.2, have had some experience of directly employing foreign workers. Of these companies the ones that could be confirmed as employing them as workers covered by health insurance were only four in number: Company AR, Company B, Company BT and Company AS. The remaining ten companies admitted that they employed these workers without health insurance cover. Six of these ten companies responded that 'the wages paid to directly employed foreign workers were not processed as wages paid to workers, but were accounted for as parts purchasing costs within the Supply Division.' Thus, the direct employment of foreign workers does not necessarily mean that the business world is employing human beings.

These types of accounting methods can also be found in the activities of service contracting companies in factories. According to the the Institution for Industrial Relations and Labor Policy, Chūbu, it is common practice in factories for the dispatching of workers by the service consulting industry to be accounted for under buying costs for each individual factory unit (Chūbu Sangyō Rōdō Seisaku Kenkyūkai 1998: 21). In the quest for cost reductions, the continued presence on a fixed scale of foreign workers, particularly workers of Japanese descent who receive relatively higher wages than part-time workers can be thought of as being related to the ability to account for this as buying parts and not as employing people.

As a result of these developments, peculiar phenomena can be detected in the existence of foreigners in regional society. The number of companies (plants) in Toyota City who are taking in large numbers of foreign workers is actually declining. Despite this, the number of foreign workers just residing in these areas is increasing. Although workplaces in Toyota City may have decreased, if there is increasing demand for foreign workers in the cities, towns and villages surrounding Toyota City to which it is possible to commute, then the increase of foreign workers in Toyota City is not at all unusual.

It is possible to catch a glimpse of the same kind of phenomenon in neighbouring Okazaki City. The companies that directly employ foreign workers in Okazaki City have formed an organisation within the Okazaki Chamber of Commerce and Industry called the Okazaki Regional Committee for the Management and Promotion of the Employment of Foreigners. This committee – taken from the ranks of a gathering of various different businesses in the Chamber of Commerce and Industry for the purposes of bringing in a foreign labour force – had its beginnings in the formation of a research group started by small- and medium-sized companies that had had no choice but to rush to employ foreigners in the midst of an absolute labour shortage. Shortly after the collapse of the bubble economy, there was a decline in the number of companies directly employing foreigners. As of 2001, companies that had participated in less than half of the golden age were in a slump. Even in these companies, foreign workers were not necessarily a strategic force that was indispensable to blue-collar workplaces. Despite this, the number of foreign residents in Okazaki City is on an upward course.

The increase in the number of foreigners living in Toyota City and Okazaki City despite the decline in places for them to work is surely the manifestation, in a social form, of increasing demand for a labour force that like workers dispatched by service contractors can be put to use as needed. In the pre-war years, Yasoji Kazahaya said of the stratum in insecure employment that 'both good and bad economic times contain the causes of destitution for them; once they encounter illness or some other calamity in their lives, this plunges them into the category of the unemployed on poor relief' (Kazahaya 1937: 23). As far as those who are familiar with the state in which present day foreign workers find themselves are concerned, Kazahaya's words apply accurately to today's foreign workers also. This is because workers who can be used when they are needed, and who it is assumed will be in the area even when they are not needed, are fulfilling the same social function as the old insecure employment stratum. In other words, 'backward looking employment strategies' is a system that begins to function when there is a poor external economy.

When wages are being set for the men and women who make up the workers who can be used as needed, just as when buying in goods; part-time workers who are not assumed to be the main breadwinners within a family; and people who have been re-employed who are assumed to be working after having received their severance payments or alternatively while receiving the age pension there is an assumption that they come without any long-term reproduction costs. *In the midst of globalisation and cost reduction pressures, demand is increasing for workers who come without the need for these sorts of reproduction costs and employment instability is increasing the supply of a labour force.* In reality, it is not at all unusual for workers who are assumed not to come with long-term reproduction costs to be the main breadwinners for a family. We have arrived at a period in time when we must re-examine the meaning and the purpose of companies, regional society and survival of the state in a global economy by returning to the starting point that people work to live.

8 The labour market for Brazilians living in Japan: service contracting companies and Brazilian workers living in Japan

Introduction

This chapter considers how the labour market for Brazilians of Japanese descent is mediated. The focus of analysis will be the 'service contracting companies' which are in direct employment relationships with these men and women of Japanese descent. This is because the majority of Brazilian workers of Japanese descent are employed in workplaces as external workers sent by service contractors and, in this sense, service contracting companies mediate the employment of Brazilians of Japanese descent. There are also Brazilians of Japanese descent who are directly employed, but the majority have found work in blue-collar areas via service contracting companies. People of Japanese descent are not exclusively to be found in the manufacturing industry – from the factories of the automobile and electronic equipment makers that epitomise Japan to their subcontractors: they are also being hired in fishing cooperatives to sort Manila and *shijimi* clams; in agricultural cooperatives to package cut flowers; in *bento* making factories that service convenience stores; and even in industrial waste management plants. The employment of people of Japanese descent can now be seen not only in the manufacturing industry, but also within the whole range of regional employment wherever they are needed.

It is the service contracting companies that dispatch to this array of workplaces. This chapter uses interview surveys with service contracting companies as the basis for examining why it is that a labour force of people of Japanese descent is being used during a period of recession.

Furthermore, as research into the employment of people of Japanese descent has shown to date, their employment and residence

problems are so closely related that they are essentially inseparable
(Yorimitsu and Sano 1992; Tsuzuki 1995 and 1998; Ishii and Inaba
1996), but this chapter will limit itself to investigating only the issue
of employment via service contracting companies. The data dealt
with here is based on the results of survey studies from February
1997 to March 1998.[1]

A definition of service contracting companies and those responsible for them

The reason why this chapter focusses its attention on service
contracting companies is because service contractors are the people
with whom the majority of Brazilian workers of Japanese descent
directly conclude employment contracts and because workers are
dispatched by service contractors to work sites, such as factories,
where work is actually carried out. It is their ability to work legally
in Japan because they have a Japanese blood relative who has
maintained the family register – a characteristic that enables people
of Japanese descent to receive a residency visa or to transfer to a
permanent resident visa – that explains why Brazilians of Japanese
descent, who are foreign nationals, can be employed in unskilled
work in Japan.[2] Resident visas are not issued for the purpose of
employment, but there is acknowledgement on a secondary level
that employment will occur, since, given the intention to settle,
it is essential to life in one's place of residence. Because of this,
people of Japanese descent and their spouses can be employed in
unskilled work. The majority of people of Japanese descent who can
be employed in unskilled work are employed by service contracting
companies and then deployed to individual work sites. Let us take
a quick look now at how we should define the service contracting
companies that directly employ people of Japanese descent and
dispatch these men and women to their respective work sites.

Service contracting companies are frequently confused with
temporary personal agencies, but they are treated differently by the
law. Under Section 9 'Contracting (numbers 632–642 of the Civil
Code),' Paragraph 2 of 'Contracts' Volume 3 'Claims' of the Civil
Code, contracting is defined as a contract for receiving remuneration for work completed as promised and the fruits of that labour.
In the sense that workers are being dispatched to sites where there
is work to be done, however, there is hardly any difference in form

between contracting and temporary employee placement. However, the Public Employment Security Law prohibits the sending of workers who have been employed by one employer to another workplace which has issued a request. This is because the Public Employment Security Law forbids businesses privately supplying labour outside the public sector. The dispatching of workers to specific sectors is acknowledged as an exception within the scope outlined in the 'Laws to guarantee the appropriate management of temporary personnel agencies and to maintain employment conditions for dispatched workers' (Temporary Staffing Services Businesses Law). Naturally, the construction industry and site operations of manufacturing industry are not included under this. In these areas, service contracting companies have an exemption under the Civil Code as their legal foundation. Put another way, service contracting companies are recognised exclusively in the manufacturing industry.

The differences between temporary personnel agencies and service contracting companies are detailed in Figure 8.1. The problem is 'whether matters such as directions regarding an order' are confined to the sphere of '"instructions by the person placing the order" or whether they are labour management directives' (Anzai 1997: 50). That is, in order to return to the definition in the Civil Code, service contracting companies make the manufacturing line the basic unit in the contract with the company to which workers are dispatched and accordingly a contract must emerge that reflects the processing fees for each individual product that is produced. Making this the first condition leads us inevitably to the second condition. Since in contracting the manufacturing line the service contracting company is shouldering responsibility for the workers' tasks and safety, it absolutely must station a supervisor from its own company on this line. In short, it needs to maintain both 'independence in terms of the management of its business' and 'independence in terms of labour management' (Hayashi 1996: 2–3).

However, as Figure 8.1 shows, it is difficult to clearly distinguish service contracting companies and temporary personnel agencies. The relationship of giving orders that distinguishes the two companies needs to be dealt with as a substantive issue in the workplace as it is not explicitly set out in written contracts. This is also clear from the nature of contracting unit costs. The agreement that binds the service contracting company with the manufacturer, the written document, bases the contract on the unit costs for each

Figure 8.1: Contract conditions requiring clarification between the service contracting company and the parent company

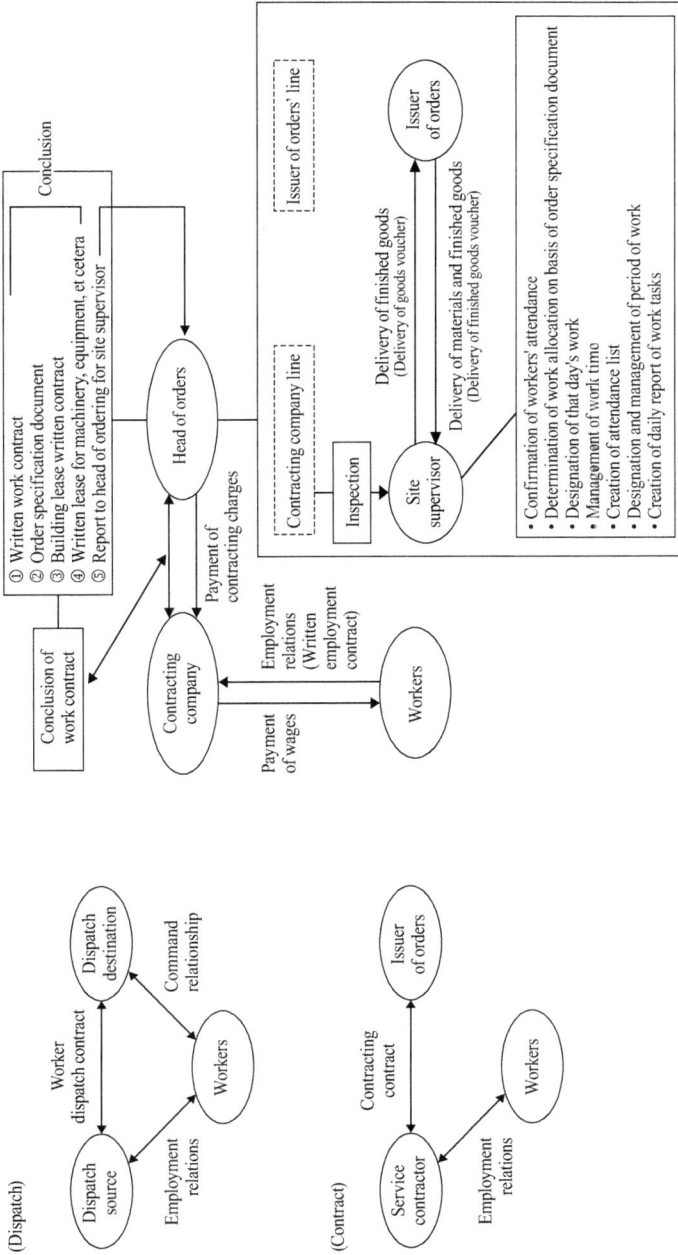

Source: Hayashi 1996: 7.

individual item of production, but this determines the contracting unit costs by multiplying hourly pay by the number of people working on the line in question; wages are not derived on the basis of unit costs (Yorimitsu and Sano 1992: 120).[3] This, however, is not apparent in the written contract document. It is thus whether or not a supervisor is required at the worksite, the second condition, which provides the point of distinction between service contracting companies and temporary personnel agencies.

However, service contractors contract multiple sites and no operator stations supervisors in all of their sites. The thinking of the client company (the user company) that contracts out its line to the service contractor plays an important role in this decision.[4] This point has already been made, but those who use service contracting companies entrust work to them on a line unit basis, in keeping with fluctuations in demand, and they look out for the benefits of using service contracting companies in a way that matches the waves of production activity in prosperous times and during recessions (Yorimitsu and Sano 1996: 140–148). We should not, however, overlook the fact that handing over the portion of work operations that is the line, establishes the premise that some contract workers will also be put to work in areas where they might be required, other than on the contracted line. Service contracting companies practically always contract multiple sites. This is because operators will contract both worksites in which their own company supervisors are stationed and worksites where they are not. Accordingly, this chapter, unlike previous research which has classified the employment of people of Japanese descent using the contract relationship between factories and workers of Japanese descent (Sano 1992; Nishizawa 1995; and Sano 1996), takes into account the fact that one service contractor is dispatching to a variety of worksites, and approaches the employment of people of Japanese descent from the perspective of relationships between the service contractor and the company that is receiving its workers.

As the reader will understand simply on the basis of what has been said already, it is not possible to discuss the true state of contracting companies in terms of a legal definition. In order to discern what we can about the true state of contracting companies let us begin with a look at how the managers of contracting companies acquire the know-how for dispatching workers and how it is that they came to embark on this business.

Table 8.1: Previous jobs of contracting company managers

Previous jobs	Number of people
Contracting company work	22
Labour supervision in parent company	5
Subcontracting factory management	5
Building industry related	3
Other	9

Note: Valid responses from 39 companies. Some managers have had expereince in more than one of the above areas and, therefore, this table is based on multiple responses from some managers.

What sorts of people are running the service contracting industry? Let us look at Table 8.1. When this survey asked the proprietors of contracting companies about their previous employment, it emerged that an overwhelming number had also been previously engaged in the service contracting industry. The next largest group had been labour supervisors in companies that received workers from service contracting companies and who had then started out independently. After this group, came people who had been managing subcontracting companies and who went on to assume responsibility for the parent company's factory line following a request from the parent company to do so. Then there were those who had been engaged in the building industry and whose business activities very closely resembled those of the service contracting industry. Apart from a small number of exceptions, in all of these cases these people had some sort of relationship with either the contracting of lines or clients to which workers were dispatched and embarked on their present businesses because of this. In the cases of managers who are Brazilians of Japanese descent, they were all previously employed as translators in service contracting companies and relied on the support of Japanese business partners when they set up independently in business. Once these people of Japanese descent are operating independently, the clients to whom they dispatch workers are either the same clients from their time as translators or clients that their business partners have secured. When we think about this, we see that the decisive issue for Brazilians of Japanese descent when starting up businesses that dispatch workers is not assembling the workers, but whether or not clients have been secured to whom these workers will be sent.

Service contracting businesses, which have a labour force as their finished product, do not require any fixed capital, such as factories or the equipment found in them, at the time of their inception. Nonetheless, as will be discussed below, in order to secure the housing in which workers will live, these businesses require more than just the capital to pay workers' wages. Just one phone call makes it possible for anyone to enter the service contracting business, however, because all that is needed is the ability to raise the capital that can ensure the provision of housing for workers. This is why, in most cases, rather than starting off by opening an office and specialising as a service contracting company, people make a gradual transition from their previous occupation to the management of the new business, which has a service contracting business as the mainstay. A business partner is sought and business affairs are initially left in his hands with people continuing to run their own factories while seeing the service contracting company as a side business. Similarly, it is an industry that anyone can enter as long as they can find clients; the expansion of client numbers, however, is not necessarily smooth going. It is first vital to win a level of trust that is sufficient to lead to being assigned a production site.

As has been mentioned, the true state of service contracting companies cannot be understood through their legal definition. Entry barriers to this industry are low if, on the basis of a history of work experience as a manger in the service contracting industry, one can secure places to which to send workers; however, business expansion requires time.

Service contracting company scale and the market

Keeping these points in mind, this section will treat the work that is contracted by service contractors as the market of the contracting business, and investigate the manner in which that labour market is stratified. In the indirect employment offered by service contractors, both the duration and the format of the contract between the contract unit and the contract client are permeated by markets of diverse quality.

The employment most widely used by service contracting companies is the sort that matches the waves in scale of production, including seasonal fluctuations.[5] However, cost reduction is a daily challenge for companies exposed to fierce competition. There is also a constant demand for that segment of employment that is essential to a stable scale of production of goods. This is why there is also service contracting in which essentially the very same production areas are contracted as those for which the main company factory has responsibility; where the same machine tools and the same labour organisation are used in one's own company factory as in the main company factory. That is, these companies become perfect primary subcontractors devoted to assembly. The first employment sector to which Brazilians of Japanese descent can gain access via service contracting companies is employment within this primary subcontractor framework and employment where the whole factory line is put out to contract at the normal scale of production. These are assumed to be the markets shown as 1a and 1b in Table 8.2.

The second employment sector exists in the form of seasonal and temporary workers and is characterised by waves of production that are exposed to constant fluctuations, and here also the employment market can be sorted into several patterns. The first of these is employment that, whilst being caught up in the wave of fluctuations, is relatively secure. Employment in this segment is employment on the line for which a contract has been concluded between the service contractor and the parent company for a set period of three, six or twelve months. On these occasions, employment contracts can also be concluded for other similar periods of time. This is the 2a market.

Below this level, contracts did not have the line as their basic unit; employment was arranged as a promise by the contracting company to dispatch a set number of people to the factory. There were on these occasions not just contracts with a factory, but also cases of coming in as a subcontractor on a line contracted by another company in the same industry. This is the 2b market. Since this 2b market is matched to an even shorter production wave than the 2a market, shorter contracts of around three to six months are created.[6] Finally, there is the most secure employment that one can enter, but in which the contracting costs – widespread knowledge of which is gained through the medium of the Portuguese language newspaper for Brazilians of Japanese descent – are even lower than the average wage.[7] This is market 2c. Employment in this market is not, generally, the usual factory line work (under ordinal optimization conditions). This is employment in areas such as family-run confectionery manufacturing businesses, fresh meat factories, sorting and pack-

Table 8.2: Classification of the market in which people of Japanese descent are used

Market segment	Market characteristics	Analysis of business people in this survey
1a Own company factory employment	Own company management of point of production	4 companies
1b Stable employment within factory	Contracting manufacturing line	4 companies
2a Fluctuating employment within factory	Contracting that concludes an agreement	14 companies
2b Fluctuating employment within factory	No agreement, but unit costs the same as 2a	11 companies
2c Insecure employment outside factory	Employment below the market price for Brazilians of Japanese descent	6 companies

Note: Valid responses from 39 companies.

aging in fishery and agricultural cooperatives, bento makers, light duties in the construction industry, and industrial waste treatment. Service contractors carry out their actual operations by combining multiple markets with a number of these as strategic markets for their own survival. A classification of all of the service contractors in this survey yields the distribution that we see in Table 8.2. Thus, service contracting companies – in the sense that they extensively contract areas of insecure employment, supplying the labour force that is required in only the quantities that are needed – are carrying out what might be called a labour force editing function.

The differences in these market sectors are plainly shown in the guidance of dispatched workers and in the nature of the supervision of these men and women depicted in Table 8.3. What this means, in effect, is that supervisors from one's own company are stationed at the place of work where a line has been contracted and that this supervisor begins by lecturing new workers about their work. This happens in markets 1a and 1b. In this survey, most of the service contractors have placed a supervisor from their own companies in places where they have dispatched more than twenty people to a single worksite.[8] What is important here is that even service contractors, who are running business operations with stable 1a and 1b markets as their own company's main market, are getting involved in 2b markets. These are markets which largely leave the guidance and supervision of workers to the client receiving those workers. Service contractors even, occasionally, participate in 2c markets. This strengthens the possibility of ending up with a new business partner in markets that are experiencing bad conditions. There are more extensive business opportunities for service contracting companies in unstable markets. The intentions of the parent companies that make use of contracting companies play a mediating role in this. This is because employers are looking for profit when they simultaneously entrust a stable workplace to service contractors and also use them as a way of getting people to move around to other parts of the factory. Service contractors run by Brazilians of Japanese descent were all clustered in markets 2b and 2c.

This kind of opening up of business opportunities where conditions are bad brings about a strangely distorted phenomenon in the relationship with the scale of a company (the number of workers dispatched). On the other hand, the proactive focus on markets that

Table 8.3: The nature of guidance and supervision of dispatched workers

	Number of independent contractors
Guidance of new workers	
Left to the recipient	27
Own company line supervisor	12
Senior worker on the line	12
Labour supervision	
Own company supervisor in place	15
Management staff patrolling	30
Left entirely to recipient	14

are inherently very dangerous gives rise to service contracting companies that require large numbers of dispatched workers. Similarly, independent contractors who make 1a their principal market are also managing factories in their own companies and have a need for a large quantity of workers in secure employment. Consequently, the larger scale service contractors find themselves in the extreme situations of focusing on stable markets and, conversely, of proactively accepting unreliable employment. Markets 2a and 2b are the focus for small scale contracting companies. In this survey, at the end of the scale at which the largest number of workers are dispatched – from over fifty to under a hundred – 1a, 2a and 2b unite to expand their operations. The picture of service contracting companies that emerges is not a simple one of companies with small scale businesses being unstable and stability increasing with an increase in the scale of businesses. This is the particular trait of service contracting companies as niche industries.

Service contracting companies within industrial society

Having examined the stratified nature of the markets to which people of Japanese descent are dispatched in the last section, we will now consider the nature of employment via service contracting companies. The markets from 1a to 2c, outlined above in 'Service contracting company scale and the market,' certainly display a degree of variation and they are areas of insecure employment that have traditionally been the domain of seasonal and part-time

*Table 8.4: Time taken by contracting companies to respond to
personnel requests (unit: number of businesses)*

Time taken	Requests for personnel increase	Requests for personnel decrease
1 day	5	5
< 3 days	5	4
< 7 days	8	7
< 14 days	8	7
< 30 days	8	11
< 90 days	2	2

Note: valid responses from 36 companies

workers. As touched on briefly previously, service contracting companies play the roles in industrial society of singlehandedly taking up this area of insecure employment and of distributing to it only the required labour. This provision of the labour required – or, to restate, the ability to effect a rapid reshuffling of the labour force once it is no longer required – positively advances the continuing expansion of the employment of people of Japanese descent in regional society within a range of types of occupations.

Let us firstly look at this from the angle of how long it takes service contractors to respond to increases and decreases in employment requests from client companies. As Table 8.4 shows, about half of the service contractors respond within a week to these upward and downward fluctuations; it is through this sort of function that they respond to demand. When service contracting companies are discussed, there is a tendency to focus on this prompt response to required labour, but there are also service contractors who merely focus on stable employment, avoiding from the outset this area in which business people seek responses in a short period of time. From Table 8.4 we see that in the case of personnel increases 27.8 per cent (10 companies) and in the case of personnel decreases 36.1 per cent (13 companies) of service contracting companies take over a month to respond to requests form the companies with whom they have a contract. However, the ability or otherwise to respond to urgent requests is an important factor for factories and others who use service contractors in determining whether they will entrust a higher market segment to a particular service contractor or whether they commence a business relationship with a separate, new service contracting company.[9] In other words, seen from the standpoint of service contractors, it is inevitable that they fall into the ambivalent circumstances of having to increase their involvement with unstable employment the more that they attempt to move into stable markets.

Let us consider this theoretically, in line with the function fulfilled by service contracting companies in industrial society. Yoshinori Shiozawa criticises General Equilibrium Theory in which the volume of all transactions in raw materials and prices are simultaneously determined and – on the basis of recognition of a process of reproduction in which the real economy is repeated year after year – he treats the real economy not as constantly producing a fixed amount, but as a process containing 'fluctuations' seen as changes in the volume of that production. Further, he thinks that the continuation of circumstances in which the quantity being produced does not necessarily match the quantity actually being sold is normal; he considers this to be a steady state (Shiozawa 1990: 33–39 and 238–241). Accordingly, he pays attention to the role of 'stock' and 'money' as features that continue even while the fluctuating economy gives rise to gaps in demand and supply. In other words, because stock enables suppliers to respond in lightning quick fashion when the demand exists and because money generally works as an equivalent to raw materials, it is possible for both parties to engage in exchange despite neither needing the other's goods (Shiozawa 1990 365–369 and 1997a: 147–164). Shiozawa calls this function 'detached equipment.' He focuses on the dimension of each company being able to act wholly independently by making use of detached equipment. Holding stock as detached equipment would make it possible for a company to continue limited operations for a time, even if another company further up the chain were to cease operations because of an accident (Shiozawa 1997a: 163–164 and 1997b 221–223; 242–243).

If we try to adapt this to the theory in this chapter, service contracting companies are not the detached equipment between production and demand but the detached equipment introduced into the interior of production activities, and decision making about the level at which detachment occurs produces the differing markets in Table 8.3. The steady state of our living economy does not only correspond to changes in stock and operating ratios, as Shiozawa assumes. We need to pay attention to the fact that the fluctuations in productive capacity that he sees as fluctuations in the steady state are also

Figure 8.2: Manufacturing industry production plan and the position of the employment of Brazilians of Japanese descent

Range of manufacturer's production plan

Manufacturing industry factory	
Line managed by main company	Line entrusted to contracting company
Main company workers Dispatched workers of Japanese descent (2b primary subcontractor)	Workers of Japanese descent employed by contracting company (1b primary subcontractor) Workers of Japanese descent dispatched by other contractors (2a secondary subcontractor)

Subcontracting factory directly run by service contractor	
Line managed by contracting company	Line entrusted to other contractor
People of Japanese descent directly employed by contracting company (1a primary subcontractor) People of Japanese descent dispatched by other contracting companies (2a & 2b secondary subcontractors)	People of Japanese descent employed by other contracting companies (1b secondary subcontractors) People of Japanese descent employed by separate contracting companies (2a & 2b tertiary subcontractors)

built into annual activities. To this extent, seasonal fluctuations within production activities are considerable. In order to maintain a degree of freedom within the Toyota Production System, which minimises stock, companies necessarily place detached equipment inside production activities.[10]

Let us now attempt to confirm the position in which Brazilians of Japanese descent are employed. Because service contracting companies that send workers to manufacturers single-handedly assume the portion of difficulties anticipated by manufacturers, they attempt to avoid risk by increasing their own complexity. This can be seen in service contracting company employment in actual factories (Figure 8.2). Service contractors by no means station workers directly employed by their own company on all lines, even when they contract lines from the main company. There are waves even in production activity on contracted lines and therefore this portion is covered using personnel from other service contractors. Similarly, in directly operated subcontracting factories where the contracted line expands and operations in one's own factory are the same as in the main company factory, the manufacturing line is sent to the other service contracting companies in the same way as the parent company. It is here that we can observe separate contractors (tertiary service contractors) sending workers to another contracting company (a secondary service contractor) that has contracted the line of a service contracting company. Thus, production activities that are responsive to fluctuations in demand are implemented via a repeated overlaying of contracting. The people who are employed in this mesh of contracting are workers of Japanese descent.

The manufacturers who receive these dispatched workers ensure that their companies achieve the planned level of productive output by combining both the factories that they manage themselves and also their factories that have been subcontracted to service contracting companies. Figure 8.2 shows that service contracting companies are even built into the normal production activities of production plans. We are able to confirm that secondary subcontracting by service contracting companies has been built into lines in manufacturing company factories that have been contracted to service contracting companies. Similarly, the contracting of lines to other service contracting companies (secondary contractors) is even occurring in factories directly run by service contracting companies, along with the further contracting (tertiary contracting) in which workers are sent to lines that are directed and supervised by yet other service contracting companies. In other words, the regular production activities of the manufacturing industry are now premised on a labour force organisation that already includes tertiary contracting as part of daily production activities.

If we now extend our argument a little further, we realise that the sending of workers in the numbers required by the manufacturing industry works in tandem with Brazilians of Japanese descent being employed in a variety of workplaces in non-manufacturing industries. There are, of course large numbers of service contractors who exclusively send workers to the factories of manufacturing industries. Whilst the focus of our investigations in this chapter is the whole of the service contracting industry that mediates the labour market for Brazilians of Japanese descent, this does not mean that we will not be examining the role being played by those places to which workers are sent in the non-manufacturing industry.

Work in non-manufacturing industries occurs in the markets referred to as 2c in the previous section. Compared with work in the manufacturing industry, this is seen as far inferior employment by service contractors in terms of contract unit price and by employees of Japanese descent in terms of hourly pay. However, establishing areas that, as far as both service contractors and workers are concerned, yield sparse profit in terms of unit price, establishes a foothold that could lead to the creation of labour markets with favourable contracting unit prices. There are also areas of employment in manufacturing industry factories where Japanese full-time employees have been replaced, but the biggest attraction of using service contracting companies for the manufacturing industry is that they can supply a labour force that corresponds to the fluctuations in production volumes. In order to stabilise supply for themselves, service contracting companies duplicate relationships for each line that they receive from the parent company and also become the subcontractor (child) within manufacturing industry factories. They cannot, however, stabilise supply for themselves merely by doing this. Even in the case of work that is unprofitable in terms of unit price, service contracting companies position themselves to be able to dispatch a labour force when a sudden need for an increase in personnel arises in the factory by ensuring that they are able to meet any request for a labour force.

Not all service contractors, however, necessarily need to engage in dispatching to non-manufacturing industry areas. This is because it is sufficient for them to have links of some sort or another with independent contractors who are engaged in sending to non-manufacturing industry areas. Consequently, when we survey all service contracting businesses, we can classify service contractors into three groups. The first are service contracting businesses that only send to factories in manufacturing industries such as automobile and appliance; the second are service contracting businesses that are engaged in also sending to non-manufacturing industry workplaces while focussing principally on manufacturing industry factories; and, finally, the third are service contracting businesses that specialise in sending to non-manufacturing industries. These are shown in Table 8.3.

Let us give a brief depiction of the differences between manufacturing and non-manufacturing industries. Generally, contracting unit prices are high in manufacturing industries and strikingly low in non-manufacturing sectors. In concrete terms, in automobile related areas, the contracting unit price – allowing for differences according to the labour strength required by particular operations – is 2,000–2,500 yen per hour. Next is the appliances industry at 1,650–1,800 yen per hour, more than fifteen per cent lower. Compared to these, contracting unit prices in the food industry vary according to scale of factory operations, ranging from 950–1,400 yen per hour. Freight operations in agriculture are charged at 1,400 yen per hour, but this amount is reached only when bonuses are applied for contracted night time operations. Contract unit prices are even lower than these figures for work at industrial waste management plants. However, demand from non-manufacturing industries is more stable than is the case with manufacturing industries. Sudden increases or decreases in personnel numbers are few and once a business relationship has been established, there are no concerns that it may be terminated.

To reiterate, employment in the contracting industry is fundamentally employment on a short term premise. Service contractors form their own businesses by concluding contracts with employment markets that arise to counterbalance increases in the number of personnel in one particular place and decreases in another. Service contracting companies, as the organisations that allow the formation of these sorts of employment markets, are unable to eliminate the range of increases and decreases in personnel numbers by dealing exclusively with one company. There are bound to be areas of mismatch. Similarly, a single company simply cannot respond to a customer's sudden request for a decrease in the size of the labour force. When we look at service contracting companies as one of the employment markets for workers of Japanese descent, we see that the networks that exist between service contractors, depicted in Figure 3.3, have a certain pattern to them, and we can identify from this that it is the fact that workers are dispatched not only to manufacturing industries but also to non-manufacturing sectors that makes a flexible labour supply possible.

The networks between these service contractors are not necessarily formed between proprietors. The truth is that networks between proprietors are extremely rare and they also tend to be very narrow in scope. It is the strength of the informal networks possessed by people of Japanese descent that are noticeable in this area. The human relationships connections of those who work in the main company as management staff for service contracting companies and those who have been assigned the role of worksite leaders are used in networks. Many of these people have lived in Japan for long periods of time. Despite the fact that there are no apparent links between the proprietors of service contracting companies, service contractors are connected via the mediation of interpreting staff. Consequently, they are able to form the sort of structure in which workers are, as it were, exchanged between service contractors. This does not mean that there are links of a cooperative nature between service contractors. Rather, the situation that exists between individual service contractors is one of relationships of rivalry as they compete for a share of the pie. In addition, some contracting company staff set out on their own without informing their former employers. Most contractors are in any case indifferent when this happens. Also, only one of the organisations in our survey had been built up cooperatively by a number of managers. However, even though there may not be any official organisation or contact between companies, as has been argued in this chapter, service contractors are linked with each other by an invisible thread and the labour market is constructed via these links.

Brazilian workers of Japanese descent within service contracting companies

Having discussed how service contracting companies connect regional employment in the previous section, let us now consider how Brazilian people of Japanese descent are positioned as workers in service contracting companies. In other words, who are these Brazilian men and women of Japanese descent replacing? Accordingly, in this section we will consider firstly how workers of Japanese descent are seen by service contractors and then the significance of service contract company workers of Japanese descent for the parent company that employs them via service contracting companies.

Firstly, there are the service contractors' views of workers of Japanese descent. As mentioned previously, however, contracting companies used to employ people of Japanese descent from the stratum of workers in insecure employment, in the days before these workers made their way into contracting companies. Japanese migrant, seasonal and fixed term contract workers correspond to this stratum of workers. However, there has been a decline in the numbers of these three types of workers compared to the volume of

work in the service contracting industry. There has been an increase
in spending on recruiting in an attempt to retrieve this working
population that has even seen a shrinking of its potential numbers. In
an effort to make use of fixed term contract workers from Hokkaidō
and Okinawa, which produce large numbers of migrant workers,
service contractors need to outlay about 500,000 yen per individual
worker in their recruiting activities.[11] In contrast to this, in the case
of Brazilians of Japanese descent, one can get away with outlaying
300–350,000 yen per person by using a tourist from Brazil.[12] If one
chooses to recruit people who are living in Japan, then there are
practically no recruitment expenses. Moreover, more importantly,
when there is an attempt to secure absolute numbers, recruitment
expenses show a gradual increase in the case of Japanese people.
When dealing with people of Japanese descent it is possible to keep
costs down, and because in addition to this there is no gradual increase in costs, calculations can be made simply on the basis of the
number of people recruited. This is the reason why service contractors who had been dispatching Japanese migrant, seasonal and fixed
term contract workers shifted to Brazilian workers.[13]

However, the reduction of the existing stratum of workers in
insecure employment and the increase in recruitment expenses have
not forced all service contractors to shift to employing people of
Japanese descent. This is because of the large effect of the ideology
of those who use service contracting companies in their factories
and moreover that of the service contractors regarding foreign
workers. Factories dislike workers coming onto the worksite with
appearances, skin colour and languages that are different from those
of their own nationals. This is why even in the actual workplaces
where people of Japanese descent are employed the factory appoints
those people who resemble Japanese in their features and skin colour
and why there are beginning to be dismissals of the dependents
of people of Japanese descent who are not of Japanese descent in
terms of family lineage. This shows that if a service contractor
were, conversely, able to assemble a labour force entirely of
Japanese workers, he would consider this to be a major advantage
as a sales point in dealing with the businesses using his service
contracting company. Since factories regard foreign workers as
being qualitatively different, it is possible to find business people
even in the ranks of service contractors who avoid foreign workers
as a matter of principle. For example, this is strikingly evident

amongst the service contractors who make up the *Association of Japanese In-House Contractors*: anyone who emp_oys foreign workers cannot be affiliated with this association and any affiliated service contractor who does employ foreign workers is immediately asked to withdraw.

The reduction in Japanese migrant, seasonal and fixed term contract workers is not simply the result of the drying up of the existing labour supply. We need to also note the fact that the service contracting industry itself grew during the 1980s. This will be discussed later, but when interviews in this survey asked in which year businesses had the greatest number of dispatched employees, the response was the 1997 fiscal year. This means that in the service contracting industry, where labour is a commodity, this was simultaneously the best year in terms of sales. All service contractors re-entered the market, strengthening their results during a period of economic recession and anticipating this situation. This does not mean that only service contracting companies that employ people of Japanese descent grew. In service contracting companies, which see people of Japanese descent as a labour force, even on the largest scale – that of the whole group – the number of workers dispatched reached the level of 6,000 people; there is only one gigantic service contracting company of this kind. However, within the ranks of service contracting companies that only dispatch Japanese workers there are numerous contractors, operating as independent companies and not as groups, which regularly dispatch more than 10,000 people. Even these enormous service contracting companies that have Japanese workers as their main force, showed a more than three-fold strengthening of sales through the 1980s.[14] We can understand from this that the service contracting industrial category as a whole was a growth field.

Service contractors encountered a relative reduction in the labour force caused by an absolute drying up of the existing labour force – in short, the Japanese migrant, seasonal and fixed term workers that they used to recruit from the Tōhoku, Shikoku and Kyūshū regions – and by the expansion of contracting markets. Therefore, service contractors who specialised in Japanese workers were forced to make big changes to their labour force supply areas in the 1980s. A certain contracting company that in September 1998 boasted the largest scale of operations, regularly dispatching 12,000 people, and also the largest sales had faced a situation through the

1980s of large reductions in employment in the Tōhoku region. This was why it had reopened its Asahikawa Employment Office and Okinawa Employment Office in 1980. It moved staff from its Sapporo Employment Office and carried out irregular recruitment activities in Asahikawa. When it needed labour from Okinawa also, this company hired community centres and set up interview venues and carried out recruitment activities by transferring staff from its Miyazaki Employment Office. The opening up of new offices shows periodic expansion of labour supply sites to more distant places in order to recruit a labour force. On the other hand, this company closed its Shikoku Employment Office.[15] It is not at all exceptional for service contracting companies that rely on a Japanese labour force to move, as this one has, in search of new labour supply areas. Up until this period, there had only been a few companies in Naha, but the number of service contracting company employment offices began to increase rapidly from 1990. Within merely two or three years, today's situation was reached with about thirty companies establishing offices there.[16] In other words, at the same time as the existing stratum of workers in insecure employment was declining, the supply zones providing insecure labour changed considerably. Service contracting companies that focus on dispatching a Japanese labour force have responded to the reduction in migrant, seasonal and fixed term Japanese workers by moving their recruitment bases to ever more remote locations. Meanwhile, service contractors who are not particularly concerned about Japanese people making up their dispatched labour force have responded to the labour short- age engendered by the expanded market by shifting to people of Japanese descent to make up their labour force.

Thus the expanded segment of the service contracting company market has come about as a result of the substitution by parent companies of service contractors for regular employees; in short, by a process of outsourcing. There follows a comparison of the costs of substituting contractors for regular employees and the expense to the parent company when it employs an individual regular em- ployee. Naturally, these costs to the parent company of contracting out to a service contracting company are not the amount that is paid to workers of Japanese descent, but an amount that includes the service contracting company's margin in addition to the work- ers' pay. This corresponds to the contracting unit price for service contracting companies.

Table 8.5: Years of greatest foreign worker numbers according to
service contracting companies (unit: companies)

Year	Number of companies
1990	2
1991	0
1992	2
1993	1
1994	4
1995	2
1996	1
1997	27

Note: valid responses from 38 companies.

Let us look at a comparative table of regular employees and
outsourcing that was used as reference data in the business
activities of a particular service contractor in order to secure new
customers – that is, new destinations to which to dispatch workers.
This is set out in Table 4.2. It can be appreciated from this that the
service contractor regards the fact that he replaces regular workers
as a selling point. Having confirmed that indirect employment
has no greater impact on productivity than direct employment in
terms of low prices, the transaction becomes practically a matter
of re-extension for the client company that has begun dealing with
the service contractor. Re-extension, as long as there is no notice
to suspend business from the parent company, is characterised by
a continuation of dealings in the form of automatic extensions to
contracting agreements in which the renewal of contracts is not
concluded via written documents.

We can also confirm, from looking at Table 8.5 that the business
world made up of indirect employment represented by service
contracting companies is spreading into the business world as a
whole. When individual service contractors were asked for the year
in which they dispatched the largest number of workers 68.4 per cent
of business people (26 companies) replied that this was 1997. The
steady increase up until 1998 of the population of people of Japanese
descent, that we see also in Immigration Bureau statistics, shows
that people of Japanese descent were steadily entering Japanese
industrial society at a time when it was said to be in recession and
that there was a definite increase in the size of the pie for contracting

Table 8.6: Requests to contracting companies from companies receiving workers and the latter's use of contracts

Requests from companies receiving workers	
Contribute to productivity	29
Wages compression	10
Work-related injury	9
Use made by companies receiving workers	
Securing absolute numbers	30
In order to compete	1
Both of these reasons	5

companies. The growth of service contracting companies does not only mean that there was an increase in workers from outside companies who were engaged in unskilled work. Unskilled work still continues to occupy a large proportion, but the employment of people of Japanese descent, including in the area of replacing regular employees, is increasingly also a search for a number of skilled workers from outside the company. As many as twenty per cent of service contractors mentioned having taken on new workers who were skilled in special skills such as welding and slinging.[17] While not a qualification, it also needs to be added that in ten per cent of companies in this survey, receiving training in the Nonius micrometre was a prerequisite for employment.

Independent contractors suggested several possible causes for the expansion in the number of service contracting companies in recent years. All of these were along the lines of: the labour shortage in the blue-collar sector until the period of the economic bubble; the decreasing of regular employee numbers in order to safeguard the employment of the remaining regular employees after the bursting of the bubble; and the replacement of employment in these areas where cuts had been made with outsourcing. These measures enabled parent companies to stabilise employment and reduce costs. This is a discourse about the stabilisation of employment by the parent company simultaneously causing an expansion of insecure employment. Different contexts prevail in the destination company and the service contracting company regarding the ways in which workers of Japanese descent are actually being used in each area of work in workplaces. In an environment in which, under the present conditions of pursuing international competitive power, there is a constant quest for cost reduction trends and no desire to increase employment even when there are upturns in the national economy, the service contracting company advertisements in Table 4.2 are attractive to companies, which scrutinise the activities of service contracting companies.[18]

As Table 8.6 shows, the foremost item sought from workers of Japanese descent is a contribution to productivity. Line operations are not outsourced in order to reduce the simple costs of the wages component which are variable capital. The reason why client companies that receive dispatched workers use service contracting companies is, as has been stated, in order to secure an absolute number of workers for the worksite in the midst of fluctuating demand for finished goods. The parent company uses numerous service contracting companies to assemble an absolute number of workers. It is possible for a sole service contracting company to dispatch numbers of workers in the order of two or three hundred, but there are also times when fifty, a hundred or all of the indirect personnel become superfluous.[19] On these occasions, if companies are dealing with multiple service contracting companies, it is possible to reduce the load placed on any one of the latter, and at times of a need for personnel increases also it becomes possible to assemble the numbers of required workers rapidly because the scale of increase for each service contracting company is small. Put another way, at times of personnel increases or reductions, particularly when these are pressing, it is networks amongst the proprietors of contracting companies and amongst staff of Japanese descent that are utilised.

It has clearly been shown that the employment of people of Japanese descent by service contracting companies supplements shortages in the stratum of workers in insecure employment who had previously been recruited from Tōhoku, Hokkaidō and Shikoku, and simultaneously that people of Japanese descent have come to shoulder the burden of the expanded outsourcing market. This has caused a diversification of types of occupations not only in unskilled work, but even in the case of work that requires an investment of time to acquire skills. The client companies hold expectations that the labour force of Japanese descent will satisfy the 'numbers strategy' and 'quality strategy' of their worksite area. Certain service contractors who managed their own factories ascribed the fall in the proportion of workers with perfect monthly attendance from ninety-eight to ninety-six per cent, when comparing the time before and after the period of the economic bubble, to a decline in the quality of Brazilians.[20]

The focus of discussions about workers of Japanese descent has shifted in recent years to the change from migrant workers who aim to take a set amount of money back with them to their hometowns to one on workers of Japanese descent of the enjoying their lifestyle type who take pleasure in a consumer lifestyle in Japan. However, this is an issue that includes the problems of other people of Japanese descent who live in Japan aside from workers working on factory worksites (see Chapter 2). In actual workplaces, they continue to be recognised as hard working workers. However, although, on the one hand, they attempt to see through employment contracts for three, six or twelve month periods, it is also a fact that the number of people renewing contracts beyond these periods has declined. Places where it was standard to have one year employment contracts were able to achieve the high re-contracting rate of over sixty per cent, but service contractors who offered three month contracts had fewer than fifty per cent of people seeing through their contract period until the end and had a re-contracting rate of around thirty per cent. The reason for comments about the aims of work having changed, despite the fact that there is still a high attendance rate in workplaces of which one can be proud, results from the fact that this sort of change in the settling down rate has been problematized.

Conclusion

One factor that can be offered up as a characteristic of workers of Japanese descent is that whether male or female they receive roughly similar levels of hourly pay throughout Japan. The uniform spread of this piece of information by the Portuguese language newspapers that are always on sale in areas where people of Japanese descent live in large numbers and the high rate of mobile phone ownership mean that this information has led to frequent movement. The trait of Brazilians of Japanese descent of moving for even a difference of 100 yen has led to the existence practically throughout Japan of the same rate per unit of time. The results of this frequent movement in which they are engaged have not simply been limited to changes in wages, but have caused considerable change to the living environment. There is a discernible rise alongside the increasing length of stay in Japan by Brazilians of Japanese descent in the former *takobeya* (labour camp) style living environment, in order to increase the settling down rate even slightly by not allowing any movement and also as an innovation for holding onto workers who have moved in. In addition to this, the stock of dwellings administered by prefectures for low income earners and those run by the Housing and Urban Development Corporation have deteriorated. The dwindling numbers of Japanese residents wanting to live in them has led to people of Japanese descent being sought as customers in order to fill unoccupied residences. In an effort to control movement and to increase the previous settling down rate, service contractors also recommend this type of residence in places where public housing and housing run by the prefecture are available for rent. Thus the service contractors' strategy for increasing the settling down rate inevitably leads to the residential problems centred on foreigners in regional areas. This is closely related to the company strategy of service contracting companies and the residential problems of people of Japanese descent which were discussed previously.

It had been anticipated at the time that with the revision of the Immigration Control and Refugee Recognition Act and the penalty provisions against employers, the employment of Brazilians of Japanese descent would move from indirect to direct employment. However, reality ran counter to these expectations, and the trend of increasing indirect employment continued unabated. As this chapter has confirmed, it is exclusively in these terms that we need to understand the intentions of the client companies who make use of service contracting companies. We can, however, say one thing: a labour supply system that compensates for mismatches between companies and between sectors that demand labour has been constructed by the spread of not just manufacturing but all types of employment into regional areas.

9 Microanalysis of the labour market for people of Japanese descent

Introduction

Service contracting companies are in-house contracting businesses that dispatch external workers primarily to worksites in manufacturing industries. Previous research can be divided into research that focuses on workers of Japanese descent as a flexible labour force (Watanabe ed. 1995a and 1995b; Nishizawa 1995; Satō 1996a and 1996b; and Tanno 1999b) and research that has as its subject workers of Japanese descent who were long-term residents in regional society (Tsuzuki 1995, 1996 and 1998). This is why the relationship between the movement of workers in factories and the movement of long-term residents in regional areas has come to be studied from separate standpoints. Through an empirical examination of just how workers of Japanese descent are deployed from the service contractors' dormitories to the factories that are in need of a labour force, this chapter makes it clear that labour problems are causing problems in regional communities. In this sense, this chapter bridges the two types of previous research referred to above.[1]

The first focus of this section is to give a concrete illustration of what is meant by labour problems being the cause of problems in regional communities. To begin with, the discussion will touch on the conflict with residents that people of Japanese descent bring about in the housing complexes that are the subject of analysis here. There will also be a simple explanation of the housing complexes of Toyota City in Aichi Prefecture, where the author carried out his participant observations. This will be followed by the main subject – a microanalysis of service contractors. This microanalysis will be conducted on the basis of the results of the author's participant observations. The nature of the service contractors' organisations in this participant observation will provide the starting point for the microanalysis. The service contracting company in which the author carried out his participant observations will be referred to as Company A in this chapter. Furthermore, the contents of the professional work that is repeated daily within the organisation will be organised chronologically from morning until evening. This will be followed by a consideration of the relationship of the content of the professional work duties of service contractors with three other actors – the proprietor of the service contracting company; the interpreting staff to whom the client company entrusts their workplace and who become the right hand of the proprietor; and the dispatched workers. There will be an examination of the role of the proprietor (hereafter Mr B), who occupies a central position in the service contracting company; the interpreting staff; and an even more detailed examination of the contents of their work and their roles within the organisation. Finally, this chapter will show concretely how the client who receives the dispatched workers from the service contracting company makes use of that company. Illustrating these areas will show that the labour problem of the employment of people of Japanese descent is inextricably linked to community problems.

Incidentally, this chapter represents research that is based on data obtained from participant observations inside a specific service contractor and as such it is very limited. At the time of the survey, this service contractor, run by husband and wife proprietors and two interpreting staff, was dispatching about fifty workers.[2]

The region and service contracting company in this survey

The service contractor dealt with in this chapter has set up his office and also all of the dormitories for dispatched workers in housing complexes in Toyota City. These housing complexes, with about 10,000 people living in them, are a group of apartment buildings made up of public housing sold as lots or leased by the Housing and Urban Development Corporation (currently Urban Renaissance Agency, and referred to hereafter as the HUDC) and housing managed by the prefecture which is leased to low income earners by the Aichi Prefecture Housing Supply Corporation. There are understood to be around 3,000 people of Japanese descent living in these housing complexes.[3] Housing managed by the prefecture is leased by individual workers, but in the case of the HUDC housing leases the HUDC will sometimes issue a corporate lease to companies;

thirteen companies including our service contractor have taken out these leases to house people of Japanese descent. When service contractors rent apartments, they frequently rent the entire dwelling, but the HUDC does not recognise long-term corporate leases and because it started issuing corporate leases after it was unable to fill empty residences, service contractors' dormitories are dotted amongst the dwellings of ordinary individuals. Table 9.1 shows the state of these housing complexes, as it was in December 1999, so as to make it easier for the reader to visualise the situation. Just a brief word of explanation: not necessarily all of the 213 apartments leased by the contractor have people of Japanese descent living in them. Because under corporate leases the question of who is to be housed is left to each lessee, even the HUDC, which is the landlord, is unable to confirm the number of people of Japanese descent living in its own leased dwellings.

The housing complexes are encircled by an outer perimeter road. In the early morning, once it has gone six, the workers waiting for the service contractor's courtesy vehicles that will take them to the factories that are their work destinations begin appearing along this road. Courtesy vehicles pick up workers that are going to their company in lots of two or three at a time as they come across them. Some vehicles would wait a while for workers who were late, but there were also those that would rush on to where the next batch of workers was waiting to be picked up because the ones they had initially waited for had not turned up. These courtesy vehicles are not only to be found on the outer perimeter road, but also in car parks within the housing complexes. The majority of workers, both male and female, wear company uniforms. Until around gone eight, when the workers who start at nine have been picked up, this scene unfolds here and there within the housing complexes. In addition to this early morning leaving for work scene, after six in the evening, there is a further manifestation of the presence of people of Japanese descent in the sole shopping centre within the housing complexes.

The increase in the numbers of workers of foreign nationality in the housing complexes began following the taking out of corporate leases by the HUDC. With the start of corporate leases, alongside the increase in the portion leased by service contractors and turned into dormitories there was also an increase in the number of people of Japanese descent renting rooms as individuals while being dispatched by service contractors. Following the increase in the

Table 9.1: Dwelling types in the housing complexes (unit: apartments)

	Public corporation housing	Housing managed by prefecture
Total number of apartments	1,653	1,350
Number of leased apartments	979	1,350
Number of sold apartments	674	0
Number of corporate lease apartments & number of apartments leased by foreigners	213	472

Note: This table shows 1,350 total managed apartments in December 1999, but the total of tenanted apartments is 1,060 and the proprtion of foreigners in the tenanted apartments is 45 per cent.

numbers of foreigners within the housing complexes, the troubles between the workers of Japanese descent and the service contractors who leased the dormitories for these workers and Japanese residents manifested itself. The bulk of the troubles were related to: 1) the way of putting out rubbish; 2) loud noises coming from windows; 3) matters of daily life such as the parking of cars on roads. Japanese residents' complaints regarding the most basic daily lifestyle practices came to a head in September 1997 with the residents putting these down in writing and sending a formal letter to Toyota City. The city then forwarded the residents' complaints to the HUDC and the Aichi Prefecture Housing Supply Corporation. This problem was even taken up by the Aichi Prefectural Parliament which had just begun a sitting at that time, resulting in the unprecedented state of affairs in which not only the service contractor as the direct employer, but also the Toyota Motor Company which stands at the summit of the region's industrial structure were criticised as being responsible for a deterioration of the living environment.[4]

It was when this situation was reached that the various departments concerned within the Toyota City Ward Office first reached out beyond the boundaries of their own respective areas and set up a conference in order for the various people in charge to exchange ideas directly with one another. Similarly, the service contractors directly employing the people of Japanese descent who were experiencing this problem as it came to a head also formed the Liaison Committee of Companies Directly Employing People of Japanese Descent (hereafter: Company Liaison Committee) which had at

its heart the Chūbu Outsourcing Kyōdōkumiai – which having felt
the worsening sense of crisis, was promoting the formation of an
organisation primarily in Aichi and Shizuoka. As of the end of
1999, periodic discussions were being held around the same table
between Toyota City as the administration; the HUDC as the landlord; neighbourhood councils of the area as representatives of the
residents; and the Company Liaison Committee for the employers.

As mentioned previously, the housing complexes were composed
of HUDC housing and housing managed by the prefecture. Housing
managed by the prefecture also included cases of individual leases
taken out by people of Japanese descent, but it was only HUDC
housing, where corporate leases were to be found, that ended up
becoming a social problem. Conversely, however, it was in housing
managed by the prefecture that one saw the greater incidence of
actual problems as far as Japanese residents were concerned, such
as the manner in which rubbish was put out. Particular features
of foreigners' residential problems in the housing complexes
account for why these have not been problematized as part of
the overwhelmingly bad aspects of the living environment.[5] The
reasons for this could be thought of as including: the fact that in
prefecture-managed housing Japanese residents form a minority in
some dwellings since, as Figure 9.1 shows, the majority of people
living there are of Japanese descent; and also the fact that as a result
of all of the housing being rental properties with none available
for sale, unlike the case with the HUDC, there is little will on the
part of Japanese to make these dwellings their final place of abode.

This is what is seen as the deterioration of the living environment
in housing complexes, and people of Japanese descent are criticised
as being its cause. There is strangely, however, practically no knowledge, aside from these problems, of the matter of how the workers
of Japanese descent who are living in the housing complexes are
deployed in the factories of Toyota City and of the surrounding cities,
towns and villages through the medium of service contractors. The
following section seeks to shed some light on this point.

The organisational form of the service contractors in this survey

The company of the service contractor in whose firm the author
carried out participant observations will be referred to here as

Company A and we will begin by looking at how Mr B, Company A's proprietor, entered the service contracting industry. This will be an attempt to summarise the type of organisational structure under which Company A is carrying out its business activities.

Before commencing with Company A, Mr B ran a consultancy business. His main line of work was general consulting at the time of the opening or refurbishment in the leisure equipment and restaurant areas, with operations spanning the whole country. In 1995, he switched to a large-scale business expansion away from the consulting industry and towards the service contracting industry. This was because he was facing the danger of his family breaking down as a result of the consulting business being one in which it was necessary, against his will, to go wherever there were clients and leave his house empty for long periods of time. Since Mr B had been giving advice regarding labour management from the time of running the consulting business and because he was also acquainted with manufacturers, he understood the business format of service contracting companies. At the time when he was thinking about making substantial changes to his business, he had an acquaintance who wished to dispatch workers and it was by dispatching to that company that Mr B made his shift to the service contracting industry.

Figure 9.2 shows the current organisational form of Company A. As the proprietor, Mr B oversees all business operations and has two interpreting staff under him who as chief clerks are each responsible for their own respective client companies and dispatch workers of Japanese descent on a daily basis to match the demand for labour from the companies in their charge. Company A has six client companies on its books (one automobile related; two food products related; one construction related; one electrical appliances; and one ceramics company), but both the electrical appliances and ceramics client companies underwent large-scale changes in their management environments in 1997 and since that time, they have not been using dispatched workers. Consequently, there are actually four companies to whom works are dispatched.

In the automobile related company, which has the best contracting unit price, there are significant changes in the daily amount of overtime hours for each area. Similarly, because the state of operations in the parent company may require using a new customer or carrying out sudden dismissals, Mr B takes direct charge of this company

Figure 9.1: Company A organisation chart and information flow regarding labour demand

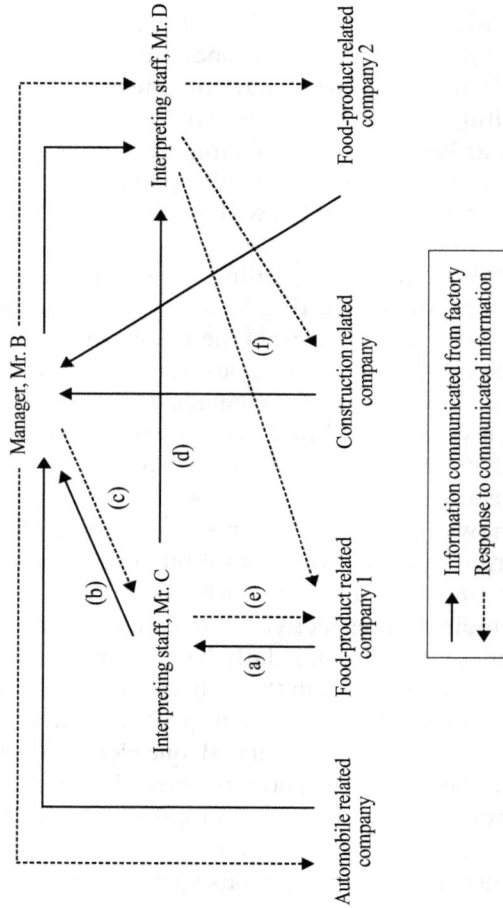

Manager, Mr. B

Interpreting staff, Mr. D

Food-product related company 2

Interpreting staff, Mr. C

Construction related company

Food-product related company 1

Automobile related company

(a) (b) (c) (d) (e) (f)

Information communicated from factory

Response to communicated information

himself. There are eleven dispatched workers. Food Company 1 is the customer that takes the largest number of the workers dispatched by Company A. The dispatching of workers to this company which has a mainly female labour force necessitates the accompanying and meeting of workers. Also, because high quality, very fresh, high grade paste products are their leading product, they are made to order and the volume produced changes considerably each day. For this reason, the number of workers required for production activities also varies daily. Mr C, an interpreting staff member, has sole charge of this company. Eighteen workers are dispatched to this company and casual workers, who have been used in a temporary capacity in the past, are added on weekends. Interpreting staff member, Mr D, on the other hand, is in charge of the construction related company and Food Company 2. The construction related company pre-cuts the wooden materials used for wooden prefabricated houses. Food Company 2, unlike Food Company 1, is a factory that produces regular amounts each day. Partly because these two companies have stable production volumes, there are few changes in their demand for labour. Furthermore, as they only employ male workers, there are no accompanying and meeting requirements. This is why interpreting staff member, Mr D, is in sole charge of two companies. Around ten workers are dispatched to each of these companies.

The nature of labour demand in each of the client companies has a big influence on the roles of the interpreting staff in Company A. Interpreting staff member Mr C who is in charge of Food Company 1 which has the most intense labour demand, is recognised as having the discretion to be able to make decisions without seeking Mr B's judgement on everything. This is because if he were to look to Mr B to make decisions, this would render him incapable of responding smoothly to clients' requests. For this reason Mr C's work is carried out largely as shown by arrows (a) and (e) in Figure 9.1. The activities of Mr B and Mr C, indicated by arrows (b) and (c) are of the sort that can be observed during the lunch hour and at the end of the day. Interpreting staff member Mr D's level of autonomy, on the other hand, is low and both client companies – the construction related company and Food Company 2 – communicate their requests to the proprietor in the first instance. All activities regarding clients are communicated to Mr D as instructions from the proprietor. The following section takes a practical look at the business activities shown in Figure 9.2.

Figure 9.2: A chronological look at the daily workflow in a contracting company office

	5:30	9:00	12:00	15:00	After 18:00
Proprietor Mr B	• Meeting at 7:30	• Government office related	• Communication of necessary matters to workers in lunch break • Interviewing newly-employed workers • Communication of production schedule from hereon by someone in managerial position in client compnay		• <u>Confirmation by FAX of the overtime workers and the work chart for that day</u> • Help Mr C with meeting workers
Interpreter Mr C	• <u>Sending off trips 5:30-9:30</u>		• Arrangements regarding absentees • Explanation to those making takt changes • Amendments to city ward office of insurance and foreigner registration details • Make new workers available for interview with factory supervisor	• Act as agents regarding workers' public utilities charges and remittances	• <u>Confirm that day's overtime workers and times when they are to be met</u> • <u>Confirm worker numbers for the next day and shifts</u> • <u>18:00–22:00 meet workers</u> • <u>Communicate next day's shifts to workers while transporting them</u>
Interpreter Mr D		7:00 Help Mr C transport workers • Explanation to those making takt changes	• Act as agents regarding workers' public utilities charges and remittances		18:00 Help Mr C with transportation of workers

Note: Underlined items indicate things that are done everyday without fail. Other items do not necessarily occur everyday

A service contractor's day

A service contractor's day begins with accompanying workers in the morning. Company A's day begins with accompanying workers going to Food Company 1 from the housing complexes. When a factory begins work at six thirty, the first trip accompanying is at five thirty and when the start time is seven o'clock, this happens at six twenty. In Company A, it is standard practice for interpreting staff to carry out these accompanying activities. However, on days when interpreting staff are not working or when there is a sudden influx of an increased number of employees, the husband and wife proprietors perform the accompanying duties. Since factories usually begin operating at seven in the morning, this means that work starts at six twenty. The courtesy vehicle that comes to meet workers is a single minivan that seats up to ten people, but at times when large numbers of workers are being dispatched in response to factory requests, two minivans are required. The minivan has a roughly twenty minute drive to the factory, and about an hour after having returned to the housing complexes, it makes its second trip and after a further hour its third trip dispatching workers to the factory. At the factory, they firstly drop off the workers at the employees' entrance and then report the number of people that they have brought with them to the person in charge of the factory. When an employee is suddenly absent, as well as communicating this to the person in charge of the factory, the interpreting staff ascertain whether the line will still run even if this person does not turn up and also whether someone must be found to replace the person concerned in the event that he simply cannot come to work. These confirmation activities are carried out with each trip.

When a substitute needs to be found for the person who is absent, the interpreting staff member firstly confirms whether the person concerned absolutely cannot make it to work and also their reason for being absent. If the person concerned confirms that they cannot come to work, a call is made to someone who is rostered off on that day and the possibility of this person coming into work on their day off is negotiated. In most cases a substitute can be found by doing this.

However, there are also days when large numbers of workers are all absent at once. On these occasions, workers are selected from a list of job applicants who had previously telephoned the office looking for work. The person selected comes into the factory for just one day as a casual. Company A says that although it has been three years since it began as a service contracting company, under the existing method, no vacancies have opened up to date in the numbers of people required by the factory. Food Company 1 is, by the way, the only place where Company A performs the task of accompanying and meeting workers. Company A has three other companies as its major clients: one automobile related company; one construction industry related company that pre-cuts wooden materials for prefabricated houses; and another food products related company. The workers that Company A dispatches to these companies are practically all males. Most of the male workers have a driver's licence. For this reason, those who own a car commute to work in their own cars and, in addition, Company A sometimes loans cars to lead workers at the workplace to be used for accompanying and meeting workers or to make it possible for them to ride to work separately.

In the case of females, however, since most do not have a driver's licence, service contractors must carry out the accompanying and meeting of workers in workplaces where females are in the majority. In mainly male workplaces, the costs associated with accompanying and meeting workers amount simply to adding an accompanying and meeting bonus to the pay of the male employees who assume these tasks. This is why the proprietors of service contracting companies find it most desirable, when possible, to dispatch workers only to mainly male workplaces.

The work of transporting workers to the factory comes to an end at nine o'clock and then there is a steady stream of other jobs to be completed before six in the evening when it is time to meet the workers for their trips home. These duties differ completely from one day to the next with no set things having to be done on any particular day. They include: seeing to office procedures related to the Nagoya Immigration Office or the Toyota City Ward Office;[6] contacting the factory to which workers are dispatched and attempting to coordinate with the company's planned production schedule; on weekdays, paying electricity, gas and water bills on behalf of the workers working in the factory; and organising remittances to their families in Brazil. In all this, relations with these offices and relations with the workers are one and the same thing. Let us examine this via a concrete example. Mr B and the interpreting staff drive workers who are rostered off on this day but who have formalities to see to at the various offices. As all of Company A's workers live in the housing complexes, this group of workers is asked to wait for the return of the courtesy vehicle at around nine thirty, either in the car park or the office, from where they are then accompanied. The author also once went along on a somewhat surprising task which involved carrying out the necessary education committee formalities in order to get children into primary and secondary schools and explaining these formalities to the worker involved.[7] As with all work on a worksite, there will inevitably be work-related accidents. In the two weeks during which the author was carrying our participant observations, two workers reported injuries. There were various tasks to be done gathering together the documents needed for reporting these injuries and for calculating paid leave. Interpreting staff members deal with the electricity, gas and water payments and also the remittances to Brazil that the workers have asked them to take care of while they are at these offices calculating paid leave.

When new workers are employed, in most cases, interviews are held at lunch time. These are not, however, Company A interviews. People who wish to become Company A employees must undergo an interview with the supervisor of the factory to which they have been sent.[8] The interpreting staff member gathers together the new workers during the factory's lunch break and accompanies them to see the factory supervisor.

Normally, as long as the various tasks do not drag on too long, managers fit in a brief break between one and around three in the afternoon. Even this brief respite, however, can vanish with the appearance of incidents such as a worker suddenly feeling unwell or an accident in the factory. From about three onwards, the office telephone begins ringing and the translating staff members' mobile telephones start ringing incessantly. The client company contacts the office by fax; informing them of the hours worked by the workers who were sent on that day and also of any overtime. The calls to their mobile telephones inform them of the numbers of workers who have returned home from Food Company 1 for which they are conducting accompanying and meeting transportation. Interpreting staff members, between completing their morning accompanying duties and before going back to pick them up in the evening, must ensure that they make a trip to Food Company 1's factory, meet directly with the supervisor, and confirm with the person in charge of overtime for the day how many will be doing overtime and also how many workers will be in the first batch to be met and driven home. There are also instances, however, of orders coming into the factory in the evening and because of this there are revisions to the numbers that had been agreed at the lunchtime meeting. This is the reason for the confirmation telephone calls.

The first trip ferrying workers home from the factory leaves the housing complexes at five thirty in the evening and reaches the factory car park at six. At this time, courtesy cars belonging to other service contractors are also in the car park. Just as in the mornings, cars are sent every hour to meet the workers. In contrast to the morning accompanying, which progresses sequentially according to the order of the factory line's production schedule, because at finishing time all lines come to a stop at once, apart from the overtime line, two vehicles need to be sent for the first trip to meet workers. Whether there will be any overtime or not and how long that overtime will last are factors that vary from day to day, but the very latest final pick up trip that the author observed was at ten at night. Company A's day would finally have ended with this trip dropping off the workers at the housing complexes.

Daily work content in service contracting companies

The previous section provided an outline of the kind of work done by service contractors by showing the passage of time in the course of a day from the first trip accompanying workers in the morning to the last trip taking them home at night. In this section, we will look at the office that issues instructions from a fixed location. We will also look at the interpreting staff who take care of the various issues assigned to them while constantly going around to the worksites with the support of the office. Finally, we will take a more detailed look at what sort of work each of the people in these roles do and at how they accomplish the matter of dispatching a labour force.

Firstly, we will look at the office. Company A's office is situated inside the public housing complexes with the residence of the couple who are the proprietors of the company doubling as their office. The work of the service contractor is, as has been described: 1) accompanying workers to and meeting them after work; 2) contact with the client company where the workers have been sent; 3) the recruitment and dismissal of workers; 4) negotiations with relevant agencies. But it is primarily 2) contact with the client company where the workers have been sent and 3) the recruitment and dismissal of workers that make up the work of the office. Contact with the client company occurs initially at the level of the interpreting staff, but in the case of urgent matters or those related to work attitudes these are also communicated to the office. Whilst contact with the interpreting staff concerns mainly issues to be dealt with that day or the next, contact from the client company to the office is mostly on the level of much more long-term information.

At the time when the author was conducting his participant observation, in September 1998, the number of workers being employed and dispatched by Company A was just short of fifty. Even at this scale, however, two to three workers are being replaced each month. Company A has not released all of its recruitment documents. There are many names in these of people who are related to workers already employed by the company, but the company also keeps the names of people who have called on a word-of-mouth basis even if there are no client companies to which to dispatch them at that time: they form a waiting list of emergency workers that is kept for when a sudden request for more personnel comes from a client. The details ascertained when people call seeking work are: name, gender, age, address (building and room number within the housing complexes), telephone number and employment history. The practice of making a point of asking the building and room number within the housing complexes under the category of address tells the story of just to what extent Company A's recruiting occurs primarily within these housing complexes. The telephone calls do not, however, come exclusively from within the housing complexes. When the author took his turn answering the telephone, there were even calls looking for work from people as far afield as Ōizumi Town in Gunma Prefecture and from Fukuoka Prefecture.[9]

Telephone applications are not Company A's main recruiting method. More so than the company, it is the workers who play the largest role in Company A's recruiting as they perform a hard sell saying that they have family members who would like to come to Japan and ask whether there might be any work for them. Operating on a scale of around fifty employees, by making the relatives of their company's existing employees the centrepiece of employment practices the company can practically manage, on average, to replace just under ten per cent of workers each month.[10] For this reason, people applying by telephone mainly end up securing casual work for just a day. In Food Company 1, where Company A provides accompanying and meeting services for workers, in addition to the usual contracting to dispatch workers for the line, Company A also supplies casual workers for the weekend. The reason why Food Company 1 needs casual workers on the weekend and why Company A sends them this casual labour force is because Japanese part-time workers will not come in to work on the weekend; they want these days off when the rest of their family members are at home. The people of Japanese descent who live in the housing complexes are aware of this casual employment with Company A and on Thursday afternoons the telephone calls start coming in from workers looking for casual work. The office receives a fax on Friday evening giving details of the numbers of casuals required. Company A gathers this number by working its way, in order, down the waiting list of people who have already called. In the case of casual work, recruitment basically only occurs within the housing complexes – except for people who have already been used for casual work in the past – because of the need to have workers who will be ready to work on the very next day after just having received a call from the factory on the Friday evening. These people are actually employed without an interview, but judgements regarding how well or how poorly people communicate in their responses on the telephone do operate in lieu of interviews.

Interviews cannot be foregone in the event of employment. Before interviews in the factory mentioned in the previous section, there are interviews with Mr B. At lunch time, Mr B gets the workers to come to the office and holds face-to-face interviews with them. During the time that the author was at Company A, one job applicant who came in for an interview was already being dispatched to another factory by a different service contractor and had taken the day off in order to come to the interview. This job applicant was a Brazilian female whose third generation Japanese descent husband had been working at Company A for three years. Taking into consideration the fact that in the course of the interview it became clear that her husband had a good work attitude she was employed despite the fact that Company A had no particular need to increase its personnel in the current conditions. However, this offer was conditional upon being able to conclude her employment with the service contractor

Table 9.2: Items on the resume of a worker of Japanese descent

Name, photograph of face, gender, date of birth and age, current address, telephone number
Birthplace, nationality, last year of school, number of trips to Japan and most recent work in Brazil, blood type
Passport number, place of issue of passport, height, weight, uniform size, shoe size
Japanese speaking ability, Japanese listening ability, ability to comprehend written Japanese[11]
Manners and attitude, interviewer's evaluation of speech and will to work[12]
Family situation in Japan, number of people in family, presence or absence of dependents, visa expiration date
Date and place of entry into Japan this trip
Date and time of interview, name of interviewer, name of dispatching company

for whom she was currently working harmoniously. Meanwhile, Mr B put together a resume for the worker to present to the person in charge of personnel in the factory. Resumes presented to the factory must address all of the items listed in Table 9.2. In the case of this worker, the interpreting staff member accompanied her to the factory on the Wednesday of the following week and while looking over her resume, the factory supervisor interviewed her and she was offered employment. It is the factory that decides whether one will be employed or not and it is only after this decision has been made that the worker can be employed by Company A.

Meanwhile, it is expected that interpreting staff will adapt the work that they do so as to be responsive to the priority assigned to the matters that they are instructed to deal with by the office. The interpreting staff members in Company A have been given the roles of chief clerks. The mobile telephone is an essential item for these interpreting staff who are chief clerks. Calls flood in incessantly on these mobile telephones from business partners, the office and workers. Calls from business partners primarily concern that day's volume of work and plans for the following day. Food Company 1, for whom they carry out accompanying and meeting activities, is the company with the most severe fluctuations in this area and at lunchtime staff are informed of the plans for the overtime line on that day and also the names of the workers who will stay back on that line. The call informing interpreting staff of the time to make the return trip to meet workers, after four thirty in the afternoon, should officially be the final call, but there are also frequently calls to staff while they are en route to pick up workers, informing them that instead of finishing at the set time the workers will now be doing overtime. The interpreting staff members need to cope with these changes.

Also, when there are changes to the line that the service contracting company is in charge of in the factory or when there are changes, including takt changes, to how the same line has been operating to date, the interpreting staff are immediately summoned to the factory where they interpret the line head's explanation of the work instructions for the workers. They also spend about an hour looking over the shoulders of workers until the latter have become familiar with the new work. There are frequently changes to the work takt in relation to that day's volume of work and labour supply – as, for example, when there are suddenly employee absences or when the amount of work increases on only one specific line in the factory. Thus, interpreting staff are endlessly being summoned to the factory whenever there are changes to the organisation of the lines within the factory.

From the workers' point of view, the interpreting staff members, as chief clerks, are their immediate bosses. Therefore, they are reliant on the interpreting staff for requests for days off and for advice regarding procedures concerning various agencies.[13] Calls regarding these matters happen mainly during the lunch period, but as most people of Japanese descent own a mobile telephone, these calls can also occur during work hours. Calls from people looking for work are also frequently received by interpreting staff. This is how the office and interpreting staff cooperate to advance the daily work of the service contracting company.

Relationships between proprietor, interpreting staff and workers concerning dismissals

In order to gain a more concrete understanding of the employment of people of Japanese descent, the discussion will now focus on the dual areas of how service contractors go about their decision making, mainly with regard to the dismissal of workers; and the nature of the relationship between Mr B, the interpreting staff and the workers.

Company A has clear, established criteria regarding matters that will lead to the dismissal of workers. The first is driving without a licence. The second is the failure of individuals to improve even after having been warned about being absent from work without permission and about go-slow tactics in the workplace. The third is when the client company cuts personnel. When these cuts in personnel occur it is the client company and not Company A that draws up the list of those who are to be let go. The client company makes its decisions regarding these cuts after a comprehensive consideration of factors related to productivity such as usual attitude to work, familiarity with the work, age and problems with the language. With the exception of those cases in which Company A expresses a clear difference of opinion, it will announce the dismissals to the workplace, basically according to the requests of the client regarding the names on the list. When the scope exists for extra labour demand within companies with whom he is dealing, Mr B tries to get these companies to take the dismissed workers. Negotiating with the client that is cutting employment and then conveying this to the workers is the role of Mr B.

Interpreting staff do not play a major role at the time of dismissals; their main role is rather at the time of employment. The reason for this lies in the fact that interpreting staff, who are constantly confirming employment conditions with the client, are the first people to be approached for their advice by workers thinking of sending for their families and also because workers pass on the telephone numbers of interpreting staff to their friends. It is usual for workers to consult the interpreting staff before raising matters with Mr B. In addition, as mentioned previously, the interpreters are the ones who directly instruct new workers and those engaged in new work duties about their work and they are also the people who act as agents regarding a variety of matters which workers cannot see to during office hours because they are working. This is why workers also end up consulting interpreting staff about small everyday matters. This does not, however, mean that workers and interpreting staff are connected by relationships of trust. There are also cases in which workers, who are sufficiently knowledgeable about indirect employment, superficially keep up appearances out of fear that their relationship with the interpreting staff will end up being included in assessments regarding dismissals.

There were two interpreting staff members in Company A, and their relationship was characterised by coexistence and competition. Each interpreting staff member was assigned clients that were entirely under their own jurisdiction meaning that they were entirely responsible for the management of those clients and the workers employed there. At the same time as seeing to the various duties concerning these workers, interpreting staff have to rush off to the factory whenever it issues requests. Because of this, if the interpreting staff were not to cover each other's work occasionally, they would not be able to resolve all that day's matters. This is why interpreting staff must also stay in contact with one another.

At the same time as cooperating as partners in their work, interpreting staff are constantly the subject of comparisons by Mr B with regard to their relationship with clients and their abilities in resolving issues that arise. During the time that the author was there, interpreting staff member, Mr D, was dismissed.[14] Mr B fired the interpreting staff member despite the fact that he then had to temporarily assume the work that the interpreter had been doing himself. It was differences in the problem solving abilities between the two of them that caused Mr B to take this decision.

When he has the opportunity to do so, Mr B chats with the workers and asks them about the current situation. The interpreting staff members are also generous in giving advice when transporting workers to and from work or when they receive calls from them. Even so, there is a line that cannot be crossed between workers and management. The two workers with whom the author shared a dormitory room were both sixty year old *issei*. *Issei* refers to foreigners who hold Japanese nationality. Under Brazilian law, foreign nationals who are out of the country for more than two years lose their permanent resident rights. For this reason, both of them, having family in Brazil, took it as a given that they had to return once a year. The period when the author was at Company A was also the time when the phenomenon of homelessness amongst people of Japanese descent began appearing, therefore, there was no guarantee that there would be any work when these two older workers returned to Japan after having gone back to Brazil.[15] They both hoped to stay working for Company A right up until the time that they had to leave for home, but they also talked to each other about what would happen if, in the worst case, they were to be dismissed. One of them left the dormitory at six thirty in the morning to start work in an automobile related company at seven and returned after eight every night. The other one left the dorm at seven in the morning for an eight o'clock start or at eleven for a one in the afternoon start at a food products company and returned home after eight at night. The one who worked in the automobile related company would have to leave early in the morning the next day therefore the only time that they had to spend with one another was roughly a mere thirty minutes as they ate dinner together after having taken their turns in the bath following their return from work. Mr B visited the dormitory on several nights during the author's stay, but with the exception of these occasions the conversation between these two older workers about how work had been that day generally turned to what would happen should they be dismissed.

This concern was not confined to older workers. Every night, the author would visit employees of Company A who were living in other public housing dormitories and prefecture run housing. The barrier between the employer and the employed that could not be crossed was visible in these places; this barrier was the 'safety net' that extended between employees. The 'safety net' is a network for reducing the dangers of sudden dismissal and safeguarding lifestyles during periods of unemployment and also for rapidly finding another place to work even if one should be dismissed. There are extremely large numbers of people who have relatives in the housing complexes and confirmation of the employment situation is carried out via, among other things, telephone calls with one's relatives and in conversations during meals together on the weekend. The state of the work situation is confirmed through the exchange of information about the conditions of work capacity and overtime hours in people's respective factories, information about conditions inside the service contractor where people themselves are directly employed and rumours that they have heard from others. Workers understand that employment through service contracting companies is fundamentally short term in nature and that when personnel cuts start being implemented they will be the first to be cut. Consequently, no matter how close the relationship between them and the proprietor or the interpreting staff, workers are not bound exclusively to a relationship with their present company; they attempt to maintain their option of being able to move to another service contractor if the opportunity arises.

Company A has a large number of people who have been employed as family units and this employment of families is quite attractive to both management and workers. As far as management is concerned, the employment of families produces a sense of security, increases the settling down rate and guarantees workers who will not lose sight of their aims because they are living together as a family. Similarly, management can plan for a rapid increase in personnel numbers by sending out a call for other family members. The standard boarding fee is 20,000 yen per person, but, depending on the situation, the boarding fee per person can be arrived at by dividing the rent for each house leased from the HUDC by the number of workers living in that dormitory.[16] If there are a large number of working families, it is possible to keep down the boarding fee per person and even if there are workers who are unemployed as a result of the inevitable personnel cuts, then as long as families cover their portion of the boarding fee, these workers can continue living in the dormitory. These people provide Company A with reserve personnel who are able to respond to the factory demand for increased personnel at any time. Workers frequently experience someone in their family becoming unemployed. Being able to meet this danger as a family living together is highly advantageous. Usually, as long as someone in the family is working for the contracting company that owns the dormitory, then even workers who work for other companies or acquaintances who are unemployed can live there too.[17]

However, when the person paying the boarding fee loses his job, then the workers must vacate the residence within a month. As is also the case for Company A, many workers have relatives within the housing complexes. This is what makes it possible for workers to continue living in the housing complexes even when they are out of work. Similarly, considering the accuracy of the information possessed by the safety net, the certainty of being able to find work by using this information and also the dangers of moving away from the housing complexes, workers who have lost their jobs choose, whenever possible, to remain in the housing complexes. The information that they are able to glean via the safety net does not come only from relatives and acquaintances who are working. It is also common practice to stay in contact with interpreting staff from previous places of employment, even after having moved to a new place of work. It is precisely the fact that interpreting staff from other companies have no direct relationship with the current employment of these workers that makes them all the more appropriate as people with whom workers directly discuss their discontent.

Human relations between proprietors, interpreting staff and workers naturally exist when these groups are in an employment relationship with one another, but they also continue even when the employment relationship no longer does. At the same time as providing a safety net for workers who have lost their jobs, this arrangement also gives employers access to a recruiting network for times when there is a sudden need for an increase in personnel in the factory or when they are looking for replacements for workers who have been dismissed. Mr B, who in spite of not placing any recruitment advertisements always manages to assemble rapidly the labour that he needs, is able to make use of the dual nature of the safety net surrounding unemployed workers that exists in their relationships with interpreting staff. The conflict with Japanese residents inside the housing complexes that were discussed above is the other side of this safety net. Viewed from the perspective of the Japanese residents, the result of this safety net is sudden increases and decreases in the number of unfamiliar residents. This then leads to a situation in which, in view of visible phenomena such as the manner in which rubbish is put out, noise levels coming from rooms and illegal parking, the employment of people of Japanese descent takes on the aspect of being the primary cause of community problems.

Clients who use a flexible labour supply

The reader will have understood from this discussion the types of activities undertaken daily by service contractors and also why it is that the issue of the employment of people of Japanese descent causes community problems. This section will now examine client companies' methods of using service contracting companies, which is the root cause of the transformation of the employment problem into a regional problem. In practical terms, this will be looked at from the perspective of demands for increased and decreased numbers of personnel and also instructions about hours of work and overtime for existing workers. As mentioned previously, Company A currently has four main client companies, but of these the fluctuations in demands for labour are greatest in Food Company 1, to and from which Company A ferries the workers that it dispatches, and also in the automobile related company. The other two companies are relatively stable and do not display the same degree of fluctuation as the two companies mentioned above. As the author was only there for the short period of two weeks, this section will discuss the relationship between workers and the client company by focussing on the companies with the greatest levels of fluctuations.

Let us begin our discussion with Food Company 1 which has the highest level of fluctuation. Aside from selling high quality boiled fish paste products such as *kamaboko* and deep-fried foods to brokers in the market, they have also opened their own company-managed counters amongst the food sales counters of a department store. It is particularly as a result of having opened up these counters that the company is undergoing rapid growth. Since it carries out sales demonstrations at these self-managed counters, it needs to take in not only finished products but also half finished goods. Because of this, this company decreases production levels considerably on the day before days when the market is closed when there will be no need to supply brokers and also the day before the department store is closed. Since it has opened up counters within a specific department store conglomerate, the company is also subject to considerable fluctuations in production based on the department store's schedule, as for example in the case of massive storewide bargain sales.

The labour force that they receive is mainly female, but there are also men working in Food Company 1. During the period when the author was there, there was a fluctuation of between thirteen and twenty three in the number of workers dispatched each day. The day with the lowest number of dispatched workers was Tuesday, the day before the day on which the department store was closed and the day with the highest number was Saturday, the day before Sunday when Japanese female part-time workers take a day off and moreover the most profitable day for department stores. Work for workers of Japanese descent is usually from the time of their arrival at the company at seven in the morning until six in the evening. They have a one hour break, but their work consists of standing up for ten hours every day. Working hours that exceed eight hours are paid at an hourly overtime rate of 1.25-fold and there is overtime every day. The hourly pay rate for women in this company is 900 yen compared to 1,100 yen for men. Out of a desire to keep overall wages costs low, the factory has put together a female overtime shift. By contrast, they have constructed work shifts for male workers that start after lunch and attract no overtime even though they finish at the same time as the end of the overtime period for the women.

It is the fact that these are high quality fish paste products that is the selling point for this company. Both a high level of quality and freshness are required. Because of this, there is practically no pre-preparation and the factory is informed the night before of the volume of goods to be sent out the next day. It is on this basis that the quantity of overtime and also the number of workers required for the following day are determined, and if there is a need for more workers than had been planned, Company A is contacted with a message to increase the number of workers. When the personnel increase is a matter of a small number of workers, it is usually interpreting staff member Mr C who is contacted and he informs the office. When the number of workers is large, five or six, then the request for an increase in personnel is communicated by the factory supervisor to both the interpreting staff member and also the office. Furthermore, when the following day's production volumes are exceedingly large, first thing the next morning there is a request from the factory for unanticipated overtime in order to be able to send out the required product. This is, as mentioned earlier, a change that occurs after the final confirmations for the day have already been made. As most Japanese part-time workers are housewives with families, not only can they not work on Saturdays and Sundays, but they also cannot be asked to do overtime at short notice. The existence of workers of Japanese descent has become indispensable to manufacturing in Food Company 1.

Let us now turn to the automobile related company. The workers sent to the automobile related company from Company A work in four areas: the presses; upholstery; metal plate; and welding. During the time that the author was there, there was absolutely no overtime in either upholstery or metal plate. On the days when there was overtime in the welding area, it was for about two hours and apart from there being around two days of overtime per week, work generally finished on time. Working hours in the press area were extremely varied, ranging from days on which there was no overtime at all to a maximum of four hours overtime. However, there was overtime on most days and there was even some work on Sundays. A total of eleven workers sent to this company during the time that the author was there were: one to upholstery; two to plate metal; four to welding; and four to the presses.

The automobile related company informs Company A of planned reductions for the following month at the end of each month. When it receives these demands for a reduction in personnel, Company A sets about putting them into action, but since there is a schedule of informing the people concerned and arrangements for the next place of work, the workers have about a three week leeway before they are dismissed. For example, when there was a request to cut personnel by four people at the end of April 1998, the response to this company's request was to allow one person to keep working until 16 May of the same year with his dismissal from the company being dated 18 May while three were kept working until 22 May of the same year and dismissed on 25 May. There have been no further requests for reductions in personnel from this company since June 1998. During the period of the author's participant observation, it was Mr B who noted that the operation of the factory was proceeding under bare minimum conditions.

Meanwhile, just as in the case of personnel reductions, when there is an increase in personnel, plans for these increases are usually communicated at the end of the previous month. Company A takes along the workers who it is able to dispatch as candidates for employment to the company and following interviews with the person in charge of the company, a decision is taken regarding whether they will be employed or not. Up until 1997, there were even sudden requests for increases in personnel to be effective the following day. However, at the time when the author was carrying out his survey, conditions were entirely different from what they had been up until 1997. In August 1998, the first planned increase in personnel numbers in a long time was received and Company A set about recruitment activities. The whole matter was settled with one person of Japanese descent being taken along, interviewed by the company, hired and even having the area where he would be working decided there and then. However, this person's employment flowed on from changes to the parent company's schedule.

The examples given above show that as far as those who make use of service contracting companies are concerned their reason for using employment via service contracting companies is not solely in order to be able to cut workers easily. In short, as with this case of the planned personnel increases being out of synch with the parent company's employment plans, *the advantage of service contracting companies is to be found in their use in effecting flexible changes to employment plans in the face of unexpected circumstances.* When the recruitment has been done by one's own company the factory cannot easily turn around and carry out the withdrawal of its own workers, arguing that schedules are out of synch. Through their use of service contracting companies, client companies gain the ability to rearrange plans over and over again. Whether food companies or automobile related companies, modern workplaces are all seeking to assemble a labour composition that matches changes in production volumes. *Workers of Japanese descent, who actively take up work on worksites that the Japanese dislike and who, furthermore, are not averse to long working hours, contribute to factories by engaging in production and in its flip side – the changes that are required to its labour force. They also assume the role of absorbing even bigger changes in factories by being withdrawn from workplaces through dismissals.*

Conclusion

Service contractors respond to the demands of factories through the sorts of activities mentioned in this chapter. The forte of service contractors that emerges from this is a passive nature that starts up businesses simply by responding to demand from factories. The use of the term passive here indicates that they are not exercising their own independent decision making regarding choices about labour – that is, goods. This is seen in the fact that in the service contracting industry where labour is a good the employment of workers requires the client company's confirmation and also in the case of the dismissal of workers where it is the client company that draws up the list of workers to be dismissed. This gives rise to the dimension of the client company-workers relationship in which dismissals are carried out ruthlessly according to the demand being experienced by one's own company and without regard to the conditions in which workers find themselves. It is the consequences of this situation that bring about social problems such as those that have typically appeared in the housing complexes.

Naturally, we cannot make the service contractor from this chapter into the archetypal service contractor in housing complexes. Similarly, it is not necessarily the case that all areas in which workers who are employed via service contracting companies live experience the same conditions as these particular housing complexes. It is the expression of the unique character of an area, strikingly apparent in the case of Aichi prefecture, which gives rise to social problems such as one in which the employment of people of Japanese descent leads to a worsening of the living environment. Ōta City and Ōizumi Town in Gunma Prefecture and Hamamatsu City in Shizuoka Prefecture, which are all well known for having large numbers of people of Japanese descent, are not confronting this sort of problem. The explanation for why problems have not arisen on the outskirts of Hamamatsu despite it being the same sort of regional city while in Aichi Prefecture the issue of the employment of foreigners and the housing problem have become one, is largely to do with the management policies of the Nagoya Branch of the HUDC and the Prefectural Housing Supply Corporation. As Ikegami et al. point out, both the fact that Shizuoka Prefecture does not engage in corporate leases and also the application of strict conditions and the fundamental exclusion of foreign nationals when people take up residence in housing run by the prefecture and the city have a bearing on this; and, even in places like Hamamatsu where there are over 10,000 residents who are people of Japanese descent, one does not come across the ghettoization of people within a specific area (Ikegami 1998: 2).

The reasons for why the housing complexes fell into the state described in this chapter can be found in a particular set of conditions. However, as long as people of Japanese descent are being dispatched by service contracting companies, then the employment issue and housing problems will, to either a greater or lesser extent, end up being linked no matter what the area. Workers cannot rely on the dormitories used by service contractors for a place to live. When indirectly employed workers on short term contracts are reliant on the employer for a place to live this means that there is inevitably a systematised turnover of the individuals living in a given place of residence. These individual residents are workers. These workers, just like Japanese fixed term contract workers and seasonal workers, are external to the company are also made to transfer from one particular company to another at the convenience of the company to which they have been dispatched. This is why service contractors obtain residences near factories. There are even companies in the ranks of service contractors that belong to the Company Liaison Committee despite having merely one employee from their company in the housing complexes. The proprietor of this particular company told the author that he was participating in the survey because he felt that given that service contractors cannot carry out their business activities without access to worker residences, the problems that are occurring in the housing complexes are problems that could occur anywhere and therefore he hoped to be able to get hold of a manual in readiness for when the same sort of problems occur in another area. Thus, the example of the housing complexes dealt with in this chapter may be an extreme example, but it occupies an important position as one test case concerning foreign workers.

Part III
The Divisions Between the Economic System and Legal Society Concerning Transnational Persons

Part III

10 An integrated migrant worker industry: changes in travel agencies and capital accumulation in Japanese-descent communities in Brazil

Introduction

It has been roughly thirty years since the employment of people of Japanese descent began in Japan. In the sending country, Brazil, the employment of people from Brazil in Japan in the 1980s led to discussions about domestic law, while in the receiving country, Japan, employment of these people was illegal before the 1990 revision of the Immigration Control Act. In the space of the thirty years from this stage until 2007 (the time of writing), it has been local travel agencies in Brazil, run by people of Japanese descent, that have consistently functioned as the body gathering together workers to go to Japan. Previously, Piore has shown that studies of institutions can explain why immigrants who travelled to the Americas from the nineteenth to the twentieth centuries live in the particular areas concerned (Piore 1979). Portes has further commented that by using the push-pull theory we can explain no more than the flow of immigrants who are already present and that it is only studies of institutions that enable us to discuss the formative process behind the flow of immigrants in the initial stages (Portes 1982).

In the case of the labour force of Japanese descent, it is travel agencies for migrant workers and service contracting businesses that correspond to the institutions mentioned by these authors. This is because the specific labour market for people of Japanese descent is formed in a manner that transcends national borders via organic ties between recruiting organisations overseas, centred mainly on travel agencies run by people of Japanese descent, and the points of production within Japan. This chapter will elucidate the nature of the formative process behind the flow of immigrants making up the labour force of people of Japanese descent by clarifying the process by which the structure linking travel agencies run by people of Japanese descent and service contracting businesses are formed. While doing this, the chapter will also examine the kind of structure that was formed as a system for transcending national borders in the year 2004. Following this, there will be a discussion ranging from the systemic changes currently underway to the future directions for migrant work.

Labour markets that transcend national borders as institutions: links between travel agencies run by people of Japanese descent and service contracting businesses

No sooner had travel agencies run by people of Japanese descent begun gathering together people than a migrant work boom erupted in the societies where they lived. In the era of migrant workers (loser migrant workers), those travelling had to find their own places of employment and prepare the documents needed for getting a visa.[1] The development of travel agencies for migrant work lowered the hurdles for working in Japan. This was because people wishing to work in Japan could, simply by communicating their intention to do this to the travel agencies, entrust the troublesome business of gathering documents and visa formalities, and even finding a place of employment, to the travel agencies.

Particularly in the period of the bubble economy, automobile manufacturers, their subcontracting automobile body manufacturers, electrical appliance manufactures and others directly carried out recruitment information sessions for workers in the major cities of Latin America. Local newspapers for people of Japanese descent reported on the influence of these job offers in Japan on Latin America, thus leading to a situation in which information about places of employment in Japan became directly available to people hoping to engage in migrant work[2] (Mori 1993; Del Castillo 1999).

Around the initial period of the migrant worker phenomenon, it was not unusual for manufacturers to develop direct recruiting activities in Latin America, but this practically disappeared following the collapse of the bubble.[3] The process of the development of a bubble economy in Japan, led to a change in recruitment activities

*Figure 10.1: Conceptual map of the efficacy of expanded announce-
ments*

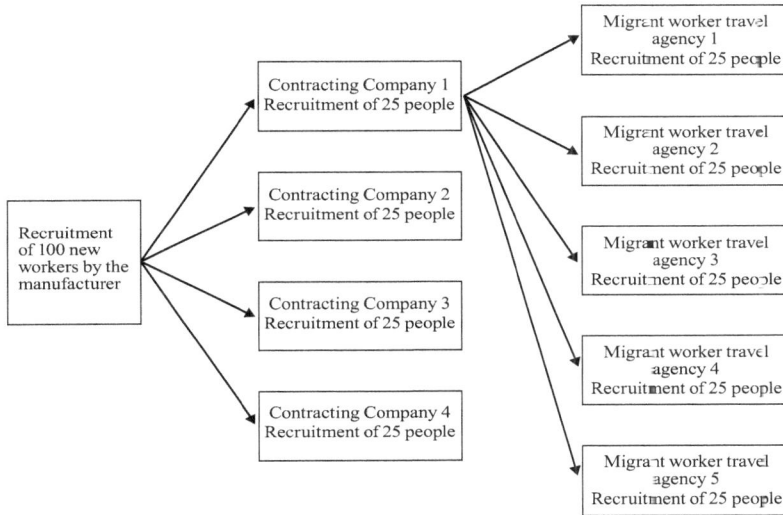

there towards a structure which had service contracting companies
at its heart. This change led to an expansion in the information
concerning migrant work and the effectiveness of announcements.

Let us now take a more detailed look at the effectiveness of announcements underpinned by increased information about migrant
work. When manufacturers directly carried out their own recruitment activities in Latin America, they held employment information
sessions with the cooperation of travel agencies with whom they
had links, and also interviews in which they explained details of the
work to the people who had come along hoping to go to Japan as
migrant workers. Those people who were successful in the interview
could take care of the formalities for the voyage, including paying
for the travel agency and their airline tickets, on the spot. Under
this arrangement the recruitment of, for example, 100 people by
a manufacturer would be circulated by its business partner travel
agency as a job advertisement for work in Japan for 100 people.

Meanwhile, when a manufacturer needs to recruit 100 people,
there are normally numerous independent service contractors that
send them a labour force. If we assume that four service contracting

companies send twenty five people each, these four companies will, at the same time as recruiting within Japan, also convey the existence of twenty five job vacancies to the migrant worker travel agency in Latin America with whom they have a business arrangement. Since independent service contractors generally have business arrangements with from five to ten migrant worker travel agencies, a minimum of twenty of these agencies (four independent contractors by five migrant worker travel agencies) set about distributing recruitment advertisements and recruiting people in Latin America. Consequently, what starts off as only a case of recruiting 100 people ends up seeing the release of advertisements for the recruitment of 500 people, as even if the twenty companies send out only one recruitment advertisement each, this amounts to twenty advertisements for twenty five people. In reality, there are independent service contractors who have arrangements with more than five migrant worker travel agencies, and these agencies also post their recruitment advertisements in several forms of media, therefore, job vacancies for 100 people will be conveyed to Latin America as more than 500 job vacancies. This is what the author means by the effectiveness of expanded announcements (Figure 10.1).[4]

Increases in the number of travel agencies run by people of Japanese descent which have given rise to the effectiveness of expanded announcements, also led to specialisation amongst travel agencies. At the same time as the change in arrangements, in 1997, in which the Japanese Consulate in São Paolo became the only office issuing visas in Brazil, the Consulate also began ranking travel agencies as A, B or C. This led to the development of a situation in which, even if one's airline ticket and the necessary documents were all in order, unless the travel agency was ranked at B or higher, restrictions were placed on the visa that was issued. This was an actual shutting out of migrant worker travel agencies, but C rank agencies attempted to survive by entrusting the Consulate formalities to A and B rank travel agencies. At the same time, this division into ranks led to a systematisation of the travel industry with A and B rank travel agencies at its core. A and B rank travel agencies were able to increase the number of ticket sales that they handled in their own companies through wholesale sales of airline tickets to affiliated C rank agencies. This rise in the volume of ticket sales increased the agencies' bargaining power with the airline companies, and, in addition to a guaranteed volume of ticket sales, it brought with it the ability to procure cheaper airline tickets.

In 2003, in opposition to these large travel agencies (A and B rank), C rank migrant worker travel agencies established the Brazilian Association of Nikkei Tourist Agencies (*Associasção Brasileira das Agencias Nikkeys de Turismo*), and succeeded in setting up an alternative for ticket sales. Their bargaining power in relation to airline tickets had, until that time, relied on the volume of tickets handled by the parent travel agency. The parent travel agency, in order to increase its own bargaining power, would determine the airline company that would exclusively sell tickets to each travel agency. However, the price of tickets was largely influenced by whether or not cheap tickets were sometimes released as a result of the management policies of individual airline companies rather than by the volume of sales. From the standpoint of migrant worker travel agencies, it was desirable to be able to make use of these much cheaper airline tickets at these points in time. Having their own price competitiveness managed on the basis of which airline company's tickets the parent company sourced at wholesale prices was an unfavourable outcome in terms of management strategy. This is why the Brazilian Association of Nikkei Tourist Agencies negotiated with airline companies to make the price of airline tickets to Japan identical. Whether one travelled with JAL, VARIG or KAL, the fee would now be the same. As far as the airline companies were concerned, this was also a favourable request as it meant that they could avoid the trap of price discounting competition with other companies. The Brazilian Association of Nikkei Tourist Agencies still manages to just exist at the time of writing (2007), but its influence has almost entirely disappeared. However, as a result of this association's actions a system of uniform airline ticket prices was established, and in 2007 uniform airline ticket prices were available even for travel agencies outside the association.

The travel agencies that have thrived through migrant work in the midst of the fixing of airline ticket prices are those of the management type known locally as *asesoria* (consultancies). Whilst leaving the details to the following section, let us take an extremely brief look at *asesoria*. Since traditional travel agencies gather together people hoping to work in Japan on the basis of requests received from the service contracting companies with whom they are affiliated, these people receive briefings, before leaving for Japan, on the region in which the factory to which they are going is located and on the type of work in which they will be employed. In contrast to this, *asesoria* do not have business partnerships with only specific service contracting companies or companies from specific industries. Their business consists of sending people who wish to work in Japan to those people who supply a labour force to the service contracting industry, which in turn supplies the independent service contractors within Japan. For this reason, *asesoria* send people who wish to work in Japan to labour suppliers in the service contracting industry even if there are no jobs at that particular point in time.[5] From the viewpoint of migrant worker travel agencies also, using *asesoria*, enables them to link their customers to employment in Japan on occasions when they are unexpectedly unable to satisfy requests from clients, or at points in time when there are no requests from clients. In addition to the formation of a group of travel agents, integrated under the umbrella of wholesale tickets, this function has led to the emergence, in recent years, of a group structure with *asesoria* at its core.

A system under ongoing modification: networks, markets and *asesoria*

This section will treat the structure which collects people in Brazil who want to work in Japan and then dispatches them as one system, and will also consider modifications to this system on the basis of the three opportunities: 'networks,' 'markets' and '*asesoria*.' As has already been argued, the fact that travel agencies run by people of Japanese descent and organisations of people from the same prefecture are intimately linked was a necessary prerequisite for the feeding into Japan of the large volumes of people arriving for work. The reason for this is because tangible recruitment activities occur via networks of personal connections; and, the more that this network becomes systematised, the better it is able to gather people from all over Brazil. In this sense, it could be said that the travel agency market place always mobilises its networks, and that it has evolved in a form that includes networks within the market place.

It was in 1997 that these relationships between networks and markets began to crumble. The changes that occurred in this year are not limited to the previously mentioned concentration of the function of issuing visas solely in the consulate in São Paolo and the ranking of travel agencies. Despite the fact that Brazilians of Japanese descent travelled to Japan with the intention of working, a considerable number went to Japan on short term (tourist) visas, and then, one after another, they modified their status to resident visas. Although the issuing of visas is supposed to be a policy control measure that occurs upon entering a country at the time of arrival, the fact that this had turned into a dead letter became a problem. From this point onwards, it became compulsory for Brazilians of Japanese descent to acquire a resident visa at the time of arrival in Japan. What is being raised as a problem here is not the fact that resident visas have become required, but the very term of validity of resident visas. Resident visas are visas that are issued for periods of one or three years, but traditional resident visas were largely issued for a one year period. Most people on a one year visa who have gone to Japan to work and then temporarily returned to their own country (this is even if they have renewed their visa in Japan), and who then want to go back to work must once again acquire a resident visa. In order to acquire a resident visa, one must have already decided on a place of employment, therefore, people attempting to travel to Japan once again had to make arrangements for the voyage on the basis of having secured a place of work at a migrant worker travel agency. This led to the new situation of the issuing of three year visas (this means that even renewals in Japan were issued for three years). At this very moment, the travel industry reached a turning point. This was because people who had returned temporarily to their own countries now came back to Japan on immigration re-entry permits, therefore, the need to re-acquire a visa at the time of return to Japan disappeared. Alongside this, there was also no longer the need to have a predetermined place of work at the time of the repeat voyage. Repeat travellers were able to go to Japan just with the purchase of an airline ticket.

In the past, the author has also interpreted the increased numbers of repeat travellers and of families setting off to do migrant work, as well as the rise in individuals experiencing migrant work as having made it possible for them to travel to Japan without relying on the migrant worker travel agency industry (Tanno 2001b). When, however, one pays attention to the nature of *asesoria*, it must be admitted that this is a mistaken evaluation of the situation. *Asesoria* dispatch people wanting to work in Japan to that country before any specific place of work has been decided for them. What makes this type of transcending of national borders possible is the fact that the *asesoria* market targets people who already hold a visa. On this point, it could be said that *asesoria* came into existence with the amendments to the policy concerning visas.

Incidentally, it is having a partner who supplies labour to independent service contractors in Japan that makes it possible to dispatch these workers to Japan before any place of work has been found for them. The author has interviewed someone in Hamamatsu who supplies labour to independent service contractors. His work throughout the day entailed sending off faxes of lists of workers who were engaged on a standby basis by independent service contractors all over Japan. This contractor's business consists of sending off the number of workers specified by independent service contractors, from amongst those on the faxed lists, to each of the contractors concerned. 'I dispatch to 600 companies. It is not possible to get through everyone on the lists in a day. Even if each company were to ask for one worker to be dispatched, I would need 600 workers a month. As there are so many people on standby, this doesn't present any difficulties.'[6]

Asesoria are also beginning to cause large-scale changes in recruiting. Recruitment notices in media such as newspapers and magazines have been declining rapidly in the 2000s. When the author conducted his first survey in Brazil in 1997, the telephone numbers used for calling people to request interviews came from glancing at the recruitment notices in the media. By November 2004, the number of companies that could be contacted via this method were no more than approximately thirty (in August 2007, there was a slight increase with it becoming possible to confirm the location of and carry out interviews with about forty companies). In those days, there were also many migrant worker travel agencies that had no need even to place advertisements, but who collected people hoping to go to Japan to work by displaying a large sign. This was confined to a small number of places around Liberdade Station. The efficacy of the expanded announcement of advertisements was drastically reduced, with the result that migrant work became invisible in the cities. However, this does not indicate that migrant worker travel agencies have disappeared. There are fourteen offices in the Pencil Building at 32X Gloria Street. Eleven of these are migrant worker travel agencies. It is unlikely that anyone would notice that migrant worker travel agencies are concentrated in this building which has no signboard or any other indication. There is, however, an endless stream of people hoping to go to Japan to work coming to the building. The location of migrant worker travel agencies has in part become the tacit knowledge of the community of Japanese descent, and the need for recruitment notices has now been severely curtailed.

There is no guarantee of speedily finding work if one turns up in Japan as an individual with only an airline ticket, without having gone through a migrant worker travel agency or an *asesoria*. Even while people say things such as 'there are only repeat travellers,' 'people heading off for migrant work for the first time are nowhere to be found' and 'migrant worker travel agencies are already a thing of the past,' migrant worker travel agencies are not disappearing. No matter how much the numbers of repeat travellers increase, and even if at a glance the numbers travelling to Japan with just an airline ticket appear to be on the rise, these are no more than superficial changes. Instead, this merely shows the changed appearance of the state of the links between migrant worker travel agencies and service contracting companies; individuals continue, as usual, to be deployed to points of production having first passed through one of these two organisations.

Continually evolving migrant worker travel agencies: the birth of an integrated migrant work industry

With the appearance of the new intermediary organisations known as *asesoria*, migrant worker travel agencies are also being compelled to make significant changes to their management form. Let us examine the modifications undergone by Company A, a well-established migrant worker travel agency known as Brazil's migrant work champion. The author has continued to accumulate continuous interviews with the siblings who manage the company and their families as well as with leading employees in the eight years that have passed since the initial interviews with Company A in 1997. In this section, an examination of the changes that Company has undergone in this period will provide the main basis for considering changes in migrant work.

Company A's headquarters are located in Vila Carrão, where large numbers of Brazilians of Okinawan descent live, and it has branches in Liberdade as well as in the Tsurumi district of

Yokohama. Another three migrant worker travel agencies, apart from Company A, have their head offices in Vila Carrão, and these are all operated by someone who has re-emigrated from Bolivia.[7] Company A was a late entrant as a travel agency amongst Bolivian travel agencies, but the first to get involved in migrant work. Company A dispatched its first workers to Japan between 1983 and 1984. The person who showed Company A that migrant work could be a business was Mr M., the eldest son of Mr N., an influential member of *Colonia Okinawa* in Bolivia. Mr M. decided to go to Japan to work for a year, partly because he was thinking of getting married and needed money, and partly on his father's recommendation.[8] When he was about to leave Japan, after having worked as a fixed term contract worker for a year, the factory for which he had been working said, 'we would like you to gather together people in Latin America who might want to come to Japan for work.' He reasoned that if he was going to assemble people wanting to work in Japan, then rather than assembling them in his birthplace of Bolivia, this would be easier to do in Brazil with its far larger population of people of Japanese descent. He asked his old friends, the brothers who owned Company A, for help with recruiting activities.[9]

Even Company A, the pioneer in migrant worker travel agencies, faced hardships in recruiting people who wanted to work in Japan up until the end of 1984. The first two rounds of trying to assemble people hoping to work in Japan were particularly difficult; no one trusted them even when they said 'You can earn money if you go to Japan.' The situation changed in 1985. When the first batch of people to be recruited returned to Brazil and began buying houses and cars, the word spread like wildfire that 'migrant work was profitable,' and then the company no longer needed to place advertisements. Company A's business partner at the outset was the service contracting business that we will look at in the following section, Company B. Company B was the very first in the service contracting industry to make a success of bringing in workers of Japanese descent; and, in 2005, it could proudly claim to be the service contracting company that was dispatching the largest number of foreign workers in Japan. Company A started off helping out Company B, and then along the way built up its business as Company B's agent. However, following Company B's exposure in Japan for breaches of the *Immigration Control Act*, Company A was also exposed for breaching the same act.

Company A treated this exposure as an opportunity to sever its ties with Company B. Another reason for this move was that Company A's business had started to undergo rapid change at this time. At the end of the 1980s, Company A began to think about immersing itself totally in the migrant work business. The majority of migrant worker travel agencies were set up to offer services to people hoping to work in Japan: in other words, seeing to preparations regarding airline tickets to Japan and positions of work. Company A, however, was not thinking of limiting its migrant work business to just these stages. People returning home after having worked in Japan would bring the fruits of their labours, their savings, with them. Hence, Company A thought that it would be able to develop businesses aimed at returnees. Accordingly, Company A established a real estate division within its own company, and began acting as agents for returnees buying homes or farmland. This is why Company A no longer needed to rely on the specific business connections that Company B had provided.[10]

When its real estate division began to show increased profits, Company A split up the company, turning this division into a subsidiary company. This was because it had become too big to operate as a part of the travel company. However, from around the middle of the 1990s, business suddenly stagnated for this real estate subsidiary. This was because repeat voyages by migrant workers had begun. People who had purchased houses as the outcome of their first experience of migrant work, did not look to real estate with the savings from their second period of migrant work. Furthermore, in this same period, Brazilian banks set up branches in cities such as Tokyo, Hamamatsu and Nagoya, where there were large numbers of Brazilians. At the time when Brazilian banks had not had any branches in Japan, migrant workers used to take their savings home in cash when they returned to Brazil. It was precisely because they returned with a large sum of money all at once that they made large purchases. When it was possible to establish Brazilian banks in Japan, the style of savings and remittances was completely transformed. Once they had set up bank accounts at a Japanese branch, by handing over one of the cards attached to that account to family back in Brazil, family members could withdraw cash when they needed it, either in Brazil or in Japan. There was no longer any need to face the risks of carrying large sums of money. This brought about a change in the spending behaviour of migrant workers away from a consumption style that made large purchases towards a style that increased daily lifestyle expenditure. The result has been that even people who still do not own any real estate have disappeared from the targets of real estate businesses.

When these changes in consumption by migrant workers became apparent, Company A curtailed its real estate business and returned once again to its original concerns, shifting its emphasis to its migrant worker business. This was why it now set up a separate migrant work referral business. The head office of Company A only sold airline tickets while its subsidiary Company AS, operated a migrant worker travel agency which included work referrals. However, Company A's curtailment of its real estate subsidiary at this time did not signal that it had abandoned business aimed at returnees. Although the previous type of consumption behaviour in which large sums of money were spent all at once had ceased, as long as there are people who go to Japan to work in order to earn money returnees, or their families left behind in Brazil, will transfer the fruits of work in Japan into some form or other of consumer activity. Company A reasoned that as long as it kept pace with change, there were still plenty of businesses for it to establish.

These newly opened businesses can be seen as the historical evolution of developments in Company A's business and also of Vila Carrão's businesses for Okinawans of Bolivian descent. Vila Carrão's Okinawans have got through the various periods that have come and gone by collecting together in one business as a single group. Beginning as stallholders (mainly selling *pastel* (a fast food snack)) at roadside and open air markets (*feiras livres*) in the 1960s, they moved into sewing businesses in the 1970s, the distribution of building materials and the management of supermarkets in the 1980s, and then the travel business from the latter half of the 1980s. Bolivian immigrants, with their shared experience of reclaiming the jungle in *Colonia Okinawa* after having been sent to Bolivia from Okinawa under the Occupation, did not hide within their own group as they succeeded at their self-run businesses; they taught each other their business know-how. This has resulted in Carrão's Okinawans of Bolivian descent having continued to gradually accumulate capital and then move into larger businesses (Mori 1998 and Mori 2001).

Company A has also engaged in a variety of businesses: laundries; supermarkets; luncheonettes; and building materials supply.

It has now sold off its laundries, supermarkets and luncheonettes, but one of the proprietor's sons has taken over the building materials supply business. There are also relatives who run a number of independent businesses and groups of friends who have lent each other a hand since their time in Bolivia. Company A zeroed in on this. It was precisely as a result of their former shared experiences that they helped one another and revealed their true intentions to each other. Company A decided to teach, for a fee, the management know-how required to start up a business to those people on the outside who lacked this set of shared experiences. Even if someone who has earned some capital through migrant work thinks of starting up a business, if that person has no previous business experience or no experience in the type of industry in which he had hoped to start a business, the undertaking is not possible. Accordingly, Company A offers advice and sends those that it advises to its acquaintances and friends who have made a success of the type of business that they hope to enter; giving them the opportunity of three to six months of On the Job Training (OJT). During this time, clients gain on site knowledge of matters such as laying in stock and how to provide service to customers, and once their OJT is over they can confirm whether or not they still have the desire to set up a business. It is understood that based on their experience up to this point, about two thirds of those being advised realise the severity of running one's own business and abandon their plans to start a business. Company A continues to provide management support to those who persist to the end, for roughly two years from the time that they start their business. This represents a move into the consultancy business. It is not possible to make a profit just from the consultancy business as it sees low levels of sales due to the management support given during the start-up period. Therefore, it does not only engage in management support: its subsidiary real estate company introduces its stores; and companies related to the son's building supply business subcontract store renovation work thus building a structure in which development occurs as one business with links between connected divisions.

Company A is still an integrated migrant labour business.[11] Migrant work is a travel package in which the airline ticket and place of work come as a set. The business of migrant worker travel agencies is fundamentally to sell this migrant worker travel package. However, Company A has become a structure that makes large sums of money not only from the areas dealing with the departure of migrant workers, but also from the travel package area by making services to returning migrant workers a pillar of their business. Generally, travel agencies of Okinawan descent have high cost travel packages. Compared to the standard migrant worker travel agency airline ticket and work place sets which are available for 2,400 dollars, these cost from 2,800 to 2,900 dollars at Company A. These are disadvantageous prices in terms of price competitiveness, but people who use Company A agree to the prices because they anticipate having access to services after they return from Japan. For this reason, Company A has succeeded in securing its own niche market, without being drawn into competition with other migrant worker travel agencies.

The present for classic migrant worker travel agencies: the dominance of Japanese service contracting businesses and the demise of migrant worker travel agencies

What has become of the classic migrant worker travel agencies that sell airline tickets and employment in Japan as a set? This discussion excludes Okinawan-type travel agencies being run by Okinawans. Compared to Okinawan travel agencies which have a lot of repeat customers, general migrant worker travel agencies run by people from the mainland have failed to turn their customers into repeat customers. Becoming repeat customers is used here in the sense of getting customers who have used one's company to go to Japan to work (migrant work) on one occasion, to use it when they once again return to Japan.

Whilst migrant worker travel agencies compete with one another, they have formed a group for mutually accommodating people wanting to work in Japan but who are a mismatch for a particular company. This section will consider the labour recruitment system, with a focus on Company B. As mentioned previously, Company B is the largest service contracting business in Japan employing people of Japanese descent; at its peak, the company boasts figures of having dispatched a labour force of 6,500 people, and, in 2005, this number was still around 5,000. It has business dealings with approximately 230 companies. Even if all of its clients were to have only one vacancy it would need 230 new workers per month. In 1984, Company B set up Company C in São Paolo, and began recruiting labour locally in Brazil. By the time of the November 2004 survey, it had extended its operations and was dispatching 30,000 people wanting to work in Japan. Meanwhile, because Company C is a local subsidiary carrying out recruitment activities for Company B, it cannot pursue profit as a standalone travel agency.[12] On this point, Company C cannot be considered as being in the same rank as general travel agencies run by people of Japanese descent.

Company B's recruitment system is an agency system. People who have come into their company are dispatched by their company, but as Company B is not able to gather the numbers of people that it needs via its own efforts, it has appointed ten travel agencies to act as its agents, and these gather people wanting to work in Japan for the company.[13] The cost, when people come straight into their company is 1,800 dollars, a cost that only includes about 1,400 dollars for the airline ticket; fees for assembling documents such as the fee for obtaining a visa; and a minimum charge for maintaining an office. In contrast to this, the ten agencies ask people wanting to work in Japan for between 2,400 and 2,600 dollars. Speaking solely from the point of view of price, going to Japan with Company C imposes a lower cost burden on those working in Japan, and Company C has an overwhelming price competitiveness in this one area. However, Company C does not actively advertise the fact that one can get to Japan for 1,800 dollars. Thinking purely in terms of gathering people, it would be a good idea to put out advertisements featuring the cost alone. However, this would make them entirely responsible for any risk. The cost of the airline ticket and employment package is paid for locally via a system known as *tatekae* (the advancing of money in expectation of later reimbursement). This is deducted from their wages at their places of employment, and is paid in five instalments by men and six instalments by women. The whole amount of the cost of travel expenses is paid to the migrant worker travel agency by the place of employment once this period of reimbursement of any monies advanced has ended. Should a worker flee during the period of reimbursement, the travel agency assumes the liability for the entire travel expenses. By getting its agencies to collect people wanting to work in Japan, Company B is able to make the agencies assume the burden of this risk. However, agencies do not go along with this unilateral taking on of risk by them. For this reason, Company C pays the agencies an incentive of 100,000 yen for each individual person wanting to work in Japan that they collect.[14] As a result, with the 100,000 yen from Company C, agencies made a profit for their businesses while charging people who wanted to work in Japan the usual migrant worker travel agency market price. In order to support this sort of structure, Company C (and its parent company, Company B) could not itself be a rival to its agencies; and for this reason, Company C made the portion of people who had once worked for Company B and were returning to Japan for a second time the exclusive market for their own company.

All ten agencies are in a state of collapse. None of these agencies can secure repeat travellers in their own companies. Whichever agency one approaches, the reply is the same, 'any relationship is just for the present. When they become repeat travellers and are ready to go again, they go with a different travel agent. The consumers choose so there is nothing to be done about it; I cannot have faith in any idea of travel agencies being able to get people to use them repeatedly.' As they cannot succeed in corralling the travellers who are their market, they are always in competition with other companies. They must make use of brokers, known as promoters, in order to assemble even one more person wanting to work in Japan than rival companies. The affiliates of Company C have dealings with twenty promoters in small agencies, and with 300 promoters in large travel agencies. At the stage of November 2004, each agency was handing promoters from 900 to 1,100 dollars for each person that they collected. Moreover, while the situation varies between agencies, the numbers of workers that can be assembled without recourse to a promoter is between five and thirty per cent of the figures achieved when promoters are used. All agencies are finding that they are unable to collect people to work in Japan without a promoter.

If the amount handed to promoters is around the 1,000 dollar mark, then, essentially, practically all of the 100,000 yen that agencies get from Company C ends up in the hands of promoters. Moreover, this price paid to promoters sometimes depends on the demand for labour. However, migrant worker travel agencies that are unable to corral people wanting to work in Japan (migrant workers), have no choice but to rely on promoters to collect the numbers required. Incidentally, each promoter does not have an exclusive contract with a specific travel agency. When a promoter has found someone wanting to work in Japan, they approach the numerous migrant worker travel agencies with whom they have dealings and end up handing this person over to the travel agency willing to pay the highest price. This is why promoters, in their relationship with migrant worker travel agencies, have considerable bargaining power as suppliers rather than subcontractors.

Considered from a business perspective, dealings with promoters do not necessarily lead to profits. We must not overlook the fact that the same type of logic is at work here as that used by the parent company, Company C, when it utilises migrant worker travel agencies. When migrant workers who were introduced by promoters flee from their workplaces during the period of reimbursement for monies advanced, the migrant worker travel agencies charge promoters for the travel costs that had been advanced. Cases of flight, during the period of reimbursement for monies advanced, by people wanting to work in Japan, who are increasingly made up of workers on repeat trips, are increasing to such an extent that mechanisms for avoiding this risk are needed. However, as mentioned previously, the use of promoters is a relationship in which there is a trade off against one's own profits; and, the more use migrant worker travel agencies make of promoters, the more inevitable it is that they are reducing their profits. In this way, migrant worker travel agencies that are unable to secure the services of repeat workers who would use them two or three times, are all drawn into a war of attrition.

September the eleventh and migrant work

The airline terror of September the eleventh also had a considerable impact on migrant work. This is because the United States government now requires a visa (transit visa) even for transit passengers who are only passing through the USA. The appearance of transit visas ended up leaving migrant worker travel agencies facing two options. The first was to use flights that do not pass through the USA. However, this option inevitably led to higher prices as the flight time increased. Secondly, the people wanting to work in Japan who are dispatched by one's own company end up being only those who hold re-entry permits. Transit visas are, as the name suggests, issued to transit passengers who must already possess an onward ticket to their destinations. Now, when people attempt to gain a residence visa, this is issued to them within three to four weeks of having applied to the Japanese Consulate, and then having received their residence visa, they must apply for a transit visa. It takes about a week for a transit visa to be issued, but one needs to allow one month at the very least for the whole process.

Job vacancies in Brazil are in competitive relations with job vacancies within Japan. Even once it has been decided that workers will be sent from Brazil, it is not unusual for other workers to have been sourced from within Japan before the foreign workers concerned actually arrive in Japan, and for the latter to have no choice but to work in a different type of industry from the one they had been told about before having been dispatched from Brazil.[15] In an attempt to avoid this happening, all of the travel agency demand has shifted to indirect flights; that is, those that do not go via the United States. As of November 2004, the vast majority of migrant worker travel agencies used Air Canada, and in cases when Air Canada flights were full, priority then passed to European carriers. Using Air Canada led to an increase in the flying time and also to a price increase in the airline ticket of around 100 dollars. However, this represented practically no difference at all from the cost of a direct flight given that obtaining a transit visa via a travel agency would cost around 100 dollars. In addition, since the Brazilian Association of travel agencies of Japanese descent had set an agreed price for only airline tickets on direct flights, price competition emerged for indirect flights. Travel agencies able to buy airline tickets at a cheaper price than other companies could expand their profits. Furthermore, making it possible for employment in Japan to begin as soon as possible also led to the perception of improved customer service.

This is how September the eleventh has come to have a significant influence on migrant work by people of Japanese descent. The scene at Guarulhos International Airport has undergone a complete change as a result of the change to indirect flights in the travel routes that had previously been concentrated on direct flights to the United States. In the 1990s, every day at nine in the evening, in Terminal Two, there would be queues that were more than five hundred metres long of people waiting to check in for the direct flights to Japan that were concentrated in the time slot from eleven at night until one in the morning. Each family would have four or five carts lined up in front of them. Each cart would be loaded up with five or six suitcases. This was unmistakably a swarm of people in search of an affluent society. These swarms of people disappeared from view at the airport. It was not that the numbers of people coming and going between Brazil and Japan had fallen. The reason for their invisibility was that as a result of the shift in demand to indirect flights, people travelling to Japan were no longer concentrated on late night flights but spread throughout various time slots.

A constantly changing system: understanding migrant worker travel agencies from a new institutional theory approach

The employment in Japan of people of Japanese descent from Latin America owes its existence to the authorisation of links between migrant worker travel agencies and service contracting businesses by legal and administrative institutions, such as the amendments to the Immigration Control Act and visa controls. For this very reason, changes to a variety of institutions have had an enormous impact on the labour market for workers of Japanese descent. The following section will examine migrant worker travel agencies from an institutional point of view.

In this chapter, the term institution is used along the lines proposed by Douglas C. North (North 2005). North firstly restricted the subject that was to be analysed using the term institution to 'the rules of the game' and clearly made a rigorous distinction between an institution and an organisation, seeing an organisation as a player within an institution, which represents the 'rules of the game' (North 2005; Chapter 5). This not only differs from the old institutional theorists such as Veblen and Commons who dealt with every possible tangible and intangible – for example, customs, value systems, norms, laws, social organisation and labour unions (Veblen [1899] 1961; Veblen [1904] 1965; Commons 1990; and John R. Commons 1995); it also differs from the new institutional theorists such as Ronald Coase and Oliver E. Williamson who carry out organisational analyses using transaction cost theory (Coase 1937; Coase 1960; Williamson 1975; and Williamson 1985).

North argues that what limits the behaviour of players, including organisations, is the institution, and that institutions are established out of the beliefs of each of the individuals who make up the players. In addition, he stresses the fact that individuals affect institutions through their belief that they can influence outcomes. However, North does not think that the links between these institutions, beliefs and individuals create a stable system. The reasons for this are that once a time axis is introduced into these relationships, there must be a constant reorganisation of the relationships between institutions, beliefs and individuals as a result of continuous changes in three factors. These factors are: 'changes in the quantity and quality of the population;' 'increases in the stock of necessary information regarding the environment;' and 'frameworks that motivate individuals with incentives.'

A summary, undertaken from this perspective, of the changes in travel agencies run by people of Japanese descent in Brazil would look as follows. First of all, there were 'changes in the framework providing incentives to individuals.' This was a change in the recognition framework regarding work in Japan, from 'loser migrant workers' to 'migrant workers heading for success.'[16] It was precisely the spread throughout the society of people of Japanese descent of the recognition framework, in which 'migrant work leading to success' was itself what provided the incentive, that led to working in Japan developing into a boom in which it was impossible to stem the flow of people. This situation led to changes in the formal rules. As pointed out by Commons, laws, by regulating 1) what can be owned as wealth, and 2) by what methods wealth must be obtained, end up determining those actions by people that can be brought about by revisions of the laws (Commons 1995; Chapter 2). If the issues dealt with by Commons are not viewed solely as legal issues but in terms of the issue of changes to formal rules, then we can say that the increased numbers of people re-entering the country and voyages in which only an airline ticket has been purchased, as well as the emergence of the new institution of *asesoria*, which resulted from consular changes to how visas are issued, are all a matter of course.

More than twenty years have already passed since migrant work began in the middle of the 1980s and, in this time, the experience and knowledge of individual migrant workers has also increased. However, it is the migrant worker travel agencies that have built up a store of experience and knowledge. This increase in experience and knowledge on the part of migrant worker travel agencies is evident in the collection methods employed by the ten agencies that Company B uses to recruit and in the way in which the labour force to be dispatched is collected via promoters for these ten agencies. This is the origin of the structure whereby subcontracting organisations are made to absorb the risk that the company as an organisation is unable to absorb. Similarly, subcontractors make sub-subcontracting organisations absorb risk in the same way. Structures for the management of risk are set up after the fact and according to a hierarchy (Williamson 1975 and Williamson 1985). This is not to treat the flight of people working in Japan as merely a probable event; structures for the management of risk are one institution that provides incentives to lower the very likelihood of these incidents by creating a structure that continues to be responsible even after the dispatching of workers. It could even be said to be an option that has abandoned controlling worker preferences.

Conversely, if it were possible to control worker preferences, different choices would surface. One suggestion for this state of affairs is Company A's tactics to secure repeat workers. By securing repeat workers Company A not only delineates its own market, but even controls its clients' preferences. Company A thus produces a virtuous circle – securing workers with a strong will to work → acceptance of expensive charges on the part of consumers → reduction of people fleeing → offering services upon their return home. The company makes it possible to secure a labour force with a strong will to work while simultaneously securing a sequence of sources of income. Neither institutions of the Company C type – that attempt to manage risk by abandoning client preferences and establishing a hierarchy – nor institutions of the Company A type – that do control client preferences – select workers from a reservoir of people wanting to work in Japan by means of an 'invisible hand;' both select workers using the 'visible hand' of risk management.

Naturally, the spread of recruitment activities that make use of promoters within migrant worker travel agencies does not simply represent institutionalisation that has accompanied an increase in knowledge on the part of travel agents. We also should not overlook, in this regard, the fact that changes are at work in the scale and quality of the potential migrant worker population. These changes include a decline in the labour force of people of Japanese descent in Latin America due to the increase in the numbers of people remaining in Japan, and a new generation of workers who, for example, are largely unable to speak Japanese. We can also conjecture that changes in the quality of this potential for hiring migrant workers are related to the changes to migrant work advertisements that were

discussed earlier in this chapter. This is because of the inevitability
of a decline in migrant work advertisements in newspapers for the
communities of people of Japanese descent once these are predom-
inantly made up of people who cannot read Japanese.

However, what needs to be appreciated through institutional
change is the transformation of Japanese descent communities
via changes in individuals and the changed appearance of migrant
worker travel agencies which reflect these changes in communities.
It is the change to an integrated migrant worker business on the
part of the Company A group that best exemplifies this changed
appearance of the community. The changes to the Company A group
show the changed appearance of the consumption propensities of
migrant workers returning home. The consumption of the fruits
of their overseas labour by migrant workers in their homeland of
Brazil is not a simple act of consumption. At the same time as being
consumption, it is also closely related to investment activities for
the purpose of asset formation. In this sense, Company A's shift,
from the real estate to the consulting business, in the core services
that it offered to people returning home does not merely indicate a
change in Company A's management strategy, but shows a change
in the very nature of capital accumulation by Brazil's community
of people of Japanese descent.

Conclusion: the endless migrant worker phenomenon

Migrant worker travel agencies have undergone considerable change.
Kōichi Mori evaluates migrant work saying, 'If the option to work
in Japan had not come up, Brazil's community of Japanese descent
would probably be in even further decline.' Migrant work is not in
any sense a problem that has been created by individuals. It is a
problem of the whole community of Japanese descent; and this is
why all of the local Japanese language newspapers that serve as community papers continue to carry stories about migrant work. While
continuing their constant broadcasting of the message by leaders of
associations of people from the same prefecture that 'migrant work
is leading to the hollowing out of the community, and the community
of people of Japanese descent is on the brink of a crisis that could
destroy it,' Japanese language newspapers ignore the fact that these
same leaders are profiting from migrant work-related businesses.

The same thing can be said about the changes to migrant worker travel agencies. Although migrant worker travel agencies are said to 'have become unprofitable,' in Liberdade alone more than 100 migrant worker travel agencies for people of Japanese descent, migrant worker travel agencies and migrant worker agents jostle with one another. Compared to the period, in 1990, when there were 230 migrant worker travel agencies just in Liberdade, this is a reduction, but if we look at the whole of the city of São Paolo, there are concentrations of migrant worker travel agencies in the area around Paulista Avenue, the location of the Japanese Consulate; Vila Carrão and Casa Verde, developed by the Okinawan community; and in the Aclimação district. There is no sense of a drastic reduction.

Contrary to the statement 'migrant work is also at an end now' the number of travel agencies has remained at a set level. Migrant worker travel agencies are implementing endless changes. Migrant work is not ending. When people who had previously been 'Japanese' immigrants stopped being Japanese, Brazilians of 'Japanese descent' came into being. Takashi Maeyama has undertaken a detailed analysis of the situation in which the various Shinto sects, which were the religion of people of Japanese descent, spread throughout the community as these people established themselves as Brazilian nationals (Maeyama 1997). What Maeyama saw as a problem was the fact that the Japanese immigrant community, made up of Japanese immigrants who had travelled to Latin America from Japan, still had no gravesites despite the passing of many generations in Latin America. These immigrants felt strongly that Japan was the place to which their spirits would return. In the 1950s, when, through the issues of winners and losers, they were compelled to choose the host society – continuing to live in Brazil – the Japanese immigrants realising that their spirits would continue to dwell in the host society, finally began to erect grave markers there, thus becoming Brazilians of 'Japanese descent.'[17]

The reason why migrant work will continue in some form or other is because the events taking place are the opposite of what Maeyama has described. No matter how much the period of work in Japan is extended, and even if there is no longer any need to lead a family life split between Brazil and Japan while not earning an income, migrant work will not disappear as long as the place to which one's spirit will return (its final resting place) is Brazil. Quite the contrary, if we take into account the reality that the accumulation of wealth in the Brazilian Japanese descent community is structured by means of employment in Japan, then migrant work will also continue to be seen as necessary to the continuance of the Brazilian Japanese descent community in future. Thus, as long as this structure persists, migrant worker travel agencies will continue to exist while making changes in the future to the contents of the services they offer as they respond to demand.

11 Socio-legal Study of Special Permission to Stay in Japan: Legal Foundations of Foreigners Living in Japan

Introduction

This chapter will examine the system of special permission to stay in Japan, in order to better understand the most fundamental issues in discussions about foreign residents in Japan. Special permission to stay in Japan is issued, pursuant to Article 50[1] of the Immigration Control and Refugee Recognition Act (hereafter referred to as the Immigration Control Act or the Act), to grant resident status to a foreign national illegally staying in Japan. In that legal status is granted to a person who fails to meet the requirements for residency laid down by law, the system is extremely similar to amnesties in European and North American countries. Whereas an amnesty legitimises the residency of migrants already residing in the country who meet a set of criteria, in the Japanese system applicants lodge a claim of eligibility and permission is granted after each claim has been individually assessed. In this respect, the Japanese system is not exactly the same as an amnesty. Furthermore, the Japanese government denies that the system is an amnesty policy. This standpoint is indicated in an item of *The Basic Plan for Immigration Control* Third Edition,[2] which says that, 'Japan has not adopted any amnesty policy which would encourage an inflow of new illegal foreign residents or an extension of illegal residency (*Shutsunyūkoku kanri hōrei kenkyū kai* (The Immigration Law Study Group) 2005: 171).' Concerned that the impression that Japan has adopted an amnesty policy would encourage more migrants to enter Japan and stay longer, the government insists that special permission is no amnesty.

Amnesty or not, special permission is definitely a hurdle which the most disadvantaged foreign residents, who lack resident status, must clear to come out of hiding. Examining the restrictions imposed on applicants for special permission affords an understanding of the minimum requirements for legitimate resident status laid down by the government. This chapter will dwell on one particular case as, having produced a landmark decision and consequently set a new precedent, it is of great significance in discussing the current system of special permission to stay in Japan. There will be a close examination of the arguments presented to the court – namely, the written request for a stay of execution of the forcible deportation order; the written opinion submitted by the Immigration Bureau regarding this request; the written opinion of the foreigner refuting the Immigration Bureau's opinion; and the ruling by the Tokyo District Court. In the course of scrutinising these documents, the very circumstances of the dispute will be the focus of the investigation.

The focus of attention will be the argumentation before the court. This is because the author holds the same view as Takeyoshi Kawashima that 'a court is a highly effective means of, and social system for, publicly recognising and supporting a struggle for a right' (Kawashima 1959: 147). The author also agrees with Kawashima's insight that a struggle over a right in court is 'a relationship between counter forces or an equilibrium maintained through opposition to each other. Equilibrium does not mean a static and peaceful relationship but, on the contrary, is the process of a struggle in which the balance is constantly lost as, in reality, the strength of a force changes and is promptly restored by its counter force' (Kawashima 1959: 146). The aim in this chapter is to bring to light how facts are acknowledged in the course of an actual struggle for a right.

In discussing the relationship of legal norms to law and order, Kawashima, furthermore, regarded legal norms or rules as law and order measures, and viewed the relationship as a social process. He also pointed out that the social process through which law and order are achieved could be construed as a process of 'social control.' Kawashima called this approach a social control model of law or, alternatively, a social structure model of law (Kawashima 1972: 328–329). The administration of immigration control has never been academically questioned from the perspective of social control. This actual case will provide a basis for looking beyond the court dispute itself and detecting the problems in Japan's immigration control policy, from the perspective of social control.

It should be noted that the decision by the Tokyo District Court on the case to be discussed in this chapter is an administrative ruling on a stay of execution; merely a part of the legal proceedings, not the final decision. The ruling is, however, worth looking at for three reasons. Firstly, it is significant that the court went out of its way to make a finding specifically on the possibility of the petitioner winning the case. It would have been sufficient for the court to have said that it could not find the case totally groundless, with regard to the requirements for a stay of execution. Secondly, through its consideration of the harshest outcome possible for foreigners living in Japan, the detention of illegal residents, the ruling revealed the government's view of foreigners and the intention behind its policies. Finally, special permission to stay in Japan was later granted after the district court decision. This extraordinary development provides important materials that are useful in the discussion of discretionary administration.

Data and methodology

In the course of conducting research on issues regarding foreign workers in Japan, the author has had the opportunity to make friends in the legal profession. Among these are numerous practising lawyers who mainly work on cases involving foreigners. They all complain about the same thing: when discussing issues of foreigners and immigration, scholars, including jurists, have only talked about immigration control policies and their legal ramifications. No one, they argue, has offered a discussion relevant to what has actually been going on in immigration control; and, to be more precise, no research that is useful to legal practitioners has been conducted. The author also often heard these friends lament the fact that Japanese scholars tended to speak a lot about the situation in other countries, such as Germany, France and the US, and then use this to cavil about the situation in Japan. The view of these lawyers was that although these discussions might be of some significance to academics, they were of no use in court. Their point was that arguments had to be presented based on our own Japanese laws and then discussed with a good understanding of current laws and precedents from past cases. Unless this occurred, they went on to say, we theorists would never be of any help to legal practitioners.

The author was lost for words when it came to responding to their critical observations.

Incidentally, the author had as an acquaintance a lawyer who had recently won a number of important precedents in cases involving foreigners. He was a senior student when the author was at post-graduate school. The author asked for the opportunity to look at the cases that he had been involved with. The lawyer accommodated this request and allowed the author to use one of the desks in his office. Conditions were imposed to protect personal information: these included 1) that the author was allowed to read freely case documents from which personal information had previously been erased and to make notes as long as these were hand-written; 2) that notes were checked each day and the author was prohibited from taking books of his notes out of the office until these had been filled to the last page of each book; 3) that the books filled with notes to their last page were checked again before the author took them out of the office; and 4) that if the author were to present a paper based on the information obtained at his office, the lawyer would read it beforehand.

Under these rules, the author read the records of cases. The lawyer and his staff also shared their knowledge of some important matters, including the implicit understandings that they had acquired through interviews with clients; this constituted tacit knowledge which was unrecorded but essential when reading the documents concerned. There were also briefings on major points of dispute in the actual court battle as well as on the expedient points of dispute. There were also explanations of the goal that they had set in the court battle; that is, their anticipated middle ground. The following discussion is based on the data collected via the above methodology.

Legal background to the current administrative practices of immigration control

This chapter will look into the 2001 *Gyō-ku 143* Case, (hereinafter referred to as this action), which concerned special permission to stay in Japan. The Tokyo District Court handed down such a landmark ruling that the full text was published in the *Hanrei Jihō* (Judicial Precedents News) (*Hanrei Jihō*, No. 1,771: 76–83). The ruling set a precedent for 1) granting a stay of execution of written deportation orders, including the detention component, and 2) finding that the issuance of a written deportation order is highly likely to be a wrongful abuse of discretionary power or a violation of proportionality even though there may be grounds for deportation. This precedent has been recognised by experts in constitutional law as one of the most remarkable decisions of recent times concerning the Administrative Case Litigation Act (hereinafter called the ACL Act) (Sasada 2002: 151). The case has become an important precedent that is often cited in court trials. Before going further into the case, let us first look at the matters which have had a prescriptive authority over the administrative procedures in immigration control.

Firstly, there are three vitally important court rulings to look at; namely, the Supreme Court decisions from 1957,[3] 1959[4] and 1978 on the case remembered as the MacLean Case. The Supreme Court decisions are said to have respectively confirmed 1) the discretion of the state over a foreign national's freedom of movement and entry to the country; 2) the complete discretion of the Minister of Justice over special permission to stay in Japan; and 3) the complete discretion of the Minster of Justice over the extension of a period of stay. An outline of the three cases follows.

In the 1957 case, Articles 3 and 12 of the Alien Registration Act were disputed in relation to Article 22 (Freedom of movement) of the Constitution. Although a concurring opinion – that freedom of movement in the Constitution was applicable to entering and leaving Japan – was appended by a minority of the bench, the ruling by the majority opinion held that,

> The provision of Article 22 guarantees no more than the freedom to choose and change one's residence and freedom to emigrate; it does not extend beyond this and, what is more, as the provision distinguishes the freedom to choose and change one's residence from that to move overseas, the former is, accordingly, clearly meant to be only applicable within the country.... In effect, Article 22 of the Constitution has no provision for entry to the country by a foreign national. This can be construed to be consistent with the international customary law that the relevant state can decide to reject entry of a foreign national at its discretion and has no obligation to approve entry of a foreign national unless there is a specific treaty that provides otherwise.

This ruling established the precedent that the state has complete discretion with respect to entry to Japan by a foreign national on grounds traceable to international customary law.

The 1959 Supreme Court decision concerned a case that was disputed as follows. A Korean male and a female Korean permanent resident of Japan became engaged prior to World War Two. The man entered Japan in August 1954 and lived in a de-facto relationship with the woman. Their child was born in March 1956. The couple could not officially marry under the particular circumstances of the diplomatic relations that prevailed between Japan and Korea at the time. They ran a shop selling rice crackers in Japan, and built up considerable assets and solid reputations. On the grounds that he based his livelihood in Japan, the man filed an action seeking special permission under the provisions of Article 50 of the Immigration Control Act. The court of first instance ruled that,

> The decision to permit or refuse a foreign national entry to, exit from and residency in the country is primarily at the discretion of the state. Where the Minister of Justice finds the objection filed against a special inquiry officer's decision groundless following investigation of the matter, it must be understood that the determination to grant special permission to stay in Japan or to declare the objection as groundless is left to the complete discretion of the minister [*Saikōsaibansho minji hanrei shū* (Collection of Supreme Court Decisions) (13 (12): p. 1,498).

Both the High Court and the Supreme Court upheld the lower court's decision, which is considered as having established the complete discretion of the Minister of Justice.

The MacLean case involved a foreign national, who came to Japan as an English language teacher in May 1968 with a visa that allowed him to stay in Japan for a year. In May the following year, he had his period of stay extended for 120 days, which he claimed he needed to prepare himself to leave the country. When he applied for another extension, the Japanese government did not grant it on the grounds of the applicant's political activities in Japan. The case was disputed in the courts before the Supreme Court found that,

> In deciding to permit or refuse an extension of the period of stay, the Minister of Justice must consider not only the propriety of the grounds given by the foreign national, but also his conduct as a whole during his stay, the domestic political, economic and social conditions in Japan, the world situation, diplomatic relations, the comity of nations and other circumstances, and make a right determination that best

fits the circumstances, from the standpoint of preserving the national interest. The goals of control over the immigration and residency of foreign nationals include maintenance of domestic security and good morals, preservation of insurance and health and stability of the labour market, which must be also taken into consideration. It is, in the nature of things, impossible to expect such decisions to be appropriate unless they are left to the discretion of the Minister of Justice, who has ultimate responsibility for the administration of immigration control.

Thus, the Supreme Court recognised the comprehensive discretion of the Minister of Justice, in a similar manner to the 1959 decision. From then on, these Supreme Court decisions were used in court disputes as a strong basis for recognition of the discretion of the Minister of Justice.[5]

In addition to judicial precedents, immigration control procedures are prescribed by departmental notifications issued by the head office of the Ministry of Justice to directors of its regional bureaus. The most important of these notifications are those issued respectively on 8 April, 1992 and on 1 August, 1996 regarding spouses of Japanese nationals (hereinafter referred together to as 'the notifications on spouses of Japanese nationals'); that issued on 30 July 1996 regarding long-term resident mothers and children (hereinafter referred to as 'the notification on mothers and children'); and that issued on 16 April 1999 which revised the notifications on spouses of Japanese nationals (hereinafter referred to as 'the direction on marriage'). The notifications on spouses of Japanese nationals announced that their status as the spouses of Japanese nationals made foreigners eligible to stay in Japan, and that a regional immigration bureau could determine to grant long-term resident status to such persons. The notification on mothers and children granted permission to stay to foreign national parents who are the breadwinners, even in cases where their own children have a Japanese parent, and held that, just as in the case of the notification on spouses of Japanese nationals, determinations could be made in regional immigration bureaus. The notification on marriage instructed that the applicant's period of residence in Japan be disregarded when considering cases of spouses of Japanese nationals.

What, by the way, is a departmental notification and what does it do? The following is the full text of the notification on long-term resident mothers and children. The direction MOJ Kanzai 2,565 was

issued on 30 July, 1996 to directors of regional immigration bureaus
and sub-bureaus from the head office of the Ministry of Justice.

*Notification regarding treatment foreign nationals supporting their
natural children where there is one Japanese parent*
The following procedures apply in regard to this issue. The director
of a regional immigration bureau will consider the various circumstances. If the director finds it appropriate to grant long-term resident
status, this is to be notified to the head office of the Ministry. This
office will then make a judgement on an individual basis, and only if it
finds that it is appropriate to grant this status, will the foreign national
parent be permitted to stay in Japan. However, further consideration
is deemed to be necessary in order to ensure that the minor, who is
the foreign national's natural child and has one Japanese parent, lives
a stable life in Japan. Accordingly, this directive requires that such
cases be treated as set out below, when an application for a change
of resident status is received from a foreign national supporting such
a dependent child.

You are also kindly requested to notify the directors of the branch
offices under your jurisdiction of this change.
1. Treatment of the application for a change of resident status by a
    foreign national parent supporting their natural children who have
    one Japanese parent
Regarding a foreign national parent, who is a minor and unmarried,
and supporting their natural child who has one Japanese parent (Note
1), a regional immigration bureau (or a branch office) may grant the
change of visa status to a long-term resident (one year) status if it
is found that the foreign national holds custody of the child and has
been raising the child for a significant period of time. Cases in which
the child has been raised outside Japan (including those in which the
child was born in Japan) and those in which the foreign national parent
having entered Japan, has been staying on a temporary visitor's visa,
should be forwarded to the head office of the Ministry, along with
those cases which are too difficult to determine at a regional bureau.

(Note 1) A natural child with one Japanese parent is defined as a
child whose father or mother has Japanese nationality at the time of
his/her birth, irrespective of whether or not the child is legitimate and
of whether or not the child has Japanese nationality. An illegitimate
child without Japanese nationality is required to be acknowledged by
his/her father of Japanese nationality.

(Note 2) To care for and raise a child is defined as supervision and protection of a minor by the holder of parental authority. The term is used in the same sense as Article 820 of the Civil Code which says, 'A person who exercises parental authority holds the right, and bears the duty, to care for and educate the child.' Where the foreign national parent is not capable of providing enough for the child but supplements livelihood with security payments, this will suffice if his/her caring for and raising of the child are confirmed as a fact.

2. Matters that require attention on application for and granting of a change of visa status

The applicant for a change of visa status should be advised to write in the 'reason' column that he/she requests long-term residency in order to live together with and support his/her natural child of Japanese parentage. At the same time, the applicant is to be asked to submit a letter of commitment that he/she will personally care for and raise the child.

On granting a change of visa status, the applicant should be advised that the change to long-term resident status has been granted because of the acknowledged necessity to support his/her natural child of Japanese parentage, and that on a future application for an extension of the period of stay, the renewal of the visa with long-term resident status may not be granted if the applicant is found not to be caring for and raising the child while he/she still needs to be cared for and raised. The fact that this advice has been given should be recorded.

3. Treatment of an application for an extension of the period of stay after the change of visa status

The long-term resident visa will not be renewed, in principle, for an applicant who has been granted the change of visa status pursuant to Section 1 if he/she is found not caring for or raising the child at the time of application while the child still needs to be cared for and raised.

4. Documents required

1) Documents to prove identity and civil status

a. Family register and certificate of residence to prove Japanese nationality

b. Certificate of birth of the child without Japanese nationality and family register with a record of the affiliation

c. Certificate of alien registration

2) Documents to prove that the applicant exercises parental authority

3) Documents relating to the raising of the child

    a. Materials relating to the child's schooling and childcare, such
    as certificates of school, childcare or nursery attendance
    b. Other certificates relating to the state of care for the child
   4) Certificate/s relating to the work and income of the person
    supporting the child
   5) Letter/s of reference from a guarantor/s residing in Japan

According to Hiroshi Shiono, 'a departmental notification provides
a point of reference that binds subordinate administrative offices.
However, its effect stops there; never being used as a norm by the
courts in relation to the general public. In that sense, a departmental
notification has no external effect (Shiono 2005a: 94). Basically, a
notification is issued by a higher section in the government to its sub-
ordinates, and it only binds the lower sections in the organisation.[6]
All of these notifications – those on spouses of Japanese nationals,
on mothers and children and on marriage – are no more than guide-
lines for administrative procedures at regional immigration bureaus.

    The Immigration Bureau has consistently failed to make most of
these notifications public. The notifications on spouses of Japanese
nationals were obtained through a personal channel by the author's
lawyer friend. The existence of the notification on marriage had not
been known until it was first mentioned in a reply, by then Prime
Minister Keizō Obuchi, to a question submitted with the help of
a Social Democratic Party member of the Diet when this same
lawyer was dealing with a relevant case. The notification on mothers
and children was the only exception, having been announced in
newspapers and other media at the time when it was instituted.
Unlike notifications regarding family registers, which are made
public in the *Koseki* (Family Register) magazine (published by
Teihan) and *Koseki Roppō* (Six Codes of the Family Register), those
relating to the administration of immigration control are announced
neither in the *Kokusai Jinryū* (International Exchange), published
by the Japan Immigration Association, or the *Nyūkan Roppō* (Six
Codes of Immigration Control). Although not all administration
based on departmental notifications is secretive, the administration
of immigration control is conducted in a significantly secretive way.
It is also worth noting that the notifications in relation to marriage,
namely those on spouses of Japanese nationals and the marriage
notification, have been abolished, the reasons for which will be
discussed later.

The current administrative procedures of immigration control are prescribed by the ghosts of judicial precedents set by the Supreme Court in the late 1950s. At the same time, the applicability of the Act varies according to the administrative body's internal documents, which, unlike laws and official notifications, are out of the sight of the public. This is the biggest problem in Japan's immigration policy. It is also the source of complaints by legal practitioners against academic researchers of law. Scholars may be good at studying publications and other readily available materials, which do not reach the reality of the immigration control policy of Japan. Nothing, however, affords better glimpses of this reality than a good grasp of documents which are not made public; namely, departmental notifications. Why? Because the administration of immigration control relies more on the unwritten sources of law such as customary law, case law and general principles of administration[7] than on what is provided for by the written law of the Immigration Control Act. With respect to customary law, we have already established that whether to grant entry to a foreigner and what rights to grant to one who has entered Japan rely on international common law.[8] With respect to case law, the author has confirmed that the rulings handed down by the Supreme Court in the late 1950s prescribe the administration of immigration control in the form of case law. Lastly, general principles of administration include the principle of administration by law, the principle of equal treatment (the principle of equality), the principle of police proportionality (the principle of proportionality), the administrative rules and the principle of good faith and sincerity. It is, in fact, these general principles of administration that will be the subject of dispute in following sections.

With this understanding of the background and principles that prescribe the administrative procedures of immigration control, let us now look at how the prescriptive forces work in concrete terms.

The circumstances of the legal action

This section will identify the points of dispute in the legal action by looking mainly at the facts found in the written motion of application for a stay of execution of deportation and the written opinion submitted by the Immigration Bureau in response to the application. The following section will be devoted to examining the view of the state in detail, which will reveal what is actually going on in respect of the administrative procedures of immigration control.

In keeping with Issue 1,771 of *Hanrei jihō*, the parties concerned in the case – a foreign national who filed the request for a stay of execution and his special permanent resident spouse – will hereafter be referred to in this chapter as A and B respectively. A entered Japan, through Narita, on 14 May, 1992 with a short term (15-day) visitor's visa, declaring that the reason for his trip was to visit friends and relatives, although his real purpose was to work in Japan to help support his family back home. Shortly after arriving, he began working for a construction company. He lost his job in the economic downturn, but found employment in another construction company (XX Industries). While employed by this company, he frequented a bar after work in Kanamachi, Katsushika Ward of Tokyo, where he met B, who was also a customer of the bar, in approximately March 1997. They began going out in June that year. In approximately September 1997, A moved out of his company's employees' dormitory to an apartment run by an acquaintance of B. At the same time, the two began to share their livelihood, using their combined income from A's employment as a construction worker and B's part-time job to support both of them and B's family (B's two immature[9] children). In December 1999, A and B registered their marriage at the Katsushika ward council office, and applied for new registration for A, based on Article 3, paragraph 1 of the Alien Registration Act. Out of consideration for the feelings of the children living with B, the couple decided that they would not co-habit until they had the children's understanding. A continued to live alone in the same apartment as before after they married.

On 6 January, 2000, A presented himself at the Tokyo Immigration Bureau Building No. 2 and reported his overstay. On 18 January, 2000 a letter from A was received by an immigration control officer at the Tokyo Bureau, who conducted an investigation into possible violations, and then entered A and B's statements into the records at the Tokyo Immigration Bureau Building No. 2 on 8 June 2000. Finding that there were reasonable grounds to believe that A fell under Article 24, Paragraph 4, Item (ii) (Overstay) of the Immigration Control Act, the officer had a written detention order issued by his supervising immigration inspector on 9 August. The order was enforced and A was transported to the immigration control officer on 11 August. On the same day, the supervising immigration inspector accorded provisional release on application from A. On that day and on 20 November of the same year, the inspector conducted an investigation into possible violations by A. On the latter occasion, he found that A fell under Article 24 paragraph 4 item (ii) (Overstay) of the Act and issued a written notice of the finding. A immediately requested a hearing pursuant to the provision of Article 48 paragraph 1 of the Act. A had admitted his overstay and expressed his desire to live in Japan with B and her children both in the investigation by the immigration control officer and in the examination by the supervising immigration inspector. In response to the request filed by A, a hearing was conducted in the presence of B on 20 April, 2001 by a special inquiry officer of the Tokyo Immigration Bureau, resulting in a decision that the finding of the immigration inspector was faultless, to which A immediately filed an objection.

In approximately May 2001, A and B started a business preparing and selling processed food, in the hope of opening a restaurant together in the future. The older child of B, who had accepted his mother's marriage to A, found a job and moved to accommodation provided by his employer. B's younger child had found it difficult to accept the marriage at first, but was beginning to open up to A. Out of consideration for the feelings of the children, A had stayed at the apartment mentioned earlier on the days when friends of the children visited their residence, before A, B and B's younger child began living together as a permanent arrangement in approximately June 2001.

On 8 August, 2001, the Minister of Justice made a determination that B's objection was without reason. A written deportation order was issued by the supervising immigration inspector on 13 August, 2001. A was promptly taken into the Immigration Bureau's detention facilities, leaving B having to carry out the food processing work which had been done by A as well as doing her part-time work and supporting her third son who was living with her. To visit A at the detention facility and have meetings with his lawyer to seek a stay of execution of the deportation order placed a heavy load on her. The loss of the main income earner made it difficult for the family to earn a livelihood, and B suffered from constant lack of sleep. On 1 November, 2001, A was moved to the Migrant Detention Facility Eastern Japan Management Centre. On 9 November, 2001, he filed an action with the Tokyo District Court against the Minister of Justice and the supervising immigration inspector of the Tokyo Immigration Bureau seeking rescission of the Minister's determination in this case and the revocation of the issuance of the deportation order by the inspector.

Questions raised by the plaintiff

The plaintiff raised the issue that the system, under Article 50, Paragraph 1 of the Act, grants special permission to stay in Japan under certain conditions, even if the Minister of Justice, in making the determination set forth in Article 49 Paragraph 3, finds that the filed objection is without reason. In contrast to the criteria under Article 50, Paragraph 1, Item (i) 'when a person has obtained permission for permanent residency' and Item (ii) of the same section 'when a person has had a registered domicile in Japan as a Japanese national in the past,' Item (iii), on the other hand, does not define any criteria, leaving room for the exercise of discretion by simply saying, 'If the Minister of Justice finds grounds, other than those in the previous items, to grant special permission to stay.'[10] In the actual administration of immigration control, however, discretionary decision-making has been substituted by perfunctory processing as prescribed by the departmental notifications, producing routine decision making. In order to produce decisions in a routine manner, there must be set criteria to work against. When regular applications for special permission to stay in Japan are considered, decisions are naturally based on whether the criteria has been met. A's representative argued that this case too must be judged against the same criteria. Next, the plaintiff's lawyer explored how the criteria were established.

He pointed out that the notifications issued respectively on 8 April, 1992 and 1 August, 1996 by the director general of the Immigration Bureau of the Ministry of Justice (the notifications on spouses of Japanese nationals) state that,

> Special permission to stay in Japan shall be granted to those suspected of illegal entry, landing and/or overstay if (1) the foreign national has been residing in Japan, whether legally or illegally, for three years or more; (2) this person is married to a Japanese national and the marriage is genuine and stable; (3) the foreign national concerned is applying for special permission to stay in Japan (in immigration control terminology: he/she has filed an objection, wishing to stay

in Japan); and (4) the foreign national meets both the requirements of wishing to stay in Japan and of having filed an objection. In cases where all of the above-mentioned criteria has been met, the determination to grant special permission to stay in Japan (the determination of the Minister of Justice) ends up being made solely by the director of the relevant regional immigration bureau.

An additional notification was issued by the director general of the Immigration Bureau on 16 April, 1999 under the heading 'Regarding delegating directors of district immigration offices to make determinations to grant the Minister of Justice's special cases permission in response to objections concerning landing or residency, filed pursuant to the Immigration Control and Refugee Recognition Act.' The notification says 'Unless the case is so important that it may have an impact on the political situation, diplomatic relations and/or public safety, if the foreign national is married to a Japanese national and the marriage is found to be genuine and stable, the director of a relevant district immigration office is delegated the authority to make the determination to grant special permission to stay in Japan in order to streamline the administrative process.' Further, the government announced its general policy principles in *the Basic Plan for Immigration Control 3rd edition* on 24 March, 2000, as follows.

Japan applies deportation procedures to illegal residents, as provided for in the Immigration Control Act, according to which the Minister of Justice may grant special permission to stay in Japan, on an individual basis, where the Minister finds grounds for giving such special permission.

Many foreign nationals granted this special permission have close relationships with Japanese nationals and others, and have actually built a foundation for various aspects of their future lives in Japan. In more concrete terms, one such example would be the case of a foreign national who is married to a Japanese national, and where they are in an actual marriage. This applies to a foreign national who has not committed any violation of laws other than the Immigration Control Act.

In determining whether to grant this special permission to stay, the Minister of Justice shall consider various aspects in each case comprehensively. These include: the reason for application for the special permission; the foreigner's family situation; living conditions; behaviour and other circumstances; the necessity for humanitarian consideration; and the potential impact on other illegal residents. Special permission to stay in Japan is granted, in principle, when it is found that the foreign national has a strong connection with the Japanese community and that a serious problem would arise, especially from the humanitarian point of view, if the said foreign national were to be deported. [...] As for an illegal resident who is recognised as having a civil status or position with a Japanese national, a permanent resident or a special permanent resident and who has strong connections with the Japanese community, appropriate measures shall continue to be taken in individual cases with humanitarian considerations.

The International Convention on Civil and Political Rights (hereafter referred to as the ICCPR) was also cited by the plaintiff's representative. Article 17, Paragraph 1 of the ICCPR says 'No one shall be subjected to arbitrary or unlawful interference with his privacy, family, home...' Article 23 of the convention says, in Paragraph 1, 'The family is the natural and fundamental group unit of society and is entitled to protection by society and the State,' and in Paragraph 2, 'The right of men and women of marriageable age to marry and to found a family shall be recognised.' Citing these provisions, A's representative argued that it would be more problematic not to grant his client special permission to stay in Japan than otherwise.

The plaintiff's lawyer also cited Article 25 paragraph 2 of the ACL Act to argue that his client's case met the requirements for a stay of execution of a deportation order. Paragraph 2 says, 'if there is an urgent necessity in order to avoid any serious damage that would be caused by the administrative disposition..., the court may, upon petition, by an order, stay the whole or part of the effect of the original administrative disposition, the execution of the original administrative disposition or the continuation of any subsequent procedure (hereafter referred to as "stay of execution".)' The plaintiff's representative further argued that, pursuant to the clause 'when there is an urgent necessity to avoid any serious damage that would result from being returned' (Article 25, Paragraph 2 of the Act), his client's case met the requirements for a stay of execution of deportation orders. Deportation orders, which, as mentioned earlier, are made up of a detention component and repatriation component, are executed as a whole. A's representative brought up the following points in relation to detention and repatriation. In relation to detention, 1) the Immigration Bureau expressed the view that detention became a humanitarian issue when it had lasted more than one year, and that a temporary release was granted to detainees once this period of time had elapsed. A's lawyer argued, however, that there was no point continuing the detention currently imposed on his client, who had maintained from the outset that he could never go back to his home country and who was clearly facing a long period in detention. 2) A's detention had been harming B's health and the actual state of her marriage with A, which also had an effect on her children. Only an end to A's detention could avert this damage. 3) If repatriated, this would severely limit A's ability to exercise the right of access to the courts, guaranteed by Article 32 of the Constitution of Japan. Furthermore, once the forcible deportation had been executed, the action seeking a stay of the execution of deportation would become meaningless and the benefits of the action would be lost. 4) Properly, a determination by the Minister of Justice had to be justified by lawful and strict examinations of evidence. The execution of deportation would make the lawful and strict examinations of evidence in A's case impossible. Therefore, A's representative argued, a stay of execution of both detention and repatriation would be appropriate.

After having demonstrated the rationale for granting A special permission to stay in Japan, A's lawyer explained that his client's marriage to B could be substantiated by the following facts: a) A and B did not co-habit at the beginning of the marriage because they considered the feelings of B's children, who would have had to live with them; b) During the time when they lived separately, B had an evening meal with A at his apartment almost every day. On the evenings when B could not visit A due to her work, she prepared his meal and/or left a note or letter for him; c) A and B had shared a livelihood, and A's detention made it difficult for B to support the family, resulting in an excessive burden being placed on B; d) B had been exhausting herself coping with the case, which had damaged her physical and mental health. A's representative argued that these were the facts that proved the genuineness of their marriage. He also pointed out e) that there had been no violation of laws or ordinances other than the Immigration Control Act before their marriage and f) that A had lost the basis of living in his home country while staying in Japan, making it barely possible for him to settle back there and even less possible to do so with his wife and her children. Having cited these points as the grounds, A's representative sought a stay of execution of the deportation order.

The State's argument in the written opinion of the Immigration Bureau

As mentioned earlier, this action has it beginnings in A voluntarily presenting himself at an immigration office to report that he was residing in Japan without legal status. Therefore, no concrete facts were disputed. The Immigration Bureau narrowed its arguments down to the following two points of dispute: 1) Whether the requirement for a stay of execution of a deportation order set forth by Article 25 paragraph 2 of the ACL Act – 'if there is an urgent necessity in order to avoid an irrecoverable damage' – was applicable to this action, and 2) whether the requirements for not allowing a stay of execution set forth in Article 25 paragraph 3 of the same act – 'when it is likely to seriously affect public welfare or when the action on the merits seems groundless' – were met in this case.

The Immigration Bureau was of the opinion that the Constitution of Japan did not guarantee a foreigner the right to enter, stay in or seek to continue to stay in Japan. The discretion of the Minister of Justice to permit an extension of the period of stay had been confirmed and made binding by the Supreme Court ruling on the MacLean case, while the power to refuse to grant special permission to stay in Japan had been conferred by the Tokyo High Court decision handed down on 28 June, 1990. Both decisions had established judicial precedents (*Shōmu geppō* (Law Suits Monthly), Vol.47, No. 10: 3,023–3,044). The Immigration Bureau further maintained that Article 22, Paragraph 1 of the Constitution (Freedom to change one's residence) guaranteed a foreign national freedom to choose and change his/her residence but not freedom to enter the country. The bureau also pointed out that, under customary international law, a state was not obliged to allow a foreign national to enter the country and that it could make a decision freely as to whether it would allow a person to enter and what restrictions it would impose on that person, which guaranteed the foreigner neither the right to stay nor the right to demand a continued stay.

The Immigration Bureau therefore contended that *the basic human rights provided for by the Constitution were guaranteed to a foreign national only inside the bounds of the residency system for foreigners based on the Immigration Control Act.* The Bureau also argued that it was far from relevant, in this case, to ask whether the ICCPR was being observed or whether the equality under law provided by the Constitution applied to foreign nationals. *In the Immigration Bureau's argument that constitutional rights were guaranteed to a foreign national only within the framework of the Act, the law was apparently placed higher than the Constitution and given the power to determine whether or not constitutional basic human rights were to be granted to a foreigner in the administration of immigration control.*[11]

The Immigration Bureau attributed the origins of this anomalous placing of the Immigration Control Act above the Constitution to: the persistent treatment, under the Act, of special permission to stay as an administrative procedure relating to the arrival and departure of foreigners; and to the fact that the matter of whether or not to grant this special permission to stay, established in Article 50, Paragraph 1 of the Act, is a matter of discretion for the Minister of Justice. As its rationale for the discretion exercised by the minister, the immigration authority pointed out that determinations of whether or not to grant special permission to stay in Japan was made following comprehensive consideration of 1) the foreign national's personal circumstances and 2) *political, economic and social conditions in Japan at the time.* In order to judge on the latter in particular, the argument continued, multipronged and specialised knowledge was needed and so was political consideration, which called for conversance with domestic and international situations and, naturally, broad discretion. The Immigration Bureau explained that special permission to stay in Japan had been created because there were indeed positive reasons for which a foreign national should be permitted to stay even if, legally, their case merited deportation, and that it could become unlawful not to grant permission under such extremely special circumstances. In defining discretion, the immigration authority was of the view that it could be unlawful to refuse to grant the permission only when there was such a positive reason for the foreign national to stay in Japan. This definition will be referred to as the view of the Ministry of Justice.

The Immigration Bureau acknowledged that special permission to stay established a provision for the granting of approval in cases where there was a need for the view of the Minster of Justice to be heard – under Article 50, Paragraph 1, Item 3 of the Act 'when there is a recognition of circumstances in which special permission to stay ought to be granted.' Meanwhile, it indicated that this same section of the Act said nothing about the requirements that it should have provided. The immigration authority contended that since there was no provision of requirements, the matter should be left to the discretion of the minister. The Bureau's argument in relation to this case was that even if A and B were telling the truth, their case failed to be accepted as constituting a positive reason for the granting of this permission, and 'this led to the view that the original claim itself had been unreasonable, resulting in the immediate dismissal of his case.' Although it seems a rather one-sided argument, the authority maintained that it was only rational to assume that even if the applicant's case were true, his request for special permission should be dismissed unless the Minister of Justice acknowledged some reason in favour of granting it.[12] According to this interpretation, the Immigration Bureau argued that the occasions on which the minister found no positive reason for granting permission were tantamount to 'occasions when the action, on its merits, seemed groundless.'

In its written opinion, the Immigration Bureau explained that it refused to grant special permission to stay and issued a deportation order due to A's bad behaviour, which included: 1) illegally staying in Japan beyond the period of fifteen days permitted by his short term visitor's visa; 2) entering the country with the intention of working illegally and staying illegally (and, of necessity, having worked illegally during this time) for more than eight years before voluntarily presenting himself at the immigration office; 3) not having been sufficiently remorseful to return home with his older brother, who had also been overstaying, at the time when the latter was deported; and 4) violating the Alien Registration Act by having failed to register himself for seven years and seven months, until he married. In addition to the bad behaviour, there were two points of reference taken into consideration when the determination by the Minister of Justice was made. Firstly, A had a family back in his country. This made it reasonable to believe that sending him back there would cause little adverse effect on his life. Secondly, even if his marriage to B were an actual marriage, it was merely one element against many others considered in making the determination.

Disputing whether 'an urgent necessity in order to avoid irrecoverable damage' existed, the immigration authority pointed out that the fact that he had appointed a representative along with today's improved means of communication would enable A to continue the action if he was deported. Therefore, the authority argued, A's right of access to courts would not be violated by the execution of the deportation order. With respect to the detention component of the deportation order, the Bureau maintained that it was necessary to stop A's activities as a resident and to place him in custody in order to execute the repatriation component. It further argued that 'irrecoverable damage' would not apply to physical restraint, restriction of freedom or psychological suffering resulting from detention because these outcomes were readily presumed to arise from detention, and fall within the permissible limit.

Finally, the Immigration Bureau presented its argument in relation to public welfare. It pointed out that even a legally residing foreigner was subject to the control of law in terms of resident status and period of stay, and that a foreigner on provisional release, even after posting bail, was restricted in terms of residence and movements. The authority warned that by granting a stay of execution of the detention component of a deportation order, the court would create a situation in which an illegal migrant was not subject to any controls or restrictions, effectively endorsing this situation. Unlike provisional release, a stay of execution of a detention order had no bail arrangements. It lacked measures to prevent the illegal migrant from escaping. If the foreigner escaped and rendered the deportation order incapable of being executed, contended the Immigration Bureau, there could possibly be a serious threat to public welfare.

Resting its case, the Immigration Bureau concluded that the requirements for a stay of execution were not met.

Immigration control policy criticised in the written opinion of the plaintiff (1), with regard to administrative practices

In response to the case presented by the Immigration Bureau, which was discussed in the previous section, the plaintiff submitted a written refutation (hereafter referred to as the written opinion of the plaintiff). Accepting no more than the existence of the judicial precedents which the immigration authority cited as the basis for its case, the plaintiff disputed all remaining arguments. The plaintiff's representative questioned, first of all, the definition of the discretion of the Minister of Justice, which was the authority on which the administration of all immigration control was based. He also questioned the determination by the Minister of Justice regarding this case, which he considered to have been unlawful because he believed that the action, on its merits, had grounds (and was eligible for stay of execution as set forth by the ACL Act).

We will now look at the plaintiff's refutation with regard to the discretion of the Minister of Justice. Before the plaintiff's representative took on the question of whether the Minister of Justice's discretion existed or not, he raised questions regarding how the system of special permission to stay was actually handled. According to the written opinion, the special permission system had started as a remedial measure for Korean residents in Japan before the Immigration Control Act was amended in 1990. In the late 1980s, the number of so-called new-comer foreigners began to increase. Even after new-comer foreigners were found to be staying for longer and/or marrying Japanese nationals, the immigration authority advocated that the special permission system continue to be practised in the same way as before. In typical fashion, the Immigration Bureau announced its view under the name of the director general in the *Japan Times* and other media, declaring that even if a relationship led to the birth of a child, marriage to a Japanese national alone did not constitute grounds for the due granting of special permission to stay in Japan. Nonetheless, admitting that it could not deny the legitimate interests that should be protected in marriage in some individual cases, the immigration authority was beginning to issue special permission on the ground of marriage to a Japanese national. It was around this time, the plaintiff's representative noted, that the notifications on spouses of Japanese nationals were issued.

In these notifications, the representative said, the authority to grant special permission to stay in Japan was delegated to the directors of regional immigration bureaus. However, all that the directors could determine was to grant the permission; they had no authority to refuse to grant the permission. A's case had been refused permission. That meant that the director of the regional immigration bureau must have passed it on to the Adjudication Division of the Immigration Bureau. Regardless of whether the case had been determined by the director of a regional immigration bureau or sent to the Adjudication Division, it was a long-established fact that inquiry was to focus on the genuineness and stability of the marriage and that the permission was granted in almost all cases, as long as it was sought on the grounds of marriage. Although Japan has never adopted an across-the-board amnesty, the special permission effectively provides amnesties on an individual basis. To make it possible for regional immigration bureaus to make determinations, departmental notifications defined models for cases that would generally be granted the permission under the delegated authority, such as those concerning spouses of Japanese nationals and permanent resident mothers and children. Consequently, although the government's official stance remains that special permission to stay in Japan is a measure for legitimising illegal residents on an individual basis, it has been popularised via its actual application.

Furthermore, the 1999 notification on marriage disregarded the period which the foreign national has stayed since entering Japan saying, 'Unless the case is so important that it may produce an effect on the political situation, diplomatic relations and/or public safety, if the foreign national is married to a Japanese national and the marriage is found to be genuine and stable, the director of a relevant district immigration office may make the determination to grant special permission to stay in Japan in order to streamline the administrative process.' Subsequently, in January 2000, the Ministry of Justice also eased the criteria for granting special permission to stay in Japan on grounds other than marriage to a Japanese national. The minister aimed to implement a new set of criteria, including 1) that the applicant has been living in Japan legally and/or illegally for a total of ten years after entering the country either legally or illegally and 2) that there is evidence of the applicant having integrated into Japanese society, such as children's schooling. If a family met the new criteria, all its members were granted special permission to stay in Japan, even if none of them had legal resident status.[13] (Nonetheless, the new criteria did not apply to delegated determinations by the director of a regional immigration office.)

In addition, the 2000 *Basic Plan for Immigration Control* stated, 'Many foreign nationals granted this special permission have close relationships with Japanese nationals and others, and have actually built a foundation for various aspects of their future lives in Japan. In more concrete terms, one such example would be the case of a foreign national who is married to a Japanese national, and where they are in an actual marriage. This applies to a foreign national who has not committed any violation of laws other than the Immigration Control Act.' Through this statement, the ministry made it public that living in an actual marriage with a Japanese national or a permanent resident comprised 'grounds for granting special case permission to stay in Japan' and that this policy would be maintained in the future.

In its written opinion, the Immigration Bureau denied that a foreign national had the right to lodge an application for special permission to stay in Japan because the Immigration Control Act contained no provision for that right. Although the term 'an application for special permission to stay in Japan' is not found in the Act, this does not necessarily mean that there is not such a thing. In judicial precedents and administrative interpretations of the Act, it is understood that the objection against an unlawful determination connotes an application (or a "request" as it is termed in the administration of immigration control) for special permission to stay in Japan, to which the Minister of Justice is obliged to respond in one way or another. In fact, the minister can determine not to grant the permission when he finds that the objection is without reason, only because he is, in effect, responding to an application (or request) for the permission. The above premise of the Immigration Bureau, on which its argumentation was based, was wrong.

Immigration control policy criticised in the written opinion of the plaintiff (2), with regard to the discretion of the Minister of Justice

The Immigration Bureau was of the view that the state was free to choose conditions to attach before and when allowing the entry of a foreigner. The plaintiff's representative pointed out that it was inappropriate for Japan to take this view while advocating the principle of international cooperation in the preamble and Article 98 of the Constitution. While the immigration authority might well take this view, he noted, the prescription of conditions to be imposed on foreigners required legislation. Therefore, the discretion must be based on legislative, not administrative, authority. The plaintiff's representative pointed out that the Immigration Control Act did not allow any room for discretion in deciding to allow the entry of a foreigner, stating in Article 9, Paragraph 1, 'If... an immigration inspector finds that a foreign national conforms to the conditions for landing prescribed in Article 7, Paragraph 1, he shall endorse the passport of the foreign national to that effect by affixing a seal of verification for landing.'[14] The representative developed his argument, saying, 'A foreign national about to enter the country generally has neither a foundation for a livelihood nor a family in Japan. Yet, the Act denies the Minister of Justice discretion in making a decision involving such a foreigner. How then could boundless discretion be given to the minister in making a determination involving a foreigner who has the foundation of his livelihood and a family in Japan?' Using the Immigration Control Act as his rationale, the plaintiff's representative established that the scope of the minister's discretion was not boundless.

As mentioned earlier, there are established intra-departmental criteria in the Immigration Bureau for considering whether or not to grant special permission to stay in Japan. The determinations are made against the criteria by the director of a regional immigration bureau, on behalf of the Minister. In theory, individual cases are supposed to be given discretionary determination. In practice, however, the determinations have become a matter of routine work, which in itself negates the Minister's discretion. On the premise that a foreigner without resident status was not eligible for protection under the law, the immigration authority argued that special permission to stay in Japan was granted *de gratia*. If the permission is a favour, however, this hardly explains the fact that departmental notifications have rendered as many as over 2,000 foreigners eligible for it annually. While the Immigration Control Act prescribes that it is a crime to overstay in Japan, it acknowledges that there are exceptional cases of such residency that deserve protection, in the form of Article 50, Paragraph 1, Item (iii), and holds the Minister of Justice responsible for this protection. This being the case, the requirements for being eligible for protection will change as humanitarian thinking advances, but the existence of legal protection regarding residency for foreign nationals is a given and not a favour.

The Immigration Bureau compared A's case with those seeking an extension of the period of stay, citing the MacLean case. The authority argued that the Minister of Justice had comprehensive discretion in making a decision about an extension of residency, let alone in making a decision about special permission to stay – a decision involving the more serious matter of resident status. Recent court rulings, including those of: the Tokyo District Court on 28 April, 1994 (*Hanrei Jihō,* No. 1,501: 90–96); the Supreme Court on 2 July, 1996 (*Hanrei Jihō,* No. 1,578: 51–55); the Tokyo District Court on 19 September, 1997 (*Hanrei Jihō* No. 1,650: 66–77); and the Osaka High Court on 25 December, 1998 (yet to be published in a collection of court decisions), have ruled on whether an extension of stay was appropriate or not. In these cases, rulings were made on the appropriateness or inappropriateness of renewing the period of residency, after having ascertained and evaluated the facts in a detailed manner. These rulings hinged on the necessity of a variety of activities having their basis in the couple's status; these covered not only the execution of the core responsibilities of couples – cohabiting, cooperation and assistance, but ranged as widely as discussions of the shouldering of the expenses of marriage and the recovering of the marriage relationship in cases where couples lived apart, as well as discussions about divorce. The plaintiff's representative also quoted from the text of the ruling in the MacLean case, 'If the determination lacks any foundation in fact or if it is patently clear that it would be inappropriate given social norms, then the determination is found to be unlawful for having gone beyond the bounds of the discretion or having abused it.'

The plaintiff's representative also considered it significant that the original 1959 decision of the Supreme Court – upon which the Immigration Bureau's case relied and which had also found that 'it is appropriate to interpret the principle of discretion as having limits' – was upheld. From this standpoint, A's lawyer argued that the Supreme Court decision had to be interpreted as follows: determinations by the Minister of Justice concerning 'circumstances in which special permission to stay ought to be granted' should be tried on the question of whether there is a lack of any foundation in fact or a patent lack of appropriateness in light of social norms; and where these cases are upheld, the failure of the Minister of Justice to grant special permission to stay must be ruled to be unlawful as an overstepping of the scope, or an abuse, of his discretion. Having demonstrated a possible interpretation totally opposite to that made by the Ministry of Justice, the representative contended that the determination by the minister constituted an abuse of his discretion as result of having gone beyond its bounds. This was explained in terms of the Minster having failed to consider the fact that needed to be considered, namely, the plaintiff's genuine marriage with B, while having considering the facts that did not need to be considered – namely, his overstaying, working illegally and failing to register himself on the alien list for eight years.

A's lawyer concluded this part of his refutation by questioning the following points: 1) The Minister of Justice took into consideration the period of overstay and illegal work in determining not to grant A the special permission. If the said period was counted as a demerit, however, it would apply to practically all of the foreign nationals to whom the minister might give the permission, making the system of the special permission doomed to extinction. 2) As a routine practice, the Immigration Bureau sought a certificate of employment from an applicant for the special permission to prove that this person was living a stable life. 3) The requirement for deportation set forth in Article 24, Item (iv-f) of the Act states, 'A person who has been sentenced to imprisonment or a heavier punishment for violation of the provisions of laws and regulations relating to alien registration, except for those whose sentences have been suspended' virtually indicating that the Act itself acknowledged that a violator of the Alien Registration Act was not particularly heinous unless he/she had been sentenced to imprisonment or a heavier punishment. Accordingly, A's lawyer rebutted the minister's determination, which cited the plaintiff's violation of the Alien Registration Act as one of the grounds for deportation, because it ran counter to the spirit of the Immigration Control Act.

Immigration control policy criticised in the written opinion of the plaintiff (3), with regard to the provision 'if there is an urgent necessity in order to avoid any irrecoverable damage' in Article 25 of the ACL Act

According to the plaintiff's representative, the immigration authority had maintained that the damage suffered by A did not qualify as irrecoverable damage, by interpreting damage which is caused by an administrative disposition or its execution as being within permissible limits, if this damage is presumed to be a natural outcome of carrying out the law on which the disposition is based. The representative began his refutation of the Immigration Bureau's argument, by calling it 'the general damage benchmark approach.' According to this approach, the Immigration Control Act presumed that a detainee was, as a matter of course, subject to detriments, such as limited freedom and psychological suffering, which are generally associated with detention. To be acknowledged as irrecoverable, the detriment estimated to have been incurred by the detainee, judging from the person's physical condition and the environment of the detention facilities must be greater than the sort of general damage that might be expected in these conditions. In other words, damage extraordinary enough to make the detention inappropriate must be predicted.

The general damage benchmark approach, the plaintiff's lawyer noted, was no longer a golden rule. He cited a decision that had acknowledged the detainee's human rights and another that had adopted the criterion of weighing the possible effects of the stay of execution of a deportation order against the seriousness of the expected damage instead of the damage generally associated with detention (the request filed for stay of execution, Case 2,000 Gyō-ku 11). These decisions had been given respectively in relation to the detention of an Afghani national on a written order of detention and that of a Pakistani national on a written order of deportation.

The plaintiff's representative explained the reasons for the decline of the general damage benchmark approach in recent years as follows: Article 25 of the ACL Act provides that, 'The filing of an action for the revocation of the original administrative disposition shall not preclude the effects of the original administrative disposition.' If this rule were adhered to, however, the recipient of a disposition could in some cases win the action on its merits, after having sustained irrecoverable damage; when the victory would come too late for remedy. To rectify this, the court had acceded to the stay of the disposition until it had made its decision on the action. The plaintiff's lawyer contended that the term 'irrecoverable' in these instances must be interpreted as describing cases in which 1) revocation of the disposition granted by the court did not provide remedy to the parties concerned and 2) even if monetary compensation were possible, the payment of money as a social convention did not compensate for any damage.

This interpretation was given in the decision of the Kobe District Court on 12 June, 1992 (*Hanrei jihō* No. 1,438: 50–70). In cases concerning the stay of execution of a deportation order, not a single ruling has denied that the repatriation component of deportation causes irrecoverable damage. Thus, although the unlikelihood of a foreign national who has been deported coming back to Japan might well be a detriment that has been presumed by the Immigration Control Act, this does not necessarily constitute a denial of the fact that this is irrecoverable damage. The ACL Act allows stay of execution of an administrative disposition 'in order to avoid irrecoverable damage' because once a disposition is executed, it has consequences for many people and it becomes a precedent, on which future cases will rely. The court has recognised the need to stay the execution of an administrative disposition in many cases involving damage which had generally been expected from enforcement. The damage disputed in these cases includes: loss of the opportunity to stage a protest sustained by demonstrators as a result of a denied permission for the rally; the stripping away of access to parliamentary activities sustained by a politician after his name was struck off the MPs' roll; and discontinuation of business suffered by a restaurant, as a result of an suspension order. It would, then, appear unreasonable to deny the irrevocability of the damage usually associated with a disposition only in the case of detention.

Incidentally, to physically detain a Japanese national, unless the person is caught in the act, warrants – both an arrest warrant and a detention warrant – are necessary. The court conducts an examination before it issues each warrant. When the person is arrested or taken into custody, a quasi-complaint quickly opens the way for a judicial review. Even after having been physically detained, the person may be set free on bail or by revocation of detention, regardless of whether there are facts constituting the charge/s or not. A foreign national, on the other hand, is taken into custody under a written deportation order, which is issued by a supervising immigration inspector, pursuant to Article 49, paragraph 6 of the Act. There is no judicial intervention before the order is issued. Article 52, Paragraph 5 of the Act allows for the foreigner to be held in custody for an indefinite period, by stipulating that, 'If the foreign national cannot be deported immediately, the immigration control officer may detain this person in a migrant detention centre… until such time as deportation becomes possible.' There are neither judicial inquiries prior to the detention nor an opportunity for the suspect to file an objection to the physical restraint. Temporary release, which lifts the physical restraint, is decided by the director of a detention centre or a supervising immigration inspector, where any judicial intervention is denied. The Immigration Control Act provides for few procedures to ensure due process of law. In fact, the only procedure found in the Act enabling the judicature to free a detainee from physical restraint is a stay of execution of the issuance of a written deportation order. The Act does not guarantee the detainee's human rights unless the procedure of stay of execution is actively used. Criticising the Immigration Control Act for failing to prescribe relevant procedures, the plaintiff's representative stressed that the requirements for 'irrecoverable damage' must be explicated more precisely than indicated by the existing text of the Act, in order to ensure the human rights of detainees.

The Tokyo District Court ruling – A new precedent more consistent with social norms

On 27 December 2001, Chief Justice Masayuki Fujiyama of Civil Court Division 3 of the Tokyo District Court handed down a judgment, the main text of which reads as follows: '1) the execution pursuant to the written deportation order issued to the plaintiff by the other party[15] on 1 August 2001 shall be stayed until the tenth day reckoned from the day of the pronouncement of the decision of the first trial of the action, on merit (line 3 of Case 316, heard in this court in 2001, requesting rescission of the dispositions including the issuance of the written deportation order). 2) The other request by the plaintiff shall be dismissed. 3) With regard to the costs of the action, the plaintiff shall bear a quarter of the costs and the other party the rest.' Two reasons were given for the judgment.

The first reason was concerned with whether or not the case met the requirement for a stay of execution prescribed by Article 25, Paragraph 2, of the ACL Act 'if there is an urgent necessity in order to avoid irrecoverable damage.' The court first defined the irrecoverable damage as damage inflicted by the application of the disposition for which neither *restitutio in integrum* or reparation in money was possible; or which, even if monetary reparation were possible, was generally accepted as being difficult to return to an unscathed state, given the nature and conditions of the damage.

Spelling out that the damage which the plaintiff would sustain was physical restraint due to detention – an abuse of human rights of the most serious kind second to murder, the court acknowledged that it would bring him significant harm, both physically and psychologically, which was, in its view, generally accepted as difficult to compensate for with money. The court accepted some of the arguments by the plaintiff's representative in establishing its benchmark for judging, by which it ruled, '*Under the Japanese legal system, it is highly exceptional to execute a proceeding that imposes such serious restriction on human rights via a mere administrative disposition. Therefore, it requires extreme caution not only on the part of the administrators who directly engage in the disposition, but also on the part of the courts that judge its propriety. The same applies to the process of determining whether or not the case meets the requirements for a stay of execution.*'

Justice Fujiyama acknowledged 1) that a period of time for adjusting had been needed at the beginning of A's marriage to B before they began to co-habit; 2) that even if such adjustment was needed, A and B had already been sharing their livelihood; 3) that the detention of A left B with an excessive burden of running the processed food business that A had started shortly before being taken into custody, having a strong impact, not only economically on the family's livelihood but also psychologically on B and her child, who had finally begun living with A; and 4) that if this continued, the family relationship between A, B and the child would be crucially affected. The court found that if the family relationship were to collapse, it would be impossible to make up the damage with money, or that if somehow possible, this restitution was generally accepted as being difficult to effect. On these grounds, A's deportation was recognised as irrecoverable damage.

In response to the Immigration Bureau's approach that any damage was presumed under the administrative disposition prescribed in the Act, the court ruled that although certain damage was a natural consequence presumed under a disposition or a law, the necessity to stay its execution must be acknowledged if this would cancel out the effects of a later court decision in favour of the plaintiff. Justice Fujiyama went on to point out that whether or not certain damage was irrecoverable did not always correlate to whether or not it was the natural consequence of a disposition; some damage resulting from a disposition could be irrecoverable, whilst other damage not presumed by the law could be easily recoverable afterward. The justice established that it was sufficient for this court to decide whether or not it could recognise the damage as difficult for the person/persons concerned to recover from, by considering the nature of the particular disposition, that of the damage as a consequence of the disposition and the circumstances of the plaintiff. He thus placed great importance on hearing facts and rejected the Immigration Bureau's approach. In relation to a stay of execution of the detention component of the written deportation order, the Tokyo District Court decision stated 'Even criminal procedures contain the principle of requiring a judicial examination based on the warrant system before the detention of a suspect. On the other hand, the procedures in immigration control are highly exceptional in that a mere administrative authority is allowed to take people into detention in the form of administrative dispositions without any judicial examination. With such dispositions, it would hardly be unreasonable if a higher proportion of cases were successful in meeting the requirements for a stay of execution, particularly those with a component of detention.' Thus, the court indicated its view that it was justifiable to set the bar to detention high.

The court also found that in most past cases that had won a stay of execution of a deportation order, only the component of repatriation had been stayed. This was because 1) whether or not there were grounds for deportation was not disputed in these cases and 2) they were judged against winning cases from earlier times when the vast majority of cases had deserved repatriation. The court acknowledged that this case had fair prospects of winning and suggested the possibility of securing a decision that deviated from previous cases – to stay the execution of the detention component – because 3) the understanding of the problem and the posing of points of issue were different in this action from those in the past.

The second reason given by the Tokyo District Court concerned the possible applicability to this case of Article 25, Paragraph 3 of the ACL Act – 'when the action, on its merits, seems groundless.' Next, the court considered the interpretation of the legal text in the Immigration Control Act that said, 'any foreign national may be deported from Japan.' 'The general view is that in cases where the legal text states that "something may be done," the legislators have expressed their intent to give the relevant government organisation certain latitude of discretion with differing scopes of leeway – complete discretion[16] or constrained discretion.'[17] Article 24 of the Act thus substantiated the discretion of the Immigration Bureau in its provision. The court pointed out that under administrative law, an administrative office could choose not to exercise its authority even if the requirements for an exercise of authority were met (administrative opportunism) and that particularly in the areas covered by police law including immigration control, where the objective of the exercise of authority by an administrative office is public safety and maintenance of order, it was generally viewed that the exercise of authority must remain minimal (the principle of police proportionality). On the premise of administrative opportunism and the principle of police proportionality, the court found it appropriate to construe that an administrative office was not allowed to exercise its authority, if relevant facts existed to meet the requirements for a disposition set forth by law. This was not only the case when in the said circumstances there was effectively no possibility of causing disturbance to public safety and order without exercising the disposition. It also applied if there was a possibility that inaction would bring about minimal harmful effect and the adverse effects of exercising the disposition would be also minimal, and the restraint of rights and freedom imposed by it would be far greater than these adverse effects.

With respect to the series of provisions for deportation, the court expounded as follows. Procedural provisions for deportation (Article 47, Paragraph 4, Article 48, Paragraph 8 and Article 49 Paragraph 5 of the Act) laid down the issuance of a written order by a supervising immigration inspector as the administrative disposition that formalised deportation of a relevant foreign national. The discretion granted by the substantiative provision for deportation in Article 24 of the Act was, in actuality, assigned to supervising immigration inspectors through the procedural provisions. Consequently, supervising immigration inspectors were authorised to use their discretion as to whether or not to issue written deportation orders (discretion on enactment) and when to issue them (discretion on timing). Lastly, the authority duly obliged immigration inspectors not to violate the principle of proportionality. Further, Justice Fujiyama found that, as well as supervising immigration inspectors, immigration control officers, immigration inspectors, special inquiry officers and the Minister of Justice were all given discretion at each level of the procedure of deportation.

After discussing discretion at all levels, the judgment document came back to the question of whether or not 'the action, on its merits, seemed groundless,' which was critical in deciding the question of staying the deportation. The answer was found in the recognition, or rather, the lack of recognition of A's marriage to B, which underpinned the determination made by the Minister of Justice pursuant to Article 49 Paragraph 3, and the issuance of the written deportation order by the supervising immigration inspector in compliance with the minister's determination. The marriage was genuine. Justice Fujiyama found that *the determination by the minister and the issuance of the deportation order had been an error of fact, which constituted deviance from or abuse of discretion* [author's emphasis], and therefore concluded that the action on the merits of this case did *not* seem groundless.

This decision was made by a lower court. New decisions by lower courts accumulate to influence higher court decisions. The Tokyo District Court ruling has been referred to in other cases for a stay of execution of a written deportation order, triggering the formation of a new "social norm."

Administrators take over in a country of laws: protecting the interests of the plaintiff by losing the court case

This Tokyo District Court decision has become one of the most significant precedents of recent years, concerning the resident status of a foreign national in Japan. Immediately after the decision was handed down, the Immigration Bureau lodged an appeal, which took the trial to the High Court of Tokyo. Arguments in the high court presented important points of dispute regarding the significance to the immigration authority of holding on to the discretion of the Minister of Justice; or in other words, of adhering to the official view of the ministry. Considerations of space do not permit a more detailed discussion of the arguments in the high court, except to say that the plaintiff lost the case in the second instance. The decision in the original case was published in full, and recognised as one of the most remarkable rulings, but was not made a final and binding judgment.

All the above notwithstanding, matters took a course that is hard to understand for those (and the author in particular) outside the world of legal practice. The Immigration Bureau won the case in the Tokyo High Court, which effectively approved the execution of the deportation order and refused A's request for a stay of execution of the detention component. The government body had every reason to continue its fierce fight against A in the action on its merits. In fact, however, the authority's reaction was quite different. On 10 May, 2002, it issued a revocation of the written deportation order of 13 August, 2001, numbered Tokyo No. 2 5,128, against A. On the same day, it granted A special permission to stay.

Why had the immigration authority appealed to the High Court? There had been two reasons. The first was the belief that the authority could not afford to let the Tokyo District Court decision become a final and binding judgment as it found some of the wording in the text unacceptable. The administrative office took such a strong aversion, in part, because of the concepts presented by the court concerning 'the discretion of a supervising immigration inspector' – 1) that it was the supervising immigration inspector, not the Minister of Justice, who held the discretion and 2) that the principle of proportionality places bounds on the discretion. The notion that the discretion rested with the supervising immigration inspector was the presiding judge's unique theory, which perplexed all concerned. The constraint imposed by the principle of proportionality interfered with the scope of the discretion, something that the authority could never accept. Had it accepted this, its theory of complete discretion would no longer have held.

The second reason for the Immigration Bureau's appeal was probably the district court finding that a stay of execution of a deportation order applied not only to the repatriation component of the order, but also to detention. Under the current law, a foreign national applies for special permission to stay in Japan on admitting living in the country without a legal status. At the time of application, the system offers the applicant only two prospects – special permission or deportation (so-called enforced repatriation). Once the written deportation order is issued and about to be executed, detention of the foreign national is necessary to ensure their repatriation. The immigration authority strongly believes that it is impossible to carry out the administration of immigration control, unless detention and repatriation are integrated into the deportation order. It admits that, in reality, a considerable number of foreigners are working and living a normal life in Japan, having been served with a written deportation order and later given provisional release. Nonetheless, from the administrative office's standpoint, this is an exceptional measure, taken on an individual basis.[18]

The law has given the Minister of Justice discretion in determining special permission to stay in Japan. The purpose of a court is to execute laws. In administrative litigation, 'the court can only make a judgment as to whether or not conduct by the government is lawful. It would be *ultra vires* for the court to rule on whether or not a determination made by a government institution, from its policy and administrative perspective, is appropriate (Fujita 2005: 98). The premise of administrative law is law-based administration. However, this comprises the "administration by law" principle. Therefore, arguments in the courts revolve, as discussed above, rather on unwritten sources of law or prerequisites to law. The Immigration Control Act may grant comprehensive discretion to the Minister of Justice, but this discretion in actual practice, has diverged from what the law stipulates. This is not, however, necessarily seen as acceptable. Although what led to its initiation is unclear, an amendment was recently introduced whereby it is now possible for the practice of the director of a regional immigration bureau in using the discretion to determine to grant special permission to stay in Japan to occur in line with the law. In line with this, the marriage notification was abolished. This indicates that a large number of cases of special permission to stay had been determined by the directors of regional immigration bureaus. It is not difficult to imagine that the change to the text of the Act allowing the directors of regional immigration bureaus to grant the permission was made in an attempt to resolve the discrepancy between what the law stipulates and what is being practised.

Throughout the trial, the plaintiff's representative raised the following issues: 1) a process that takes someone into custody and forcibly removes them from a country cannot be left to the complete discretion of anyone at all. The scope and nature of the discretion as well as the rights that are affected may vary depending on whether the person is a national or a non-national, but it must, at least, be ensured that the proceedings taken by the state are fair. 2) What is seen as fair may vary with the changing times and social situations, but can be objectively defined with a certain latitude at any given time with reference to the Constitution and treaties such as the International Convention on Civil and Political Rights and the Convention on the Rights of the Child. It is this prescribed latitude that forms the scope within which the discretion may be exercised. 3) Fairness is inevitably sought and found on an ad hoc basis when there are still a small number of cases to handle. As the number of cases increases, however, there arises the need to maintain equality and objectivity. In making a discretionary determination, the authority granted to the state may be primarily for seeking what is fair in a case, but at the same time the state is obliged to handle cases of the same circumstances equally, once it has decided on a matter. 4) The delegation to directors of regional immigration bureaus of the authority to make a discretionary decision regarding the special permission, under the above-mentioned departmental notification, is an indication of the fact that proceedings 1)–3) have been increasingly difficult to achieve/have come to a standstill in practice. It is not problems with the discretion but with the principle of equality that have been making the proceedings difficult. 5) The state, however, regards problematizing the discretion as a means of letting itself off the hook regarding the principle of equality. The lawyer raised these five points as his strategy in questioning the current immigration control administration.

Incidentally, the true beginning of the trial was when A turned himself in at an immigration office, and asked to apply for special permission to stay in Japan. The special permission was refused, which kick-started the execution of a written deportation order – its detention component, to be precise. The circumstances left him no choice but to file a request for a stay of execution of the deportation order, while, needless to say, he wanted more than the stay. His ultimate goal was to secure special permission to stay in Japan. In the end, A's lawyer protected the interests of his client even though he failed to win in the High Court or have the epoch-making district court decision confirmed.

Departmental notifications have shifted the administration of immigration control from the discretion of the Minister of Justice to the standardised judgment of regional bureaus. As a result, more than ten thousand illegal residents are being made legitimate annually today, after little public debate on the matter. In contrast, the 1990 Immigration Control Act amendment triggered the controversy between the camps for and against opening up the country to migrants and became the subject of deliberation in the Diet. Public discussions of this sort since then have died out almost completely, while the number of cases granted the special permission has increased more than thirty-fold. Considering that this change has been caused exclusively by a shift in the administrative procedures of immigration control, our country of laws seems to have been taken over by an administrative state.

The state power of Japan from the perspective of foreigners

Throughout the process leading to the district court decision, A's representative kept asking if his client came under the categories of cases routinely given special permission to stay in Japan. This led him to inquire into what procedures were taken to exercise the special permission system and what kinds of cases were granted the permission. Changes in recent years in the number of cases granted special permission to stay in Japan are shown in Figure 11.1. It is worth noting that the number has been higher than ten thousand annually since 2003. Since the amendment of the Immigration Control Act in 1990, the illegal residents given legitimate resident status have totalled 55,741, although special permission was granted to no more than about 500 annually for the five years preceding 1995.

In comparison to the numbers of illegal migrants legitimised in other countries, the numbers being granted the special permission in Japan is not small. In 1987–88 in the United States, 1.8 million were granted legal resident status in general amnesties and another 1.27 million under the Special Agricultural Workers program, totalling more than 3 million legitimised. France has a far smaller scale of legitimisation – 130,000 in 1981–82 and 78,000 in 1997–98 (Kondō 2001: 290–295).

In European and North American countries where amnesties are offered, they often coincide with a major change of the system, such as a revision of immigration laws. The large-scale legitimisation of illegal migrants in 1987–88 in the US, for example, was offered following the 1986 legislation of the Immigration Reform and Control Act.[19] Such a major change may be made to the system every now and then, but nobody knows when the next one will come. On the other hand, Japan has been legitimising a mass of illegal migrants every year. The accumulated number of those regularly

*Figure 11.1: Number of cases of special permission to stay at each
year end*

Number
of cases

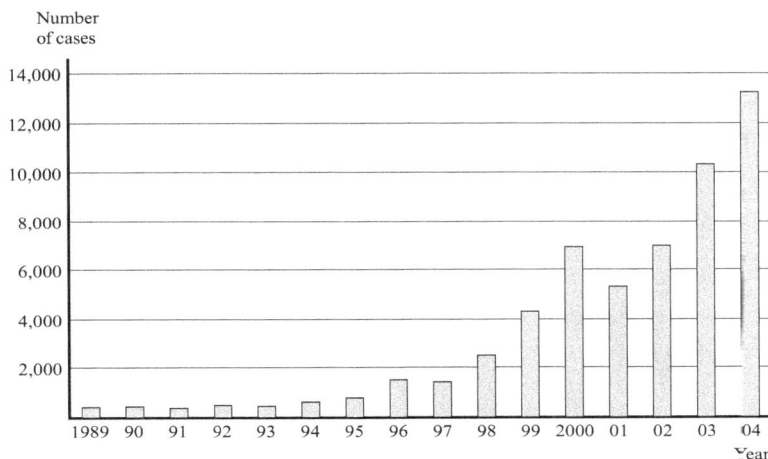

legitimised in Japan is far from small, compared with those given
amnesties sporadically by the Western countries over the years.

Special permission to stay in Japan has been granted in considerable numbers and is expanding. In principle, every case is judged
individually. However, the sharp increase in the number of cases
granted the special permission is hard to explain other than that they
are being processed routinely following standardised procedures,
as the plaintiff's representative suggested. In Japan, legitimisation
of illegal migrants in numbers not significantly fewer than in the
Western countries is being carried out without undergoing any more
scrutiny than that found in the administrative procedures within an
administrative office.

The dramatic increase of legitimisation of illegal migrants is
closely linked to the rationale adopted within government departments and agencies. This link is evident in, among many things,
a passage in the government's third Basic Plan for Immigration
Control,

> The Ministerial Meeting against Crime formulated an 'Action Plan
> for the Realisation of a Society Resistant to Crime' in December 2003.
> According to this action plan, the government will aim to reduce the

number of illegal foreign residents by half in the next five years to
ensure that the people of Japan can live with peace of mind. It also
indicates that it is necessary to eliminate unreasonable suspicion
towards most of the foreigners who are staying in Japan peacefully
and legally.

It is not difficult to imagine that the policy approved by the
cabinet led to the sharp increase in cases being granted the special
permission. Evidently, as one of the measures 'to reduce the number
of illegal foreign residents,' the government is legitimising illegal
migrants, or in more concrete terms, granting special permission
to stay in Japan.

From the perspective of the history of ideas, Masao Maruyama
pointed out that the modernisation of Japan was Westernisation in
form only; Japan had developed its own ideas by flexibly adapting,
modifying and embracing all sorts of foreign ideas (Maruyama
1961). On its website, the Ministry of Justice began in 2003 to
disclose some of the cases in which it granted special permission
to stay in Japan. The Supreme Court has also been offering, on its
website, the texts of some of the important decisions and rulings in
cases concerning stays of execution of written deportation orders,
as a part of the information that it provides on administrative case
litigation. The cases disclosed on these websites in recent years show
that the phenomenon described by Maruyama in his *Nihon no Shisō*
(Japanese Thought) has been occurring in the legal system of this
country.[20] The system of special permission to stay in Japan has
been evolved by flexibly and profusely accommodating extremely
diverse cases. However, if consideration is given to the fact that this
system exists as an exceptional provision established by law, then
the free and unfettered manner in which the granting of special
permission to stay has developed is not, in itself the problem. The
problems are: 1) that the system is still continuing after having
had to undergo repeated rehashes as the original purpose of the
legislation became out of touch with reality; and, more importantly,
2) that no questions are raised about the fact that internal criteria and
departmental notifications have been working virtually as sources
of law, even if under administrative law, as the legislative branch
of the government has been failing to fulfil its function.

As has been discussed in this chapter, the quantitative increase
in the number of cases granted special permission to stay in Japan

has been caused by the shift in procedures from discretionary determination on individual cases to determination according to the criteria set by departmental notifications.[21] Such shifts, initiated by rationales adopted within the government administration, give outsiders the impression that the system is prone to highhanded changes of the procedures. They also make it extremely difficult to understand how Japan accepts foreign migrants. This is probably where the system of special permission to stay in Japan fails as a social control measure. Although the Immigration Bureau won the case, A was granted special permission to stay in the end.[22] The outcome is not only confusing to foreigners wanting to apply for the special permission but also practically impossible for Japanese people to understand. If the system of special permission to stay in Japan were to arouse suspicion among both foreign and Japanese residents, it would not help achieve stable law and order. To ensure that law and order are maintained, the state must review the significance of the special permission system in today's context. Japan has a position in the world today that is totally different from the one it had when the policy was enacted. Prior to the war, when Japan was struggling to catch up with European and North American countries, it was a poor country, exporting its excess population out to Manchuria, the Korean Peninsula, the South Pacific islands and Central and South America. The situation has changed. Today, people come to work in Japan from under-developed countries and it is mostly to those people that the government grants special permission to stay in the country. When an illegal resident from a country such as the United States and France is deported back home, special permission is hardly an issue. This is because special permission to stay in Japan is, in practical terms, operating as 'a means to secure human rights on a global scale.' If the special permission could be presented as such, it would be recognised as a system to help achieve law and order, giving the discretion its rightful place. Furthermore, it is impossible to consider the propriety of the system of special permission to stay in Japan, without discussing the connections between the complicated court decisions and the precedents that have been approved in the immigration administration. Nonetheless, it is not necessarily best for the issue to be decided by national debates, which are subject to emotional public opinion and the trend of the times. As this is an extremely sensitive issue concerning the protection of the rights of minorities, it most certainly requires rational discussion; and, in the interests of achieving this, there cannot be any denial of the involvement of the discretion of administrators if this system is to survive. This is, however, on the proviso that the application of the discretion can be monitored, as it is an extraordinary use of power to detain someone and banish them from a country.

Conclusion: freedom, equality and Takeyoshi Kawashima

This book has been an attempt to form an understanding about foreign workers in Japan, both through a theoretical approach and a thorough analysis of the present situation. This author's conclusion is that, with regard to foreign workers, rifts have been opening up in Japanese society between economics and the law and between people's lives and politics, and that these have been patched up with fabrications, or in other words, with lies.

The chapters in this book have discussed the increasing detachment of economics from people's lives and from politics, using the term 'invisible permanent residents' as a key word (Takamichi Kajita, Kiyoto Tanno, Naoto Higuchi 2005). In an earlier section, the discussion went a step further and revealed that the discrepancies between what was going on in economics and other spheres of society essentially originated from legal definitions in relation to foreigners, and that the contradictions in the law were made good by fabrications.

The lawyer who gave the author the access to information says that a foreign worker is like a *nue*, a legendary creature from Japanese fables. Although its body consists of parts from several different animals, a *nue* is none of those animals. It is a liminal being, eluding the network of classifications. Appendix Table 1 shows the classification of resident statuses granted according to their work contents. One of these is the status of trainee. According to the definition of this resident status, trainees are not workers but they are foreigners who are in Japan to undergo training in order to become full-fledged workers. Appendix Table 2 gives classifications of visas granted on the grounds of applicants' personal status with regard to residents with special permission, long-term residents, permanent residents and their spouses. One of the categories is workers of Japanese descent, who are not counted as foreign workers but regarded as long-term resident foreigners. Trainees and Japanese descendants both work in Japan as foreign labour, but they are not considered to be so by the Immigration Control Act. These were the observations made by this lawyer. It would seem that it is the law that is lying here. Citing rulings by the legendary magistrate Ōoka Echizen from eighteenth century Japan, Suehiro argues that a good judgment, in essence, does not bend a law but interprets the facts in such a way that they conform to the law. In other words, it reconciles facts with the law by saying that what happened did not happen and/or that what did not happen did: that is lying. This was discussed in the introductory chapter.

To bridge the law and facts with misrepresented truths, however, is to commit a grave sin. Trainees, who are not supposed to be workers, have no freedom to choose either their job or employer. Without any means of having their voices heard, trainees have no choice but to stay at the same workplace even under bad working conditions. Unlike them, workers of Japanese descent have the freedom to choose any employment. As this book has revealed, however, the choices available to them are practically limited to jobs within the service contracting industry. Nonetheless, people of Japanese descent supposedly choose short term temporary jobs of their own free will. This leads to their problems being categorised, not as issues of foreign workers, but as those of contract labour, illegal temporary staff placement and fraudulent subcontracting. Although the employment issues facing people of Japanese descent may be discussed as part of the comprehensive job security issue, the major premise that they are not foreign workers prevents them from being given a legitimate place in the government's labour policy.

The author has discussed workers of Japanese descent in an essay titled 'Status: A Foreign Labour' (Tanno 2001b). There are more than 300,000 Brazilian nationals of Japanese descent living in Japan. Together with those from Peru, Argentina and Bolivia, foreign workers of Japanese descent total more than 370,000; and most of these are contract labourers. The figures could be interpreted as a social problem of discrimination against them in recruitment and employment. Should this happen in a country which subscribes to the idea of affirmative action, major businesses would, more than likely, be allotted a quota: – for example, one per cent of its new regular employees would have to be foreigners of Japanese descent. They may be treated more favourably than other foreigners, but people of Japanese descent are made to remain in non-regular employment because they are, after all, foreigners. Their foreign nationalities work like a status, which further entrenches their social class. All these baneful effects have been produced by the lies that have been told.

Everybody knows that foreign workers are the ones who bear the burden of unskilled work in Japan. Newspapers played up this topic in their reports on the series of reviews announced in May 2007 in relation to the overseas trainee and technical intern system. The deception about the trainees and interns, however, has never been questioned, not even in newspaper reports. In effect, they are workers. Legally, they are not. They are trapped in a *nue*-like existence. This has placed the national and local governments in an impasse in their policies on foreign workers. The sequence of the departmental notifications from those on spouses of Japanese nationals to those on marriage, and then to those on permanent resident mothers and children corresponds to the changes in the life of a female foreigner – from being single to being married to a Japanese national or a permanent resident, and then to being divorced with a child or children. In fact, the last two notifications coincided respectively with the time when marriages of female foreigners to Japanese men became an issue and the time when foreigner mothers and children from broken marriages became an issue. This course of events shows that foreign workers may be dealt with by labour policies when they are not yet married, but that once they stay longer in the country and start families, further policies are needed to accommodate these changes. In short, labour policies do not work unless they are supported by social policies. While labour policies control the environment where the workers earn the income to support their families, social policies must be implemented to respond to the problems which accompany their prolonged residence in Japan: health insurance and pensions, children's education and the ageing of the workers. In reality, however, Japan's failure to acknowledge foreigners as workers has prevented it from introducing labour policies for them. As long as no labour policies are in sight, waves of challenges for social policies are building up bit by bit. Without labour policies to take care of them, foreign workers are rarely entitled to enough income to survive. In this situation, foreign workers will end up being a burden on society acting only to increase the social security expenditures.

As globalisation has progressed, Japan's social system based on life-time employment and seniority-oriented wages has been replaced by that of diversified employment. A proposal by *Nikkeiren* (Japan Business Federation), titled '*Shinjidai no nihonteki keiei shisutemu* (Japanese-style management system in a new era)' in 1995 was instrumental in the shift to the combined use of differentiated personnel groups. Being a group of workers differentiated in terms of rights (as the equality guaranteed to non-Japanese nationals naturally differs from that for Japanese nationals), foreigners found their niche by jumping on the wagon of the service contracting industry, which played a major part in expediting the differentiation in employment. The niche was reproduced beyond the national borders of Japan, as discussed in Chapter 10. When the employment system of service contracting differentiated labour disregarded international boundaries, the industry as a whole was reproduced in the countries from which the workers come.

Citing Neil Smelser's concept of primordialism (Smelser 1991: 39) as 'fundamental cultural values and beliefs that are the first premises for organising and legitimatizing institutions, roles and behaviour,' Christian Joppke argued that British immigration policy was defined by primordialism (Joppke 2004). In relation to foreign workers in Japan, this primordialism could be seen as having been the principle of *jus sanguinis* or principle of family lineage.

As mentioned in the introduction to this book, the author has some reservations about the research undertaken by Kajita in his later years (1999, 2001 & 2002). One often hears these works being criticised for having accepted bureaucrats' statements unquestioningly. From the perspective of 'primordialism defining immigration policy,' however, Kajita's analysis is not too far off the mark. His only error was that he missed a very important question, or probably failed to distinguish it. The critical question concerned not how the bureaucrats understood the facts, but the rationale that made them say what they said. Had he distinguished 'the formation process' of legislation – the process of drawing up the legal text, and the 'implementation process' of legislation – the process of enforcing the law in accordance with the legal text, this would have provided useful evidence that 'the fundamental ideas of our social system' (or 'primordialism' to borrow from Smelser) had been developed logically during the latter 'implementation process' (namely, the process of enforcing the law).

One fundamental idea of the Japanese social system is, judging from its Nationality Act, the principle of *jus sanguinis*. Japanese descendants suited this view extremely well. The rationale for accepting them was found in primordialism; having Japanese blood. This could be readily used as good grounds for the legitimisation of their residency. Thus, the mythology of bloodline opened the door for Japanese descendants to work in Japan. The mythology then collapsed. The acceptance of foreigners of Japanese descent was pronounced a mistake by the Ministry of Justice. As of April 2006, a Japanese descendant is required to produce certificates of a clean criminal record both in Japan and at home at the time of new entry and visa renewal. The state has admitted that Japanese descendants do not necessarily share Japanese cultural values. What are the different lights in which we can see the foreigners who belong to this category? The author believes that the category based on bloodline is meaningless, but sees some significance in it in the context of labour policies. This category allows controlled acceptance of foreign labour into Japan. A scheme that only admits Japanese descendants and their families to the country to work makes it possible to impose limits on the foreign labour entering Japan. If the scheme fails, the disaster will not be infinite. In Brazil, for example, there are said to be 1.3 to 1.4 million Japanese descendants. Therefore, the number of people entering Japan from Brazil under the scheme will not exceed 1.4 million. As the category of Japanese descendants has this use, it will always be a key concept in the government's policy making and also be subject to controversy. However, if the people in this category remain unacknowledged as workers, the problems that it faces today will continue, no matter how much tinkering there might be.

Now, let us ask what lets Japan off the international human rights regime. As was true with the case discussed earlier in this chapter, Japanese courts rarely decide whether or not there has been a violation of the International Human Rights Agreement or the Convention of the Rights of the Child, to both of which Japan is a signatory. It would be no exaggeration to say that whilst Japan has ratified international treaties on human rights, it is hardly bound by them. This conceals a structural problem typical of the legal world of Japan. The international human rights regime normally takes effect when an international treaty on human rights is ratified by a country. It is a system in which the courts of the country are required by the Vienna Convention (the International Agreement on Treaties) to use the judicial precedents of the treaty's other signatories in the same way as its own. This regime is practised because an individual who is unsatisfied with a decision on human rights by the highest court in the country is entitled to appeal to international judicial organisations, which use judicial precedents from all the signatory nations. Japan, however, ratified the treaties excluding the provisions for the right of an individual to appeal to international judicial organisations (called the right of individual petition). For this reason, there is no court higher than the Supreme Court of Japan to which an individual may appeal, and the courts in Japan do not make decisions using precedents from other signatories to the treaties.

It is this very stance that makes Japan less capable of dealing with problems involving foreigners. No device exists for controlling the alliance of travel agencies run by people of Japanese descent and independent service contractors who make up the employment system that transcends borders. Something akin to this transnational employment system is practised in bringing foreign trainees and interns to Japan. The recruiting system leaves Japan few means of control, except issuing and refusing visas, at the other end – the points of emigration for foreign workers. In effect, the state cannot control the system itself. Although it is the Japanese government's forte to guide an industry and its businesses towards goals that it sets as being fair, administrative guidance cannot achieve the objective that it expects, with respect to caring for the people moving to Japan under this system. The Japanese legal system must respect such people as individuals with inherent rights, something which it tends to be less than enthusiastic about doing, and build up a device which those who have had their rights violated can use to petition. Only by doing so, will it be possible to give a human face to the transnational employment system. As Kawashima pointed out, the modern times were made modern by the fact that people could form an equal, if nominal, relationship with the other party in a transaction. What is required most of all now is the establishment of legal provisions designed to enable foreigners to enter the market as equal parties to a transaction, particularly in the context of the Japanese labour market. Needless to say, the first step is to remove the lie that has resulted in foreign workers not being counted as workers under the law, despite the fact that socially they are workers. This cannot, in any likelihood, lead to foreigners being treated in the same way as Japanese workers, who are citizens, in all respects. And herein lies the precise reason why they must be given a legal footing as "foreign workers."

12 Japanese citizenship and Japanese descent: boundaries and the significance of connecting to the first Japanese

Introduction

The Birth of International Marriage: the path to 'Japan as a civilised country,' by Itsuko Kamoto, was highly acclaimed for its treatment of the history of international marriage in Japan and its relationship with Japanese nationality. The author still recalls having obtained a copy relatively soon after its publication and reading it avidly. And yet, partly because the author's research theme was mainly the foreign worker labour problem, he did not give this book that much thought. However, the problem of workers of Japanese descent cannot be avoided in considerations of the foreign worker problem. It is one's links with Japanese nationality that form the basis for differentiations in rank amongst foreign workers. If this point is kept in mind, one will inevitably arrive at the same problem consciousness as Kamoto. The problem is one of the boundaries of Japanese nationality.

Only workers of Japanese descent are allowed to work without restriction despite being foreign workers.[1] One argument assumes that the lack of work restrictions is based on a visa category that regards people of Japanese descent as long-term residents and not foreign workers. The actions of the Ministry of Health, Labour and Welfare in the midst of the world-wide recession that followed the Lehman Brothers Shock of 2008 — spending state funds, from April 2009 until March 2010, on a repatriation assistance scheme that urged unemployed workers of Japanese descent and their families to go home — make it perfectly clear for everyone to see that people of Japanese descent are foreign workers.

Why is it that only people of Japanese descent have been accepted into Japan without the application of any of the work restrictions of the Immigration Control and Refugee Recognition Act? The standard response is that this is a consequence of the 1990 revision of this Immigration Control Act. The author would like to consider, firstly, why it was that within the Japanese legal system, including these revisions to the Immigration Control Act, people of Japanese descent were the only ones not to have work restrictions placed on them; and, secondly, what was the origin of the thinking that underpinned the foundation for granting special status to people of Japanese descent alone? As I re-read Kamoto's book with these thoughts in mind, I realised that, on a number of points, a wide gulf exists between the sociological and legal understandings of nationality.

The aims of this chapter are, firstly, to indicate the points of conflict between sociological and legal understandings of nationality, and then to elucidate why it is that it is permissible to grant special status only to people of Japanese descent. There will, moreover, be a discussion of the fact that differences between the use of the term people of 'Japanese descent' as a result of administrative measures and references to people and societies of people of Japanese descent in Brazil's *'colonia'* lead to various misunderstandings.

Becoming Japanese

What it is to be Japanese is not at all self-evident. And precisely for this reason there are numerous cases every year of claims being filed regarding requests for confirmation of nationality. As a result, the higher courts – the Supreme Court and the High Court – have accumulated a number of precedents. Nevertheless, there is an endless stream of suits being filed involving cases seeking a determination of recognition of nationality. Cases seeking confirmation of nationality, which ask for a judgement regarding whether the person concerned is a Japanese national or not, are for the most part international marriages,[2] making it natural that Kamoto, who was dealing with international marriage, should take up the discussion of nationality.

Incidentally, people who hold Japanese citizenship are also necessarily listed on a family register. Conversely, 'in the event that a foreigner has mistakenly been recorded in a family register, this entry must be deleted as it is not legally permitted (Tanaka 1966: 110).' This is why Japanese are required to submit their family register when they apply for a Japanese passport. However, it is not exclusively Japanese who appear in family registers,[3] and some people are not listed despite the fact that they were originally Japanese. Considering an example of a recent social issue will make this easier to understand: there are children who are not listed in family registers because of the so-called 300 day provision in civil law which says that children born to a mother within 300 days of her divorcing become the children of her former husband. This is an issue that has been dealt with increasingly in national magazines and newspapers as well as on television. Even in all of the editorials and special feature articles that have dealt with this issue, what has been lacking, despite the understanding that this is a problem of not having a family register, is a viewpoint that sees this as a problem of statelessness. Socially, also, the result of not having a family register is the emergence of some degree of doubt regarding whether these children are Japanese nationals. The issue of the 300 day provision is one that relates to Japanese women. Given that the mothers in these cases are unquestionably Japanese, the fact that this problem leads to children not being listed on a family register can be said to be a natural outcome of a Nationality Act that adopts a principle of family lineage, which is based on the family lines of one's current parents.

A child with a Japanese mother becomes a Japanese national regardless of marriage issues. For this reason, problems under the 300 day provision, in which there are no doubts about the birth mother being Japanese, present no problem whatsoever under the Japanese Nationality Act. However, when the father is Japanese, this not the case at all. Even if it is certain that the birth father is Japanese, the child could be deemed either a foreigner or Japanese simply on the basis of procedural matters. The problem of a child's nationality changing wholly as a result of these sorts of formalities was questioned by a judgement about the unconstitutionality of the Japanese Nationality Act handed down by the full bench of the Supreme Court on 4 June 2008. The issue in this case was the questioning of the reasonableness of having split the nationality of two children born to a Japanese father and Filipina mother, who were in a de facto relationship. One child was given Philippine and the other Japanese nationality on the basis of whether there had or had not been an application for recognition of unborn children for the purposes of nationality. The Supreme Court ruled that it was unreasonable to change nationality simply on the basis of the existence or absence of an application for the recognition of unborn children; said that the child who was a Philippine national should also be legally recognised as Japanese; and brought down its decision that the Japanese Nationality Act was unconstitutional.[4] Even someone who, until the day before, had been a foreigner could become Japanese through the recognition of the courts. What it is to be Japanese is not at all self-evident.

What has been the opinion of the Ministry of Justice?

Legislators, more so than the Japanese Nationality Act, could be said to determine who is Japanese. Within the Civil Affairs Bureau of the Ministry of Justice, it is Civil Affairs Bureau Section Five that deals with the Japanese Nationality Act and Civil Affairs Bureau Section Two that deals with the Family Registration Law. The postwar heads of each of these sections have written several volumes of outlines, on a case by case basis, of the Japanese Nationality Act and the Family Registration Law. These works are a consolidation of the thoughts of the authors, and the opinions in them do not represent the opinions of the Ministry of Justice. However, those responsible for the practical implementation of the law could well think that the Ministry of Justice's opinion regarding nationality, on a case by case basis, is revealed in these detailed discussions of how one ought to make judgements about the intent behind the application of the laws.[5]

Let us look first at how Kenta Hiraga, the drafter of the post-war new Japanese Nationality Act, saw nationality. According to Hiraga, nationality is 'a close political relationship between the individual and the state' and 'an individual's qualification as a member of a particular state' (Hiraga 1950: 1). The principle of territorial jurisdiction and the principle of birthplace (*jus soli*) were adopted as a result of 'the state being conceived of as the territory of the ruler, namely the lord' in the medieval feudal state. With the advent of modern times, the concept of the principle of family lineage emerges as a result of the understanding that community – that is a people, sharing various elements such as language, religion, customs and literature and the arts, which altogether make up culture – constitutes a 'country' (Hiraga 1950: 2). In any event, connections with the community that have been established in a country are decisive when considering nationality.

In feudal society, people were, essentially, permitted no freedom of movement either in terms of status or geographically, and, with the exception of communes, people, particularly the peasants who formed the vast majority of the population at that time, were instead possessions that came with the land. In this period, people's concept of residence was directly linked to their concept of nationality. They were able to concretely and realistically confirm that 'that person lives on that land – in other words, that that person is a member of a community with regional bonds formed by people who permanently reside on a fixed piece of land.' However, as people's mobility increases, a state of affairs arises in which it cannot be said that the fact of living in a particular area directly builds a community. This is seen in the various understandings of where one lives as: 'simply a *place* for a person to stay temporarily,' 'a *place of temporary residence* as a place of more or less continuous stay' and 'a *residence* as the living base where an individual's daily life is constantly carried out'[Emphasis inserted by author]. Residence and place of temporary residence are conceptually distinct: the former is not merely restricted to a place where an individual stays. The individual is drawn into a variety of social relationships in that place, and the concept of address designates a place that has been given a certain position by the surrounding society. Thus, as people's mobility increases, it is not only the pragmatic relationships between individuals, of the sort that had existed until medieval times, that form the connections between land and individuals; these connections turn into highly abstract concepts of nationality within the modern concept of nationality.

The idea behind reexamining the membership of the community, in response to this situation in modern society, was the principle of family lineage. Hiraga commented that the principle of territorial jurisdiction directly links the concept of nationality with the concept of residence. 'The acquisition or forfeiture of the qualifications to be the inhabitant of a country is nothing other than the acquisition of a residence in the country,' but the principle of family lineage 'comes into existence when regional connections with a land have been abstracted from the concept of nationality.' Also, the separation and independence of this concept of nationality from the concept of residence is expressed in the adoption of the principle of family lineage (*jus sanguinus*) as opposed to the principle of birthplace in which where one was born formed the legal basis for the acquisition of qualifications to be an inhabitant of a country.' This is because 'in the principle of family lineage, a child acquires his mother or father's nationality at birth. Accordingly, the acquisition or forfeiture of the qualification to be an inhabitant of a land is, understandably, not dependent on the place of birth (Hiraga 1950: 9–10).'

When Hiraga first covered the fundamental concept of nationality, he did not simply embark on a commentary on the Japanese Nationality Act. This is because the thinking that provides the key for considering the structure of Japanese nationality – in short, the essence of the principle of family lineage for Japan – is contained within it. Hiraga explains that:

> Japan's family register system embodies the official stance that the qualification to be recorded in a family register is restricted to Japanese citizens and that all Japanese citizens are recorded in family registers. It is, on the other hand, however, permanent residence (*honseki*) that provides the foundation for the family register system. *One's permanent residence does not necessarily bear any connection to where one's real residence may be, and yet, even so, it is one of the prescribed places in this land of ours.* If that is the case, then all Japanese citizens, by virtue of being entered in a family register, have a permanent residence; and, by virtue of having a permanent residence, even if only conceptually, they possess connections with the land of Japan, in the form of regional bonds (Hiraga 1950: 12–13).' [Emphasis inserted by author.]

In short, the adoption of the principle of family lineage functions not only to make citizens of the children of citizens; it grants a concrete status to the individual as a member of the community that is the family. It achieves this by connecting nationality with the family register system, which controls families. In this way, the principle of family lineage simultaneously guarantees a conceptual connection between these children and the land of Japan, via the mediation of their permanent residence (honseki).[6] As a result, the Japanese concept of nationality includes an element of the principle of territorial jurisdiction.

Incidentally, according to Hiraga, the adoption of the principle of family lineage does not immediately lead to those people defined under the Japanese Nationality Act becoming citizens. Up until the first half of the nineteenth century, the people defined under the Japanese Nationality Act were not modern citizens; they had had a former existence: that is, as 'inhabitants of the country.' The need to consider nationality within the concept of the citizen arose following the latter half of the nineteenth century. This required a state of affairs in which there was 'the creation of an awareness of one's own people as a state in contrast to other people and the formation of the idea of citizens as a means of henceforth distinguishing a member of one's own people from other people. And this not only made possible self-awareness on the part of these citizens as participants in politics as members of political bodies, it even led independent individuals to develop a distinct consciousness (Hiraga 1950: 34).'

In addition, Hiraga explains the principle of family lineage in the following terms. The principle of family lineage is an arrangement whereby the children of citizens systematically become citizens. However, the original need for this principle arose once people began to move around, under the principle of territorial jurisdiction; and this placed people with a common culture, language and a variety of social customs outside the state and the community. At the same time, it was no longer possible to retain the unity of the community by making people, who while having been born in the country had different languages, cultures and customs, into citizens. At the foundation of this way of thinking is the idea that individuals form couples as communities of men and women, and then as children are born to couples, communities of parents and children are established. These children acquire the language, culture and various social customs that exist in the variety of large and small communities within the nation through their families; in communities of couples and communities of parents and children. It is in this sense that the children of citizens become citizens (Hiraga 1950: 108–110; 1951: 201–202).

Hiraga's successors have also adopted the stance that up until the first half of the nineteenth century we cannot talk of a modern concept of citizen. The person who has shown this most clearly is Aritsugu Tashiro:

> Japan, before the opening up of the country in the Meiji period, was a pre-modern nation, but, in addition to being a nation, it should also be noted that Japan had substantial nationality laws (the Customary Nationality Act). In addition, the substance of the Customary

Nationality Act can be thought of as having been that "the inhabitants are a people sharing the same thoughts" (Tashiro 1974: 55).'[7]

However, as Tashiro is well-known for his extreme stand on the principle of family lineage with regard to nationality, some caution is required. He goes as far as saying that his views, which seem to repudiate Hiraga's principle of family lineage, are that '"family lineage" means a blood relationship, in other words, physiological blood ties (Tashiro 1974: 45).' He says that 'whether – aside from "natural family lineage (physiological family lineage)" – there exists any leeway for considering matters such as "legally mandated family lineage," where there are no physiological connections between parents and children, is a fundamental question for the Japanese Nationality Act.' Tashiro even asserts that 'we must interpret family lineage in the Japanese Nationality Act as being confined to physiological family lineage (Tashiro 1974: 45–46).'[8]

Incidentally, all of the works that have been treated as stating the opinion of the Ministry of Justice by the author also discuss the development of the Japanese Nationality Act. These all seek the beginnings of the Japanese Nationality Act in Edict Number 103 issued by the Grand Council of State in 1873 (hereafter the 1873 Edict).

Although Kamoto also makes the 1873 Edict, as the first Japanese Nationality Act, the main analytical focus of her book, she includes a discussion of the fact that international marriages were occurring, in a similar manner, within the international marriages that took place before the 1873 Edict. The stress in Kamoto's book is on continuity. However, none of the books mentioned as having been written by government officials stating the opinion of the Ministry of Justice contain any reference whatsoever to the international marriages or to international marriages prior to 1873. This is most likely because the legal approach treats international marriages, including those that pre-date the 1873 Edict, as falling outside the category of the Japanese Nationality Act. Why is it that a gap emerges between the treatment of nationality within legal and sociological approaches?

What was Japan's principle of family lineage? Finding the Japanese progenitor

Differences between the legal and the sociological approaches began to emerge in the handling of the Family Registration Law of 1871 (the law upon which the Jinshin Family Register was established), which was proclaimed in April of that year through Edict Number 170 of the Grand Council of State. Incidentally, the author has, up until this point, read Kamoto's approach as a sociological approach, but this is not accurate. Rather, Kamoto's way of approaching family registers has been to rely on the historical demographer Akira Hayami; making it more appropriate, perhaps, to refer to the Kamoto-Hayami approach. A straightforward illustration of this is that while referencing Hayami, she argues that 'this family register has its origin in Chōshu domain's *tojaku* (family register).' Kamoto continues, 'However, if we consider the functional dimension of understanding the population through "family" units, we see that even the Edo Period Register of Religious Faith and Relationships of Village Members played the same role (Kamoto 2001: 21).' Kamoto sees the Jinshin Family Register as stretching back to the family register system that preceded it, and, bringing a functionalist viewpoint to bear, considers the Jinshin Family Register from the aspect of continuity with the Register of Religious Faith and Relationships of Village Members.

However, within a legal approach, there is a clear demarcation of the Jinshin Family Register and the preceding family register system. The discussion of this point, in the following section, will show that it is not possible to discuss the international marriages that Kamoto talks about in this chapter – from the beginning of the Edo period to the very early Meiji period (before the establishment of the Jinshin Family Register) – in terms of connections with the current Japanese Nationality Act. As far as the Japanese Nationality Act is concerned, the Jinshin Family Register contains the names of the Japanese progenitors: it is the first setting out of who is Japanese.

As we saw in the preceding section, there is not necessarily a common understanding regarding what the Japanese principle of family lineage denotes, even amongst those in the Ministry of Justice who are responsible for putting this into practice. There is, however, agreement on the point that the principle of family lineage holds that the children of citizens become citizens. In other words, this is the logic that Japanese are the children of Japanese. In order to establish this proposition that the children of Japanese are themselves Japanese, it is essential to be able to point to the first Japanese. A perusal of Tomohei Taniguchi's *Family Registration Law* (1957), in Yūhikaku's collection of the complete works of

jurisprudence, shows that the family registration system began
with the eight hereditary titles designated by Emperor Tenmu in
684 (*Yakusa no Kabane*). Moreover, despite this book having been
published in the post-war period, the date is recorded with reference
to the imperial era.[9] This, once again, drives home a feeling of just
how intimately the family register system and the emperor system
are linked. The family register that becomes problematic in terms of
the Japanese Nationality Act is not, however, a family registration
system that has continued unbroken from ancient times.

It was Tashiro, with his insistence that the principle of family
lineage is the same as the principle of blood relations, who
exemplified this point most clearly. He argues that there is no other
way of sustaining the principle of citizen's children becoming
citizens apart from tracing back sequentially to establish the
knowledge of whether one's parents were Japanese or, even better,
whether back in time one's grandparents were Japanese. Moreover,
'as one traces back through the principle of family lineage, there
must have been a first, founding, Japanese person in the past. We
call this founding Japanese person "the progenitor Japanese person."
Firstly, this progenitor Japanese person comes into existence, and
then his descendants are born; the Japanese people who will inherit
his nationality. "In the beginning, there was the progenitor Japanese
person." This is the essence of the Japanese Nationality Act built
on the principle of family lineage (Tashiro 1974: 52).'

The progenitor Japanese person is to be determined in the
following way: since the new nationality law is enacted by replacing
the old nationality law, the people who are Japanese in the new
law are those who were also Japanese under the old law. Before
the old nationality law, there was no nationality law based on legal
statements; it was a case of '"one's nation was one's nationality,"
and given the existence of a nation, it could be said that a law
whose purpose it was to determine the nationality of the members
of this nation – in short, (essentially) a nationality law – existed
naturally (Tashiro 1974: 54).' As mentioned previously, the
essential nationality law before the opening up of the country was
a Customary Nationality Law based on the idea that the inhabitants
are a people sharing the same thoughts. From this point of view,
Tashiro locates the 1873 Edict as the first nationality law.

He argued that 'a foreign woman who becomes the wife of a
Japanese man acquires Japanese nationality, and both members of

the couple become Japanese. Conversely, a Japanese woman who becomes the wife of a foreign man forfeits her Japanese nationality and both people in the couple become foreigners. Because this, ultimately, comes down to an official stance that both people in a couple should be of the same nationality, it was thought that children born to a couple were governed by the principle that assumed that they should acquire the same nationality as their parents. In short, the principle of both people in a couple having the same nationality can be seen as having naturally implied the principle of parents and children having the same nationality. This further implied the principle of family lineage – that is, that children would inherit their parents' nationality, and it is here that we can see signs of the beginnings of the principle of blood relations with regard to biological principles (Tashiro 1974: 59).' That is to say, the 1873 Edict stated that newly-arrived foreigners who entered Japan following the opening up of the country would be foreigners and that those Japanese who had left to go overseas would remain Japanese. Tashiro perceives this as including revisions to the Customary Nationality Act which held that inhabitants were citizens. As an axiomatic view can be taken of citizens who are the children of citizen couples – the core citizens, even if this area were to be left to custom, no great confusion would occur. Since, conversely, custom alone will not suffice with regard to fringe areas it is inevitably provisions based in law that must provide clarification with regard to these matters. In short, we are able to treat provisions which at a glance appear to apply only to the fringes as a nationality law that is not limited to fringe areas.[10]

The first nationality law, in the form of the 1873 Edict, was an edict concerning marriages with foreigners. The subjects of this edict were Japanese marrying foreigners, but it is absolutely impossible to find provisions in the wording of this edict that indicate who is Japanese. However, in order to establish the edict as legal text, it goes without saying that the parties concerned who must gain the permission of the Japanese government when they marry foreigners are Japanese nationals, despite the lack of provisions setting this out. Who, then, were the subjects of this law? They were the people recorded in the Jinshin Family Register which was compiled as a family register of 'the general subjects' on the basis of the 1873 Family Register Law. The first consolidated national family register provides the first record of registration of the Japanese people. Also, the people recorded in the Jinshin Family Register are, in terms of the Japanese Nationality Act, the first Japanese nationals.

Why seek the progenitor Japanese person amongst the entries in the Jinshin Family Register?

Incidentally, why is it then that the progenitor Japanese person is sought in the Jinshin Family Register? Claiming that this is simply because it is the first record of Japanese people will not suffice. Let us, therefore, look at some family register research done by lawyers. This discussion will refer primarily to two works. The first is Masao Fukushima's *'Ie' Seido no Kenkyū* (An Investigation of the 'Family' System) (a main volume and three volumes of documents), published between 1959 and 1967. The second work is *Nihon no Shihonshugi to 'Ie' Seido* (Japanese Capitalism and the 'Family' System) (1967); a compilation of Fukushima's research on the family system. The reasons for having chosen to use Fukushima's research as a representative example of research undertaken by jurists are twofold. Firstly, in his three volumes of documents, Fukushima has assembled detailed arguments and documents which show the process of the establishment of the Family Registration Law in the early Meiji period; and, furthermore, his opinions are based on documents concerning the administration of family registration in cases that actually occurred in each domain and prefecture. Secondly, of all the treatments of family registration in works relating to the Japanese Nationality Act that the author has read to date, it is Fukushima's opinions that provide the best basis for a straightforward understanding of Japanese nationality.

According to Fukushima, before the 1873 Family Registration Law, the Kyoto Prefecture Family Registration Civil Law was promulgated in 1868, and then the following year, it was enacted by the Ministry of Popular Affairs, and placed under the direct control of the government. This law was made up of: the Urban Family Registration Civil Law, enforced in urban areas; the Rural Family Registration Civil Law, enforced in rural districts; and, others including, the Samurai Registration Law, enforced by family type; the Low-ranking Samurai Registration Law and the Shrines and Temples Registration Law. In amongst these, the family registration law that related to the common people was the *Tojaku*, which had its origins in the domain of Chōshu.

It is thought that the operation of a family register began in 1869 with the Tokyo Metropolitan Family Register Ordinance, which was based on the Kyoto Prefecture Family Registration Civil Law. This register contained a number of revisions such as: making use of the new sections of landholding register, leased land register and leased retail premises register; and also the inclusion in city registers of people from other countries and resident for a certain period of time. However, both the Tokyo Metropolitan Family Register Ordinance and the Kyoto Prefecture Family Registration Civil Law were social status family registers which set out differences in terms of urban and rural areas; they were not uniform family registration systems (Fukushima 1967: 77–82). Moreover, these family registration systems, which were able to include the common people living in rural areas within rural family registers, were premised on the fact that peasants could not leave the land; they were family registration systems that not only maintained the status system (which is why family registration by family membership came into being, but were steeped in feudal traditions that stretched back to the Tokugawa political power system in which peasants were tightly bound to the land).

However, the 1871 Family Registration Law is understood as having been a complete departure from the family registration system that had existed to date. Firstly, 'the 1871 Family Registration Law was a precursor of the abolition of the feudal domains and the establishment of prefectures. Alongside having paved the way for these changes, after the abolition of the feudal domains and the establishment of prefectures, the Family Registration Law was one of the most important laws to the political power of the Restoration, which unified national political rule (Fukushima 1967: 42).' Unlike the previous registers, which had been based on family membership, the new register had a single format that transcended status differences, and in imposing the same duties on everyone it stresses the birth of the ideology of 'the equality of the four social classes.' In short, this is a legal approach that pays attention to the ideological aspects of family registers, and not the functionalist understanding of family registers of the Kamoto-Hayami approach.

Moreover, Fukushima seeks the ideological source of the 1871 Family Registration Law in Kōchi domain's reforms of its administration. Taisuke Itagaki regarded as decisive the official notice of the great reform of the domains, promulgated in November 1870, in whose drafting Takachika Fukuoka – who drafted the Charter Oath of the Council of State – participated as an influential Councillor of State. This official notice consisted of: 1) 'the establishment of a bureaucracy within the domain government structure;' 2) 'the imposition of conscription on all four social classes;' 3) 'the dissolution of hereditary samurai status and the establishment of stipend bonds;' 4) 'the abolition of low ranking samurai;' 5) 'the liberation of samurai, farmers, peasants and artisans from the class system;' and then in order to give effect to items one to five, 6) 'the establishment of a general family register by the domain government.' This was an internal matter for Kōchi, but the construction of a general family register for samurai and commoners alike abolished the inheritance of samurai status; applied conscription to all classes; and, by abolishing the old class system, its intention was to bring about the possibility of occupational and geographic mobility within the region (Fukushima 1967: 53–57).

Kōchi domain's reforms were, when all is said and done, a microcosm of Japan. With their abolition as a group, the samurai had no choice but to find employment in some occupation or other. This would not have been possible in the former situation in which there were registers for each respective status group. With the inclusion of all people in a general register, occupational mobility became possible and with the creation of these registers there was a recognition of intermarriage between people of different status, which had been prohibited in the past, and, as a result of these various factors, there was also a recognition of movement within the region (the freedom to travel). The consolidation of family registers into one system is not simply a matter of having all people recorded in one document; it was a step that had an impact on the whole social system, bringing about this sort of mobility between social groups (in today's terms: social class mobility and social rank mobility) and also mobility within the region.

Fukushima places particular stress on Itagaki's experiences at the time of the Battle of Aizu. Lamenting the fact that the common people were indifferent at the time that the warriors of Aizu were fighting, Itagaki states: 'there is separation between the upper and lower classes. The warrior class monopolizes a comfortable way of living without sharing it with the ordinary people.' Itagaki emphasises undertaking reform by means of having the will to 'dispense with the accepted practice of the samurai, create a system of equality amongst the four social classes, and enforce the principle of universal conscription[11]. Itagaki also notes that, at the time of the Kōchi domain reforms, when Kōchi domain sent a letter of inquiry to the administrative supervisor of the Grand Council of State (*benkan*) in order to carry out what was known as the 'general family register of samurai and commoners,' this became a 'general family register of the people,' and then, in the 1871 Family Registration Act, this changed to 'subjects in general.'

> Called the 'general family register of samurai and commoners' in the Ordinance and referred to as the 'general family register of the people' in the letter of inquiry to administrative supervisor of Grand Council of State, ... the ideological origins of this linked up with what Itagaki called 'a system of equality between the four social classes' and 'patriotism.' It can also be seen as being linked, as the systematic development of these, to the term 'subjects in general' which appears in the 1871 Family Registration Act (Fukushima 1967: 57).

Included within Itagkaki's ideas was the establishment of a new government structure and a patriotic citizenry. These correspond to what we would now call state or nation building. The equality of the four social classes resides in one conceptual value; however, the primary objective of positioning this conceptual value is the creation of a rich country and a strong army. With it being critical that people from all status groups and classes participate in the establishment of a modern country and in the army, it was assumed that the equality of the four social classes would mobilise the people and act as an incentive towards these ends. The national law that was constructed with this idea as its basic ideology is the 1871 Family Registration Law, and this could be seen as the reason why it provides the springboard for modern Japan. These are sufficient grounds for regarding people who are related to those appearing in the Jinshin Family Register as the first citizens.

Ideation of the family register concept and Japanese people from the viewpoint of nationality

Incidentally, there is an additional reason for regarding the *Jinshin* Family Register as containing the names of the first Japanese and also for considering the first Japanese to be the starting point for the subsequent Japanese Nationality Act, based on the principle of family lineage. Paragraph one of the first Family Registration Law of 1871, determined that,

> Since under the existing, status-based, family registration system it is not possible to gain a complete understanding of the entire populace, this system will be reformed and a unified family register compiled. By making use of the place of residence principle (the idea of achieving an understanding of the populace on the basis of residence), these family registers will include everyone, without a single person being omitted. Therefore, on the basis of the newly compiled law, we should make every effort to record complete details for all Japanese subjects (namely, nobles, warriors, soldiers, Shinto and Buddhist priests, and commoners) and their place of residence.

Fukushima maintained that this was 'an argument for realising that there was a fundamental defect in the existing system of the status-based family register, under which it was not possible to capture the whole of the population, and also for reforming this to establish a unified family register which as result of relying on the principle of place of residence would be comprehensive and omit no one (Fukushima 1967: 22).' In short, the Jinshin Family Register, by a thorough application of the principle of place of residence, differed as a register and in its actual conditions from both preceding and subsequent family registers. It is a register not simply of the concept of, but the actual progenitor Japanese.

Within a very short time of the drawing up of the Jinshin Register, however, the family register ceased reflecting the actual situation. With freedom from the strict ties that had bound them to the soil in the feudal period, and under the ideology of equality between the four social classes, there was increasing spatial and social mobility on the part of people. However, the recording of people in the books of the family register, strictly tying them to the family register rather than to the soil, gave rise to the situation that while people continued to be entered in the records of the family register, some individuals were not living in the location of these registers. In extreme cases, circumstances arose in which not a single person from a family lived in the location of the family register. The family register ceased to reflect reality.[12]

In addition, the family register was changing form. The Jinshin Family Register was 'established on the basis of "house" (house-

hold) units, which were in turn based on address; and, in addition
to listing matters such as permanent domicile, full name, age,
patron Shinto deity, Buddhist sect and crimes it also recorded
the family seal.' Then, in 1887, the family register took the form
of 'establishing a system of registration lists which included three
additional lists: additions to the register; instances of removal of
names; and movements. Exclusively items related to movements in
status were recorded in these.' Then, the format of the 1899, family
register was one in which 'alongside essential reform of the family
registration system and as a result of the creation of a system of
recording social status, the family register came to be established
on the basic unit of the "family," which in turn was based on the
main domicile. Consequently, the family register added the extra
columns of "Relationship to former head of household" and "Reason
for assuming family headship and date." The column, "Relationship
to family," was also added for people other than the head of the
house (Takiguchi 1966: 357–359).' The family register, having been
based on the principle of place of domicile, was moving in the direction of being perfected as an account of status relationships with
regard to the head of the household on the basis of the principle of
main domicile.

Did the loss of information, from families, in the family register
regarding their actual residential state invite danger for the family
registration system? Not at all. Fukushima refers to Izutarō
Suehiro's comments that 'The family, under our civil law, is not
an organisation with an actual social existence; it is no more than
a legally designated type of family organisation that only exists
ideologically. This is an ideological existence that endures vertically
as the continuous repository of the spirits of the ancestors; it is
not a horizontal organisation that actually exists (Suehiro 1940:
259–260).' Citing Suehiro's portrayal of these families that exist
not in reality but as ideological concepts as 'families as "types,"'
Fukushima argues that 'even if all the members of a family pass
away and the family register of that "family" is removed from the
family register archive (an extinct family), the "family" does not
cease to exist; it continues to exist as in the past as an ideological
concept, and it is precisely for this reason that extinct families can
be revived (Fukushima 1967: 6).' The continuation of the family
system, even when it has lost its basis in reality, emphasises the
existence of enforcement by means of a national law – the Family

Registration Law. As a national law, the Family Registration Law provides ongoing security for the efficacy of the family as a system. Accordingly, by bringing about the ideological nature of the family as a type and by compelling members of the family to practise ancestor worship with its vertical ties, family registration continues to be a mere empty shell, but it provides the reality for the family system, which is created via the mediation of family registration.

In this way, the process of the family registration system becoming a mere empty shell is linked to the processes, on the other hand, of the family system becoming a concept and an ideology. The conceptualisation of the family registration system leads us to anticipate that it is functioning as ideology with regard to nationality also. The author believes that by arriving at a concept of nationality that is linked to the process of the family registration system becoming ideological, we will be able to discern the reasons for the introduction of disparities into Japanese nationality, which is based on the family registration system of the imperial period. In short, using the family register as the classification we introduce hierarchical relationships between Japanese nationals in two ways. Firstly, because the Jinshin Family Register was based on the principle of place of domicile, we are able to acknowledge that the people listed in it are the first Japanese, who were alive at the time of its compilation. Secondly, we can connect the people listed in the Jinshin Family Register and their descendants to the historical circumstances that have built the Japanese nation-state. That is, we have people who are Japanese nationals on the basis of the domestic register: Japanese nationals on the Taiwanese Register who became Japanese with the cession of territory that occurred under the Treaty of Shimonoseki; and Japanese nationals on the Korean Register, which was based on personal and territorial sovereignty for Koreans under the Japan Korea Annexation Treaty.

In fact, on 2 April 1966, shortly after the conclusion of the Treaty on Basic Relations between Japan and the Republic of Korea, Yoshimi Ieyumi, head of Civil Affairs Section Two at the time, issued the following Notification No. Kō 1,025 by the Chief of Civil Affairs Bureau (*Minjikyokucho Kaito No. Kō 1,025*).

Furthermore, as a postscript, when Koreans who have been residing in Japan have become naturalised or when they have relinquished their Japanese nationality, they are officially listed, by the Ministry of Justice, in the Korean Register as "nationality Korean" or "in possession of Korean nationality." However, this "Korean" listing is apparently being used with exactly the same intent as a listing in the nationality column under the alien registrations, in line with the unanimous opinion of the government announced on 26 October last year. In other words, Koreans resident in Japan *come under their former Korean nationality* and fall under special circumstances in which as they continue to reside in Japan they lose their Japanese nationality and become foreigners. Because this results in them not possessing a passport or nationality certificate that could stand in its place, they have been listed under the name "Korean" as an expediency measure. In this sense, we are of the opinion that the "Korean" listing – as a term that indicates Koreans who have come to Japan from the Korean Peninsula which was formerly a Japanese territory – does not indicate any sort of nationality at all (emphasis inserted by author) (Ieyumi 1966: 252).'

It is precisely in the family register, more than in the recording of nationality, that we can find the origins of differentiation

The transformation of the principle of family lineage into the principle of a register – from the viewpoint of Brazilians of Japanese descent

The application of the Japanese Constitution 1947 rejected the family system that had existed to date, and led to the placing of the highest value on the dignity of the individual. The Family Registration Law was also revised with the post-war version stating that 'Married couples and children of the same lineage form the basic unit for the establishment of family registers; and the one register cannot list generations beyond the third generation or more than two couples. Family registers formed according to this same law have a different foundation for their establishment from family registers under the old law, which were established with the family of the old Civil Code as their basic unit: they differ considerably in both their contents and form (Iwasa 1959: 205).' The Family Registration Law had significantly altered its principles of establishment.

Did the meaning of family registration also change then as far as the Nationality Law was concerned? Nothing of the sort happened. As discussed above, Japanese nationals are invariably listed in family registers, but there are also cases in which parents may not have made a notification; despite parents having made a notification, officials may not have followed all of the formalities accurately; and there may even have been false reporting of family registers. For these reasons, it cannot be said with certitude that as long as one is listed in a family register, then one is a Japanese national; people listed in family registers are held to be Japanese nationals failing any proof to the contrary.

However, there are limits to proving that a family register is a fabrication. If the actual person who lied or related parties are still alive and able to give evidence, then it is possible to disprove, but if the parties concerned are no longer alive, and it is no longer possible to provide evidence that it is a fabricated family register, then it becomes impossible to overturn. A situation in which it is impossible to undermine the contents of 'the "old family registers" by producing proof to the contrary is actually similar to having a public-reliance effect. Also, *a Nationality Act based on the principle of family lineage regards people listed in the "old family registers," which can no longer be overturned, as definitely Japanese (actual progenitor Japanese), and, on this basis, decides whether or not their descendants are to have Japanese nationality* [emphasis added by author] (Tashiro 1974: 78).' Thus, 'the nationality of old ancestors must inevitably rely on a listing in a family register, and when this is the case, the predetermined foundation for deciding actual nationality comes to reside instead in the family register (Tashiro 1974: 77).' Just as the Edict of 1873, which was the first Nationality Act, had regard to the people listed in the Jinshin Family Register, the inevitability of the emergence of family register problems as problems of the predetermination of nationality[13] also conforms to the logic of the legal history of the Nationality Act.

Even though there is a new Nationality Act and a new Family Registration Law under the new constitution, there has been no change to the arrangement whereby only people who are connected to a family register, which serves as a record of citizens, can become citizens. Also, as is clear from looking at the acceptance of people of Japanese descent, even though Japan has changed to a new Family Registration Law that rejects the family system, the new family registers are still connected to the old family registers. In the new and old family registers alike, those people connected with a family register, lead an existence in which they are classified differently from ordinary foreigners and foreign nationals. *The structure of the law which mandates that people who are Japanese citizens must be listed in a family register makes possible the granting of special status to foreigners who have links with a family register, even though they are foreigners, if they can confirm their place on this register.* Ideologically also they are given a basis which considers them to have a standing as the descendants of members who participated in the building of modern Japan.

Kiyoshi Ando (pen name: Zenpachi Ando), one of the leaders of the post-war community of Brazilians of Japanese descent and also a founding member of the São Paolo Institute of Humanities, has given a compelling explanation of the need for the absorption in Brazil of the Japanese immigrant society that has existed from the pre-war period. He considered that the level of Japanese language proficiency attained from Japanese language education in the post-war *'colonia'* of *Nikkei* ought to be around the fourth grade of elementary school, and, in order to put this into practice, he made and distributed textbooks to each *'colonia.'* The fact that Japanese language education in post-war Brazil was at this level is well-known amongst people who are familiar with Latin American society. And the recognition of the right to work for people of Japanese descent, under the amendments to the 1990 Immigration Control and Refugee Recognition Act, plausibly speaks to consideration having been given to their cultural ties to Japan, but, from the viewpoint of people who know the real situation, this opinion in itself is an indication of the ideological nature of the term 'Japanese descent.'

Ieyumi, who was mentioned earlier, refers to the decision of the full bench of the Supreme Court on 5 April 1961[14] in arguing,

> The foundation for the loss of Japanese nationality by Koreans, as a consequence of this decision by the Supreme Court, is to be found in Clause (a) of Article 2 of the Peace Treaty. The extent of loss is not due to the principle of consanguinity; it is *based on the principle of family registration*, and at the time that the treaty came into effect, they were recorded in the Korean Family Register or as people who had a reason for why they should be registered [emphasis added by author].

Ieyumi treats people who were listed in the Korean Register and who had their names removed from the Domestic Register – even those people who were Japanese according to the principle of consanguinity via social status actions such as marriage or the adoption of an heir (people who Tashiro thought ought to be Japanese) – as having lost their Japanese nationality along with the coming into effect of the Peace Treaty (Ieyumi 1966: 244). Clearly, the use of the words 'principle of family registration,' indicates that the distinctions that exist in nationality ought to be sought in the family registers.

The author had thought that the differences between the descendants of those people on the Korean Family Registers as well as the Taiwan Family Register and the descendants of those on the Domestic Family Register – that is, people of Japanese descent – were differences of treatment between the descendants of the, as it were, now independent former colonies and the descendants of the suzerain state. However, if one considers these differences in treatment in terms of the descendants of people who participated in the building of the Meiji nation state of Japan and those who did not, then the explanation for the difference between people of Japanese descent – upon whom there are no restrictions regarding residence, work or being accompanied by family members – and Japanese who are citizens is merely the presence or absence of voting rights. If we think in these terms, under the principle of family lineage, the concept that indicates links with people who are recorded in the family register, which serves as a list of the nation's people, is that of family line, and what one must prove is not the nature of one's links (which is precisely why there is no recognition of the Japanese nationality of people who, although being Japanese by virtue of family lineage, have been entered on the Korean family Register), but whether or not one has a record of being a Japanese person in the form of a family register (Domestic Family Register) that precedes these links.

Endnotes

Preface

1 Kawashima maintains that 'the lives of individuals in agricultural communities are subsumed within the group (collective) in the following ways: 1) a large part of an individual's life is prescribed by the group and joint relationships exist in large parts of people's lives; 2) generally, there is complete mutual understanding between people regarding other people's lives, emotions, thoughts (value systems) and actions; 3) people equate other people's standpoints and interests with their own and identify with these sentiments and judgements (psychological restraints exist regarding individual actions taken apart from the group); 4) consequently, it is anticipated and expected that people will have fundamentally the same feelings and thoughts and behave in the same ways (there is a prohibition on and suppression of individuals acting apart from the group). I have decided to call this kind of individual versus group relationships the *principle of "united into one"'* (Kawashima 1982a: 262).

2 Makoto Kumazawa (1989), Makoto Sataka (1991), Hiroshi Kawahito (2006) and others too numerous to list.

3 The progressive inflation in the number of university graduates accompanying increases in both the number of people continuing on to university and in the number of universities is also likely, however, to have some bearing on this.

4 The author feels a strong sense of unease about discussing people of Japanese descent as foreign workers.

5 Meanwhile, in this four year period, the numbers of Indonesians have shown a consistently decreasing trend. This company has continually built up the number of factories that it has in Southeast Asia throughout the 1990s. During this period of overseas company start-ups, companies took in management trainees and people who would become leaders locally, and gave them in-house training. Subsequently, until the time that they were able to carry out worker training in their overseas factories, this parts maker accepted them as trainees and allowed them to study the structure of factories in Japan. There is, however, decreasing sense to sending people to Japan under the Indonesian trainee phenomenon as technical education and the transmission of technical skills – including the cultivation of talented people – becomes possible within these overseas factories after the passage of around ten years.

6 Clearly, this does not mean that there was no knowledge of who was working in any individual workplace. It is simply that they did not exist according to official records.

7 This is based on verbal comments made during a survey conducted in Toyota City in Aichi Prefecture in May, 2003. However, significant truths are concealed within these words.

8 The author has, in the past, said that the direct employment of workers of Japanese descent in this company was the 'employment of foreigners from a long-term perspective (Tanno 2000; Kajita, Tanno & Higuchi 2005), however, he now acknowledges that this was a mistaken assessment.

9 The contract unit price also falls in proportion to the portion of the social insurance burden not borne by the company.

10 In addition to this, there is, naturally, an increase in the demand for female labour because of the cheap contract unit costs.

11 These comments were made at a study group held at a Yokohama law firm in February 2007.

2 See Tanno (2006a) for a more detailed explanation of Tables 1 and 2 in this chapter.

13 There would hardly be anyone who sees professional foreigners, who have a high social standing and are highly paid – such as foreign lawyers and accountants working on international transactions and foreign top management figures like Carlos Ghosn – as a problem. The term, the foreign worker problem, as it is used in this book, indicates a foreign worker problem in the area of unskilled labour. Accordingly, it is only the trainees and skilled trainees who represent a problem in Table 4.1 in the book.

14 There is a whole back story to the consigning to oblivion of the employment approval system: at the time of the reform of the Immigration Control Act in 1990, the Ministry of Justice – which would have been deprived of the work of conferring legal status on foreigners – voiced vehement opposition to the (then) Ministry of Labour which was attempting to construct an employment approval system to bring in people of Japanese descent.

15 Ranks from A to C that are attained by permanent workers are further divided into categories 15–20. Workers rise through the categories within these ranks on the basis of their experience. In order to rise in status to another rank, an exam must be taken. This division into ranks only occurs in the case of blue-collar work; engineers and office staff are all on the one level.

16 That is, work at D rank requires no experience.

17 Since there are many trainees and skilled trainees who are employed for the sum of 300 yen per hour (around 60,000 yen per month) with this fact being reported in newspapers, the labour force is seen as being extremely cheap. The amount of remuneration received by workers is certainly extremely low, but when seen from the perspective of the cost to the factory, including the fees paid to the organisation that accepts trainees and introduces them to companies, this is not at all the cheap work force that one might have expected. The fees incurred are more than twice the minimum wages for the region.

18 It is not that this company has not thought at all about making Brazilians regular employees, but after the comments quoted in this passage, the following was said, 'the recruitment of Brazilians proceeds along a totally different route from that for the recruitment of Japanese and for us to engage them in our company we would need to deploy Portuguese

speaking staff in our personnel department. We are not considering a labour force that would require us to incur that level of cost. The most appropriate option for us is to make a request of the service contracting firm that has been sending us workers to date as a labour relations package.

19 On this point, Koike (2005) *The Economics of Work, 3rd Edition* is correct. The author is of the same opinion as Nomura (2003) regarding whether or not even blue-collar workers on the work site embody intellectual skills, but it is possible to argue that a dividing line between regular and irregular employment emerges as a result of the company making decisions as to whether or not they possess adequate levels of what Koike calls intellectual skills.

20 It is not that there are no companies that turn Brazilian contract workers into regular workers. In the companies where the author conducted his interviews, there are also more than twenty previous cases of Brazilians being raised up from irregular workers to regular employees. However, these types of examples are still extremely limited in number.

21 What one must be mindful of, however, is the influence of the revised Temporary Staffing Services Law which came into effect from April 2004. The General Affairs Department of Toyota issued instructions, with regard to primary subcontracting, to the effect that workers being obtained from service contractors were to be substituted with dispatch workers.

22 The meaning of 'the living law is the standard reality: namely, what exists as people's actions in society' (Kawashima 1982a: 131). There are also some extremely loose versions in use when it comes to definitions of Kawashima's living law.

Chapter 1

1 Before starting on his own argument, Hatta says: 'In what ways is the market useful to our lives and when should the government intervene in markets? In the market, the most excellent individuals and companies succeed in supplying the goods and services that others require. In this way, the market plays an important role in improving the people's standard of living. In economics, "the market distributes resources efficiently"' (Hatta 2006: 2). There is, however, no explanation of why excellent individuals and companies succeed in the market. It is not necessarily the case that technological excellence will win out when a new market is being established: many will recall the struggles in Japan between VHS and Beta surrounding the standard for videotapes; and, on the world market, struggles between Microsoft and Apple, as well as other makers concerning operating systems for personal computers. Was not the clear message of these conflicts in the marketplace that technologically superior products do not necessarily conquer the market; rather, even inferior products will succeed as long as they capture the market?

2 Williamson, Oliver E. (1985), *The Economic Institution of Capitalism*, Free Press; North, Douglas C. (1990), *Institutions, Institutional Change and Economic Performance*, Cambridge University Press (Translated by Kōshi Takeshita, (1994, *Seido, seido henka, keizai seika*, Kyoto: Kōyōshobō); Eggertsson, Thrainn and Douglass C. North (eds.) (1996), *Empirical Studies in Institutional Change*, Cambridge: Cambridge University Press;

Furubotn, Erik G. and Rudolf Richter, 2000, *Institutions and Economic Theory: The Contribution of the New Institutional Economics*, Ann Arbor: The University of Michigan Press; Yanagawa, Noriyuki (2000), *Keiyaku to soshiki no keizaigaku* (The economics of contracts and organisations), Tokyo: Tōyō keizai shinposha; and others.

3 Coleman, James S. (1990), *Foundations of Social Theory*, Cambridge, Massachusetts: The Belknap of Harvard University Press; Granovetter, Mark (1995), *Getting a Job: A Study of Contacts and Careers* 2nd ed. Illinois: Chicago University Press; Seiyama, Kazuo (1995), *Seidoron no kōzō* (The Composition of Systems Theory Tokyo: Sōbunsha); and others.

4 Harrison, Jeffrey L. (1995), *Law and Economics*, Minnesota: West Publishing Company (Translated by Yasumi Kobayashi & Katsumi Matsuoka (2001), Taga Shuppan; Richard A. Posner, (1998), *Economic Analysis of Law* 5th ed., Aspen Law & Business; Eric Posner, (2000), *Law and Social Norms*, Cambridge, Massachusetts: Harvard University Press; Katsuzō Ōta (Chief translator) (2002), *Hō to shakai kihan: seido to bunka no keizai bunseki* (Law and social norms: an economic analysis of systems and culture), Tokyo: Bokutakusha; and others.

5 Hideo Fukui distils the following three main points from the Coase Theorem. 'Firstly, the law ought to precisely determine the contents of rights; secondly, the law ought to determine procedures for minimising transaction costs; and thirdly, the law ought to determine the initial distribution of rights so as to decrease the sum total of transaction costs' (Fukui 2006: 15). If the Coase Theorem were to be realised with regard to the initial distribution of rights then, whatever the distribution conditions, the ultimate distribution problem would finally have been resolved. Therefore the problem is to establish three standards: '1) If the transaction costs incurred in order to realise B's rights when rights are distributed to A and the transaction costs incurred in order to realise A's rights when rights are distributed to B are equally small, then an initial distribution of rights may occur for both. 2) If the transaction costs incurred in order to realise B's rights when rights are distributed to A are small, but the transaction costs incurred in order to realise A's rights when rights are distributed to B are considerably larger, then the initial distribution of rights ought to be to A. 3) If the transaction costs incurred in order to realise B's rights when rights are distributed to A and the transaction costs incurred in order to realise A's rights when rights are distributed to B are both quite large, then the initial distribution of rights ought to be to the party which is assumed to value the worth of the rights most highly (Fukui 2006: 9).

The author naturally understands that the rights that Fukui considers a problem are exclusive access rights regarding transferrable goods as represented by property rights. However, is it not exclusive to limit the use of what is expressed by the word rights to those things that are concerned with economic opportunities? In Japan in particular the word rights can be seen as largely being used to indicate a political or social meaning. If the concept of rights used in the three standards mentioned above were to include a political and social meaning – where A was hypothesised as being irregular employment (or foreign workers) and B regular employment (Japanese workers), would people who emphasise law and economics be able to reach the conclusion that 'A ought to receive the initial distribution of rights?' The author thinks that if Fukui's three standards were to be established, then 2) would apply in this case.

6 In the section before the quoted sentences, Hatta refers to the Constitution: 'The people's right to pursue liberty and happiness, without interference from the government, can be interpreted as meaning that the government should not intervene in the market. Moreover, if we interpret the words "to the extent that it does not oppose public welfare" as "to the extent that the market does not fail," then we can see the guarantee of liberty by the constitution as reflecting the viewpoint of a division of roles between an economics-style market and the government along the lines of "there ought not to be any policy intervention in the market as long as there is no failure of the market"' (Hatta 2006: 16) It could be said in general of people who accept the "law and economics" stance that they would give this a different reading and interpret 'to the extent that it does not oppose public welfare' as 'to the extent that the market does not fail.' However, is it not a matter of deception to think that this is possible? If it were possible for all people to participate on an equal footing in the market, then it may be possible to re-read it in this way. However, the foreign workers who form the main subject of this volume, are inevitably in a different position form that of citizens in terms of the legal system. Also, people who live with a handicap of the mind or body cannot be equal on the physical level. Moreover, because of the costs of fulfilling one's role as a parent, which one is socially expected to shoulder, single mothers and single fathers – as sole parents – cannot compete in the labour market on an equal footing with parents who have a partner. Why is it that people are indifferent to the roles that some people must play and to the encumbrances under which they operate as they participate in the market?

7 However, this is not directly connected with an expansion of workplaces using foreign workers. This is because not all Japanese service contractors use foreign workers; the contractors using foreign workers constitute just one portion of subcontractors.

8 This reference to foreign labour 'having become public in terms of the system' does not mean that the Japanese government recognised the introduction of foreigners to work in unskilled jobs. The labour force made up of workers of Japanese descent was legalised according to the legal logic that this did not mean the introduction of unskilled labour. What the author is attempting to say is that workers of Japanese descent became public in the sense that, irrespective of having come to be socially recognised as a labour force and irrespective of their having acquired a legal basis, their existence was no longer covered up in Japanese employment. Speaking figuratively, it could be said that 'they no longer had to work in hiding.'

9 I have drawn on the work of Takashi Uchida (1990) *Keiyaku no saisei* (The Extension of Contracts), Kōbundō for the motif of this section – the demise of the foreign worker labour market as a principle and the foreign worker labour market as a phenomenon.

10 The realisation of the prevalence of these types of contracts – economic relationships – is typically to be found in the conditions that Marx and Engels commented on in the *Communist Manifesto*: 'The bourgeois classes,

having gained control, destroyed all relationships – feudal, paternalistic, patriarchal and pastoral. They relentlessly severed the variety of feudal bonds that connected people with their elders in blood relationships leaving no other bonds in place between people apart from naked profit and "monetary considerations."'

11 Economics and sociology, which have adopted this viewpoint, give a theoretical explanation for the appearance of continuous transactions as a social phenomenon. The social phenomenon (fact) and theory (interpretation) are in agreement on this point. In law, however, as Yoshio Hirai argues, it would appear that there are no inconsistencies regarding continuous transactions between interpretations based on the practice of law (precedents) and interpretations based on theory (theory). Hirai (1996), 'Iwayuru danzokuteki keiyaku ni kansuru ikkōsatasu: "shijō to soshiki" no hōriron (A consideration of so-called continuous contracts: from the viewpoint of legal theory of "markets and organisations"),' in *The Establishment of and issues in Studies of Japanese Civil Law: Eiichi Hoshino Seventieth Birthday Commemorative Edition, Volume 2*, Tokyo: Yūhikaku, p. 705.

12 The advance of globalisation that has accompanied the expansion of the contract sphere takes labour management relations back to labour capital relations. As a result of this, the revival of labour capital relations inevitably leads to the need for a reservoir of labour that can be used freely as total capital while individual capital does not bear the long-term costs of the reproduction of the labour supply.

13 Seiyama, Kazuo (1995), *Seidoron no kōzō* (The Composition of Systems Theory), Tokyo: Sōbunsha.

14 In addition to the issues raised here, even if the new economic approach of the New Institutional School can discuss the functional aspects of the existing institution, it cannot explain how the existing institution came into being. Kagami has studied the Japanese post-war subcontracting system and concludes that there existed decisive differences in the relationships between new companies and subcontracting companies in the 1950s and 1960s with the in-company subcontracting, which is seen as characteristically Japanese, becoming the dominant form in the 1960s. Accordingly, he made it clear that it is not possible to consider in-company transactions as a continuation of the pre-war system and that the birth of company transactions does not emerge internally from the logic that dominated the 1950s relationship between new companies and subcontracting companies. Kazuaki Kagami (2001), 'Shitauke torihiki kankei ni okeru keiretsu ni keisei to tankan (The formation and development of keiretsu in subcontracting transactions relationships),' in Tetsuji Okazaki (ed.), *Torihiki seido no keizaishi (Economic History of the Transactions system)*, Tokyo: Tokyo University Press.

15 Munger, Frank (ed.) (2001), *Laboring Below the Line*, Russel Sage Foundation.

16 Even if improvements in overall efficiency are sought, without the guarantee of a minimum level at which the people living in that society can individually feel satisfaction, those people who can only enjoy insufficient (or unsatisfactory) contentment, are not likely to see society as legitimate. Hatta's logic in saying that 'irregular employment is better

than unemployment' might be permissible in the short term, but when it continues amongst people as a permanent state and when the number of people permanently in this situation rises above a certain number, then it becomes a double-edged sword that jeopardises even the political system.

Chapter 2

1 The knowledge that can be gained via the present book on this point is not knowledge deduced from theory; it is observed knowledge derived inductively from the accumulation of facts (Lakatos 1970).

2 The argument, at heart, is not that we cannot see any movement from India; the sense is rather that while India is a heavily populated country like China, there is still only limited movement to Japan.

3 See Todaro (1997) for an opinion that is representative of neoclassicism.

4 Propagandists for the theory would probably say that these changes are decisive. The author's stance that there are no fundamental differences provides a mirror-image reflection of real movements by immigrant workers.

5 Sassen (1995) provides a theoretical explanation of this point, and Sassen (2002) raises the problem as one of the ethnography of poverty.

6 In addition, we could cite the often repeated criticism of global city theory's omission of the explanatory framework of the state and the difficulties that this occasions in using it to explain the case of Japan, where the influence of state actors is substantial.

7 For example, at Seiko-Epson, the labour union – harbouring a sense of impending crisis regarding the improved skills of the workers of Japanese descent that had been dispatched by the service contractor – proactively negotiated a policy that accepted a results-based wage structure. The bringing about of terms of competition that included a substantial reduction in wages by regular workers who were not facing any competition is a good example of the introduction of foreign workers into the workplace.

8 'Pinpoint migration,' in the jargon used by staff at a shelter in the city of Yokohama, *Josei no ie salaa*, indicates people who know nothing about Japan despite having lived there for long periods of time. One of the staff members, Chieko Nishioka, was the first person to use this term.

9 I learnt of the following point about the links between the beginning of exchange relationships and the 'Japan-America Airlines Agreement' from managers of Japanese descent who had been running local travel agencies in São Paolo from the 1960s. The relationship between the beginning of direct flights to São Paolo and the 'Japan-America Airlines Agreement' is accepted opinion amongst the participants in the travel industry that has long linked Japan and Latin America. A total of five people lectured the author on this point.

10 The embassy and seven consulates issued visas in Brazil. With the possibility for Brazilians of Japanese descent to gain employment in Japan that accompanied the revision of the *Immigration Control Act*, the Japanese government intensified the workload of issuing visas for the consulate located in São Paolo which had a large population of Brazilians of Japanese descent. As at the year 2002, in contrast to the situation in other consulates where consuls carry out other consular duties in addition

to issuing visas, two extra consuls have been deployed in the consulate in São Paolo with sole responsibility for issuing visas. People aspiring to go to Japan as foreign workers and the travel agents for Brazilians of Japanese descent who assist them in this say that the situation that has arisen is one in which 'visas are issued promptly in São Paolo, but that a lot more time and effort is required at other consulates.' As a result of this, travel agencies for Brazilians of Japanese descent that had operated in other cities to gather people and send them off to Japan before the revision of the *Immigration Control Act* had collapsed and then moved their head offices to São Paolo.

11 Table 2.2 shows not only changes brought about by the revision of the *Immigration Control Act* from 1989 to 1990 but also by changes to another system. From 1996 to 1997 the duration of short term visas was reduced while that of residence visas increased. The majority of people of Japanese descent came to Japan on short-stay (tourist) visas and then changed to residence visas after starting work. Because of this immigration authorities integrated the issuing of visas to people of Japanese descent, whom they knew would already be working, into residence visas. Changes to the operation of this system are also reflected in the statistics.

12 Kōichi Mori (1992) is also very detailed on the situation in this period.

13 The Foundation *Nippon Rikkōkai* can be offered as an example of a representative organisation that promoted the acceptance of the siblings of immigrants for the purpose of experiencing Japan, the country of their ancestors.

14 In the early period when working abroad started, it was the airline companies rather than the Japanese government that thought that there were no markets for Japanese direct flights on routes that made use of beyond rights from America. Consequently, direct flights to São Paolo first began as freight flights, with Japanese airline companies reacting when voyages by workers travelling to work abroad in Japan led to increases in connecting flights for European and American airline companies. The airline companies reduced the proportion of freight flights and, ultimately, turned all flights into passenger flights.

15 The prefectural association organisations were not the only organisations used. Brazilians of Japanese descent ran Cotia, the largest agricultural cooperative in Latin America, and they made use of every connection that they had including the youth groups attached to this sort of agricultural organisation; university old boys networks in the cases of people who had been industrial migrants in the post war period; and even more so class reunions from pre-migration days based on migration agencies (later: JICA).

16 The *Nippaku Mainichi Shinbun and the Paulista Shinbun,* partly as a result in the decline in population of people of Japanese descent who can read Japanese, have merged to become the *Nikkei Shinbun*.

17 Figure 2.4 is based on the results of a joint survey conducted by Takamichi Kajita, professor in the Sociology Department of the Graduate School of Hitotsubashi University; Naoto Higuchi and Yukie Takahashi in the doctoral course at the Graduate School; and the author who was also in the doctoral course (all titles were current at that time). This survey was made up of a questionnaire survey of 2,054 workers of Japanese descent;

an interview-based survey of 77 ethnic businesses being operated by people of Japanese descent; an interview survey of service contractors at 50 companies; and an interview survey of 69 local Latin American companies (67 of these in the city of São Paolo) – travel agencies run by people of Japanese descent and brokers. See Kajita (editor) (1999) for the results of this survey.

18 The handling of the rent in cases of the human trafficking of foreign women is carried out in the following manner. Brokers buy local women and then become their prostitution managers. The organiser of managed prostitution who bought the women regards the amount of money for which he bought them from his personal broker to be the women's debt, and withholds their freedom until they have finished paying off the amount. The women pay money to local brokers in order to get to Japan, and this is the rent that the women pay to the brokers. However, the organiser of managed prostitution who bought them from the broker shifts the rent that he himself paid to the broker onto the women as their debt thus leading to the women being the only ones who are constrained to pay rent.

19 People who are undocumented workers, even workers who come to Japan from Latin America, are unable to find work for a work introduction fee of one thousand dollars. For example, the debt amount levied on people who come to Japan from Thailand to work in the night entertainment industry is, as can be seen in Figure 2.5, around the three million yen level, but in the case of those from Colombia, it is not unusual for this figure to be around eight million yen.

20 The author heard of a particular travel agency in São Paolo where the receipt of a 100,000 yen commission was concluded at the time of the agent's contract for each person sent to factories that were in Japan. For that reason, up until 1997, this travel agency did not receive a fee for work introductions (rent for workers) to people who went to work abroad in Japan. It set prices for going to Japan that were lower than those of other companies, but the news that prices were much lower than at other companies had the contrary effect, leading to mistrust and to the company not being able to gather up the number of people that it needed. Accordingly, having decided to risk seeking to recoup its rent burden from those aspiring to go to Japan, they were able to gather together the necessary workers by issuing tickets at prices that included a work introduction fee.

Chapter 3

1 In a strict sense, movement from small- and medium-sized companies to large companies was not closed. What is being referred to here is limited exclusively to movement within conglomerates which have business dealings with one another. However, even if we look beyond these to the whole of the labour market, movement from large to small- and medium-sized companies and the other way around is largely a case of changing occupational category; and, in contrast, movement amongst small- and medium-sized companies is mostly made up of movements within the same occupational category (Ono 1997).

2 Employment rules amongst the companies concerned with blue-collar work have been established via the mediation of a certain type of cartel-

like activity. In the case of the automobile industry, for example, the people in charge of employing fixed term contract workers for the head company in each of the manufacturers periodically hold a meeting and exchange information about matters including: how many fixed term contract workers are currently employed in each of their respective companies' factories; how much they currently pay in recruitment payments; the amount of assistance that they are providing with dormitory and meal costs; and the size of dormitories. When the wages of fixed term contract workers have risen too much, the leading company will reduce its wages. In addition, they also suppress the wages market place for fixed term contract workers as all companies follow their lead. This is, however, simply a gentleman's agreement, not a stipulated item, and in periods of prosperity there are companies that do not abide by the agreement. (This is based on interview surveys in November and December of 2000 with the people in charge of the personnel departments in the head companies of automobile Company A and Company B.)

3 It is not that every single manufacturing company has stopped carrying out recruitment activities; they continue to carry out recruitment in the form of direct employment in the area known on site as 'casual' employment in which they employ students during their long vacation periods as fixed term contract workers just for the duration of this vacation (Tanno 2000b). It is, however, in the area of migrant work which is premised on long term and direct employment that Japanese manufacturing companies play practically no direct role these days. See Chapter 7 of this book and Tanno (2000b) for concrete examples. For concrete examples of the system for the recruitment and distribution of the labour force, see Sano (1997) and Satō (1996a, 1996b).

4 The 'interface mechanism' referred to in this chapter is taken from Herbert Simon. See Simon (1996: 1999) for more details. Simon (1997a, 1997b), Kaneko (1986), Imai and Kaneko (1988) and Shiozawa (1997a) were consulted for ideas regarding the relationships between organisations and networks.

5 In interviews with companies, the author had doubts about the position of foreign workers who, although employed directly, were not covered by social insurance. Even in the case of large companies, blue-collar foreign workers were not covered by work insurance or social insurance; in practically all of these companies they got by on foreign travel accident insurance. Upon asking what kind of accounting process was used in paying workers' wages, the author realised, from all of the replies received, that they came under the heading of procurement costs in the Purchasing Division. According to the *Report of the Institution for Industrial Relations and Labor Policy, Chubu*, it is standard procedure in factories to account for the dispatching of workers as procurement costs within individual factory units (*Report of the Institution for Industrial Relations and Labor Policy, Chubu* 1998: 21).

6 From 1998 until 1999 Naoto Higuchi, Associate Professor at Tokushima University, and the author conducted field work amongst the Japanese descent communities in the states of São Paolo and Parana in Brazil and also Colonia Okinawa located in Warner County in Bolivia. We interviewed migrant worker pioneers who were employed in a relatively

early period of migrant work for people of Japanese descent, 1983 to 1984, and who, when they returned home, were entrusted with the assembling of workers in Latin America by Japanese factories. According to these workers, in the initial period of migrant work, from 1984 to 1988–1989, wages were roughly the same as those for part-time workers or a little lower than those for casuals. They told us that even though the pay was low: 1) as a result of hyperinflation in Latin America, the currency in their countries fell and the dollar rose in value; 2) a black market in U.S. dollars was created because demand was concentrated on the stable American dollar rather than their own countries' currencies; and 3) consequently, when they returned home to Latin America having converted the money that they had saved in Japan into American dollars they were able to build up a fortune. Similarly, the people who had been assembled and sent over to Japan by the older, experienced migrant workers in 1984 and 1985, had returned home after working abroad for two years and a number of them had been able to build houses. From around 1987, migrant work had come to be mythologised as something that enabled one to make a fortune.

7 As Figure 3.3 shows, the diversification of workplaces was originally planned via a labour marketplace in which the diversification of types of work acted as a network; that is, as a system for multiple service contractors. Because of this, if we just look at individual service contractors, we can detect both service contractors who rush to the diversification of areas of work and service contractors who, conversely, only specialise in their areas of strength.

8 Former Prime Minister Obuchi's private advisory committee, the colloquium known as 'Ideas for 21st Century Japan,' can be offered up as representative of this kind of tone. In the midst of the progressive decline in the birth rate and the ageing of the population, this colloquium put forward the proposal for a policy of accepting immigrants as an essential policy matter for the future.

9 The female labour referred to in this chapter denotes the labour force in the insecure employment area that consists primarily of part-time work. For a discussion that locates this female labour see Ōsawa (1993) and Kimoto (1995).

10 There are service contractors who specialise in dispatching workers who have overstayed their visas, such as workers from Peru, Nepal and the Philippines. In addition, there are also contractors who, without calling themselves contracting companies, specialise in dispatching Chinese who stay in Japan as trainees. The existence of these sorts of contracting companies that deal with undocumented workers can be explained by their ability to transform into selling points the fact that these workers for whom there are few employment opportunities 1) have a high rate of remaining on the job; 2) will work even when working conditions and the labour environment are unfavourable; and 3) attract low wages in discussions with clients. In a certain service contractor, in metropolitan Tokyo, who dispatches both people of Japanese descent and undocumented workers, the hourly pay rate for sending workers to factories is: 1,400 yen for male Brazilians of Japanese descent (with a contracting unit price of 1,800 per hour) and 1000 to 1100 yen for Nepalese (contracting unit price: 1,300 to 1,400 yen per hour).

Chapter 4

1 *Toyota City Statistics* publishes the total amount of cash wages paid by all plants within the city, with each plant clustered according to a scale based on the number of employees. Table 4.1 has been calculated by dividing the total amount of cash wages in the cluster units by the total number of workers in each cluster.

2 Since service contractors stay in the same dormitories as the workers, the contracting company dormitories are largely of the mixed, rather than single, residence type with many workers sharing accommodation. It is not only communication difficulties that arise when workers from different countries live together, but a multitude of other troubles. There are cases of increased costs being incurred – as a result of prejudices towards other countries – when, for example, workers from different countries cannot be put to work on the same line; separate lines are established to avoid this type of issue; and there is a need to station extra supervisors. As service contractors have experienced and are familiar with these sorts of difficulties, they tend to assemble people from specific countries.

3 As a result of the revision of the Immigration Control and Refugee Recognition Act, workers of Japanese descent became eligible to work, however, this recognition extended only as far as the third generation.

4 Large companies, represented by a portion of listed companies, are sensitive to the appearance of their companies' names in the newspapers. If workers dispatched by service contractors cause incidents that are reported in the newspapers, dealings with that contractor are terminated. As it is mostly the case that once on a company's blacklist of terminated transactions, all transactions opportunities are lost thereafter service contractors who have made it into the largest companies do their utmost to ensure company efforts to avoid hiring any people who are masquerading as workers of Japanese descent. This takes the form of service contractors drawing up family trees of people of Japanese descent. Large-scale service contractors who employ Peruvians draw up family trees and exclude employment hopefuls possessing documents which show that their parents have an excessive number of children.

5 For a detailed discussion of strategic instrumentality please see Okuno and Suzumura (1988); Okuno (1993); and Aoki, Kim and Okuno (1996).

6 On the recruitment of workers of Japanese descent in Latin America, please see Mori (1992); Sano (1996); Del Castillo (1999), Tanno (2000b); and Higuchi (2001).

7 On the measures that dismissed workers are able to take and also the tangible problems that they face, please see Shimoi (1990); Motohisa (2000); Li (2000); and Okuno (2000).

8 In order for companies to carry out personnel cuts for the purposes of reducing the workforce, they must act on the basis of precedent and fulfil four principles of personnel cuts. First, there must be just reasons for why it is necessary to carry out workforce cuts; second, no other measures but workforce cuts are left open to the company following all efforts having been made to avoid the dismissals; third, the selection of those to be dismissed is reasonable; and fourth, all has been adequately explained to the workers. On the basis of the second principle, if the employment

of irregular workers is continuing at the time when regular workers are being laid off, then it is to be concluded that the company is not making sufficient effort to avoid the dismissals.

9 There are also cases in which it is not the labour unions but NGOs that support foreigners that resolve labour problems. One also comes across many cases in which the resolution of labour problems is advanced via cooperation between groups that support foreigners and labour unions. Shipper (2008) provides a detailed discussion of this point.

10 The Kanagawa City Union is one labour union that has succeeded in organising Peruvians of Japanese descent. There is little research on the foreign worker labour movement, but an exceptional amount of research into the Kanagawa City Union is provided by Ogawa (2000a) and Ogawa 2000b.

11 The author is a member of the Yokohama City Union (YuniYoko) in which foreign workers have made up half the membership since 1998. The following discussion is based on the results of conversations with foreign workers who are also members of this union during the author's participation in union activities as a member of YuniYoko.

Chapter 5

1 This does not mean that contracting companies do not employ undocumented foreign workers. They cannot pay the high wages that are given to workers of Japanese descent, but the demand for workers who can be dismissed easily is high.

2 The author got the idea of using a game theory approach to the diversification of foreign workers from Ostrom (1995).

3 Adam Smith said: 'Their wages are not greater than those of common labourers at the port which regulates the rate of seamen's wages. As they are continually going from port to port, the monthly pay of those who sail from all the different ports of Great Britain, is more nearly upon a level than that of any other workmen in those different places; and the rate of the port to and from which the greatest number sail, that is, the port of London, regulates that of all the rest.' (Smith [1789]; 2000: 193–194) [The translator has used a copy of Adam Smith's work available as a Penn. State Electronic Classic Series Publication at: *http://www2.hn.psu.edu/faculty/jmanis/adam-smith/Wealth-Nations.pdf* (p. 95).

4 See Sen [1982] 1989 regarding the relationship between 'choice' and 'preference.'

5 This matter was touched on in Chapters 2 and 3, but Chapter 7 gives a specific view of the realities through case studies of group companies. Chapter 8 provides a detailed investigation of its functioning.

6 This does not mean that companies under secondary subcontractors receive absolutely no reinforcement personnel from companies under tertiary subcontractors. It is not unusual for secondary subcontractors, which are large-scale companies, to rely on tertiary subcontractors for personnel reinforcements.

7 This is according to the preliminary calculations of the Chūbu Outsourcing Cooperative. Information obtained by the author in June 2007.

8 As a result of this, the first coexistence argument that takes the stance that people ought to get along well with one another morally and ethically, expresses the wish that the foreigners who have newly joined a region will understand the host country. With regard to Japanese society that takes them in, the hope of the argument is that it will show open-minded understanding towards the foreigners. This is a wonderful ideal, but it cannot produce a counter-proposal for solving tangible regional problems such as 'putting out the rubbish,' 'noise' and 'illegal parking.' In the second argument about the primacy of the community, the formation of community ends up being omitted from discussions because the starting point is the community.

9 The suggestion that the type of organisation that is outlined in Figure 2 is possible comes from Keohane (1984); Dasguputa and Maler (1992); Ostrom (1995); and Martin (1995). The discussion in this chapter is confined to the national level. When considering present social conditions, it is, however, extremely important to scrutinise how games that work on an essentially international level operate in games on the national level. Global-level games of companies' international competitiveness exert a powerful influence particularly on the three games at work within companies: the 'business-to-business rules game;' the 'role within a company group game;' and the 'individual company's social and geographic conditions game.'

Chapter 6

1 Unfortunately, the interest of most researchers is drawn to questions of how to prevent a decline in the welfare of groups with vested interests and because of this, in the author's opinion, the areas of labour research can still be seen as being made up largely of works that fall within the framework of workers as citizens and the national economy.

2 The source regarding the numbers of people who were foreigners hoping to gain employment come from annual editions of *Immigration Control Statistics* and worker numbers, such as those for people of Japanese descent that have been published on the basis of values estimated by the Ministry of Health, Labour and Welfare using documents published by the Immigration Office of the Ministry of Home Affairs.

3 The fourteen employment qualifications are: teaching; the arts; religion; journalism; investment and management; law; accounting services; medicine; research; education; technology; specialist in humanities; international affairs; in-company transfers; entertainment industry; and technical skills.

4 The term proto-migrant workers is not in general use. The author has decided to use proto-migrant workers to refer to people who went abroad to work before the mid-1980s so as to be able to contrast them with those who went abroad to work from the mid-1980s onwards. The use of the phrase 'loser migrant workers (*make inu no dekasegi*)' should be seen as being used as a procedural concept in this book; in contrast to other places where it is used as a descriptive concept.

5 When people of Japanese descent make the voyage to Japan they no longer seek a short-stay visa (tourist visa), but rather seek to acquire a resident visa.

6 Revisions to the Immigration Office's policies regarding foreigners are related to changes from settlement visa to permanent resident visa.

7 Company T, which boasts the largest scale for travel agencies for people of Japanese descent, not only sells tickets to individuals who come in looking for an airline ticket, it is also a wholesaler of airline tickets to travel agencies for people of Japanese descent that sell tickets which include work referrals. This travel agency issues sixty to seventy per cent of return tickets between Japan and Brazil. It also has branch offices in Tokyo and Nagoya; and whilst there has been no change to the total number of ticket sales since 1997, significant changes are visible in the issuing of return tickets. There has been a change from Brazil to Japan as the point of departure for return tickets. Accompanying this, operators in Brazil have changed considerably; one change has been an increase in reconfirmations when returning on tickets issued by branch offices in Japan; a move away from the traditional focus of ticket issuing. Because of this, since 1970, there has been a change from multiple branches in the city of São Paolo to a set-up in which the head office is the sole store.

8 The system that has been established to be like this is described by Hayek: 'equilibrium, once arrived at, will continue only to the extent that there continues to be a match between the given external conditions and the various expectations shared by the members of this society,' and this can be understood as one state of equilibrium (Hayek [1949: 41] 1990:57 in translation).

9 In this sense, it may be more accurate to say that migrant workers from Latin America were not turned into part of the urban miscellaneous stratum, but that service contracting businesses have been turned into business people who supply urban miscellaneous labour.

10 The case of the Okazaki Regional Conference Promoting the Management of the Employment of Foreigners, found in Okazaki City in Aichi Prefecture, can be given as an example of the fact that, as a result of changes in the social environment, the employment of foreigners in companies has changed significantly. This conference recognised the workforce of Japanese descent as an essential workforce and attempted to promote direct employment. When, however, changes in the economic environment were accompanied by the appearance of a pool of Japanese workers in irregular employment, the number of companies employing people of Japanese descent on the basis of regular employment declined, and in 2002 the activities of the conference ceased.

11 However, since the social environment for amassing assets with the money that had been earned in Japan had collapsed, outcomes were confined to temporary places of employment with expectations remaining unrealised.

12 However, even in these cases, regular employment will be limited to meaning direct employment covered by labour insurance (unemployment insurance) and social insurance (health insurance); it does not mean the opening up of a new market in employment with no fixed time limits.

13 The consequences of this are that because the motivations of individual workers regarding working abroad will remain fixed on the building up of assets even as the labour market for people of Japanese descent evolves in a reactive manner to employment conditions, there will be an expansion of the divergence between expectations and outcomes on the part of workers

and a decline in the probability of any coincidence between expectations and outcomes.

14 People who come to Japan with previous work experience in Japan or who have recourse to family or friends who have already made the trip and are living in Japan make up the mainstream of the workforce that is arriving having crossed borders.

15 The disappearance of migrant work as a path for achieving success following the bursting of the bubble economy can be perceived as a theme in the stories of the personal experiences of people who worked abroad, in the pages of migration history magazines published in Latin America in the 1990s (Pan-Amazonian Japan-Brazil Organisation 1994 and The Publishing Committee of the Forty Year History of the South American Industrial Development Youth Group 1997).

16 Workers continue working in the same workplaces and in the same manner as before, but having been forced into secondments and transfers they work as employees of other companies in their former workplaces. This is exactly the same principle as when service contractors are used.

17 Nomura (2003) provides a stimulating discussion of Japanese dualism. However, while there may be questions on the point of the amount of pay, the workforce of Japanese descent that is under discussion in the current work, in definitional terms, falls neatly within Doeringer and Piore's secondary sector (1971).

18 As can be seen in the Employment and Human Resources Development Organization of Japan (2001) also there are, in the case of workers from Asian countries such as China considerable numbers of people working not only in the blue-collar workforce, but also in the white collar sector (regular employment) in engineering and special skilled work. The extremely low numbers of these types of examples in the case of the workforce of Japanese descent is one of its characteristics.

19 The contradictions brought about by the ways of working in the contract age have been pointed out not only by researchers, but also by lawyers and labour union activists (Mori 2003 and Nakano 2003).

Chapter 7

1 The survey of plants was conducted by renting a room for seven months and living in in the Homi Danchi (Homi housing complexes) and Housing and Urban Development Corporation Residential Apartments.

2 As is clear from the fact that Toyota City, the subject of this research, is the head office of a large automobile maker (referred to as Company A hereafter), most manufacturing companies are related in some way or another with Company A. However, new factories are being set up in neighbouring Okazaki City and Nagoya City by Mitsubishi Motors (which in 2001 shut down the Nagoya Ōe Factory) and in Suzuka City by Honda. There are thus also plants that supply parts to these companies in Toyota City, and it is not at all necessarily the case that all manufacturing plants in the region are only being built by Company A and its subcontractors.

3 According to an interview survey of Company A's Global Personnel Division on 11/12/2000. In an interview on 14/12/2000 the person in

charge of Personnel Division appointments also said that seventy-five per cent resided within the city.

4 As at 1/10/2000 the total population of the city was 350,282 people, broken down into 120,399 Japanese families making up 341,092 people and 4,513 foreign families accounting for 9,190 people.

5 The number of questionnaire surveys sent out was 1,493 with 22 of these being undeliverable because the forwarding address was unknown and 5 having gone out of business. The number of valid recipients was 1,466. With 740 responses received, the response effectiveness rate was 50.48 per cent. Refer to Toyota City (2000) regarding the results of this survey.

6 The foreign employees in Company A are mainly engineers employed in American and European design centres and R&D centres and also local subsidiary employees who are employed in overseas local subsidiaries (factories) and they all come under the oversight of the 'Global Personnel' Section. The Global Personnel Section manages personnel matters not only for foreign employees who come to Japan from foreign subsidiaries for training, but also for employees from the head company who are transferred from Japan to overseas subsidiaries.

7 This figure has been compiled with reference to Nomura (2001).

8 Industry K, a primary subcontractor, was still employing workers of Japanese descent as of 2000, but only two; an extremely small number.

9 This reference to the introduction of foreign workers denotes the entry of foreign workers working as blue-collar workers into workplaces. For this reason, it does not include people who have been transferred within the company from overseas subsidiaries.

10 So as to be able to expedite having workers sent to them once help wanted requests were made, the companies that concluded contracts with travel agencies in Latin America sent off documents such as the proprietors' tax withholding at the source statements, tax declaration certificates and certificates of residence.

11 It is not unusual for those in subcontracting relationships with Company A to be summoned by a factory in the *keiretsu* when there are defective products in the parts and components deliveries and also for meetings about design changes. During these visits, companies have discovered that people who used to work in their own company are now in the factories of other companies and that they have transferred to service contractors.

12 The labour shortage that lasted from 1989 to around 1990 had a serious impact on Parent Company A as well. Even the Personnel Division of Company A seriously considered bringing in foreign workers as blue-collar, fixed-term contract, labour (from an interview with the Personnel Division of Company A).

13 The pay during this period of training is that of an apprentice; approximately half that of the pay for regular workers. The pay may amount to no more than half that of regular workers, but because there is a scale-based wages differential, when compared to the wages for which they had been working in secondary or tertiary subcontractors, there is not such a discernible decline in their earnings even at the apprenticeship pay rate.

14 Parent companies that display this type of awareness are primary subcontracting companies. It is not that there are no cases at all of workers

from secondary subcontractors having become workers in Company A at the apex of the subcontracting structure, but they are extremely rare. The movement from subcontracting companies to parent companies under discussion here largely denotes movement from secondary to primary subcontractors.

15 In the sense that this is voluntary movement by workers, it is certainly not a case of scouting. However, the companies being left described this phenomenon to the author using the term 'scouting.' Seen from the subcontractor's point of view, movements occasioned by changes to company-to-company rules on the part of the parent company can only be thought of in terms of scouting.

16 Merely one of the companies related to Company A has ceased having workers sent to it from contracting companies. This low number, within the sphere of companies related to Company A, that have stopped dealing with service contracting companies can be seen as related to the fact that Company A maintained favourable results even during the period of recession.

17 Including the perfect attendance bonus in daily and monthly pay, monthly pay reached 320,000 to 340,000 yen. There is a gap in that people starting for the first time as fixed term contract workers receive a daily wage of 9,000 yen, but as the number of times that one returns as a fixed term contract worker increases (the number of times that a contract is renewed) this goes up by 200 yen. An upper limit has, however, been set at 9,600 yen.

18 For this reason, companies are conducting research into the development of tools that do not require physical strength and are easy for women and older workers to use. They are also looking into installing lines that are easy for people of limited physical strength to operate.

19 When receiving workers dispatched from service contacting companies, even female workers come with a unit cost of from 1,300 to 1,400 yen. If they are part-time female workers, then their hourly pay is about half that of the pay for workers sent by contracting companies and even when welfare expenses are included, these part-time workers make up a cheaper labour force.

20 Compared to an hourly unit cost of 1,900 yen for male workers of Japanese descent, in the case of older Japanese (over fifty-five) companies can get by with paying a contracting unit cost of 1,750 yen.

21 This is why, as Inagami points out, companies cannot help but have differing employment strategies based on how the companies concerned are included within the class, spectrum, of company society (Inagami 1992).

22 The concept associated with *faux frais* (incidental expenses) as it is used in this chapter comes from Satake (1994). In this work, Satake defines *faux frais* by saying that 'the disappearance into idleness of the results of the human labour that is included in goods before they are consumed through sales is called *faux frais*.' He then goes on to locate Company A's production system: 'The first project advanced for effecting the reduction of *faux frais* in the large volume production system that had developed was the Toyota Production System' (Satake 1994: 1).

Chapter 8

1 A total of 52 service contractors agreed to participate in the survey and valid responses were received from 45 of these. The locations of the service contractors from these 45 companies were: 15 in Hamamatsu City in Shizuoka Prefecture; 7 in other places in Shizuoka Prefecture; 7 in Toyohashi City in Aichi Prefecture; 2 other places in Aichi Prefecture; 4 inside Nagano Prefecture; 5 in Gifu Prefecture; 2 in the Tokyo metropolitan area; 2 in Kanagawa Prefecture; and 1 in Gunma Prefecture. The total number of foreign workers directly employed by these companies and dispatched to factories is 14,029 with 13,634 of these workers being Brazilians of Japanese descent.

2 Before the 1990 revision of the Immigration Control and Refugee Recognition Act (referred to hereafter as the Immigration Act) third generation people of Japanese descent as well as the spouses of second and third generation people of Japanese descent were deemed ineligible to work.

3 The issue being pointed out here was confirmed in an interview with the person who is both editor in chief and company president of the Portuguese newspaper *Novo Visao* in March 1996. In the period before being engaged in the editing of this Portuguese language newspaper, acting as a member of staff of a contracting company, he had directly managed the dispatching of Brazilians.

4 Several service contractors responded that they dispatch workers to lines directly controlled and supervised by manufacturers other than those whose lines they have contracted. In one service contractor, where the author was actually allowed to observe and study the factory, it was possible to see two approaches: one in which 'labour dispatched within the factory' took the form of reinforcement from the contracted line; and another in which 'reserve personnel' were contracted beforehand as one line and then sent to the points where they were needed.

5 The waves that accompany these sorts of production activities are borne by the insecure employment stratum. However, in order to distinguish the portion of people in insecure employment who have become thoroughly incorporated into the company's activities – as in the case of the Brazilians in this chapter who despite being in insecure employment are expected to deliver higher levels of productivity than regular employees – they are, as in the table below, dealt with as two different markets, Market 1 and Market 2. This distinction of 1 and 2 are based on Piore and Berger's dualism argument (S. Berger and M. J. Piore 1980: 17–24).

6 In this employment sector – whether in order to force service contractors to compete or in order to assemble a particular number of workers which would be outside the abilities of one company alone – one often comes across employment in which there is no fixed time period in the contracting agreement that is concluded and in which the factory includes multiple contractors.

7 At the time of the 1997–1998 survey, the hourly wages for Brazilians of Japanese descent were 1,300–1,400 yen for men and 900–1,100 yen for women.

8 Moreover, at clients where more than fifty people have been dispatched to the one worksite, a room is borrowed within the factory to which workers have been dispatched and an office set up within it. Regular contacting company staff members are stationed in this office within the factory and they are engaged exclusively in supervising worksite leaders, maintaining contact with the main contracting company and holding business meetings.

9 However, the ability of a service contracting business to respond to big changes is largely a constraint of scale. In order to be able to respond to these changes, one service contractor ensures that it has a certain number of people available by housing thirty Brazilians of Japanese descent in its company dormitory as reserve personnel, who are always on call, and paying them a wage. When a request for additional personnel is received, the company dispatches workers from this pool of reserve personnel to the company that has contracted its services. Similarly, when the number of reserve personnel drops below twenty people, recruitment activities begin anew.

10 Stock as a form of detached equipment has been abandoned in the Toyota Production System that serves as the current model production system, and the freedom that companies used to gain from the function served by stock is now being maintained via fluctuations in the subcontractors' volume of production and via fluctuations in the volume of work through service contracting companies. Let us look at a tangible example of this. Subcontractors are all required to pursue productive activities that match the production rhythm of the main company and they are required to take delivery from the main company of products that are to be used on the production line twenty minutes in advance.

11 A contractor who has opened an office in Kyūshū (main office: Hamamatsu) and a service contractor who has opened local offices in Kushiro and Obihiro (main office: Ōta ward, Tokyo) conduct interviews at these local offices. However, according to the companies that responded to the latest survey, whilst it is possible to obtain people of Japanese descent via agents for only 300,000 yen, they still end up having to spend an average of around 500,000 yen per person as a result of the need to secure dormitories in which to house these men and women. When these matters are taken into consideration, we see that in order to open up a service contracting company that dispatches people of Japanese descent one initially faces large expenses.

12 There are, however, also many cases amongst people of Japanese descent of those who have not properly submitted their own birth certificates or documents concerning their parents' marriage registration or who have lost these documents. Simply the costs incurred by service contractors who are relied on to gather the necessary documents when people have problems with their documents and the costs of getting around inside Brazil, given that some have settled in the far reaches of the Amazon, amount to more than 500,000 yen.

13 It is possible to confirm that the system used by service contracting companies who have been recruiting Japanese migrant, seasonal, and fixed term contract workers continues to function in a similar manner in the recruitment of Brazilians of Japanese descent in Brazil. Kōichi Mori looks closely at the recruitment advertisements placed by service contractors

in Japan and by local travel agents who assemble people in response to a request from service contractors to recruit people of Japanese descent locally in Brazil. Having pointed out that there has been 'a) a move to a new job allowance of 20,000 yen; b) a work cash bonus of 480,000 yen; c) a retirement bonus of 240,000; d) a special new job allowance of 50,000 yen; and e) a special commuting to work allowance of 20,000 yen,' Mori concluded that the appearance of this set of circumstances has resulted from the difficulties of assembling people in Brazil (Mori 1992: 150–151). However, the items that Mori has raised are incentives that service contractors have been using in order to supply migrant, seasonal and fixed term contract workers from Japan's regions and to help ensure that they fulfil their contract periods. In the December 1997 Okinawa Survey and the March 1998 Hokkaidō Survey, numerous service contractors were using items mentioned by Mori as incentives to assemble people in their local offices and this information is also available from the Public Employment Exchange. Incidentally, in both Okinawa and Hokkaidō, service contractors carrying out recruiting activities are aiming to secure a labour force using a) the payment of a moving to a new job allowance and all travel expenses; b1) a monthly good attendance bonus of 20,000 yen; b2) a half yearly good attendance bonus of 200,000 yen; and c) a retirement bonus of 300,000 yen.

14   From the May, July and September 1998 surveys of local recruitment offices in Okinawa.

15   The Shikoku Employment Office was closed down, but the company still has a business office in Sendai. However, in the past, the Sendai office had held the position of the recruitment and employment base. Currently, its main work is centred on the labour management of dispatched workers to the factories of electrical appliance makers in the region who are clustered around Miyagi Prefecture and also to around 100 offices. (From the July 1998 survey of contracting companies' Okinawan local offices.)

16   From interview surveys conducted at the Naha Public Employment Exchange.

17   In addition to these, requirements regarding matters such as Japanese conversational ability and age are stressed at the time of new employment.

18   According to the answers given by about one in five (nine companies) of the service contractors who participated in this survey, the composition of sales for service contractors, on the scale of total sales, were about twenty per cent gross profits and the remaining eighty per cent were workers' wages. However, the proportion of ordinary profit once maintenance costs for offices and dormitories as well as personnel expenses for management staff have been deducted is around three per cent.

19   The manufacturers who receive dispatched workers say that the advance of this sort of scattered transaction began around 1993. In September of that year, a company that manufactured motors for industrial use in Kosai City in Shizuoka Prefecture suddenly dismissed over 300 workers of Japanese descent who had been dispatched to it from a contracting company. Because the dismissed workers gathered at the Labour Standards Office and the Public Employment Security Office day after day and this was reported by the mass media it became a social issue. Following this, there was an observable trend towards increasing the number of client companies.

20 Even amongst service contractors for whom there is no other detailed data, the perfect attendance proportion never exceeds ninety per cent. However, even contractors who said that the quality of people of Japanese descent has declined stated that this was still not comparable with Japanese in the stratum of workers in insecure employment.

Chapter 9

1 The survey which informs this chapter is based on the results of participant observations from 14–27 September 1998. During this time, the author took his turn answering the office telephones of a particular service contractor who had his company office in the housing complexes of Toyota City in Aichi Prefecture. The author also lived in the dormitory with this contractor's workers of Japanese descent, who were sent to companies as external workers, seeing them off as they left for the factories and greeting them upon their return.

2 As service contracting companies are not authorised operations, they can be set up by anyone. Company A dispatches small numbers and its manager, Mr B, is operating having obtained qualifications as a special visa application agent from the Nagoya Immigration Office.

3 The calculation that there are 3,000 Brazilians living in the housing complexes is based on an estimate by Toyota City.

4 'Demands Concerning the Improvement of the Living Environment,' dated 30 September 1997, were formally presented to Toyota City by the four neighbourhood councils that make up the housing complexes area.

5 To give one example of the changes in the housing complexes that forms part of the reality that surrounds people of Japanese descent: on the days on which rubbish was to be put out in the public housing, service contractors mobilised workers from their own companies and stationed them as sentries at the rubbish accumulation points where they checked the manner in which people of Japanese descent put out the rubbish.

6 Changes to visa status, renewals of visa period and applications for re-entry make up the bulk of the Immigration Office related work. Formalities regarding alien registration and national health insurance made up the jobs related to the city ward office.

7 On 16 September, 1998, Mr B, a second generation mother of Japanese descent, her eldest son who was thirteen, his younger brother who was nine and the author went off to the Toyota City Education Committee. On this occasion, foreigner registration was confirmed and the formalities for going to school were speedily concluded. Following this, as it was again necessary to go through formalities and explanations at the school that they planned to go to, the company decided to do this on 26 September, the Saturday of the following week when the factory where the mother worked was closed. It was decided that the mother would see to the preparations for ensuring that the children had all of the materials that they would need to go to school once she had received this month's pay and that the children would start attending school the following month. The second generation mother of Japanese descent only aspired to seeing her second boy attend school; her hopes for her eldest son were that he would start working in the factory as soon as possible. Only after Mr B had spent around an hour explaining

that those under fifteen were not permitted to work in factories in Japan and that even if he were to work in a factory, he would need Japanese did she consent to him being enrolled in the older boy's middle school.

8 Service contractors must exercise independence when it comes to both business management and labour management. Thus, the fact that the receiving company has hold of the decisive power on this most important of personnel issues – whether to hire or not to hire – gives rise to organisational problems.

9 The calls that caught my attention during my turn answering the telephone were those from callers who only asked the hourly rate or gross amount of pay.

10 There are actually large numbers of people in Company A who are working there with their families. In September 1999, around a little over half of the twenty seven members of Group 10 were employed as families, including husbands and wives, parents and children and siblings. One particular family had six members living in the Prefecture run housing with five of them being dispatched by Company A. The amount that Company A paid to all of the family members in August 1998 was 1,380,000 yen.

11 These items are evaluated on a four point scale of Good, Average, Low and None. Speaking and listening are judged to be good if there is no particular need for explanations or help in a foreign language with the interview which is conducted in Japanese. Reading comprehension of written Japanese are graded as average or low, with an item for the ability to read katakana between the two.

12 These items are also evaluated on a four point scale of Good, Average, Low and None.

13 There are occasionally calls to interpreting staff that are not only from workers in their own companies but also from workers who were once dispatched by Company A but are now being dispatched by a service contractor and from people who have acquired the interpreting staff member's mobile telephone number by word of mouth and who call regarding matters that have nothing to do with direct employment.

14 This happened on 23 September, 1998.

15 The appearance of homeless Brazilians of Japanese descent in Hamamatsu City and in Oizumi Town in Gunma Prefecture was a major topic of discussion for these two men.

16 In the case of people who wish to live together with their families or relatives, the boarding fee is split between the number of workers employed by the company and are they are each asked to pay that amount. In these cases, there are times when one person may end up paying more than 20,000 yen.

17 Sunday wages are paid at 1.25-fold the rate for working on holidays during regular work. Because of this, when workers who came into Company A's office from the automobile related company worked on Sundays this was dealt with and reported as overtime in employee attendance records.

Chapter 10

1 People who were first generation immigrants and held a Japanese passport were able to enter Japan freely and faced low procedural barriers, but those

who were second generation or later and held Brazilian nationality faced difficulties in collecting the documents that they needed on their own. The required documents included one's own birth certificate (*nascimento*); parents' marriage certificate (*casamento*); one's own marriage certificate, if married; and, in addition, an official copy of the family register for one's parents or grandparents. In cases where official copies of the family register have been lost due to the chaos of the Second World War or as a result of repeated changes of address, one needs to contact Japanese government offices (the city, town or village ward office) and have these sent by them.

2 For example, Mitsubishi Motors's Okazaki Plant directly dispatched a person in charge of human resources to São Paolo where he assembled a fixed term contract factory labour force.

3 In the course of the author's fieldwork, the only company to directly engage in recruitment activities locally under its own name after 2000 has been Isuzu Motors, which targeted university students during their summer holiday period and recruited them for a three-month period of 'casual employment' as fixed term factory contract workers.

4 By conveying the message that there is a greater volume of job vacancies than is the case in reality, the image of lots of work openings in Japan has spread throughout the community of people of Japanese descent. Consequently, in areas where there is a concentration of migrant worker travel agencies, such as São Paolo, Lima and Buenos Aires, the myth has arisen that going to one of these agencies will open the path to work in Japan; and, thus, they see a steady influx of people who expect to find work in Japan. This fact has seen new migrant worker travel agencies flocking to areas which already have concentrations of migrant worker travel agencies.

5 In 2003, the Brazilian Consulate in Nagoya identified the suppliers of labour to service contractors with ties to Brazilian *asesoria*. They, then, had these labour suppliers in Japan expose to the Brazilian federal police those *asesoria* who were sending Brazilians when there were no jobs for them. This resulted in the occurrence of a chain of bankruptcies for migrant worker travel agencies with connections to *asesoria* that were dispatching people who wanted to work in Japan.

6 The manager of a service contracting company which has its Head Office in Toyohashi City commented to the author, 'We once looked into how many contractors there were in the local area, and were able to establish that there were 300 companies just taking into account service contractors with offices in the cities of Iwata and Hamamatsu. There are, however, likely to be at the very least twice as many contractors that we were unable to identify.'

7 Carrão is also the name of a station on the east-west line of São Paolo's municipal subway, but the area of this name in which Okinawans live in large numbers is Vila Carrão, situated in the environs of Carrão's main street, Conselheiro Carrão, about fifteen minutes from the station by bus. However, this area called Vila Carrão is not known by this name for administrative purposes; it is a popular regional name for Okinawans which 'indicates the area in which members of the Vila Carrão branch of the Association of Okinawans Living in Brazil are to be found, and is

based on the customary regional subdivisions of people from Okinawa Prefecture' (Ishikawa and Machida 1986: 126).

8 Mr N, the father, even said that 'since Bolivia is a carefree country, it wouldn't do him any good to stay. My son had done nothing but sleep until that point. I thought that he had to learn about Japan's strict society so I sent him to Japan. After having lived with other people, he has changed a lot. Going to Japan to work also has a social education aspect to it here.'

9 The sibling owners of Company A say that, in reality, numerous people had approached them with the same sort of request as that of Mr M. They decided to venture into the travel business following the realisation, after having been approached by so many people with this proposition, that this was not a passing phenomenon.

10 Company A had dispatched approximately 10,000 people to work in Japan before being exposed.

11 When the author sought Kōichi Mori's opinion regarding Company A having become an integrated migrant work business, he commented, 'I do not think that Company A came up with this model. Wasn't it rather N Travel Agency, the creators of Group Okinawa, that employed this kind of business model? However, while they may do it for a fee, what is new is that they surpass even the Bolivian immigrants at passing on know-how (November 2004).' See Mori (2001) for a detailed discussion of N Travel Agency and Group Okinawa.

12 The head of the company said, 'Looked at as a single entity, Company C has as yet to post a profit. This results from Company C not existing as a travel agency, but being positioned as Company B's division for carrying out recruitment activities. Therefore, it is not being asked to show a profit but to collect people (October 2004).'

13 Only the travel agencies in the states of São Paolo and Paraná have maintained continuous dealings with Company C following 2000. Until the middle of the 1990s, the company had also had agencies and agents in Buenos Aires, Asuncion (Paraguay) and Lima.

14 S Travel Agency, a Japanese service contracting business like Company C, has opened an office on the floor above Company C's office. From October to November 2004, S Travel Agency paid an incentive of 110,000 yen for each person wanting to work in Japan brought to them by agencies. Because the agencies working for S Travel Agency paid a high promoter fee, Company C's agencies found collecting people wanting to work in Japan a struggle.

15 Amongst the increasing numbers of people obtaining re-entry permits, those setting off for their first round of migrant work practically all choose flights not requiring transit visas. These migrant workers choose flights that do not go via the United States for the added reason that they want to get to Japan as quickly as possible.

16 This author has dealt with this change using the terminology of 'loser migrant workers' and 'migrant workers heading for success,' which travel agencies were using at the time of conducting the survey of Brazil's local travel agencies. Mori (1995a), however, consolidates this in terms of a move from 'migrant workers' sense of shame' to 'the appearance of a discourse affirming migrant workers.'

17 It seems that the removal of graves began to occur in Vila Carrão, the area where post-war immigrants were concentrated; this is currently progressing with the initial removal of mortuary tablets from Okinawa to Brazil. The removal of graves was not purely a matter of the movement of physical symbols such as mortuary tablets, the remains of the deceased and the iconic censers. Okinawan religion is based on ancestor worship, and the reproduction of shamans in Brazil has become problematic (Association of People from Okinawa Prefecture in Brazil 2000; Chapter 11 and Mori 2005).

Chapter 11

1 The special permission to stay in Japan discussed in this chapter had been issued pursuant to Article 50, Paragraph 1, Item (iii) of the Immigration Control Act. In a recent amendment, an item concerning victims of the trafficking in persons was added to the paragraph as Item (iii). Accordingly, the original Item (iii) was moved down in order to Article 50, Paragraph 1, Item (iv) of the Act.

2 The full text of this document can be accessed at *http://www.moj.go.jp/ nyuukokukanri/kouhou/press_000300-2_000300-2-2.html.*

3 The Grand Bench of the Supreme Court handed down its decision on Case 1954 (a) No. 3,594 on 19 June 1957.

4 The case is included in *Saikōsaibansho minji hanrei shū* (Collection of Supreme Court Decisions) (13 (12): 1493–1499). The original decision on the case was made by Civil Court Division 3 of the Tokyo District Court on 22 April, 1958.

5 In Shiono's book (2005a), one of the most notable textbooks on administrative law, the MacLean case is introduced as an example of the 'recognition of requisite discretion' in the 'increased scope of discretion' (Shiono 2005a: 116–118). This is also cited in Shibaike as an example of administrative discretion (Shibaike 2005: 13–14).

6 Shiono continues, 'When an administrative disposition is made, using the construction indicated in a departmental notification as a point of reference, and the lawfulness of the disposition is disputed in court, the court must judge the case from its own independent standpoint by construing and applying relevant laws and regulations. The court need not take into account what has been indicated in the notification. Rather, it must not consider it at all (Shiono 2005a: 94).

7 Shiono says, 'As sources of administrative law, written laws are important. To complement them, however, unwritten sources of law cannot be disregarded. These include customary law, case law and general principles of administration (Shiono 2005a: 54–55).'

8 The plaintiff's representative regarded the state's explanation for the reliance on international common law as groundless. Firstly, he noted that the state had not proved the existence of such international common law although it had claimed that broad discretion on whether to grant entry and/or stay to a foreign national belongs to the state – that is, the Minister of Justice. Secondly, he doubted that the state's stance in giving absolute priority to international common law was consistent with its stance of

denying that the International Convention on Civil and Political Rights (ICCPR) and other explicit international treaties were judicative law. If this was consistent, the lawyer said, the state was picking and choosing only what was convenient to its argument.

9 'Immature' is the Japanese legal concept of living with and being dependent on a parent/parents; someone as yet not economically self-supporting.

10 The Immigration Bureau argued that the very fact that Article 50, Paragraph 1, Item (iii) does not define criteria for applicable cases, warrants the Minister's discretion. The plaintiff argued that the lack of a definition may leave the judgment to the discretion of the Minister, but that it does not mean that the Minister can hand down any decision he likes.

11 The judgment that the Constitution only applies to a foreigner within the framework of the Immigration Control Act is also found in the Supreme Court decision on the MacLean case, which says, 'Whether or not to grant a foreign national permission to stay in Japan is left to the discretion of the state. Foreign nationals who reside in Japan enjoy no constitutional guarantee of the right to reside in Japan or the right to demand ongoing residence in Japan. They are only granted, under the Immigration Control Act, the status of having their period of stay extended if the Minister of Justice finds at his discretion that there are grounds for recognising the extension as appropriate. The finding, *therefore, is that constitutional human rights are guaranteed to foreign nationals within the framework of the above-mentioned system of residency of foreign nationals.*

12 This logic is easier to understand if one considers that an administrative disposition has validity and official force in reality, even if it is unlawful. In its argument, the Immigration Bureau asserted limitless validity. See Shibaike (1999: 146) regarding the issue of validity.

13 The new criteria are believed to have been established in response to the incident in which overstaying foreign nationals, accompanied by a group of supporters, collectively gave themselves up in 1999 at an immigration office, seeking special permission to stay in Japan.

14 Article 9, Paragraph 1 of the Act denies an immigration inspector discretion over entry by a foreign national. Article 10, Paragraph 6 and Article 11, Paragraph 3 respectively deny a special inquiry officer or the Minister of Justice discretion over entry of a foreign national.

15 The other party here is the relevant supervising immigration inspector of the Tokyo Immigration Bureau.

16 The following definition of complete discretion, by Tokiyasu Fujita, helps to make it easy to understand. 'When a law delegates comprehensive authority to an administrative office…, it is normally expressed as a law granting the administrative office (complete) discretion. A proceeding carried out according to its policy-related and administrative judgment at its discretion is called a discretionary proceeding or discretionary disposition (Fujita 2005: 95).'

17 Fujita says 'Where the text of a law does not seem to identify the sole and single option to be taken, if it is considered that an administrative office is not allowed to use complete discretion and that there exists an

objective criterion presumed by the law, then the discretion is normally called statutory discretion or constrained discretion, in the studies of administration law (Fujita 2005: 95).'

18 In this way, Japan's immigration control administration is producing large numbers of people who are in limbo. It is widely assumed that the costs of deporting foreign nationals to their countries of origin are paid by the Japanese government. In principle, however, these expenses are paid by the deportees. Those who have saved money while working in Japan are expected to buy their own tickets with these savings. In the case of people without savings, their families in the home countries are asked if they could bear the costs. When a deportee's family also seem unable to afford the airline ticket, and if the deportee has a strong will to go home, which they acknowledge by signing a declaration that they are most unlikely to escape, provisional release is granted, during which they are expected to earn the money with which to buy their tickets.

19 A simple comparison of the numbers does not lead to a useful discussion. In European and North American countries, immigration laws and nationality regulations have changed since the 1990s. As a result, it has become easier for the children of migrants to obtain citizenship. The numbers do not tell the facts hidden by these sorts of changes to laws and regulations.

20 The practice of now disclosing some, if not all, of the cases so that the public has access to how the discretion of the Minister of Justice is exercised – something which has previously been as mysterious as a black box – is to be applauded.

21 On the other hand, the principle of discretionary determination on an individual basis still persists. To verify the discretion of the Minister of Justice and directors of regional immigration bureaus, officially, there are not supposed to be any judging criteria ("public standards"); some may, however, exist unofficially ("de facto standards"). If there were to be a set of public standards, then the special permission would have to be given to applicants who met these and there would be no room left for discretion.

22 The state claimed that this system was favour-bestowing, possibly because of cases like this one in which the immigration authority wins in the court, but still grants the losing party special permission to stay in Japan.

Chapter 12

1 Other people who are free of work restrictions despite being foreign nationals include Japanese residents from South and North Korean and also from Taiwan and China. However, since these men and women who reside in Japan as a result of former colonial connections cannot be treated as foreign workers, the discussion in this book regards only workers of Japanese descent as foreign workers who face no work restrictions.

2 Aside from international marriages, there are also numerous disputes concerning cases such as those of children who were born abroad without the consulate having been notified of their births, and children who were born before or during the war in Japanese colonies and who had not been able to return to Japan.

3 Atsushi Toriyama (2010) provides a very interesting analysis of this issue.
4 There is a detailed discussion regarding the judgement paper and commentary on this case in a special report in the 2002 issue of '*Hanreijihō*
   (Judicial Precedents Report)' and in Issue 1,267 of '*Hanrei Taimuzu*
   (Judicial Precedents Times).'
5 In this book, the items that are treated as having exemplified the opinion of
   the Ministry of Justice regarding nationality are: volumes one and two of
   The Japanese Nationality Act written by Kenta Hiraga, who wrote the draft
   of the post-war Japanese Nationality Act as Head of Civil Affairs Section
   Five; *An Article by Article Commentary on the Japanese Nationality Act* by
   Aritsugu Tashiro, who was employed as the Head of Civil Affairs Section
   Five in the 1970s; and *The Foreign Affairs Act* and *The Japanese Nationality
   Act* written by Tadamasa Kuroki and Kiyoshi Hosokawa who were in Civil
   Affairs Section Five at the time of the change from the principle of the
   patrilineal family line to the principle of the family line of both parents.
6 'The original basis of nationality was having a domicile that was where
   one's life was lived within the country, and the family registration system
   was an institution for registering, in their place of domicile, those people
   who had a residence in the country. However, since both nationality and
   family registration shared the same concept of domicile as their basis,
   "permanent domicile," which has taken on a thoroughly notional existence
   these days, can be considered a relic and a transformation of the concept of
   nationality mentioned above. Furthermore, under the official stance of the
   existing legal system, it can be maintained that the concept of nationality
   has lost its pragmatic links with the land, however, it does not reject these
   links conceptually (Hiraga 1950: 178–179).'
7 Chapter One of Kamoto's *The Birth of International Marriage* begins with
   the relationship between William Adams and his Japanese wife, Oyuki;
   however, in light of the Ministry of Justice's opinion, this probably cannot
   be considered as having been an international marriage. If we consider
   this case in terms of the assumption that Adams was an inhabitant who
   shared the same thoughts as the rest of the people, then the fact that he
   was given the Japanese name Miura Anjin by Tokugawa Ieyasu, to say
   nothing of the fact that he established a family in Japan, and, ultimately,
   passed away in Japan as he was unable to return to his native land, Adams
   can be thought of as having become Japanese.
8 Hiraga emphasises that children are socialised in families with Japanese
   parents, and, for this reason, does not adopt the same sort of principle
   of family lineage as Tashiro. There is a link between this and the stance
   that Hiraga takes regarding parents and children under the Japanese
   Nationality Act, which has at its foundation a legal view of parents and
   children. Hiraga's stance is that the parent child relationship that is
   essential for the determination of nationality is persistently the parent
   child relationship in law not the parent child relationship based on blood
   connections. As for Tashiro, he emphasises that the vast majority of parent
   child relationships in law are also relationships in which there are blood
   connections, and insists on a thorough principle of blood connections.
9 Before reading this work, the author had read Taniguchi (1959 and 1986).
   In these essays, Taniguchi rationally discussed to what extent there could
   be any matching of constitutional values with social circumstances in

which there remained the old custom of parent child relationships, when under the post-war constitution respect for the individual was valued. Having failed at first to notice the use of the imperial dating system, despite its use from the very first page of Taniguchi's *Family Registration System*, the author simply thought that it was printing error. It was yet another case of being surprised by the strength of the ties between family registers and the emperor system.

10 In the view of the author, this opinion held by Tashiro, is as far as the legal approach is concerned a premise requiring no explanation and, therefore, nationality acts, written by lawyers, all begin with the 1873 Edict.

11 Itagaki discusses the same intent in *Jiyūtōshi* (History of the Liberal Party). 'Although Aizu was known as one of the major domains, only five thousand members of the samurai class sacrificed themselves to their clan at the time of falling into ruin, with peasants, traders and craftsmen deserting in support of the enemy forces. Observing the situation, I was deeply ashamed and could not help feeling an intense patriotic concern. In my view, if the people of Aizu had fought in unity and loyalty without regard to distinctions of social standing, as one of the strongest domains, it should have been able to defeat with ease the imperial forces, which numbered less than a mere five thousand soldiers. Why is it that the commoners ran away to avoid the calamity of war, lacked the mettle to return generations of debt owed to their lord and showed indifference to the downfall of their domain? I would attribute all this to the separation of the upper and lower classes and the failure of the latter to share any of their comforts and pleasures. In not sharing these, how could both classes share hardships and sufferings?

Feudal power is declining and the time is ripe for it to be totally replaced. At this juncture, we are attempting to implement the strategy of "enrich the nation and strengthen the military" as our imperial nation soars high on the front of the eastern sea. To achieve our goal, we should administer state affairs in such a way as to bring the upper and lower classes together in harmony, sharing the joys and sorrows of life with the common people and thus achieving the unity of the whole nation. Indeed, the nation must be built on a foundation of the united power of every national. Never should we believe that it is sufficient to rely merely on the power of one class. Accordingly, we must act, at this very time, to abolish the class system immediately; to end the monopoly of power held by the warrior class; to engage together in the protection of the nation with everybody on an equal footing; and thus mark the beginning of everyone sharing joy and misery, happiness and unhappiness' (Itagaki 1957: 28–29).

12 This is why, quite apart from family registers, the system of certificates of residence was devised to provide an understanding of where people lived.

13 The adoption of a nationality law based on the principle of family line necessitates the prior establishment of the identity of the parents of a child who is born for the purposes of determining the nationality of that child. In order for the determination of the relationship between parents and children, as a precondition for nationality, to exist, one's status under the Civil Code and the family Registration Law needs to be established.

14 The papers for this judgement can be viewed in *Saikōsaibansho Minjihanreishū* (Collection of Supreme Court Civil Precedents), volume 15, number 4, pages 657–694.

Bibliography

Aoki, Hideo (2000), *Gendai Nihon no toshi kasō: yoseba to nojukusha to gaikokujin rōdōsha* (Modern Japan's urban underclass: *yoseba*, the homeless and foreign workers), Tokyo: Akashi Shoten.

Aoki, Masahiko (2001), *Hikaku seido bunseki e mukete* (Toward Comparative Institutional Analysis), Tokyo: NTT Shuppan.

Aoki, M., M. Okuno and K. Muramatsu (1996), 'Kigyō no koyō shisutemu to senryakuteki hokansei (Employment System and Strategic Complementarity),' in M. Aoki and M. Okuno (eds), *Keizai shisutemu no hikaku seido bunseki* (Comparative Institutional Analysis of Economic Systems),' Tokyo: University of Tokyo Press, pp. 123–152.

Anzai, Masaru (1997), *Rōdōsha haken hō no hōritsu jitsumu* (The worker dispatch law in legal practice), Tokyo: Sōgōrōdō Kenkyūjo.

Arai, Kazuhiro (2001), *Bunka, soshiki, koyōseido: Nihonteki shisutemu no keizai bunseki* (Culture, organisations and the employment system: an economic analysis of Japanese systems), Tokyo: Yūhikaku.

Arakawa, Ryu (1998), 'Nikkei Burajirujin mondai ga tou "Nihon" – musuko o ushinatta ryōshin no uttae ("Japan" questions the issue of Brazilians of Japanese descent: appeal by parents after losing son),' *Shūan kinyōbi* (Friday Weekly), 230.

Asanuma, Banri (1997), *Nihon no kigyō soshiki: kakushinteki tekiō no mekanizumu* (Japanese business organisations: innovative adaptation mechanisms), Tokyo: Tōyō Keizai Shinpōsha.

Asao, Uichi (1994), 'Jidōsha buhin mēkā ni okeru rōmukanri to Nikkeijin rōdōsha (Labour management and workers of Japanese descent in automobile parts makers),' *Shakai seisaku gakkai nenpō* (Report of the society for social policy (38).

Association for the Historical Commemoration of 60 Years of Japanese Migration to the Amazon (1994), *Amazon: Nihonjin ni yoru 60 nen ni ijūshi* (Amazon: a 60 year history of migration by Japanese people), Belém: Pan-Amazonian Japan and Brazil Association.

Boribia Nihonjin Ijū 100 Shūnen Ijūshi Hensaniinkai (2000), *Boribia ni ikiru – Nihonjin ijū 100 shūnen shi* (Living in Bolivia: magazine commemorating the 100th anniversary of Japanese migration), Santa Cruz: Federation of Societies of Bolivians of Japanese Descent.

Chūbu Sangyō Rōdō Seisaku Kenkyūkai (1994), *Chōki koyō no henshitsu to jinji, rōmuseisaku no yukue: chūkyōchiku jidōsha sangyō ni jirei kara* (Transformation and human resources in long-term employment, the future course for labour management policy: the case of the automobile industry in Nagoya and the surrounding area), Nihon rōdō kenkyū kikō itaku kenkyūchōsa hōkokusho (Questionnaire survey research report of the Japan Institute of Labor), Toyota: Chubu Industries Society for the Study of Labour Policy.

Chūbu Sangyō Rōdō Seisaku Kenkyūkai (1998), *Rōdō no tayōka ni muketa rōshi no yakuwari* (The role of labour and management under a labour diversification orientation), Nihon rōdō kenkyū kikō itaku kenkyūchōsa hōkokusho Toyota: Chubu Industries Society for the Study of Labour Policy.

Chūma, Hiroyuki (2001), 'Kōnai ukeougyō katsuyō no jittai to bunseki – inobēshon no shinten kara (The true state and analysis of the in-house use of contracting businesses: from the viewpoint of the development of innovation),' *IT jidai no koyō shisutemu* (Employment systems in the IT era), Tokyo: Nihon Hyōronsha.

Eguchi, Eiichi (1957) 'Rōdō shijō no mondai (Labour market issues),' Fukutake, Tadashi (ed.), *Kōza shakaigaku* (Sociology lectures) *dai 6 kan* (Vol. 6), Tokyo: Tokyo Daigaku Shuppankai.

Eguchi, Eiichi (1980), *Gendai no 'teishotokusō' naka: 'hinkon' kenkyū no hōhō* (Inside modern 'low income groups (Vol. 2):' 'poverty' research methods),' Tokyo: Miraisha.

Fujita, Eishi (1999), 'Shakai keizai kankyō henka to seisan ka hatsu taisei no saihensei (Changes in the socio-economic environment and production reorganisation of the development system),' in Uichi Aso, Masaki Saruta, Hikari Nohara, Eishi Fujita and Motohiko Yamashita *Shakai kankyō no henka to jidōsha seisan shisutemu* (Changes in the social environment and the automobile production system),' Kyoto: Hōritsu Bunkasha.

Fujita, Tokiyasu (2005), *Gyōseihō 1 (sōron) [daiyonhan] kaiteiban* (Administrative law 1 (general remarks) [volume 4] revised edition),' Tokyo: Seirin Shoin.

Fukui, Hideo (2006), *Shihō seisaku no hō to keizaigaku* (Law and Economics for the Administration of Justice Policy),' Tokyo: Nihon Hyōronsha.

Fukui, Hideo and F. Ohtake (eds) (2006), *Datsu kakusa shakai to koyō hōsei: hō to keizaigaku de kangaeru* (Employment legislation and society without disparities: thinking in terms of law and economics), Tokyo: Nihon Hyōronsha.

Fukushima, Masao (ed.) (1959), *'Ie' seido no kenkyū* (Studies of the institution of the 'family),' Tokyo: Tokyo Daigaku Shuppankai.

Fukushima, Masao (ed.) (1962), *'Ie' seido no kenkyū; shiryōhen II* (Studies of the institution of the 'family; source materials II),' Tokyo: Tokyo Daigaku Shuppankai.

Fukushima, Masao (ed.) (1967), *Nihon shihonshugi to 'ie' seido* (Japanese capitalism and the institution of the 'family),' Tokyo: Tokyo Daigaku Shuppankai.

Genda, Yūji (2001), *Shigoto no naka no aimaina fuan* (A vague unease inside work), Tokyo: Chūōkōron shinsha.

Gushiken, Kōtei (1998), Yutaka Terui (ed.), *Okinawa ijūchi: Eoribia no daichi to tomo ni* (Colonia Okinawan migration: together with the vast land of Bolivia),' Naha: Okinawa Times Company.

Han Amazonia Nippaku Kyōkai (1994), *Amazon: Nihonjin ni yoru 60 nen no ijūshi* (Amazon: 60 years of Japanese migration),' Para State, Belem: Han Amazonia Nippaku Kyōkai.

Handa, Tomoo (1966), *Imanao tabiji ni ari: ichi Nikkei imin no ayunda michi* (Still on a journey: the road travelled by one person of Japanese descent),' São Paolo: Humanities Institute of São Paolo.

Handa, Tomoo (1970), *Imin no seikatsu no rekishi: Burajiru nikkeijin no ayunda michi* (History of the lives of immigrants: the roads travelled by Brazilians of Japanese descent),' São Paolo: Humanities Institute of São Paolo.

Hatta, Tatsuo (2006), 'Kōritsuka gensoku to kitokuken hogo gensoku: futatsu no seisaku hyōka kijun no hikaku (The principles of optimization and of protecting vested interests: a comparison of the evaluative basis for both policies),' in Hideo Fukui and Ohtake Fumio (eds), *Datsukakusa shakai to koyō seido: hō to keizaigaku de kangaeru* (Disparity-free society and the employment system: thinking from law and economics),' Tokyo: Nihon Hyōronsha.

Hayashi, Takaharu (1996), 'Gyōmu ukeougyō ni tsuite (About service contracting businesses)' *Infomēto Nagoya* (Infomate Nagoya),' Nagoya: Nagoya Ginkō Kurashi to sōdan sentā.

Higuchi, Naoto (2001), 'Burajiru Paranashū ni okeru Nikkeijin rōdōsha assen soshiki (Service organisations for workers of Japanese descent in Parana State, Brazil),' *Tokushima Daigaku Shakaikagaku Kenkyū* (Tokushima University Social Sciences Research) No.14.

Higuchi, Naoto (2002), 'Kokusai imin ni okeru mezoreberu no ichizuke: makuro-mikuro moderu o koete' (Positioning the mezzo level in international migration: beyond macro-micro models),' *Shakaigaku hyōron* (Japanese Sociology Review) 52 (4).

Higuchi, Naoto; Tanno, Kiyoto; and Rika Higuchi (1998), 'Ekkyō suru shokubunka to imin nettowāku: zainichi musurimu imin no zōka to harāru shokuhin sangyō no hatten (Transnational food cultures and migrant networks: the increase in Muslim immigrants living in Japan and the development of a Halal food industry),' *Shokuseikatsu kenkyū* (Eating habits research) 19 (3).

Higuchi, Naoto and Kiyoto Tanno (2000), 'Shokubunka no ekkyō to harāru shokuhin sangyō no keisei: zainichi Muzurimu imin o jirei toshite (Food cultures crossing borders and the formation of the Halal food industry: the case of Muslim immigrants living in Japan), *Shakaikagaku kenkyū* (Sociology studies) 13.

Hiraga, Kenta (1950), *Kokusekihō jō* (Nationality Law, I), Teikoku Hanreihōki Shuppansha.

Hiraga, Kenta (1951), *Kokusekihō ge* (Nationality Law II), Teikoku Hanreihōki Shuppansha.

Hiraga, Kenta (1959), 'Shinzokuhō kaisei no mondaiten (Problems with the revisions to the Family Law),' in Zenkoku rengō koseki jimu kyōgikaihen (National Alliance of Family Register Offices (ed.), *Kosekishi daihyakugo kinen ronbunshū: mibunhō no genzai oyobi shōrai* (Collection of essays celebrating the 100th issue of the Family Registration Magazine: present and future of the Family Law), Tokyo: Teihan.

Hirai, Yoshio (1996), 'Iwayuru danzokuteki keiyaku ni kansuru ikkōsatsu: "shijō to soshiki no hōriron" no shiten kara (A consideration of so-called continuous contracts: from the perspective of "legal theory of markets and organisations"),' *Nakagawa Yoshinobu et al. (eds), Nihon minpōgaku no keisei to kadai: Hoshino Eiichi sensei kokishukuga kinen* (ka) (The formation of and issues in Studies of Japanese Civil Law: Professor Eiichi Hoshino 70th birthday commemorative edition Volume 2), Tokyo: Yūhikaku.

Hirano, Yoshitarō (1934), *Nihon shihonshugi shakai no kikō* (The organisation of Japanese capitalist society), Tokyo: Iwanami Shoten.

Hosokawa, Kiyoshi and Yoshimune Ebihara (1986) 'Jo (Preface'), in Kiyoshi Hosokawa and Yoshimune Ebihara (eds), *Kosekishi daigohyakugo kinen ronbunshū, kazokuhō to koseki: sono genzai oyobi shōrai* (Collection of essays celebrating the 500th issue of the family registration magazine, family law and family registration: present and future), Tokyo: Teihan.

Ieyumi, Yoshimi (1966), 'Zainichi Chōsenjin no kokuseki oyobi junkyohō ni tsuite (On family registration and compliance laws for Koreans living in Japan),' in Takanashi, Masayuki et al, *Koseki jihō hyakugō kinen, kazokuhō to koseki no mondai* (Commemorating the 100th issue of the family registration report, issues with family law and family registration), Tokyo: Nihon Kajo Shuppan.

Igarashi, Yasumasa (1999), 'Shokuba no dōryō/buka toshite no gaikokujin (Foreign workers as co-workers/subordinates in the workplace),' *Ōhara shakai mondai kenkyūjo zasshi* (Journal of the Ōhara Institute for Social Research) *491*.

Iizasa, Sayoko (2007), *Shitizunshippu to tabunka kokka: Ōsutoraria kara yomidoku* (Citizenship and multicultural countries: lessons from Australia), Tokyo: Nihon Keizai Hyōronsha.

Ikegami, Shigehiro (1998), *Burajirujin shūchū kyojū chiku ni okeru chiiki shakai no genjō to kadai: Hamamatsushi no jirei kara* (Present conditions and challenges in regional societies in areas with concentrated numbers of Brazilian residents: the case of Hamamatsu City), *Heisei 9 nendo Shizuoka kenritsu daigaku gakuchō tokubetsu kenkyūseika hōkokusho* (Report of the president of Shizuoka Prefectural University on special research accomplishments for the 1997 fiscal year), Shizuoka: Shizuoka Kenritsu Daigaku Tanki Daigakubu.

Ikegami, Shigehiro, Kumiko Iijima and Natsuko Ōta (1998), 'Shizuoka ken seibu chiiki ni okeru nyūkamā no zōka to gyōsei no taiō: kosaishi no jirei o chūshin ni (The increase in newcomers in the western districts of Shizuoka Prefecture and the administration's response: a focus on the case of Kosai City),' *Chiiki no kokusaika ni tomonau bunkateki masatsu to sono kaihi* (The cultural friction that accompanies the internationalisation of the regions and its avoidance), Report of the president of Shizuoka Prefectural University on special research accomplishments for the 1997 fiscal year, Shizuoka: Shizuoka Kenritsu Daigaku Tanki Daigakubu.

Imada, Takatoshi (1986), *Jiko soshikisei: shakai riron no fukkatsu* (The nature of self-organisation: the revival of social theory), Tokyo: Sōbunsha.

Imai, Kenichi and Ikuyō Kaneko (1988), *Nettowāku soshikiron* (Network organisation theory), Tokyo: Iwanami Shoten.

Imin hachijūnen shi hensan iinkai (Editorial committee of eighty years of immigration history) (1991), *Burajiru Nihon imin hachijūnen shi* (Eighty year history of Brazil's Japanese immigrants), São Paolo: Burajiru Nihon Bunka Kyōkai.

Inagami, Takeshi (1973), 'Rōshi kankei (Labour management relations),' in Shizuo Matsushima (ed.), *Sangyō shakaigaku, "Shakakigaku kōza* (Industrial sociology, "Sociology Lectures) *6,"* Tokyo: Tokyo Daigaku Suppankai.

Inagami, Takeshi (1990), *Gendai Eikoku rōdō jijō: satchaizumu, koyō, rōshi kankei* (Present day labour conditions in the United Kingdom: Thatcherism, employment and labour management relations), Tokyo: Tokyo Daigaku Suppankai.

Inagami, Takeshi (1992), 'Keiei senryaku, gaikokujin rōdō shijō: jirei kara mita supekutoramu kōzō (Management strategies, the foreign worker labour market and employment control: the structure of the spectrum seen through cases),' in Takeshi Inagami, Yasuo Kuwahara, Kokumin kinkōko sōgo kenkyūjohen (National Finance Corporation General Research Institute) (eds), *Gaikokujin rōdōsha o senryokuka suru chūshō kigyō* (Small- and medium-sized companies that make foreign workers work-ready), Tokyo: Chūshō kigyō risāchi sentā.

Inoue, Shigeru (1973), *Hōchitsujo no kōzō* (The structure of the legal order), Tokyo: Iwanami Shoten.

Inoue, Tamiji and Makoto Katō (eds) (1993), *Hana ni hikiyoserareru dōbutsu: hana to sōfunsha no kyōshinka* (Animals drawn to pollen: the coevolution of flowers and pollinators), Tokyo: Heibonsha.

Ishi, Angelo (1995), '"Dekasegi bijinesu" no hassei to seikatsu kankyō no henka: shokuseikatsu, rejā, media nado no kanten kara ('Origins of "migrant worker businesses" and changes to their living environment: from the viewpoint of factors such as food lifestyle, leisure and media),' in Masako Watanabe (ed.) *Kyōdō kenkyū – dekasegi Nikkei Burajirujin 1, ronbunhen* (Joint research – Migrant worker Brazilians of Japanese descent 1, Discussion), Tokyo: Akashi Shoten.

Ishii, Yuka and Nanako Inaba (1996), 'Jūtaku mondai: kyojū no chōkika no naka de (Housing problems: in the midst of lengthening periods of residence),' in Takashi Miyajima and Takamichi Kajita (eds) *Gaikokujin rōdōsha kara shimin e: chiiki shakai no shiten to kadai kara* (From foreign workers to citizens: from the point of view of and challenges in regional society), Tokyo: Yūhikaku.

Ishikawa, Yuki and Munehiro Machida (1986), 'Burajiru ni okeru Okinawaken shusshin imin no shūdan keisei: São Paoloshi bīra karaon chiku no baai (Group formation amongst immigrants from Okinawa Prefecture in Brazil: the case of the Vila Carrão district in the city of São Paolo),' Ryūkyū Daigaku hōbungakubu chirigaku kyōshitsu (Department of Geography, Faculty of Law and Literature, University of the Ryukyus), *Nanbei ni okeru Okinawaken susshin imin ni kansuru chirigakuteki kenkyū: Boribia Burajiru* (Geographic studies of immigrants from Okinawa Prefecture in South America: Bolivia and Brazil), (Ministry of Education Academic Research Grant, 2008, Issue no. 60043053), Department of Geography, Faculty of Law and Literature, University of the Ryukyus.

Isomura, Kentarō (1998), 'Sogaikan tsuyomeru Burajirujin: fukyō de roteishita gaikokujin sabetsu no haikei (Brazilians' growing sense of alienation: the background to prejudice against foreigners exposed by recession),' *AERA* 40.

Itagaki, Taisuke (General Ed.), Shigeki Tōyama and Shigerō Satō (1957), *Jiyūtōshi 1* (History of the Liberal Party, 1), Tokyo: Iwanami Bunko.

Iwasa, Setsuro (1959), 'Kyūhō koseki no kaisei to uji ni tsuite (Regarding the redrawing of family registers and lineage),' in Zenkoku rengō koseki jimu kyōgikai hen (National Alliance of Family Register Offices, ed.) *Kosekishi daihyakugō kinen ronbunshū: mibunhō no genzai oyobi shōrai* (Collection of essays celebrating the 100th issue of the Family Registration Magazine: present and future of the Family Law), Tokyo: Teihan.

Josei no ie Salaa (2002), *Josei no ie Salaa 10 nen no ayumi: gaikokuseki josei e no bōryoku no jittai* (The 10 year progress of Salaa's house for females: the realities of violence against females who are foreign nationals), Yokohama: Josei no ie Salaa.

Kagami, Kazuaki (2001), 'Shitauke torihiki kankei ni okeru keiretsu ni keisei to tankan (The formation and development of keiretsu in subcontracting transactions relationships),' in Tetsuji Okazaki (ed.), *Torihiki seido no keizaishi* (Economic history of the transactions system), Tokyo: Tokyo University Press.

Kagono, Tadao, Ikujiro Nonaka, Kiyonori Sakakibara and Akihiro Okumura (1983), *Nihon kigyō no keiei hikaku* (A Comparison of management in Japanese companies), Tokyo: Nihon Keizai Shinbunsha.

Kajita, Takamichi (1998), 'Gyōshuku sareta ijū saikuru: Nikkeijin ni miru dekasegi no henyō (The condensed immigration cycle: changes in migrant work observable in people of Japanese descent), *Hikaku bunmei 14* (Comparative civilisations 14).

Kajita, Takamichi (1999), 'Kairisuru nashonarizumu to esunishiti: "Nikkeijin" ni okeru hōteki shikaku to shakaigakuteki genjitsu no aida (Nationalism and ethnicity as alienating factors: between the legal qualifications of people of Japanese descent and the sociological realities),' in Kazuo Aoi, Akira Takahashi and Kōkichi Shōji (eds) *Shiminsei no henyō to chiiki, shakai mondai: 21 seiki ni shimin shakai to kyōdōsei; kokusaika to naimenka* (Changes in the nature of citizens and regional and social problems: 21st century civil society and cooperation – internationalisation and internalisation), Tokyo: Azusa Shuppansha.

Kajita, Takamichi (ed.) (1999), *Toransunashonaruna kankyōka de no aratana ijū purosesu: dekasegi 10 nen o heta Nikkeijin no shakaigakuteki chōsa hōkoku* (New immigration processes in a transnational environment: a sociological survey report of people of Japanese descent with 10 years' experience of migrant work), Kagaku gijutsu shinkō chōseihi (Special Coordination Funds for the Promotion of Science and Technology), 'Ningen no shakaiteki shokatsudō no kaimei, shien ni kansuru kibanteki kenkyū ni okeru "Toransunashonaruna kankyōka ni okeru bunkateki kyōsō ni kansuru kenkyū hōkokusho" ("Research report on cultural co-generation in a transnational environment" in basic research on elucidating and supporting people's various social activities),' Tokyo: Hitotsubashi Daigaku Shakaigakubu.

Kajita, Takamichi (2001), 'Mitsu no "shitizunshippu:" "mitsu no gēto" ron ni yoru seiri (Three "citizenships:" regulation using the "three gates" argument),' (NIRA Shitizunshippu Kenkyūkai eds), *Tabunka shakai no sentaku* (Choosing a multicultural society), Tokyo: Nihon keizai hyōronsha.

Kajita, Takamichi (2002), 'Nihon no gaikokujin rōdōsha seisaku (Japan's foreign worker policy), Takamichi Kajita and Takashi Miyajima (eds) *Kokusaika suru Nihon shakai* (Japan's internationalizing society), Tokyo: Tokyo Daigaku Shuppankai.

Kajita, Takamichi, Kiyoto Tanno and Naoto Higuchi (2005), *Kao no mienai jūminka* (Invisible Residents), Nagoya: Nagoya Daigaku Shuppankai.

Kamoto, Itsuko (2001), *Kokusai kekkon no tanjō: "bunmeikoku" e no michi*

(The birth of international marriages: the road to a civilised nation), Tokyo: Shinyōsha.

Kaneko, Ikuyō (1986), *Nettowākingu e no shōtai* (An invitation to networking), Tokyo: Chūkō Shinsho.

Kaneko, Masaru (ed.) (1996), *Gendai shihonshugi to seifuti netto: shijō to hishijō no kankeisei* (Present day capitalism and the safety net: the nature of the relationship between market and non-market), Tokyo: Hōsei Daigaku Shuppankyoku.

Kawashima, Takeyoshi (1959), *Kindai shakai to hō* (Modern society and the law), Tokyo: Iwanami Shoten.

Kawashima, Takeyoshi (1972), '"Hō" no shakaigaku riron no kisozuke (Establishing the basis of the sociological theory of "law"), in Takeyoshi Kawashima (ed.) *Hōshakaigaku kōza 4: Hōshakaigaku no kiso 2* (Lectures on legal sociology 4: The basis of legal sociology 2), Tokyo: Iwanami Shoten.

Kawashima, Takeyoshi (1982a), *Kawashima Takeyoshi chosakushū, daiikkan, Hōshakaigaku 1, ikeru hō to kokka hō* (Collected works of Takeyoshi Kawashima, volume 1, Legal sociology, Living law and national law), Tokyo: Iwanami Shoten.

Kawashima, Takeyoshi (1982b), *Kawashima Takeyoshi chosakushū, daigokan, Hōritsugaku 1, Hōritsugaku no hōhō to kadai* (Collected works of Takeyoshi Kawashima, volume 5, Methods and issues in jurisprudence), Tokyo: Iwanami Shoten.

Kazahaya, Yasoji (1937), *Nihon shakai seisaku shi* (History of Japanese social policy), Tokyo: Nihon Hyōronsha.

Keiei rōdō seisaku iinkai (Labour policy committee) (2003), *Keiei rōdō seisaku iinkai hōkoku: tayōna kachikan ga umu dainamizumu to sōzō o mezashite* (Report of the labour policy committee: aiming for dynamism tht gives rise to diverse value systems and creativity), Tokyo: Nihon Keidanren Shuppan.

Kimoto, Kimiko (1995), *Kazoku, jendā, kigyō shakai: jendā apurōchi no mosaku* (Family, gender and company society: striving for a gender approach), Kyoto: Mineruba Shobō.

Kochia sanso chūōkai kankō iinkai (1987), *Kochia sangyō kumiai chūōkai 60 nen no ayumi: 1927–1987* (60 years of progress of the central group of the Cotia industrial union 1927–1987),' São Paolo: Cooperative Agricola de Cotia-Cooperative Central.

Kochia seinen renraku kyōgikai (2006), *Kochia seinen: ijū 50 shūnen, 1955–2005* (Cotia Youth: 50th anniversary of migration, 1955–2005),' São Paolo: Cotia Youth Contact Association.

Kodama, Kōichi (2005), 'Taikyo kyōsei kara no kyūsai to jinken jōyaku (Assistance in avoiding forceful deportation and human rights treaties), in Shigeo Miyagawa (ed.) *Gaikokujinhō to rōyaringu: riron to jitsumu no kakyō o mezashite* (The Aliens Act and lawyering: aiming to build bridges between theory and practice), Tokyo: Gakuyō Shobō.

Koike, Kazuo (2005), *Shigoto no keizaigaku* (The Economics of Work, 3rd Edition), Tokyo: Tōyō keizai shinposha.

Koike, Yōichi (1995), 'Sengo no Burajiru keizai hatten to nihon kigyō no shinshutsu (Post-war economic development of Brazil and the progress of Japanese companies), Nihon Burajiru shūkō 100 shūnen kinen jigyō soshiki iinkai (Committee of business organisations celebrating 100 years of Japan-Brazil friendship), *Nihon Burajiru kōryūshi: nippaku kankei 100 nen no kaiko to tenbō* (History of Japan-Brazil interaction: 100 years of recollections and future prospects), Shadan Hōjin Nihon Burajiru Chūō Kyōkai.

Komai, Hiroshi, Ichirō Watado and Keizō Yamawaki (eds) (1999), *Chōka taizai gaikokujin to zairyū tokubetsu kyoka: kiro ni tatsu Nihon no shutsunyūkoku kanri seisaku* (Overstaying foreigners and special permission to stay: the immigration control policy of Japan at the crossroads), Tokyo: Akashi Shoten.

Komuro, Naoki (1972), 'Kihan shakaigaku (Normative sociology),' in Takeyoshi Kawajima (ed.) *Hōshakaigaku kōza 4, Hōshakcigaku no kiso 2* (Legal sociology lectures 4, Foundations of legal sociology 2), Tokyo: Iwanami Shoten.

Kondō, Atsushi (2001), *Gaikokujin no jinken to shiminken* (Human rights and citizenship of foreigners), Tokyo: Akashi Shoten.

Koronia Okinawa Nyūshoku yonjū shūnen kinenshi hensan iinkai (1995), *Uruma kara no tabidachi: koronia Okinawa nyūshoku 40 nen kinenshi* (Departure from Uruma: commemorative magazine of forty years of settlement in Colonia Okinawa),' Santa Cruz: Okinawa-Bolivia-Japan Association.

Kōshiro, Kazuyoshi, Rengōsōgō seikatsu kaihatsu kenkyūjo hen (Research Institute for the Advancement of Living Standards (ed.)) (1995), *Sengo 50 nen: sangyō, koyō, rōdōshi* (50 post-war years: industry, employment and labour history), Tokyo: Nihon Rōdō Kenkyū Kikō.

Kosugi, Reiko (ed.) (2002), *Jiyū no daishō/furītā: gendai wakamono no shūgyō ishiki to kōdō* (The price of freedom/freeter: the sense of employment and actions of modern day young people), Tokyo: Nihon Rōdō Kenkyū Kikō.

Koyama, Yoichi (1985), *Kyodai kigyō taisei to rōdōsha: Toyota no jirei* (The system of corporate giants and workers: the case of Toyota), Ochanomizu Shobō.

Koyō Nōryoku Kaihatsu Kikō (Organisation for employment and capacity development (2001), *Iwayuru hitode busoku no kanten kara mita gaikokujin rōdōsha koyō mondai no jittai ni tsuite* (On the realities of the foreign worker employment problem, as viewed from the perspective of so-called labour shortages), Tokyo: Zaidan hōjin koyō kaihatsu sentā.

Kumazawa, Makoto (1989), *Nihonteki keiei no meian* (The bright and dark sides of Japanese style management), Tokyo: Chikuma Shobō.

Kumazawa, Makoto (1997), *Nōryokushugi to Kigyō shakai* (Meritocracy and company-dominated society), Tokyo: Iwanami shinsho.

Kuroki, Tadamasa and Kiyoshi Hosokawa (1988), *Gendai gyōsei hōgaku zenshū 17, Gaijihō, kokusekihō* (Complete works of modern administrative jurisprudence 17, Foreign Affairs Law, Nationality Law), Tokyo: Gyōsei.

Kuwahara, Yasuo (1993), 'Gaikokujin rōdōsha mondai no seijikeizaigaku: bunseki, seisaku ritsuan no tame no wakugumi (The political economy of the foreign worker problem: an analysis and policy making framework),' in Tadashi Hanami and Yasuo Kuwahara (eds) *Anata no runjin: gaikokujin rōdōsha* (Your neighbours: foreign workers), Tokyo: Tōyō Keizai Shinposha.

Li, Tei (2000), 'Kaiko no tetsuzuki (Dismissal formalities),' Nihon rōdōhō gakkai (Japanese labour law society) (ed.), Kōza 21 seiki no rōdōhō (Lecture 21st century labour laws), *Rōdō keiyaku* (Labour contracts), Tokyo: Yūhikaku.

Maeyama, Takashi (1981), *Hisōzokusha no seishin shi: aru Nikkei Burajirujin no henreki* (History of the spirit of non-successors: the travels of some Brazilians of Japanese descent), Tokyo: Ochanomizu Shobō.

Maeyama, Takashi (1997), *Ihō ni "Nihon" o matsuru* (Worshipping "Japan" in a foreign land), Tokyo: Ochanomizu Shobō.

Maruyama, Masao (1961), *Nihon no shisō* (Japanese Thought), Tokyo: Iwanami Shinsho.

Marx, Karl and Friedrich Engels (1951), Hyōe Ōuchi and Itsurō Sagisaka (trans.), *Kyōsantō sengen* (The Communist Manifesto), Tokyo: Iwanami Bunko.

Miyagi, Shōsei (1998), *Burajiru no Okinawa-kenjin, toppu rīdā* (Top leaders of Brazilians from Okinawa prefecture), São Paolo: Shikaban.

Miyao, Susumu (2004) Jinbun kenkyū sōsho (Studies of humanity series), *Bōdāresuka suru Nikkeijin* (People of Japanese descent becoming borderless), São Paolo: San Pauro Jinbun Kagaku Kenkyūjo, Katsunori Wakisaka (trans.) (2005), *Nipo-Brasileiros Process de Assimilação*, São Paulo: Centro de Estudos Nipo-Brasileiros.

Mizutani, Hideo (1997), 'Rōdōsha haken jigyō no arikata o meguru kadai (Issues concerning the state of worker dispatch businesses),' *Hōritsu no hiroba* (Legal forum) 50 (8).

Mori, Kōichi (1992), 'Burajiru kara no Nikkeijin "dekasegi" no suii (Changes in "migrant workers" of Japanese descent from Brazil),' *Ijū kenkyū* (Immigration studies) 29.

Mori, Kōichi (1993), 'Nikkeijin no "dekasegi" o meguru jōkyō no henka (Changes in the circumstances concerning "migrant workers" of Japanese descent),' Masato Ninomiya (ed.) *"Dekasegi" genshō ni kansuru shinpojūmu hōkokusho* (Report of the symposium on the "migrant worker" phenomenon), Burajiru Nippon Bunka Kyōkai.

Mori, Kōichi (1995a), 'Burajiru kara no Nikkeijin dekasegi no tokuchō to suii (Special characteristics and changes in migrant workers of Japanese descent from Brazil),' Masako Watanabe (ed.) *Kyōdō kenkyū, dekasegi Nikkei Burajirujin, 1, ronbunhen* (Cooperative research, Brazilian migrant workers of Japanese descent, 1, text, Tokyo: Akashi Shoten.

Mori, Kōichi (1995b), 'Nikkeijin no "dekasegi" o meguru jōkyo no henka (Changes in the circumstances concerning "migrant work" by people of Japanese descent),' in Masato Ninomiya (ed.), *"Dekasegi" genshō ni kansuru shinpojūmu hōkokusho* (Report of the symposium regarding the phenomenon of "migrant workers"), São Paolo: Burajiru Nihon Bunka Kyōkai.

Mori, Kōichi (1998), 'Sengo ni okeru Okinawakei imin no esunikku shokugyō toshite no *costura*: midoruman mainoritī e no michi (*Costura* (the garment industry) as the ethnic occupation for post-war Okinawan immigrants: the path to middleman minority),' *Jinbunken* (Humanities research) *1*.

Mori, Kōichi (2001), 'Okinawaken imin no keizaiteki tekiō senjutsu to toshi esunikku comyuniti no seisei: São Paoloshi "Karon" chiku no Okinawakei esunikku comyuniti no jirei (Economic adaptation tactics of immigrants from Okinawa prefecture and the formation of urban ethnic communities),' *Jinbunken* (Humanities research) 5.

Mori, Kōichi (2005), 'Burajiru Okinawakeijin no sosen sūhai no jissen (Ancestor worship practices of Brazilians of Okinawan descent),' *Ajia yūgaku* 76 (Asian study abroad 76)

Mori, Tateshi (2003), 'Koyō kankei no henka o dono yōni toraeruka (How are we to treat the changes in employment relations?),' Shakai seisaku gakkai hen (Society for Social Policy (ed.)), *Shakai seisaku gakkai shi 9* (Magazine of the Society for Social Policy 9).

Morita, Kirirō (1987), *Kokusai rōdōryoku idō* (Movements of the international labour force), Tokyo: Tokyo Daigaku Shuppankai.

Morita, Kirirō (1995), *Sekai keizairon: "sekai shisutemu" apurōchi* (Theory of a world economy: a "world system" approach), Kyoto: Mineruba Shobō.

Motohisa, Yoichi (2000), 'Ihō kaiko no kōka (The effectiveness of illegal dismissal),' Nihon rōdōhō gakkai hen (Japanese labour law society (ed.), (Japanese labour law society (ed.), Kōza 21 seiki no rōdōhō (Lecture 21st century labour laws), *Rōdō keiyaku* (Labour contracts), Tokyo: Yūhikaku.

Murakami, Yasusuke and Shimpei Kumon (1974), 'Soshiki genri (Principles of organisation), in Kenichi Tominaga (ed.), *Kōza shakaigaku 8, keizai shakaigaku* (Sociology Lectures 8, Economic sociology), Tokyo: Tokyo Daigaku Shuppankai.

Nakamura, Takafusa (1993), *Nihon keizai: sono siechō to kōzō (Daisanhan)* (Japanese Economy: its growth and structure (3rd edition)), Tokyo: Tokyo Daigaku Shuppankai.

Nakano, Mami (2003), 'Rōdō haken no kakudai to rōdōhō (The expansion of the dispatching of workers and labour law),' Shakai seisaku gakkai hen (Society for Social Policy (ed.), *Shakai seisaku gakkai shi 9* (Magazine of the Society for Social Policy 9).

Nanakorobiyaoki (2005), *Buenos dias Nippon* (Good morning Japan), Tokyo: Ratīna.

Nanbei sangyō kaihatsu seinentai 40 nen shi kankō iinkai (Publication committee of the 40 year history of the South American industrial development youth group (1997), *Seinentai: 1956–1996* (Youth group: 1956–1996), São Paolo: Nanbei Sangyō Kaihatsu Seinentai 40 Nen Shi Kankō Iinkai.

Nanbei Sansui Dōsōkai Shi Henshū Iinkai (Editorial Committee of the South American Sansui Class Reunion) (2004), *Mawarimichi o shita otokotachi* (Men who took a detour), São Paolo: Mie Daigaku Nōgakubu Nanbei Sansui Dōsōkai Shi Henshū Iinkai.

Nihon Keieisha Dantai Renmei (Japan Federation of Employers' Associations) (1995), *Shinjidai no "Nihonteki keiei" – chosen subeki hōkō to sono gutaisaku* ("Japanese management" for a new era – challenges that ought to be taken and concrete plans), Shin-Nihonteki keiei shisutemu nado kenkyū purojekuto hōkoku (Report of the research project into matters such as a new Japanese management system), Tokyo: Nihon Keieisha Dantai Renmei.

Nihon Keieisha Dantai Renmei Kantō Keieisha Kyōkai (Japan Federation of Employers' Associations, Kanto Employers' Association) (1996), *Shinjidai no "Nihonteki keiei" ni tsuite no forōuppu chōsa hōkoku* ((Follow-up report on "Japanese management" for a new era), Nihon Keieisha Dantai Renmei Kantō Keieisha Kyōkai.

Nikkeiren Rōdō Mondai Kenkyū Iinkai (Japan Federation of Employers' Associations, Labour Issues Research Committee) (2001), *Rōdō Mondai*

Kenkyū Iinkai Hōkoku – tayōna sentakushi o motta keizai shakai no jitsugen o (Report of the Japan Federation of Employers' Associations, Labour Issues Research Committee – the realisation of an economic system with diverse choices), Tokyo: Nikkeiren Shuppanbu.

Nikkeiren Rōdō Mondai Kenkyū Iinkai (Japan Federation of Employers' Associations, Labour Issues Research Committee) (2002), *Rōdō Mondai Kenkyū Iinkai Hōkoku –kōzō kaikaku no suishin ni yotte kiki no dakai o: kōkosuto taishitsu no zesei to koyō no iji, sōshutsu* (Report of the Japan Federation of Employers' Associations, Labour Issues Research Committee – breaking the crisis through the promotion of restructuring: correction of high cost structures and the preservation and creation of employment), Tokyo: Nikkeiren Shuppanbu.

Nishiguchi, Toshihiro (2000), *Senryakuteki autosōshingu no shinka* (The progress of strategic outsourcing), Tokyo: Tokyo Daigaku Shuppankai.

Nishiguchi, Toshihiro and Alexander Bourdais (1999), 'Kaosu ni okeru jiko soshikika – Toyota gurūpu to Aishin Seiki kasai (Self-organisation in chaos – the Toyota group and fire at Asia Precision Machinery), *ORC Soshiki Kagaku* (ORC organisational science) 32 (4).

Nishino, Rumiko (1999), *Erukurano wa naze korosaretanoka: Nikkei Burajirujin shōnen shūdan rinchi satsujin jiken* (Why was El Crano killed? The case of the mob lynching murder of a Brazilian youth of Japanese descent), Tokyo: Askashi Shoten.

Nishiyama, Kenichi (1997), *Fukuzatsukei toshite no keizai – yutakana monobanare shakai e* (Economics as a complex system – towards an affluent society that is no longer interested in buying things), Tokyo: Nihon Hōsō Shuppan Kyōkai.

Nishizawa, Akihiko (1995), *Inpei sareta gaibu – toshi kasō no esunogurafī* (The concealed exterior – ethnography of the urban underclass), Tokyo: Sairyūsha.

Nishizawa, Akihiko (2002), 'Gurōbaru shiti no kasō mainoriti – kangeki o nū (Minority underclasses in global cities – stitching up the gap), in Kajita, Takamichi and Takashi Miyajima (eds), *Kokusaika suru Nihon shakai* (Japan's internationalizing society), Tokyo: Tokyo Daigaku Shuppankai.

Nohara, Hikari and Eishi Fujita (eds), (1988), *Jidōsha sangyō to rōdōsha* (The automobile industry and workers), Kyoto: Hōtsu Bunkasha.

Nomura, Masami (1993), 'Nihon ni okeru "jukuren" ron no nagare – Koike riron wa naze hiromattaka (The course of the "skills" debate in Japan – Why the Koike theory became widespread,' *Ōhara shakai mondai kenkyūjo zasshi* (The Journal of the Ohara Institute for Social Research), 416.

Nomura, Masami (1998), *Koyō fuan* (Employment insecurity), Tokyo: Iwanami Shinsho.

Nomura, Masami (2001), 'Nihon no seisanshugi to rōdōsha – kokusaiteki shikaku kara mita Nihon no rōdō shakai (Japan's production principle and workers – Japan's work society viewed from an international perspective),' in Hideo Totsuka and Shigeyoshi Tokunaga (eds), *Gendai Nihon no rōdō mondai – atarashii paradaimu o motomete [zōhoban]* (Present day Japanese labour issues – in search of a new paradigm [enlarged edition]), Kyoto: Mineruba Shobō.

Nomura, Masami (2003), *Nihon no rōdō kenkyū* (Japanese labour studies), Kyoto: Mineruba Shobō.

Ogawa, Kōichi (2000a), 'Nihon ni okeru gaikokujin rōdōsha no soshikika, 1 – Kanagawa shiti union no kēsu sutadi o tōshite (The organisation of foreign workers in Japan, 1 – a case study of Kanagawa) City Union),' *Rōdō hōritsu junpō* (Labour law ten day report), June 1–10 issue.

Ogawa, Kōichi (2000b), 'Nihon ni okeru gaikokujin rōdōsha no soshikika, 2 – Kanagawa shiti union no kēsu sutadi o tōshite (The organisation of foreign workers in Japan, 2 – a case study of Kanagawa) City Union),' *Rōdō hōritsu junpō* (Labour law ten day report), July 1–10 issue.

Ōkōchi, Kazuo (1944), *Shakai seisaku no kihon mondai [zōteiban]* (Fundamental issues in social policy) [revised and enlarged edition]), Tokyo: Nihon Hyōronsha.

Ōkōchi, Kazuo (1962), *Nihon no rōdō mondai* (Japan's labour issues), Tokyo: Kobunsha.

Ōkubo, Takeshi (2001), 'Nikkeijin rōdōsha ni okeru rōdō shijō no kōzō (Structure of the labour market amongst workers of Japanese descent), *Nihon rōdō shakaigakukai nenpō, 12* (Annual Review of Labor Sociology, 12).

Okinawa rōdō keizai kenkyūjo (Okinawa labour economics research institute) (1988), *Okinawaken rōdōryoku no kengai idō ni kansuru chōsa kenkyū hōkokusho – keizai jiritsu ni mukete rōdō shijō no yakuwari o saguru* (Survey research report regarding migration outside the prefecture by Okinawa prefecture's labour force), Naha: Zaidan hōjin Okinawa Rōdō Keizai Kenkyūjo.

Okuno, Masahiro and Kōtarō Suzumura (1988), *Mikuro keizaigaku II* (Microeconomics II), Tokyo: Iwanami Shoten.

Okuno, Masahiro (1993), 'Gendai Nihon no keizai shisutemu – sono kōzō to henkaku no kanōsei (Japan's current economic system – its structure and reform possibilities), in Tetsuji Okazaki and Masahiro Okuno (eds), *Gendai Nihon keizai shisutemu no genryū* (The source of the present day Japanese economic system), Tokyo: Nihon Keizai Shinbunsha.

Okuyama, Akira (2000), 'Koyō shūgyō keitai no tayōka to kintō taigū (Diversification of and equal treatment in hiring and employment forms), Nihon rōdōhō gakkai hen (Japanese labour laws society ed.), *Rōdōsha no jinkaku to byōdō "Kōza 21 seiki no rōdōhō"* (Workers' personalities and equality, Lecture 21st century labour laws), Tokyo: Yūhikaku.

Onai, Tōru and Eshin Sakai (eds) (2001), *Nikkei Burajirujin no teijūka to chiiki shakai – Gunmaken Ōta Oizumi chiku o jirei toshite* (Settlement by Brazilians of Japanese descent and regional society – a case study of the Ōta and Oizumi Districts, Gunma prefecture), Tokyo: Ochanomizu Shobō.

Ono, Akira (1997), *Henka suru Nihonteki koyō kankō* (Changing Japanese employment practices), Tokyo: Nihon Rōdō Kenkyū Kikō.

Ōsawa, Mari (1993), *Kigyō chūshin shakai o koete – gendai Nihon o "jendā" de yomu* (Moving beyond a company centred society – reading present day Japan through "gender"), Tokyo: Jiji Tsūshinsha

Ōuchi, Tsutomu (1952), *Nihon shihonshugi no nōgyō mondai* (The agricultural issue in Japanese capitalism), Tokyo: Tokyo Daigaku Shuppankai.

Raten America Kyōkai (Latin American Association) (1969), *Burajiru ijū 60 nen: Burajiru Nikkei shakai no kenkyū* (60 Years of Brazilian immigration:

studies of Brazilian Japanese descent societies), Tokyo: Raten America Kyōkai.

Rōdōshō shokugyō antei kyoku (1995), *Gaikokujin koyō taisaku no genjō* (The present state of measures regarding the employment of foreigners), Tokyo: Rōmu Gyōsei Kenkyūjo.

Sakanaka, Hidenori (2005), *Nyūkan senki* (Immigration bureau histories), Tokyo: Chūō Kōronsha.

Sakanaka, Hidenori and Toshio Saito (2006), *Shutsunyūkoku kanri oyobi nanmin nintei hō chikujō kaisetsu, kaitei (daisanban)* (An article-by-article explanation of the Immigration Control and Refugee Recognition Act, revised (3rd edition)), Tokyo: Nihon Kajo Shuppan.

Sano, Tetsu (1996), *Wākā no kokusai kanryū* (Return currents of international workers), Tokyo: Nihon Rōdō Kenkyū Kikō.

Saruta, Masaki (1999), 'Ōte jidōsha mēkā no seisan to rōdō – henbō suru Toyota no seisan rōdō shisutemu no rōmu kanri (Production and labour in the large automobile makers – the labour system and labour management in a Toyota undergoing transformation), in Mitsui Itsutomo (ed.), *Nihonteki seisan shisutemu no hyōka to tenbō – kokusaika to gijutsu rōdō bungyō kōzō* (Evaluation of and prospects for the Japanese production system – internationalisation and the structure of technology, labour and specialisation), Kyoto: Mineruba Shobō.

Sasada, Eiji (2002), 'Kenpō 2' (The Constitution, 2), *Hōgaku kyōiku 266* (Legal education, 266).

Sataka, Makoto (1991), *Hishakai ningen no susume* (The Encouragement of Non-social Beings), Tokyo: Kodansha bunko.

Satake, Hiroaki (1994), 'Tairyō seisan hōshiki to muda (kūhi) – NPS Kenkyūkai no jikken ni kansuru chōsa to bunseki (The mass production system and futility (wastefulness) – Survey and analysis of the actual experiences of the NPS Research Group), *Ōhara shakai mondai kenkyūjo zasshi* (The Journal of the Ohara Institute for Social Research) *431*.

Satō, Hiroki (1998), 'Hitenkeiteki rōdō no jittai (The realities of atypical work),' *Nihon rōdō kenkyū zasshi* (The Japanese Journal of Labour Studies), *462*.

Satō, Shinobu (1996a), 'Nikkei Burajirujin no koyō kanri – reitō shokuhin kakō mēkā no jirei (Management of the employment of Brazilians of Japanese descent – the case of frozen foods manufacturers),' *Ōhara shakai mondai kenkyūjo zasshi* (The Journal of the Ohara Institute for Social Research), *453*.

Satō, Shinobu (1996b), 'Kōnai shitauke to Nikkei Perūjin – zōsen gyō no jirei o megutte (In-house subcontracting and Peruvians of Japanese descent – the case of the shipbuilding industry),' *Ōhara shakai mondai kenkyūjo zasshi* (The Journal of the Ohara Institute for Social Research) *454*.

Seiyama, Kazuo (1995), *Seidoron no kōzu* (The composition of systems theory), Tokyo: Sōbunsha.

Shibaike, Yoshikazu (1999), *Gyōsei hō sōron kōgi [daisanpan]* (General remarks on Adminstrative Law, lectures [3rd ed.]), Tokyo: Yūhikaku.

Shibaike, Yoshikazu (2005), *Hanrei gyōsei hō nyūmon [daiyonhan]* (An introduction to precedents in administrative law [4th ed.]), Tokyo: Yūhikaku.

Shibaike, Yoshikazu (2006), *Gyōsei kyūsai hō kōgi [dai sanpan]* (Lectures on administrative assistance laws [3rd ed.]), Tokyo: Yūhikaku.

Shimoi, Takashi (1990), *Rōdō kijun hō* (Basic labour law), Tokyo: Yūhikaku.

Shiono, Hiroshi (2005a), *Gyōsei hō I, gyōsei hō sōron [daiyonhan]* (Administrative law I, general remarks [4th ed.]), Tokyo: Yūhikaku.

Shiono, Hiroshi (2005b), *Gyōsei hō II, gyōsei hō kyūsai hō [daiyonhan]* (Adminstrative law II, assistance law [4th ed.]), Tokyo: Yūhikaku.

Shiozawa, Yoshinori (1990), *Shijō no chitsujo gaku* (Scholarship on the market system), Tokyo: Chikuma Shobō.

Shiozawa, Yoshinori (1997a), *Fukuzatsusa no kiketsu* (The consequences of complexities), Tokyo: NTT Shuppan.

Shiozawa, Yoshinori (1997b), *Fukuzatsukei keizaigaku nyūmon* (An introduction to complex systems economics), Tokyo: Seisansei Shuppan.

Shirai, Kunihiro (2001), 'Seru seisan hōshiki to jinzai katsuyō (Cellular manufacturing method and the practical application of human resources),' in Tsuyoshi Tsuru (ed.) *Seisan shisutemu no kakushin to shinka – Nihon kigyō ni okeru seru seisan hōshiki no shintō* (Reform and progress of the production system – permeation of cellular manufacturing in Japanese companies), Tokyo: Nihon Hyōronsha.

Shishido, Zenichi and Atsushi Tsuneki (2004), *Hō to keizaigaku: kigyō kanren hō no mikuro keizaigakuteki kōsatsu* (Law and Economics: microeconomic considerations of company law), Tokyo: Yūikaku.

Shutsunyūkoku Kanri Hōrei Kenkyūkai (Immigration control laws and ordinances research group) (2005), *Chūkai hanrei, shutsunyūkoku kanri gaikokujin tōroku jitsumu roppō, heisei 17 nen* (Precedents and commentary, six laws in the practice of alien registration under the Immigration Control and Refugee Recognition Act, 2005), Tokyo: Nihon Kajo Shuppan.

Suehiro, Izutarō (1940), *Minpō zakkichō* (Civil code registry), Tokyo: Nihon Hyōronsha.

Suehiro, Izutarō (1923), *Nōson hōritsu mondai* (Rural legal issues), Tokyo: Kaizōsha.

Suehiro, Izutarō (1988), Takeyoshi Kawashima (ed.), *Uso no kōyō 1* (The efficacy of lies 1), Tokyo: Toyamabō Hyakka Bunko.

Suehiro, Izutarō (1994), Takeyoshi Kawashima (ed.), *Uso no kōyō 2* (The efficacy of lies 2), Tokyo: Toyamabō Hyakka Bunko.

Sumiya, Mikio (1960), 'Nihon shihonshugi to rōdō shijō (Japanese capitalism and the labour market),' in Seiichi Tōbata (ed.), *Nōson kajō jinkō ron* (The surplus rural population argument), Tokyo: Nihon Hyōronsha.

Sumiya, Mikio (1960), 'Rōdō shijō ron no kaiko to tenbō (Retrospectives on and prospects for labour market theory),' in Shakai seisaku gakkai (ed.), *Rōdō shijō to chingin* (The labour market and wages), Tokyo: Yūhikaku.

Sumiya, Mikio (1964), *Nihon no rōdō mondai* (Japan's Labour Problems), Tokyo: Tokyo Daigaku Shuppankai.

Sumiya, Mikio (1966), *Nihon no rōdō undō shi* (History of the Japanese labour movement), Tokyo: Yūshindō.

Sumiya, Mikio (1969), *Rōdō keizai ron* (Labour economics theory), Tokyo: Chikuma Shobō.

Sumiya, Mikio (1975), 'Rōdō shijō ron nōto – Nihon ni okeru kenkyū shi (Labour market theory notebook – history of research in Japan), *Keizaigaku ronshū* (Economics essay collection) *41 (2)*.

Suwa, Yasuo (2002), 'Rōdō o meguru "hō to keizaigaku" – soshiki to shijō no kōsaku ("Laws and economics" concerning labour – a blend of institutions and markets), *Nihon rōdō kenkyū zasshi 500* (Japanese labour research magazine 500).

Tachibanaki, Toshiaki (2000), *Sēfutinetto no keizaigaku* (Economics of the safety net), Tokyo: Nihon Keizai Shinbunsha.

Tajima, Hiroshi (2006), 'Gaikokujin keiji bengo to nyūkan hō (Criminal defence of foreigners and the Immigration Control and Refugee Recognition Act),' Tokyo bengoshikai gaikokujin no kenri ni kansuru iinkai hen (Tokyo lawyers association committee for the rights of foreigners (ed.), *Jitsumuka no tame no nyūkan hō nyūmon [kaiteiban]* (Introduction to the Immigration Control and Refugee Recognition Act for business-minded people [revised edition), Tokyo: Gendai Jinbunsha.

Takiguchi, Susumu (1966), 'Shōrai no koseki: yōshiki o chūshin toshite (Family registers of the future: form as central),' Masayuki Takanashi et al., *Koseki jihō 100 go kinen, kazoku hō to koseki no mondai* (Family register newsletter 100th commemorative issue, issues of family law and family registers), Tokyo: Nihon Kajo Shuppan.

Tanaka, Katō (1966), 'Shōgaiteki koseki teisei (Revision of family registers domestically and abroad),' Masayuki Takanashi et al., *Koseki jihō 100 go kinen, kazoku hō to koseki no mondai* (Family register newsletter 100th commemorative issue, issues of family law and family registers), Tokyo: Nihon Kajo Shuppan.

Taniguchi, Tomohei (1957), *Hōritsugaku zenshū 26, kosekihō* (Jurisprudence complete works 26, family registers law), Tokyo: Yūhikaku.

Taniguchi, Tomohei (1959), 'Kyogi shusse todoke ni yoru koseki no teisei to shinzoku hō kaisei ni tsuite (Regarding amendments to family registers on the basis of false birth registrations and revisions of the law on relatives),' Zenkoku rengō koseki jimu kyōgikai hen (National alliance of family register offices (ed.)), *Kosekishi daihyakugō kinen ronbunshū: mibunhō no genzai oyobi shōrai* (Collection of essays celebrating the 100th issue of the Family Registration Magazine: present and future of the Family Law), Tokyo: Teikoku hanrei hōki shuppansha.

Taniguchi, Tomohei (1986), 'Iwayuru tokubetsu yōshi seido ni tsuite no jakkan no kansō (Some thoughts on the so-called special adoption system),' Kiyoshi Hosokawa and Yoshimune Ebihara, *Kosekishi daigohyakugo kinen ronbunshū, kazokuhō to koseki: sono genzai oyobi shōrai* (Collection of essays celebrating the 500th issue of the family registration magazine, family law and family registration: present and future), Teihan: Tokyo.

Tanno, Kiyoto (1998), 'Tsukuridasareru rōdō shijō – higō hō shūrōsha no idō no mekanizumu (The manufactured labour market – mechanisms for the movement of people who are hired illegally),' *Ōhara shakai mondai kenkyūjo zasshi* (The Journal of the Ohara Institute for Social Research), *478*.

Tanno, Kiyoto (1999a), 'Gaikokujin rōdōsha no hōteki chii to rōdō shijō no kōzōka – Nihon ni okeru nishi, minami Ajiakei shūrōsha to Nikkei Burajirujin shūrōsha no jisshō kenkyū ni motozuku hikaku bunseki (The legal status of foreign workers and the structuring of the labour market – a comparative analysis based on experimental research on workers from west and south Asia and Brazilian workers of Japanese descent),' *Kokusaigaku ronshū* (International studies essays) *43*.

Tanno, Kiyoto (1999b), 'Zainichi Burajirujin no rōdō shijō – gyōmu ukeōgyō to Nikkei Burajirujin rōdōsha (The labour market for Brazilians of Japanese descent living in Japan – the contracting industry and Brazilian workers of Japanese descent),' *Ōhara shakai mondai kenkyūjo zasshi* (The Journal of the Ohara Institute for Social Research) *487.*

Tanno, Kiyoto (2000a), 'Nikkeijin rōdō shijō no mikuro bunseki – Nikkeijin koyō to chiiki komyuniti (A micro-analysis of the labour market for Brazilians of Japanese descent – the employment of people of Japanese descent and regional communities),' *Ōhara shakai mondai kenkyūjo zasshi* (The Journal of the Ohara Institute for Social Research) *499.*

Tanno, Kiyoto (2000b), 'Nikkeijin rōdōsha no koyō to toshikan ijū (The employment of people of Japanese descent and migration between cities),' *Toshi mondai* (Municipal Problems) *91 (9).*

Tanno, Kiyoto (2001a), 'Koyō kōzō no hendō to gaikokujin rōdōsha – rōdō shijō to seikatsu yōshiki no sōhosei no kanten kara (Transformation of the employment structure and foreign workers – from the viewpoint of the complementarity of the labour market and lifestyle),' in Takamichi Kajita (ed.), *Kokusaika to aidentiti* (Internationalisation and identity), Kyoto: Mineruba Shobō.

Tanno, Kiyoto (2001b), 'Mibun toshite no gaikokujin rōdōsha – shokuba ni okeru ichi to kenri (Foreign workers as social status – position and rights in the workplace),' in NIRA shitizunshippu kenkyūkai hen (NIRA citizenship research group (ed.)), *Tabunka shakai no sentaku – "shitizunshippu" no kanten kara* (Choices of multicultural societies – from the perspective of "citizenship"), Tokyo: Nihon Keizai Hyōronsha.

Tanno, Kiyoto (2002a), 'Nihonjin ni okikaerareru gaikokujin rōdōryoku – gaikokujin rōdōsha, josei soshite kōreisha ni yoru shūhenbu rōdō-ryokukan kyōsō (jō) (The foreign labour force being replaced with Japanese – competition within the peripheral labour force amongst foreign workers, women and the elderly (1)),' *Rōdō hōritsu junpō* (Ten day labour law report), *No. 1534.*

Tanno, Kiyoto (2002b), 'Nihonjin ni okikaerareru gaikokujin rōdōryoku – gaikokujin rōdōsha, josei soshite kōreisha ni yoru shūhenbu rōdō-ryokukan kyōsō (ge) (The foreign labour force being replaced with Japanese – competition within the peripheral labour force amongst foreign workers, women and the elderly (2)),' *Rōdō hōritsu junpō* (Ten day labour law report), *No. 1536.*

Tanno, Kiyoto (2002c), 'Gurōbarizēshonka no sangyō saihen to chiiki rōdō shijō – jidōsha sangyō ni miru shūhenbu rōdōkan kyōsō (Industrial reorganisation under globalisation and the regional labour market – competition within the peripheral labour market in the automobile industry),' *Ōhara shakai mondai kenkyūjo zasshi* (The Journal of the Ohara Institute for Social Research) *528.*

Tanno, Kiyoto (2003a), 'Burōka no shakaigaku – "pinpoint ijū" to chiiki rōdō shijō (The sociology of brokers – "pinpoint migration" and regional labour markets), *Gendai shisō* (Modern thought), *31 (6).*

Tanno, Kiyoto (2003b), 'Keiyaku no jidai to Nikkeijin rōdōsha – gaikokujin rōdō to shūhenbu rōdō shijō no saihen (The contract age and workers of Japanese descent – foreign workers and the reorganisation of the peripheral labour market),' *Rōdō shakaigaku nenpō* (Annual Review of Labor Sociology) *14.*

Tanno, Kiyoto (2004), 'Gurōbarizēshon to rōdō shijō no kaikaku (Global-isaiton and reform of the labour market),' *Kikan Pīpuruzu puran* (Quarterly people's plan) *28*.

Tanno, Kiyoto (2005), 'Naze shakai tōgō e no ishi ga hitsuyōka (Why a will for social integration is necessary),' *NIRA seisaku kenkyū* (NIRA policy research) *(18 (5)*.

Tanno, Kiyoto (2006a), 'Jidōsha sangyō ichiji shitauke ni okeru hiseiki koyō no henka (Changes in irregular employment in primary subcontracting in the automobile industry),' *Yoseba 19*.

Tanno, Kiyoto (2006b), 'Sōgō dekasegigyō no tanjō – Nikkei ryokōsha no henyō to Burajiru Nikkei komyuniti no shihon chikuseki (The birth of integrated migrant work businesses – the transformation of travel agencies run by people of Japanese descent and capital accumulation in Brazilian Japanese descent communities),' *Ōhara shakai mondai kenkyūjo zasshi* (The Journal of the Ohara Institute for Social Research) *573*.

Tanno, Kiyoto (2007), 'Zairyū tokubetsu kyoka no hō shakaigaku – Nihon de kurasu gaikokujin no hōteki kiso (The legal sociology of special permission to reside – the legal base of foreigners living in Japan),' *Ōhara shakai mondai kenkyūjo zasshi* (Journal of the Ōhara Institute for Social Issues) *582*.

Tanno, Kiyoto, Kaori Mutō, Chieko Nishioka and Hisano Niikura (2003), 'Jinshin baibai no shakaigaku – sherutā ni nogarete kita torafikkingu higaisha kara miete kuru mō hitotsu no shimin shakai (The sociology of people trafficking – another civil society revealed by victims of trafficking who have escaped to shelters),' *Jinbun gakuhō* (The Journal of Social Sciences and Humanities) *338*.

Tashiro, Aritsugu (1974), *Kokuseki hō chikujō kaisetsu* (An article-by-article commentary on the Nationality Law), Tokyo: Nihon Kajo Shuppan.

Toriyama, Atsushi (2010), 'Kokumin no rekishi ishiki o toinaosu (Questioning the historical consciousness of the people), in Tetsurō Katō, Hikaru Tanaka, Hajime Ono and Takashi Horie (eds), *Kokumin kokka no kyōkai* (Borders of the nation state), Tokyo: Nihon Keizai Hyōronsha.

Toyotashi (Toyota City) (2001), *Toyotashinai sangyō oyobi chiiki shakai ni okeru kokusaika shinten no eikyō chōsa hōkokusho* (Survey report on the impact of the progress of internationalization on industries in Toyota City and on regional society), Toyotashi.

Tsuneki, Atsushi (2006), 'Fukanbi keiyaku riron ni motozuku kaiko hōsei hōri seitōka no mondaiten (Problematic issues in the justification of legal control principles based on the principle of imperfect contracts),' in Hideo Fukui and Fumio Ōtake (eds), *Datsukakusa shakai to koyō hōsei – hō to keizaigaku de kangaeru* (Disparity-free society and employment laws – a legal and economic consideration), Tokyo: Nihon Hyōronsha.

Tsutsui, Miki (2001), 'Gaikokujin rōdōsha to kōsotsugyōsha no koyō daitai – "kansetsu koyō ni yoru masu daitai" no purosesu to inpakuto (Employment substitution of foreign workers and high school graduates – the process and impact of "mass substitution through indirect employment"),' *Nihon rōdō shakaigaku gakkai nenpō* (Yearbook of the Japanese labour sociology society) *No. 12*.

Tsuzuki, Kurumi (1995), 'Chihō toshi to esunishiti – Aichiken Toyotashi

H-danchi ni okeru Nikkei Burajirujin to chiiki jūmin (The ethnicity of regional cities – Brazilians of Japanese descent and regional residents in the H-apartment block in Toyota City, Aichi Prefecture),' in Yasushi Matsumoto (ed.), *Zōshoku suru nettowāku* (Multiplying networks), Tokyo: Keisō Shobō.

Tsuzuki, Kurumi (1996), 'Chihō sangyō toshi ni okeru Nikkei Burajirujin ukeire to chiiki no henyō – kattō, kinchō o hete kyōsei e (The acceptance of Brazilians of Japanese descent in regional industrial cities and the transformation of the regions – towards living together through conflict and tension),' *URC toshi kagaku* (URC urban sociology) *30*.

Tsuzuki, Kurumi (1998), 'Esunikku komyuniti no keisei to "kyōsei" – Toyotashi H-danchi no kinnen no tenkai kara (The formation of ethnic communities and "living together" – considered from the expansion of H-apartment block in Toyota City in recent years),' *Nihon toshi shakai gakkai nenpō* (Yearbook of the Japanese urban sociology society) *16*.

Uchida, Takashi (1990), *Keiyaku no saisei* (Reconstruction of contracts), Tokyo: Kōbundō.

Uchida, Takashi (2000), *Keiyaku no jidai – Nihon shakai to keiyaku hō* (The contract age – Japanese society and contract law), Tokyo: Iwanami Shoten.

Ujihara, Shōjirō (1953), 'Daikōjō rōdōsha no seikaku (The character of workers in large factories),' Nihon jinbun kagaku kyōkai hen (Japanese Social Sciences Association (ed.)), *Shakaiteki kinchō no kenkyū* (Studies of social tension), Tokyo: Yūhikaku.

Ujihara, Shōjirō (1957), 'Rōdō shijō ron no hansei (Reflections on labour market theory),' *Keizai hyōron* (Economic Critique), Feb. 1957.

Ujihara, Shōjirō (1966), *Nihon rōdō mondai kenkyū* (Studies of Japanese labour issues), Tokyo: Tokyo Daigaku Shuppankai.

Ujihara, Shōjirō (1989), *Nihon keizai to koyō seisaku* (The Japanese economy and employment policy), Tokyo: Tokyo Daigaku Shuppankai.

Umemura, Mataji (1964), *Sengo Nihon no rōdōryoku – sokutei to hendō* (The post-war Japanese labour force – measurements and changes), Tokyo: Iwanami Shoten.

Umemura, Mataji (1971), *Rōdōryku no kōzō to koyō mondai* (The structure of the labour force and employment issues), Tokyo: Iwanami Shoten.

Usaki, Masahiro, Sadao Morone and Naoki Kobayashi (2006), 'Hanrei kaiko to tenbō, kenpō (Recollections of and outlook for judicial precedents, the constitution),' *Hōritsu jihō, hanrei kaiko to tenbō, 2005, 6 gatsu rinjizōkangō* (Legal newsletter, recollections of and outlook for judicial precedents, June special edition issue).

Wagatsuma, Sakae (1987), *Hōritsu ni okeru rikutsu to ninjō [dainihan]* (Reason and empathy in the law [2nd ed.], Tokyo: Nihon Hyōronsha.

Watanabe, Masako (ed.) (1995a), 'Kyōdō kenkyū dekasegi Nikkei Burajirujin – ronbunhen shūrō to seikatsu (Cooperative research, Brazilian migrant workers of Japanese descent –text volume: employment and lifestyle),' Tokyo: Akashi Shoten.

Watanabe, Masako (ed.) (1995b), *Kyōdō kenkyū dekasegi Nikkei Burajirujin – shiryōhen taiken to ishiki* (Cooperative research, Brazilian migrant workers of Japanese descent – sources volume: personal experiences and consciousness),' Tokyo: Akashi Shoten.

Yamada, Moritarō (1934), _Nihon shihonshugi bunseki_ (An analysis of Japanese capitalism), Tokyo: Iwanami Shoten.

Yamaguchi, Genichi (2004), 'Kokuseki, koseki, mibun kankei (Nationality, family registration and status relationships),' Tokyo bengoshikai gaikokujin no kenri ni kansuru iinkai hen (Tokyo lawyers association committee for the rights of foreigners (ed.), _Jitsumuka no tame no nyūkan hō nyūmon [kaiteiban]_ (Introduction to the Immigration Control and Refugee Recognition Act for business-minded people [revised edition), Tokyo: Gendai Jinbunsha.

Yamamoto, Kiyoshi (1980), _Nihon chinrōdō shiron_ (A historical discussion of Japanese wage labour), Tokyo: Tokyo Daigaku Shuppankai.

Yamamoto, Kiyoshi (1982), _Nihon no chingin rōdō jikan_ (Japanese wages and working hours), Tokyo: Tokyo Daigaku Shuppankai.

Yamamoto, Kiyoshi (1994), _Nihon ni okeru shokuba no gijutsu, rōdō shi 1854 – 1990 nen_ (Techonolgy in Japanese workpalces and the history of labour 1854 – 1990), Tokyo: Tokyo Daigaku Shuppankai.

Yamamoto, Kiyoshi (2002), 'Tanno Kiyoto _Gurōbarizēshonka no sangyō saihen to chiiki rōdō shijō – oya kigyō no keiei senryaku ga hikiokosu shūhenbu rōdōkan kyōsō_ (2002 nen 1 gatsu, hōkokuyō pēpā) ('Comments on Kiyoto Tanno's "Industrial reorganisation under globalisation and the regional labour market – competition within the peripheral labour market brought about by management strategy in parent companies" (January 2002 report paper), Tokyo: Kokusai Rōdō Sentā.

Yamanaka, Keiko and Eunise Koga-Ishikawa (1996), 'Nihon Burajirujin no Nihon ryūnyū no keizoku to idō no shakaika – ijū no shisutemu ron o tsukatte (The continual influx into Japan of Brazilians of Japanese descent and the socialisation of movement – using a systems theory of migration),' _Ijū kenkyū_ (Immigration studies) _33_.

Yanagawa, Noriyuki (2000), _Keiyaku to soshiki no keizaigaku_ (The economics of contracts and institutions), Tokyo: Tōyō Keizai Shinposha.

Yashiro Naohiro (1997) _Nihonteki koyō kanko no keizaigaku_ (The economics of the Japanese style employment environment). Tokyo: Nihon keizai shinposha.

Yashiro, Naohiro (1999). _Koyō kaikaku no jidai: hatarakikata wa dō kawaru ka_ (Age of employment reform: How will ways of working change?), Tokyo: Chūkō shinsho.

Yashiro, Naohiro (2003), 'Kisei kaikaku o tsūjita kōheisei no kakuho (The maintenance of fairness via regulatory reform),' Higuchi Yoshio, Zaimushō Zaimu Sōgō Seisaku Kenkyūjo (hen) (Ministry of Finance, Policy Research Institute, ed.), _Nihon no shotoku kakusa to shakai kaizō_ (Income disparities in Japan and social classes), Tokyo: Nihon Hyōronsha.

Yokota, Kisaburō (1972), _Hōritsugaku zenshū 56 Kokusai shihō II shinpan_ (Jurisprudence complete works 56, Interantional private law II, new edition), Tokyo: Yūhikaku.

Yokoyama, Masahiro (1997), 'Pāto taimu rōdō no kikan rōdōryokuka no haikei to hōkō (Background to and orientation of part-time work becoming the nucleus of the labour force),' _Ōhara shakai mondai kenkyūjo zasshi_ (The Journal of the Ohara Institute for Social Research) _460_.

Yorimitsu, Masatoshi and Tetsu Sano (1992), _Chiiki sangyō no koyō kaihatsu senryaku: chiiki koyō mondai no genjō to kadai_ (Employment development strategies of regional industries: the realities and challenges of regional employment issues), Tokyo: Shinhyōron.

Zaihaku Okinawaken Jinkai (Association of people from Okinawa in Brazil) (1987), *Burajiru Okinawa imin shi* (History of Okinawan migration to Brazil), São Paolo: Zaihaku Okinawaken Jinkai.

Non-Japanese Sources

Alston, Lee J. (1996), 'Empirical work in institutional economics: an overview,' in Eggertsson, Thrainn and Douglass C. North (eds), *Empirical Studies in Institutional Change*, Cambridge Mass.: Cambridge University Press.

Aoki, Masahiko, H. K. Kim and M. Okuno-Fujiwara (1996) *The Role of Government in East Asian Economic Development*, World Bank, translated as Masaki Shiratori (supervising translator), Masahiko Aoki, Hyung-ki Kim and Masahiro Okuno (Fujiwara) (1997), *Higashi-Ajia no keizai hatten to seifu no yakuwari – hikaku seido bunseki apurōchi* (The role of government in East Asian economic development – a comparative systems analysis approach), Tokyo: Nihon Keizai Shinbunsha.

Berger, S. and M. J. Piore (1980), *Dualism and Discontinuity in Industrial Societies*, Cambridge Mass.: Cambridge University Press.

Bulow, J., J. Geanakoplos and P. Klemperer (1985), 'Multimarket oligopoly: strategic substitutes and complements,' *Journal of Political Economy* 93, pp.488–511.

Coase, Ronald H. (1937), 'The nature of the firm', *Economica* No.4, pp. 386–405.

Coase, Ronald H. (1960), 'The problem of social cost,' *Journal of Law and Economics* No.3, pp. 1–44.

Coleman, James S. (1990), *Foundations of Social Theory*, Cambridge Mass.: The Belknap of Harvard University Press.

Commons, John R. (1995), *Legal Foundations of Capitalism*, Jeff E. Biddle and Warren J. Samuels (eds), New Brunswick: Transaction.

Commons, John R., 1990, *Institutional Economics: Its Place in Political Economy* Vol.1, New Brunswick: Transaction.

Cornelius, Wane S., Philip L. Martin and James F. Hollifield (eds) (1992), *Controlling Imigration: A Global Perspective*, Stanford: Stanford University Press.

Dasgupta, Partha and Karl G. Maler (1992), *The Economics of Traditional Commons*, Oxford: Clarendon Press.

Del Castillo, A. (1999), *Los Peruanos en Japon* (Printed in Japan), Tokyo: Gendai Kikaku Shitsu.

Doeringer, Peter. B and Michael Piore (1971), *Internal Labor Markets and Manpower Analysis*, Lexington Mass.: Heath Lexington Books.

Dore, Ronald P. (ed.) (1967), *Aspects of Social Change in Modern Japan*, Princeton, N.J.: Princeton University Press.

Eggertsson, Thrainn (1996), 'A note on the economics of institutions', Lee J. Alston, Thrainn Eggertsson and Douglass C. North (eds), *Empirical Studies in Institutional Change*, New York: Cambridge University Press.

Eggertsson, Thrainn (2003), 'Open access versus common property,' Terry L. Anderson and Fred S. Mc Chesney (eds), *Property Rights – Cooperation, Conflict, and Law*, Princeton, N. J.: Princeton University Press.

Engerman, Stanley (1997), 'Cultural values, ideological beliefs, and changing labor institutions: notes on their interaction' in John N. Drobak and John

V. C. Nye (eds), *The Frontiers of the New Institutional Economics*, San Diego: Academic Press.

Engestrom, Yrjo (1993), 'Developmental studies of work as a testbench of activity theory: the case of primary care medical practice,' in Seth Chaiklin and Jean Lave (eds), *Understanding Practice – Perspectives on Activity and Context,* Cambridge Mass.: Cambridge University Press.

Engestrom, Yrjo (1999), 'Activity theory and individual and social transformation,' Yrjo Engestrom, Reijo Miettenen and Raija-Leena Punamaki (eds), *Perspectives on Activity Theory,* New York: Cambridge University Press.

Frank, Andre G. (1978), *Development Accumulation and Under Development,* New York: Monthly Review Press, translated as Kenji Agō (trans.) (1980), *Jūzokuteki chikuseki to teikaihatsu* (Dependent accumulation and underdevelopment), Tokyo: Iwanami Gendai Sensho.

Furubotn, Eirik G. and Rudolf Richter (2000), *Institutions and Economic Theory – The Contribution of the New Institutional Economics,* Ann Arbor: The University of Michigan Press.

Granovetter, Mark (1998), 'Coase revisited: business groups in the modern economy,' in Giovanni Dosi, David J. Teece and Josef Chytry (eds), *Technology, Organization, and Competitiveness: Perspectives on Industrial and Corporate Change,* Oxford University Press.

Greif, Avner (1997), 'On the interrelations and economic implications of economic, social, political, and normative factors: reflections from two late medieval societies,' in John N. Drobak and John V. C. Nye (eds), *The Frontiers of The New Institutional Economics,* San Diego: Academic Press.

Grief, Avner (2005), 'Institutions, markets, and games,' in Victor Nee and Richard Swedberg (eds), *The Economic Sociology of Capitalism,* Princeton, N. J.: Princeton University Press.

Harris, Jose and Michael P. Todaro (1970), 'Migration, unemployment, and development: a two-sector analysis,' *American Economic Review* 60 (1), pp. 126–142.

Harrison, Jeffrey L. (1995), *Law and Economics,* St. Paul, Minn.: West Publishing Co. [Japanese translation by Kobayashi, Yasumi and Katsumi Matsuoka, *Hō to keizaigaku,* Tokyo: Taga Shuppan.

Hayek, Frederic A. (1949), *Individualism and Economic Order,* London: Routledge & Kegan Paul, translated as Motō Kaji and Sayo Kaji (trans.) (1990), *Kojinshugi to keizai chitsujo,* Tokyo: Shunjūsha.

Hayek, Frederic. A. (1952), *The Sensory Order,* London, Routledge and Kegan Paul, translated as Takanori Akiyama (trans.), (1989), *Kankaku chitsujo,* Tokyo: Shunjūsha.

Hayek, Frederic. A. (1960), *The Constitution of Liberty,* London: Routledge & Kegan Paul, translated as Kenzō Kiga and Katsujirō Koga (1987), *Jiyū to hō: jiyū no joken II,* Tokyo: Shunjūsha.

Hayek, Frederic. A. (1961), 'Freedom and coercion – some comments on a critique by Mr. Ronald Hamowy,' *The New Individualist Review* 1 (2).

Hayek, Frederic (1966), 'Personal recollections of Keynes and the "Keynesian revolution,"' *The Oriental Economist* translated as Hideo Tanaka and Masaharu Tanaka (trans.) (1986), *Shijō, chishiki, jiyū,* Kyoto: Mineruba Shobō.

Hirschman, Albert (1970), *Exit, Voice, and Royalty: Responses to Decline in*

Firms, Organizations, and States, Cambridge, Mass.: Harvard University Press.

Joppke, Christian (2004), 'Primordial beliefs and immigration policy: the case of Britain's patrials,' in Jeffrey C. Alexander, Gary Marx, and Christine L. Williams (eds), *Self, Social Structure, and Beliefs: Explorations in Sociology*, Berkley: University of California Press.

Keohane, Robert O. (1984), *After Hegemony: Cooperation and Discord in the World Political Economy*, Princeton: Princeton University Press, reprinted in Japanese as *Hakengo no kokusai seijigaku*, Kyoto: Kōyōshobō.

Keohane, Robert O. and Elinor Ostrom (1995), 'Introduction,' Keohane, Robert O. and Elinor Ostrom (eds), *Local Commons and Global Interdependence: Hegemony and Cooperation in Two Domains*, London: Sage.

Keynes, John M. (1921), *A Treatise on Probability*, London: Macmillan.

Keynes, John M. and Piero Sraffa (1938), 'Introduction,' John M. Keynes and Piero Sraffa (eds) *An Abstract of a Treatise of Human Nature 1740: A Pamphlet Hitherto Unknown by David Hume*, London: Cambridge University Press.

Kuutti, Kari (1996), 'Activity theory as a potential framework for human-computer interaction research,' in Bonnie A. Nardi (ed.), *Context and Consciousness*, Cambridge, Mass.: The MIT Press.

Lakatos, Imre (1970), 'Falsification and the methodology of scientific research programmes,' in Imre Lakatos and Alan Musgrave (eds), *Criticism and the Growth of Knowledge*, Cambridge: Cambridge University Press.

Lave, Jean (1993), 'The practice of learning,' in Seth Chaiklin and Jean Lave (eds), *Understanding Practice: Perspectives on Activity and Context*, Cambridge: Cambridge University Press.

Lueck, Dean (2003), 'First Possessions the Basis of Property,' Terry L. Anderson and Fred S. McChesney (eds.), *Property Rights: Cooperation, Conflict, and Law*, Princeton: Princeton University Press.

March, James G. and Johan P. Olsen (1989), *The Organizational Basis of Politics and Rediscovering Institutions*, New York: Free Press, translated as Yūshi Enta (trans.) (1994), *Yawarakana seido*, Tokyo: Nikkan Kōgyō Shinbunsha.

Marsden, David (1999), *A Theory of Employment Systems*, Cambridge: Cambridge University Press.

Marsden, David (2003), 'Can reform of the employment relationship help create jobs?' in Antonio Argandona and Jordi Gual (eds), *The Social Dimensions of Employment: Institutional Reforms in Labour Markets*, London: Edward Elgar.

Marsden, David and P. Ryan (1990), 'Institutional aspects of youth employment and training policy in Britain,' *British Journal of Industrial Relations*, 28 (3), pp. 351–370.

Martin, Lisa L. (1995), 'Heterogeneity, linkage and commons problems,' in Robert O. Keohane and Elinor Ostrom (eds), *Local Commons and Global Interdependence: Heterogeneity and Cooperation in Two Domains*, London: Sage.

Munger, Frank (ed.) (2001), *Laboring below the Line*, New York: Russell Sage Foundation.

Nardi, Bonnie A. (1996), '"Studying context:" A comparison of activity theory, situated action models, and distributed cognition,' in Bonnie A. Nardi (ed.), *Context and Consciousness*, Cambridge, Mass.: The MIT Press.

Nash, June and Maria Patricia Fernandez-Kelly (eds) (1983), *Women, Men and the International Division of Labor*, New York: State University of New York Press.

North, Douglass C. (1990), *Institutions, Institutional Change and Economic Performance*, Cambridge: Cambridge University Press, translated as Kōshi Takeshita (trans.) (1994), *Seido, seido henka, keizai seika*, Kyoto: Kōyōshobō.

North, Douglass C. (2005), *Understanding the Process of Economic Change*, Princeton, N. J.: Princeton University Press.

Ostrom, Elinor (1990), *Governing the Commons: The Evolution of Institutions for Collective Action*, New York: Cambridge University Press.

Ostrom, Elinor (1995), 'Constituting social capital and collective action,' in Robert O. Keohane, and Elinor Ostrom (eds), *Local Commons and Global Interdependence: Heterogeneity and Cooperation in Two Domains*, London: Sage.

Ostrom, Elinor, Roy Gardner and James Walker (1994), *Rules, Games, and Common-pool Resources*, Ann Arbor: University of Michigan Press.

Pareto, Vilfled (1917), *Traité de Sociologie Générale*, Lausanne: Librairia Payot & Cie, translated as Akira Hirota and Tatsubun Itakura (trans.) (1987), *Shakaigaku taikō*, Tokyo: Aoki Shoten.

Piore Michael P. (1979), *Birds of Passage: Migrant Labor and Industrial Societies*, New York: Cambridge University Press.

Posner, Eric (2000), Law and Social Norms, New York: Harvard University Press. [Japanese translation by Ota, Katsuzo, *Hō to shakai kihan: seido to bunka no keizai bunseki* (Law and social norms: an economic analysis of systems and culture), Tokyo: Bokutakusha.]

Posner, Richard A. (1998), Economic Analysis of Law 5th ed., New York: Aspen Law & Business.

Portes, Alejandro (1982), 'International labor migration and national development,' in Mary M. Kritz (ed.) *U.S. Immigration and Refugee Policy: Global and Domestic Issues*, Lexington, Mass.: Lexington Books.

Portes, Alejandro (1997), *The Economic Sociology of Immigration*, New York: Russell Sage Foundation.

Putnam, Robert D. (1993), *Making Democracy Work: Civic Traditions in Modern Italy*, Princeton, N.J.: Princeton University Press, translated as Junichi Kawata (trans.) (2001), *Tetsugaku suru minshushugi: dentō to kaikaku no shiminteki kōzō*, Tokyo: NTT Shuppan.

Ramsey, F. P. (1990), 'Truth and probability,' in D. H. Mellor (ed.) *F. P. Ramsey: Philosophical Papers*, Cambridge: Cambridge University Press, translated as Kunitake Itō and Kōji Hashimoto (trans.) (1996), *Ramujī tetsugaku ron bunshū*, Tokyo: Keisō Shobō.

Sable, Charles F. (1981), *Work and Politics: The Division of Labor in Industry*, Cambridge: Cambridge University Press.

Sandler, Todd (2004), *Global Collective Action*, Cambridge: Cambridge University Press.

Sassen-Koob, Saskia (1983), 'Labor Migration and the New Industrial Division of Labor,' in June Nash and Maria Patricia Fernandez-Kelly (eds), *Women, Men and the International Division of Labor*, New York: State University of New York Press.

Sassen, Saskia (1988), *The Mobility of Labor and Capital: A Study in International Investment and Labor Flow*, New York: Cambridge University Press, translated as Kirirō Morita et al. (trans.) (1992), *Rōdō to shihon no kokusai idō: sekai toshi to imin*, Tokyo: Iwanami Shoten.

Sassen, Saskia (1995), 'Immigration and local labor markets' in Alejandro Portes (ed.), *The Economic Sociology of Immigration: Essays on Networks, Ethnicity, and Entrepreneurship*, New York: Russell Sage Foundation.

Sassen, Saskia (2002), 'Deconstructing labor demand in today's advanced economies: implications for low-wage employment,' in Frank Munger (ed.), *Laboring Below the Line: The New Ethnography of Poverty, Low-Wage Work, and Survival in the Global City*, New York: Russell Sage Foundation.

Sen, Amartya (1982), *Choice, Welfare and Measurement*, Oxford: Basil Blackwell, translated as Takashi Ōba and Kenji Kawamoto (trans.) (1989), *Gōritekina orokamono: keizaigaku=ronrigakuteki tankyū*, Tokyo: Keisō Shobō.

Simon, Herbert A. (1996), *The Science of the Artificial* 3rd edition, Cambridge, Mass.: The MIT Press, translated as Motoyoshi Inaba and Hideki Yoshihara (trans.) (1997), *Shisutemu no kagaku [daisanhan]*, Pāsonarumedia.

Simon, Herbert A. (1997a), *Models of Bounded Rationality: Empirically Grounded Economic Reason*, Cambridge, Mass.: The MIT Press.

Simon, Herbert A. (1997b), *Administrative Behavior: A Study of Decision-Making Processes in Administrative Organizations* 4th edition, New York: The Free Press.

Smelser, Neil (1991), *Social Paralysis and Social Change: British Working Class Education in the Nineteenth Century*, Berkeley: University of California Press.

Smith, Adam (1766): 1937 *Lectures on Jurisprudence*, Glasgow: Glasgow University Press, translated as Hiroshi Mizuta (trans.) (2005), *Hōgaku kōgi*, Iwanami Bunko.

Smith, Adam (1789), *An Inquiry into the Nature and Causes of the Wealth of Nations*, A Strahan: London, translated as Hiroshi Mizuta (supervising trans.) and Chūhei Sugiyama (trans.) (2000), *Kokufu ron 1*, Tokyo: Iwanami Bunko.

Smith, Tony (2000), *Technology and Capital in the Age of Lean Production – a Marxian Critique of the "New Economy,"* New York: State University of New York Press.

Snidal, Duncan (1995), 'The politics of scope: endogenous actors, heterogeneity and institutions,' in Robert O. Keohane and Elinor Ostrom (eds), *Local Commons and Global Interdependence: Heterogeneity and Cooperation in Two Domains*, London: Sage.

Tanno, Kiyoto, 2002, 'Who governs the ethnic migrant labor market in Japan?: Pakistani and Iranian labor turnover before and after 1990,' Yasuro Hase, Hiroyuki Miyake, and Fumiko Oshikawa (eds), *South Asian Migrants in Comparative Perspective: Movement, Settlement and Diaspora*, JCAS Symposium Series 13, The Japan Center for Area Studies (JCAS), Osaka: National Museum of Ethnology.

Todaro, Michael P. (1997), *Economic Development* sixth edition, London: Longmans, translated as Yasuo Okada (supervising trans.) (1997), *M. Todaro no kaihatsu keizaigaku*, Tokyo: Kokusai Kyōryoku Shuppankai.

Veblen, Thorstin (1904), *The Theory of Business Enterprises*, New York: Charles Scribner Sons Ltd, Keiji Ohara (trans.) (1965), *Kigyō no riron*, Tokyo: Keisō Shobō.

Veblen, Thorstein, 1998, *The Theory of the Leisure Class*, New York: Prometheus Books, translated as Keiji Ohara (trans.), *Yūkan kaikyū no riron*, Tokyo: Iwanami Bunko.

Williamson, Oliver E. (1975), *Markets and Hierarchies: Analysis and Antitrust Implications*, New York: Free Press.

Williamson, Oliver E. (1985), *The Economic Institution of Capitalism*, New York: Free Press.

Williamson, Oliver E. (1998), 'Transaction cost economics and organization theory,' in Giovanni Dosi, David J. Teece and Josef Chytry (eds), *Technology, Organization, and Competitiveness – Perspectives on Industrial and Corporate Change*, Oxford University Press.

Wittgenstein, Ludwig (1921), *Tractatus Logico-Philosophicus*, London: Routledge & Kegan Paul, translated as Takashi Hashimoto and Hidetoshi Sakai (trans.) (1968), *Ronri tetsugaku ronkō*, Tokyo: Hōsei Daigaku Shuppankyoku.

Yandle, Bruce (2003), " Property Rights or Externalities?" Terry L. Anderson and Fred S. McChesney (eds.), *Property Rights: Cooperation, Conflict, and Law*, Princeton: Princeton University Press.

Name Index

Subject Index

www.ingramcontent.com/pod-product-compliance
Lightning Source LLC
Chambersburg PA
CBHW060305030426
42336CB00011B/939